Growing Up With Divorce

Growing Up With Divorce

Helping Your Child
Avoid Immediate
and Later
Emotional Problems

Neil Kalter

THE FREE PRESS
A Division of Macmillan, Inc.
NEW YORK

Collier Macmillan Publishers
LONDON

The Free Press
A Division of Macmillan, Inc.
866 Third Avenue, New York, N.Y. 10022

Collier Macmillan Canada, Inc.

Printed in the United States of America

printing number

1 2 3 4 5 6 7 8 9 10

Library of Congress Cataloging-in-Publication Data

Kalter, Neil.
    Growing up with divorce : helping your child avoid immediate and
later emotional problems / Neil Kalter.
      p.   cm.
    Includes bibliographical references.
    ISBN 0–02–916901–1
    1. Children of divorced parents—Psychology. 2. Emotional
problems of children.   I. Title.
HQ777.5.K35   1989
306.89--dc20   89–16922
                                                          CIP

Contents

Preface   vii

1. Introduction   1
2. The Stages of Divorce   5
3. Communicating With Children   25
4. The Divorce Experience for Infants and Toddlers   41
5. Helping Infants and Toddlers Cope   73
6. The Divorce Experience for Preschool Children   93
7. Helping Preschoolers Cope   133
8. The Divorce Experience for Early Elementary School
   Children   161
9. Helping Early Elementary School Children Cope   205
10. The Divorce Experience for Later Elementary School
    Children   241
11. Helping Later Elementary School Children Cope   275
12. The Divorce Experience for Adolescents   309
13. Helping Adolescents Cope   351

Afterword   393
Notes   397
Index   403

Preface

This book has grown out of fifteen years of working with families that have experienced divorce. Initially, my efforts were focused on those families which sought professional help for children who were having difficulties accepting and adjusting to their parents' divorce. In my role as a clinical practitioner and a supervisor in the outpatient clinic at the University of Michigan's Children's Psychiatric Hospital, and at the University of Michigan's Center for the Child and the Family, I have had the opportunity to observe over 500 families in which a divorce had occurred. This in-depth clinical work, often consisting of three to twelve months of weekly contacts with each family, taught me a great deal about the ways in which parents and children react to, struggle with, and often cope successfully with the stresses of divorce.

At the same time, I had questions about how much of what I saw in a clinical, helping context was also true of families that did not seek professional help. Since 1981, my colleagues and I at the University of Michigan have been conducting research with children and adolescents attending public schools in suburban and rural communities in southeastern Michigan. Using a variety of research approaches, including semistructured interviews and standardized personality tests, we have examined nearly a thousand youngsters, approximately half of whom had experienced parental divorce and half who had not. In a series of investigations published in professional journals, it became clear that many children wrestle with stresses and conflicts related to divorce for years after their parents separate. Though the majority were progressing well developmentally, compared to youngsters whose parents had not divorced, it required active efforts on their part. Divorce-related issues were never far from their minds, and a substantial number of them were experiencing problems in their development that children whose parents had never divorced did not have to face.

As it became clear that divorce was a continuing presence in the psychological lives of the great majority of the children we saw, I established the Family Styles Project at the University of Michigan. The aim of the project was to develop, implement, and test the effectiveness of a supportive, brief group intervention for children whose parents had divorced. Since 1982, we have served approximately 2,000 youngsters in grades one through nine. Several thousand other children have participated in this program, as it has been adopted both by schools in Michigan and other states.

Though our emphasis was on developing a preventive intervention program for children of divorce, there was another serendipitous by-product of these groups: they provided a new window for observing and understanding children's reactions to divorce and how they coped. In the safety of a group context conducted in the familiar setting of their school, these youngsters told us and each other a great deal about how they felt and what they thought about divorce. They illuminated for us the impact on them of parental fighting and arguing, becoming caught in the middle of these conflicts, seeing one or both parents in great emotional distress, having reduced or no contact with their noncustodial parent, parental dating, and remarriage. In the group sessions, they shared their privately held, rarely voiced (especially in the context of formal research endeavors) feelings and ideas about divorce. We were stunned by the long-term concerns of children, and began to conceptualize divorce as a process consisting of a series of events that unfold over many years.

However, we were also impressed by how well many of these youngsters were doing. The majority seemed to be coping well. Some seemed to be especially resilient, perhaps by temperament, and able to meet even the most disconcerting changes wrought by divorce with equanimity. Others had a particularly sturdy custodial parent who adjusted well to the divorce and was able to shelter the children from the more dramatic stresses that can arise in the context of divorce. Still others had parents who could put their own hostilities and distress to rest and effectively coparent after the marital separation. We learned from the children who participated in our groups that there are several avenues to good adjustment after divorce.

Collectively, these clinical, research, and intervention experiences have led me to think about divorce in terms of the stresses for children created by marital separation. The nature of these stresses appears tied to the stages of the divorce process. In chapter 2, I describe the three stages of divorce and the stresses that seem especially common to each. This stage model of the divorce process is carried through each of the chapters focused on the ways in which youngsters experience their parents' divorce.

At the same time, it is clear that the ways in which children react to, feel about, understand, and cope with the psychosocial stresses at each stage of the divorce process are largely determined by their cognitive, emotional, and social development. Each child, at any level of development, is certainly a unique person. However, clinical and research investigations have demonstrated that a good deal of the enormous variability in children's responses to their parents' divorce is related to their level of psychological development. Thus, a child's stage of development is a central, organizing feature of this book.

The ways in which a child processes and understands information about divorce, the reasons for it, and the changes it brings about are largely determined by his cognitive abilities, which in turn are very much tied to his age. Similarly, the kinds of concerns children have about divorce, the expectations parents and youngsters have of each other, the nature of parent–child relationships, and the coping styles of boys and girls are all decisively linked to their level of psychological development.

Levels of child development will be divided into five stages. These stages will be delineated according to age: infancy and toddlerhood (birth to two-and-a-half years old); the preschool years (three to five); early elementary school years (six to eight); later elementary school years (nine to twelve); and, adolescence (thirteen to seventeen years old). Though the age of the youngster is used to define her point in development, it is the levels of cognitive, emotional, and social growth that are the key issues. Some youngsters will exhibit a level of psychological development which is at a higher or lower stage than would be expected given their chronological age. And it is not unusual for a child to have reached a particular level of development in terms of cognitive growth and yet be at a different stage emotionally or socially. It will be helpful for the reader to examine the stage immediately above and the one just below the level indicated by a child's actual age. This is especially true if the youngster's age is on the border between two levels (for example, the child who is six years old frequently evidences development at both the early elementary school stage she is in as well as the preschool level just left).

A word needs to be said about the illustrations provided in this book. I have taken great care to disguise the identity of the parents and children who served as the basis for these examples. At times, composites have been used to further protect the confidentiality of the families. Fortunately, through direct clinical practice, the supervision of others in training, and the willingness of colleagues to share their professional experiences, I have knowledge of a sufficient number of families to have several examples at each stage of divorce and of child development with very similar experiences. And in all illustrations, the words of the children, parents, and mental health professionals are direct quotes or close paraphrasings of what was said.

I also wish to underscore the fact that the children who appear in these pages were not suffering from an emotional illness. They were reacting to the stresses associated with the divorce process. They came to the attention of mental health professionals because either one or both parents, or some other concerned adult in their lives, were sensitive to their distress. My experience, through research interviews and our school-based support groups, with youngsters who never had any contact with a mental health professional, leads me to be convinced that the children who served as the basis for these examples are not atypical.

I think it is also important to note that many children do well after divorce because one or both parents are intuitively aware of the issues put forth in this book. These parents understand the stresses confronting their youngsters and act effectively on their behalf. For parents who are successfully meeting the challenges of parenting after divorce, this book will serve to confirm their approaches and may help make more understandable why their efforts have been effective. For other parents, struggling with the vicissitudes of raising children in the context of divorce, this book can provide insights and ideas for helping their youngsters cope well with divorce and, therefore, grow and prosper in its aftermath.

This book is aimed at more than one audience. It is for parents who wish to understand the challenges and stresses divorce presents to children and learn how to be helpful to them. But it is also for other concerned adults who touch the lives of children whose parents have divorced and are in a position to facilitate a child's good adjustment. Pediatricians and family practitioners are often "front-line" professionals who regularly have contact with children. They can be of enormous help to parents and children who are coping with divorce-related stresses. Attorneys, judges, and court-based case workers are often in the position of assessing the impact of particular divorce circumstances on children, talking with youngsters and parents about divorce issues, and making recommendations regarding postdivorce family arrangements. They, too, can facilitate youngsters' successful adjustment to divorce. Teachers often spend as much or more time with children than parents. They see the ways in which children are affected by and cope with divorce and can provide their charges with understanding on a daily basis. This book is also addressed to my colleagues in the mental health professions. When parents come to us with a youngster who is having difficulties adjusting to a divorce, how we understand the child and what we convey to parents can shape in powerful ways the self-perceptions, feelings, and actions of parents and children, alike. This book can provide ways of intervening with families to empower parents in their efforts to raise their children effectively. The focus here is not one of psychological disturbance but of divorce-specific stresses and how to cope with them.

Finally, I would like to acknowledge the considerable efforts of many who have contributed to my work with and understanding of divorced parents and their children. I am indebted to the past and current members of the Family Styles Project, who began with me as energetic, enthusiastic graduate students and have become valued colleagues. I also wish to thank the Office of Prevention Services of the Michigan Department of Mental Health for their generous financial support. Under the directorship of Ms. Betty Tableman, the Office of Prevention Services has provided us with resources to develop our school-based support groups and glean the insights these groups have afforded us. Similarly, the financial support of the Washtenaw County (Michigan) Community Mental Health Center, under the direction of Mr. Saul Cooper and subsequently Dr. Lucy Howard, has been invaluable. The Psychology and Psychiatry Departments of the University of Michigan, chaired by Professors Albert C. Cain and John Greden, respectively, have contributed handsomely to the financial base needed to carry out the clinical and research missions of the Family Styles Project.

School personnel, including principals, teachers and secretaries, too numerous to mention by name, who have graciously facilitated our prevention program and research efforts deserve special thanks. Without their help, our research and intervention programs with youngsters and their parents could not have been possible. And the children and parents who participated in our groups and research projects, and those who sought special help, who taught me about the pain of divorce and how to cope with and transcend it, merit my heartfelt appreciation.

I am especially thankful for the close collegial relationships I have enjoyed with Professors Albert C. Cain and K. Gerald Marsden. I appreciate beyond words their wisdom, their confidence in me, and their friendship over the past two decades. I also wish to acknowledge the invaluable assistance and guidance provided by the editors at The Free Press. Ms. Laura Wolff helped me find an effective format for expressing my ideas and guided my efforts through the first half of this book. Ms. Gioia Stevens kept me on track for the remainder of the book and firmly but gently kept the reality of deadlines before me. I also wish to thank Ms. Paulette Lockwood for typing this manuscript and retaining her good humor throughout revisions.

Last, and by no means least, I am immensely grateful to my family for their patience and understanding throughout my career. My parents, my mother- and father-in-law, and my children (most of the time) have endured my long hours at the office, and therefore less than full involvement in family matters, with grace, humor and support. My wife, more than anyone, has kept the home fires burning with the sustaining and renewing force of her love. It is therefore to her that this book is dedicated.

1

►◄

Introduction

There was a dramatic increase in the rate of divorce in the United States between 1960 and 1980. Before 1960 about one child in nine saw his or her parents divorce. By 1980 this number had jumped to one child in three.[1] Though the rise in the divorce rate has leveled off since 1980, the United States Bureau of the Census is projecting that for the 1990's, 40 percent of all children growing up in America will experience a parental divorce.

Our society has become much more aware of the fact that marriages can be personally unfulfilling, emotionally painful, or even physically dangerous for many adults. Religious institutions, state legislatures, and the courts have relaxed their restrictions regarding divorce and have become more tolerant and accepting of divorce as a solution to marriages that are not working.

There is a debate among professionals about which is more upsetting and difficult for children: parents staying in a seriously troubled marriage or getting divorced. Research on this question suggests that either choice presents difficulties for children. The idea that it is good for parents to stay together "for the sake of the children" has not been confirmed by clinical reports or empirical research. Families are remarkably different from one another in terms of how they function as a unit, how they deal with conflict, or how they might deal with the parents' decision to separate. It is very unlikely that there is only one "right way" for adults to handle their marital conflicts. Some marriages can be preserved by mutual commitment to examine and correct individual and interpersonal problems that contribute to marital difficulties. Other marriages are best ended for the good of the adults and the children.

The ending of the social and legal contract of marriage can be seen as something like social surgery, in which the bonds between husband and wife are cut by divorce. Just as physical surgery has potential benefits and risks so too does the social surgery of marital dissolution. In physical surgery, the most common aims are to correct conditions that are painful, disfiguring, limiting, and/or life threatening. And there are risks. These include infection, adverse reaction to anesthesia, and blood loss, any of which can result in serious complications, physical damage, and even death.

Possible benefits from the social surgery of divorce are relief from emotional pain, avoiding personal "disfigurement" or limitations through lack of individual growth and fulfillment, and/or escape from a physically abusive and possibly injurious home environment. But here, too, there are risks. Divorced men are more likely than married men to have psychiatric problems, serious accidents, and to be in poor health generally.[2] Divorced women often experience depression and frequently suffer from markedly reduced and even impoverished economic circumstances.[3] The children of divorce become more vulnerable to developing a wide variety of social, behavioral, emotional, and academic problems.

The risks to healthy, wholesome child development that appear linked to divorce include an increased probability that the following problems may emerge: (1) angry and aggressive behavior; (2) sadness, low self-esteem, and depression; (3) impaired academic performance; and (4) trouble with intimate relationships in adolescence and adulthood.

For some youngsters these difficulties are short-lived, and within a year or two of the parental separation they regain their developmental stride and are able to put the problems behind them. However, there is mounting evidence now that a substantial number of children, perhaps as many as 30 percent to 50 percent, bear the painful and disruptive legacy of their parents' divorce for years.[4]

Though these figures are alarming, it is important to keep them in perspective. If 30 percent to 50 percent of children of divorce experience lasting, divorce-linked difficulties, then it follows that 50 percent to 70 percent do not. Researchers and mental health professionals agree that nearly all children wrestle with conflicts and upset feelings for up to a year or two after their parents separate. Smooth growth in the areas of cognitive, emotional, social, and/or behavioral development is often disrupted, at least temporarily, by the turmoil and changes usually accompanying divorce. But the majority of youngsters do not appear to have long-lasting problems attributable to divorce.

Medical advances, most less than a century old, have illuminated the nature of the risks of surgery and, therefore, what can be done to reduce their consequences. Information about the patient's general health history and current health status, knowledge of the disease or injury affecting the patient, awareness of how infection occurs, and increasingly sophisticated methods for administering and monitoring anesthesia and for typing and closely cross-matching blood for possible transfusion have made most surgical procedures relatively safe and often routine. The likely outcome of a simple appendectomy in the 1980's is far better than it was in the 1880's. Mental health professionals and child development experts are at the very beginning of a struggle to make the consequences of parental divorce for children as benign and positive as medical science has made many kinds of physical surgery.

It is the aim of this book to integrate what we know about how youngsters grow and develop cognitively, emotionally, and socially, and what we understand about the divorce process in order to arrive at methods for reducing the risks of divorce for children. The material in this book will provide parents, therapists, educators, pediatricians, attorneys, and judges with a framework for understanding the ways in which divorce can affect the lives of children. Using the framework will permit these groups of concerned adults to help children adjust to and cope effectively with life after divorce.

2

►◄

The Stages of Divorce

In order to determine how parents and professionals can help children cope successfully with divorce, it is essential to understand the major factors influencing the child's reactions and adjustment to divorce. Three key factors contribute to how youngsters experience their parents' divorce:

1. The stage of the divorce process
2. The child's level of development
3. The child's gender

Each must be considered in order to enable parents and other concerned adults to facilitate children's healthy adaptation to divorce.

Years ago divorce was considered a single, legal event. Parents would separate and eventually "the divorce" would be granted by the court. As we began to study divorce more closely, it became clear that rather than being an isolated occurrence, divorce is a *process* unfolding over many years. This process can be divided into three *stages*, each with its own characteristic life events. From a child's perspective there are specific *psychosocial stressors* accompanying each phase of divorce. That is, there are certain life circumstances at each stage that are stressful for children. In order to be helpful to youngsters, it is important to understand the nature of these stressors.

The three stages of the divorce process are the immediate crisis phase, the short-term aftermath, and the long-range period. The boundaries between these stages of divorce are not firmly drawn. For some families the crisis stage lasts only up to a month or two after the parents physically separate; for others, the stage can continue for a year or two past the point of separation. Similarly, the short-term aftermath phase may end as early as six months after parental separation. But for some families, especially where parents are embroiled in a bitter, corrosive divorce with serious financial and/or custody disputes, it becomes a protracted phase of the divorce going on for years. It is not so much time alone that determines the stage the divorce process is in, but rather the specific life circumstances. The degree to which conflicts are being resolved and new patterns of living established are the hallmarks of transitions from one stage of divorce to the next. And it is precisely these factors that impinge in different ways on the lives of children and, therefore, require different kinds of help and support from parents and professionals.

The Immediate Crisis Stage

The first stage of the divorce process begins as parents separate and/or a petition for divorce is filed. The fact that parents are seeking to dissolve their marriage becomes public; children now realize that the conflict or emotional distance between their parents is not merely a normal part of family life that will continue indefinitely. Changes in the household become apparent as one parent leaves and children begin to sense that their lives will be altered dramatically. For youngsters this initially is a time of shock and disbelief; regardless of the amount of parental conflict that had existed, perhaps accompanied by open threats or discussion about divorce, children are nearly universally surprised, frightened, and saddened by the knowledge that divorce will occur.[1] This is a wrenching realization for most children who have held onto the belief that their parents would never get divorced. The implicit unspoken promise of parents that the family will always be together is shattered.

Conflict between parents is one of the most serious stressors a child encounters during the immediate crisis of parental divorce.[2] When one or both parents decide to separate, conflict between them is very frequently intense. Often one parent feels rejected by the other's decision to leave the marriage. Even the parent who initiates a separation may feel that he or she has been provoked into doing so. In either case at least one parent typically feels painfully wounded by his or her spouse. The message is clear: You are no longer loved, and (in many instances) you are no longer lovable or even worthy.

When people are hurt deeply a common and automatic self-protective response is to become angry. The wound to pride and self-esteem is often treated almost reflexively; the impulse is to heap disparagement and fury on the source of the pain. Even in men and women who are usually on an even keel emotionally and are not given to uncontroll-able, angry outbursts, the level of rage can be palpable. The usual sensitivity to and thoughtfulness about their children's needs, character-istic of so many parents, temporarily disappear in the maelstrom of intense anger. It is not at all unusual for youngsters to hear loud arguments and name-calling and to observe parents shoving and slap-ping one another, or worse. The raw, uncontrolled fury of these storms of rage is highly disturbing to youngsters of all ages.

However, even in the most rancorous separations, not all conflicts between parents take the form of pitched battles. Interspersed with these explosively angry exchanges, and sometimes in place of them, parents can demean and derogate one another in more controlled, quieter tones. At times this appears as verbal jousting matches:

Spouse A: [when the child is being dropped off for a visit] I told you I was taking Greg to a movie tonight at 7:00. You're late.

Spouse B: You didn't tell me that. You must have forgotten to mention it. Sometimes your memory goes as you get older.

Spouse A: Maybe it's your hearing that's going! Next time I'll write it down for you.

Spouse B: Maybe it's your thinking that's going! Besides, he's seen that movie already. Don't you know what your son has seen? Don't you listen to him?

And so on. While this sort of conflict can escalate into an explosion, some couples can keep it going at this level while children silently, or not so silently, watch the two people they care most about tear at each other with little mercy. Yet some parents who engage in this more quiet devastating warfare insist that they do not fight, scream, or argue in front of the children. They are genuinely surprised to learn how painful it is for youngsters to witness exchanges of this sort.

An alternative and even more subtle style parents sometimes use to express conflict is to criticize their (ex-) spouse within earshot of the children.

Father: [to his children when they are with him for dinner] Let's get something good to eat for a change. You must be real tired of those dry hamburgers your mother fixes.

Children: They're not so bad.

Father: Sure, if you like to eat leather with too much salt [laughing]. You must be starved. Look at that shirt, Johnny! Did your mother forget to do the laundry again? She's got a great memory, like an elephant—one that's had brain surgery!

Mothers can also use this method to demean their (ex-) husband.

Mother: [to her children who have just returned from a weekend with their father] Did you have a nice time? How did it go at your dad's?

Children: Ok, it was all right.

Mother: You mean your father actually got off the couch to do something with you? I don't believe it! I always thought he stuck to couches like he was glued to them.

Children: We went to see a movie.

Mother: Great! Well, he never was much at talking to people. At a movie he can just stuff his mouth with popcorn and ignore you. By the way, speaking of popcorn, is he still on his diet, or is he back to beer and pretzels for dinner?

Sometimes parents are so caught up in their hurt-angry feelings that they are not aware of how frequently they make these sorts of belittling, hostile comments. Many parents will truthfully report that their separation is going fairly smoothly, that they do not fight or discuss things in front of their children. They characterize their beginning divorce proceedings as "civilized." Yet their youngsters are constantly being reminded of how little one parent thinks of the other, as real or imaginary faults are magnified.

A few parents experience their divorce as "friendly." Not only are explosive, angry outbursts, verbal jousting, and put-downs absent, but both members of the couple seem calm. They may even take time for pleasant conversations over coffee at one another's homes when the children are being picked up or dropped off. Mutual respect and caring feelings are still very much in evidence. At times this may take on the quality of too much closeness for a couple that is separated and headed for divorce. Family dinners may continue regularly or sporadically, father may come over to mow the lawn, and he may sleep over from time to time. While this "friendly" divorce may be enormously reassuring to youngsters, it poses another more subtle problem. For many children it becomes more difficult to understand the need for a divorce. It also makes it much harder for children to give up the common, treasured wish for parents to eventually sort out their disagreements and get back together again. The fueling of this reconciliation wish leaves many youngsters even more deeply saddened and upset about the divorce. After all, if parents get along so well and seem to like and care for each other, why should they live apart? The hope for a fully reunited family is kept in front of the child, tantalizingly but frustratingly just out of reach. A moderate level of conflict between parents is surprisingly helpful to youngsters as they begin the task of coming to terms with the reality and finality of their parents' divorce.

The first stage of the divorce process is usually psychologically painful for one or both parents. Regardless of how much a couple wants a divorce and believes it is essential to their personal well-being, it is one of the most socially, emotionally, and financially dislocating experiences of adulthood.

Divorce requires each parent to carve out a new social identity as a divorced, unpartnered adult after years of functioning as a member of a couple. Divorced men and women find themselves not being invited to get-togethers they used to attend as a part of a couple. They may begin to feel socially isolated. And most adults find the prospect of reentering the dating scene confusing, unsettling, and downright frightening.

The spouse who feels most responsible for the decision to separate often experiences guilt and remorse along with relief, while the one who feels left must grapple with a sense of being unlovable and unworthy. It is ironic that both of these sets of feelings, guilt-remorse and a sense of being unlovable-unworthwhile, often produce the same psychological problems: depression or attempts to avoid being depressed. It is not at all unusual for children to see a parent crying, sleeping too much, feeling unable to get off the couch to get dinner or do the laundry, being inattentive to them, losing interest in eating, or generally appearing joyless. One major alternative to being depressed is to be chronically angry or irritable. This not only leads to the kinds of warfare between parents described above but also makes many parents less patient and more snappish with their children. Common ways of trying to escape depression and anger include immersing oneself in work activities or beginning a rollercoaster-like social life. Both result in children seeing much less of their parents.

Financial distress is also prominent during this stage of the divorce process, particularly for women who have primary responsibility for children after the marital separation.[3] Many mothers have left the job market or interrupted their education to raise children and manage the family household. Others have given up full pursuit of a career and worked only part-time outside the home in order to devote themselves to their families. Entry into the full-time job market is extremely difficult for mothers who have not developed the necessary competitive skills and experience. Even women who have continued to work full-time outside the home are generally paid substantially less than men for comparable positions and efforts. Child support payments, which are intended to provide economic resources and security to youngsters, are often made irregularly, partially, or in many instances not at all.[4]

Men, too, experience economic stresses after marital separation. Maintaining two households is obviously more expensive than having a shared residence. Add to that the considerable legal costs of divorce, child support payments, and the expenses associated with continuing to see one's children (for example the cost of transportation, extra clothing, bedding, and toys) and it becomes clear that divorcing fathers who are conscientious about their responsibilities also are frequently strapped for money. Financial demands become even more draining when a man remarries and begins to support a new family too.

The first stage of divorce has been labelled as a period of "diminished parenting capacities."[5] Social isolation, loneliness, irritability, depression, and anxiety collectively threaten to overwhelm even the psychologically best-adjusted parent. It is nearly impossible to be as attentive, caring, tolerant, and empathic a parent as one usually is in the face of these emotional pressures. But the escape routes from the tensions usually wind up taking parents from their children, as newly separated men and women throw themselves into work, job retraining, or social activities. As involvement in parenting is reduced, children are increasingly left in the care of others, or more typically in the case of older children on their own. Clearly, to the extent that at least the primary, custodial parent can manage these stresses and adapt quickly to the multitude of changes ushered in by the initial marital separation, the less distress the children will experience.

Approximately 90 percent of all minor children live primarily with their mother after parents separate. Nonresident fathers typically have less than biweekly contact with their youngsters, and their involvement declines as time goes by.[6] For most children, divorce means either the complete or partial loss of the relationship with their father.

Many parents are puzzled by their youngsters' openly expressed yearnings for more contact with their father, the children's excited anticipation of a scheduled time with him, the especially good behavior displayed by many boys and girls when they are with their father, their attempts to please him, or conversely, their upset feelings over having little or no contact with him. Mothers often point to how little time the children had spent interacting with their father before the marital separation. Others may note that the youngsters see their father nearly every week and wonder why that is not enough. What many adults fail to recognize is that having a father present in the home feels very different to most children than seeing him regularly and even fairly frequently when he lives apart from the rest of the family. Brief interactions around dinnertime, specific chores, help with homework, a good-night kiss, comments about an upcoming school event, and the like create an *atmosphere of father-presence* that is lost when he is no longer living under the same roof.

Even when fathers are able to see their children regularly and frequently (that is, at least once a week), the nature of the relationship is altered substantially. The easy give-and-take of brief everyday interactions gives way to extended periods of time during which fathers and their children are together for the clear purpose of seeing one another. The structure of the father–child relationship becomes more a set piece with an emphasis on planned activities. Dinners at fast-food restaurants, shopping trips to a mall, and going to movies are tightly and carefully scheduled and now rarely occur spontaneously. And the activities are supposed to be fun! Thus, fathers are placed in the role of "Disneyland Dad" rather than a full-fledged parent concerned about homework, chores, and the myriad of day-to-day family rituals such as mealtime and bedtime activities.

The loss of the relationship with the nonresident parent is mitigated to a great degree by a newly emerging arrangement known as *joint physical custody*. Here parents spend equal or nearly equal time (usually defined as no more imbalanced than a 70 percent-30 percent split) with the children. It is distinguished from *joint legal custody*, though both are loosely referred to as "joint custody," in which both parents legally maintain a voice in key decisions affecting their children such

11

as religious training, educational plans, and medical care. Joint legal custody does not carry with it any implications at all for how much time the youngsters live with each parent.

On the face of it, joint physical custody appears to eliminate the stress of losing one parent: the child lives with each parent for regular periods of time, which are usually spelled out in interim court orders during the first stage of the divorce process and in final court orders after that. The "Disneyland Dad" (or Mom) phenomenon is largely avoided as both parents stay centrally involved in the lives of their children. Parents continue to experience themselves, and are experienced by their youngsters, as full-fledged parents.

However, as with most choices there are trade-offs. Parents who have joint physical custody arrangements must interact with each other more and make more joint decisions. And they need to do so at precisely the time that they find themselves in greatest disagreement and emotional turmoil, namely during the earliest phase of the divorce process. The danger of intensifying conflicts between parents and emotionally upsetting one or both parents, two important potential sources of stress for children during the immediate crisis stage of divorce, is increased through joint physical custody. There is also considerable stress for many children as they move back and forth between two residences and, possibly, two entirely different neighborhoods. It is not surprising that joint physical custody works best when parents can cooperate on behalf of their children, keep their conflicts at a minimum when interacting around matters having to do with the children, and generally coparent efficiently.[7]

The Short-Term Aftermath Stage

This phase of the divorce process usually lasts for up to two years after the immediate crisis has passed. The turmoil and shock of the first stage gives way to a deepening recognition of the realities of divorce. The legal process of negotiation and/or adversarial conflict between spouses finally yields a divorce decree during this time. Patterns of economic support, custody, and visiting schedules set down in the initial period of the separation become routine.[8]

Conflict and hostility between parents continue to be common and serious sources of stress for children. Though parents live apart, the process of resolving disagreements around custody, division of prop-

erty, level of child support, and visiting arrangements for the nonresident parent can sustain and exacerbate the wounded feelings, anger,
and general rancor of the predivorce relationship and first phase of
the divorce process.

Older children frequently are drafted by their parents to participate
in this conflict as allies, pawns, or go-betweens. It is not unusual
for a hurt, angry parent to turn to a child for help in this ongoing
war. Many parents try to justify their position in the divorce to a
youngster and in doing so burden the child with private, adult aspects
of the divorce. An (ex) spouse's drinking, sexual activities, insensitivity, or other shortcomings are presented to the child as evidence for
self-vindication.

Mother: When you see your father this weekend, remind him that
he's late again with the support check. You can tell him he's only
hurting you when he's late.

Father: Is your mom going out with that same guy? Does he stay
overnight sometimes? Someone ought to tell her that she's acting
like a real jerk.

Mother: I'm sorry you can't go to camp this summer. Your dad's
still drinking away his money instead of thinking about you. That's
why we got divorced in the first place. I hope you don't wind up
like the bum he is.

Father: If your mother doesn't buy you some new clothes, I'm
just going to quit sending her all that money. You know I send
her $500 a month. What does she do with it? Five hundred dollars
a month! She could buy you a lot of things with that.

Mother: I don't know if you can go to your father's place this
weekend. He's three months behind in his support checks. Why
should he get to see you if he doesn't even care enough about
you to send us the money he's supposed to. Maybe I should get
the court on him.

Father: I know things are hard at your mom's house. She never
could get things organized; she's always been a flake. You're getting
old enough to tell the judge you want to live with me. Wouldn't
you like that?

Children often hear comments of this sort. In their own anger and
frustration parents can forget that they, not their children, are the
ones getting the divorce. They will have an ex-husband or ex-wife

but children do not have ex-mothers or ex-fathers. A youngster's emotional ties are usually strong to each parent. Regardless of how true statements of this nature are, missiles aimed at an ex-spouse will more readily lodge in the heart of the children, wounding and frightening them.

Lonely parents, suffering the dislocation of divorce, will many times turn to their children as sources of emotional support and comfort. It is not at all uncommon for parents to sleep in the same room or even the same bed with youngsters. Mothers frequently say that their children are lonely or frightened at night, so they permit young children to climb into bed with them or allow their older children, even young adolescents, to sleep in the same bedroom in a sleeping bag. Fathers often explain bed or room sharing with youngsters in terms of living in the very small apartment they rented after they moved out of the family home. They claim there is not enough space to permit separate sleeping quarters. In nearly every instance, these are rationalizations for the parents' own unconscious wishes to feel especially close to a child and to relieve their own feelings of loss and isolation.

Though children may enjoy these sleeping arrangements, they are emotionally costly to them. Sleeping apart from parents is a developmental achievement for youngsters. They acquire a firmer sense of independence, autonomy, and competence by being able to manage this sort of separation from parents. Having a child in the same bed, or even bedroom, with a parent is equivalent to a vote of "no-confidence" in the child's abilities to be on his own and can affect feelings of independence in school and with friends. For some children sharing the intimacy of close sleeping arrangements with a parent of the opposite sex may also be inadvertently stimulating. Even if there is no sexual activity at all, the very closeness of sleeping with a parent can be exciting to children. This kind of excitement has a forbidden quality to it and can provoke intense feelings of guilt and shame. Children who regularly sleep with or near a parent often seem to feel more conflicted with that parent, almost as if they have to make up for the closeness at night by being distant or uncooperative during the day.

Parents who feel lonely and overwhelmed by the interpersonal conflicts and financial burdens of divorce along with the stresses of single-parenting sometimes turn to their children for yet another kind of support. Children are given the tasks of regularly preparing meals, looking after younger siblings, doing laundry, and generally keeping

14

up the household. The child, in effect, becomes parent-like. The "parenting child" provides realistic help to beleaguered parents, but at the cost of partially sacrificing important elements of childhood. At the time in their lives when it is developmentally appropriate to loosen the emotional ties to parents in favor of building and consolidating peer relationships while exploring the possibilities of the world beyond the family, these youngsters become stuck in day-to-day responsibilities at home. They become old beyond their years, forego the freedom of childhood to find and develop new interests and abilities, and often experience long-lived resentment over the burdens placed upon them.

In addition to continued hostility between parents and parental neediness, the deepening sense of loss of the relationship to the noncustodial (or nonprimary) parent, typically father, is another potential source of stress for children in the short-term aftermath stage of divorce. Most children see their father less than once a month during this period.[9] The father's role as a model of masculine development for his sons diminishes, as does his contribution to his daughters' emerging sense of femininity and comfort in interacting with males.[10] Boys and girls are also at risk for becoming overly enmeshed with their mother in the absence of a relationship with their father as if all their emotional eggs were in one basket.

However, although more attention is usually paid to fathers' tendency to become peripheral in their children's lives, many youngsters also suffer a partial loss of their relationship with their mother as well. The economic necessity for mothers to return to the work force, increase the time already spent at work, or engage in some educational/vocational training reduces the time and energy available for child-rearing. The appropriate and understandable need to begin to construct a whole new social life further decreases the availability of mothers. In effect there is a double-barrelled loss of parents: the obvious shift in the father–child relationship and the more subtle but equally important changes in the mother–child relationship. For most youngsters, these losses are painful as they learn to do without the comfort, security, and pleasure of close, supportive parent–child relationships. Fortunately, many children learn to cope well and eventually develop a precocious sense of independence and competence.[11] But others seem to get stuck in their social-emotional growth and languish on the shores of childhood, feeling too frightened and alone to attempt to set sail into the waters of adolescence and young adulthood.

Children must also begin to contend with a new source of stress during the short-term aftermath stage of divorce. For the first time in their lives the majority of youngsters face the conflicted prospect of fully acknowledging their parents' sexuality. Parental dating often becomes a part of life during this phase of divorce. Until this time children are usually able to maintain the fantasy that their parents are not sexual beings and, thus, can avoid the burdens, curiosity, and conflicts this realization brings. Though by middle elementary school grades most children are aware of the biological connection between sexual intercourse and having children, they are not prepared to accept emotionally that their parents can become sexually aroused and like it! For their parents to have had sex for procreative purposes is barely acceptable to elementary school-age children and well understood by adolescents. For a parent to be sexually active for the pleasure of sex with someone besides the child's other parent, even in the context of a mature, intimate relationship, is unacceptable to most youngsters of any age. Dating, which may mean having more than one partner, is even more difficult for children to experience as appropriate behavior for a parent. When the child's opposite-sex parent is dating, it stirs uncomfortable feelings of curiosity and excitement. When it is the child's same-sex parent who is dating, it raises conflicted possibilities (through modeling and identification) for similar behavior on the part of youngsters. This can be especially troubling to adolescents who are wrestling with their own emerging sexuality and are struggling to find appropriate ways of coping with it.

Parental dating stirs up conflicts other than sexual ones as well. Regardless of which parent is dating, children are confronted by a new competition for their parent's time and affection, making them even more vulnerable to worries about being unimportant to parents. The obvious pleasure a parent takes in a new dating partner threatens a child's sense of importance to that parent. The spectre of losing the relationship with the parent looms large indeed. Secondly, the parent's dating also interferes with a fond, though sometimes secret or apparently only casual, wish most youngsters have that their parents will reconcile their differences and get back together again. The hostility or aloofness many parents report their children have toward a dating partner stems in large measure from these two worries.

To the extent that parents continue to be at war with one another and enlist their children in the conflict, feel lonely and turn to their children for companionship, feel overwhelmed by the demands of single-parenting and seek to shift these responsibilities to their children, are anxious about financial pressures and throw themselves into work or retraining to the near exclusion of parenting, are pained by the social isolation of this stage of divorce and immerse themselves in the pursuit of new intimate relationships without awareness of or attention to a child's reactions to parent dating, youngsters will suffer new and ongoing stresses related to the unfolding divorce process. Parents are understandably vulnerable to the multiple stresses associated with this stage of the divorce process. When parents can acknowledge and then cope with these pressures without abandoning their role as a parent, children are considerably less distressed. Grandparents, friends, religious affiliations, parent support groups, and individual counseling are resources many parents and children find helpful during this difficult time of divorce transition.

The Long-Range Period

The long-range phase of the extended divorce process typically begins two to three years after the initial separation. However, at times the first two stages can be prolonged due to battles over custody, visitation, and/or financial settlements, or conversely, because of an enmeshed couple's difficulty in achieving a final emotional separation and legal divorce. In fact, these often go hand-in-hand, with bitter disputes in evidence on the surface accompanied by a deeper, perhaps unconscious, need to stay mutually involved. This is a manifestation of the old adage, "We can't live together, but we can't live without each other."

A major stressor for children in the long-range phase of the divorce process is continued interparental hostility. It is precisely because one or both ex-spouses are having difficulty in coming to terms emotionally with being separated that long-lasting, intense conflicts between parents persist. This has a very different flavor from the anger and hurt feelings so common during the first two stages of divorce. Rather than a reaction to the understandable pain and general distress associated with the earlier phases of the divorce process, protracted, bitter conflict is nearly always indicative of a serious problem in accepting the finality of the divorce.

Frequently one parent believes that the divorce is a much needed, adaptive solution to an intolerable marital relationship, while the other is unable to relinquish that bond. This may take the form of jealousy and continued efforts to ''court'' the ex-spouse and press for a reconciliation. Expressions of extreme dependency that the person is not consciously aware of are not unusual: an adult may drink heavily, become physically ill, or provoke being dismissed from a job. These may be put before the ex-spouse with indirect or direct pleas for support and involvement.

But perhaps the most common form of persistent enmeshment is when one parent feels so deeply wounded and enraged that he cannot let go of the relationship. The motive for the continuing conflicts is neither reconciliation nor emotional support. The tie that binds this relationship is made up of self-justification and punishment of the ex-spouse. The milder but nonetheless maddening forms of this conflicted enmeshment include frequent lateness in paying child support, regularly picking up or dropping off a child at the wrong time, and requesting many small but irritating changes in visiting schedules and/or financial arrangements. Or the provocation can be more direct, ranging from refusal to follow court orders regarding support payments and visitation to harassing telephone calls and repetitive litigation. More recently there seems to be an increase in use of the ultimate nuclear strikes of divorce-related parent warfare: kidnapping and false accusations of child abuse.

While some irritability and disagreement is not unusual even years after the initial separation, youngsters who are faced with ongoing, serious conflicts between their parents at this stage of the divorce process are at a significant risk for developing emotional and behavioral disorders. The cumulative effects of such persistent and corrosive interparental hostility are compounded by the virulent nature of parental warfare occurring so late in the divorce process. Every effort should be made to limit, and hopefully end, serious conflict at this stage of divorce. This may include seeking individual psychotherapy to work out the underlying issues that fuel the conflict, consistently refusing to accept an ex-spouse's invitations to perpetuate this destructive dance, altering the mode of communication with an ex-spouse (for example, insisting on written communication about visiting schedules in place of explosive verbal communication), and if necessary, obtaining legal counsel with the aim of reducing any direct contact with an ex-spouse.

Though many parents continue to date during the long-range stage of divorce, the great majority eventually marry during this period.[12] Thus, the stresses for children of parents dating give way to those that remarriage brings. Frequently a parent's marriage is preceded by an informal and intermittent or more formal live-in arrangement. It is common to have a progression in which dating leads to a commitment to date one person exclusively and for that to result in the new partner beginning to spend occasional nights sleeping at the parent's home. Gradually the number of "overnights" increases until for all practical purposes the couple is living together. Since youngsters are most directly affected by live-in arrangements and the remarriage of their custodial parent, and most children reside with their mothers after a marital separation, further discussion will assume that context.

When a mother takes a part-time or full-time live-in partner, she also changes the interpersonal dynamics of the entire household. Her children are more fully aware of the fact that she has a serious commitment to another adult. The competitive feelings youngsters often have toward their mother's dating partner can be intensified. They observe directly her affectionate, caring, and even exciting feelings toward him and may worry about their own place in her heart. Will she leave them and go away with her new partner? Will she still love them? Most children do not articulate these feelings to themselves or their parents. Instead they feel generally uneasy, irritable, and/or frightened. They know they do not like the situation but are not sure why.

In addition to these competitive feelings and the worries they spawn, children often resent their mother's live-in partner because he is a threat to a cherished, if unspoken, wish: the hope that mother and father will reconcile their differences and get back together. If mother really loves this new man, she may marry him and then she and father will never get back together.

Children are not only affected by their feelings and fantasies about the relationship between mother and her new partner. They also have a relationship with him that is filled with mines ready to explode. If he is nice and likeable, many children are faced with feeling disloyal to their father for enjoying the company and activities they share with mother's boyfriend. One important reason youngsters can be prickly and uncooperative with him is to avoid just such a loyalty conflict. If he is too distant or unfriendly, children feel rejected by him and even more dramatically excluded from the relationship between mother and her partner. It begins to feel to them that they are superfluous bystanders to the new couple's relationship.

Perhaps the greatest source of stress for youngsters, one they will verbalize openly if given the opportunity, is the enormous outrage they feel toward mother's boyfriend when he tries to discipline them or assign them chores. From his point of view, he may feel that he is helping out his new partner who has been struggling with the considerable pressures of being a single parent. From the children's perspective, he is exercising an authority to which he has absolutely no legitimate claim. How dare he ask them to do the dishes, take out the garbage, or worse, ground them for some infraction! Who does he think he is?

Mother: [to her ten-year-old son] It's 8:20 and the dinner dishes are still in the sink. You know it's your job to wash them on Tuesdays. Let's get to it.

Son: But there are so many! Why did you have to cook such a big meal?

Mother: It's no worse than most nights. Come on, the faster you get to it, the quicker it'll get done.

Son: [whining] Can't I wait 'til this T.V. program is over?

Mother: [twenty minutes later] Hey, it's getting close to bedtime. Come in here and do the dishes.

Son: [sullenly] I don't feel like it. Can't I do the dishes tomorrow night? There are too many tonight.

Boyfriend: [slightly irritated] Come on now. Your mother let you watch the end of your program. Now it's time to get the dishes done.

Son: [upset] I'm tired. Besides there are too many dishes. I'll wash the dishes tomorrow night.

Boyfriend: [more irritated] Your mother told you to do them tonight, young man. Now do what your mom said. Don't give her a hard time.

Son: [angrily] I'm not gonna do them tonight. I told you I'd do them tomorrow.

Boyfriend: Your mom said tonight! Do them now unless you want to be grounded!

Son: [running to his room] I don't have to do them! You can't ground me. I'm not doing them.

Mother's boyfriend feels he is helping his beleaguered partner deal with an uncooperative son. He stays out of it until he begins to sense that she is frazzled and is getting upset. He intercedes to support her

20

and tries to add his firmness to mother's position. The son quickly becomes irritated, the boyfriend feels ineffective and then threatens a disciplinary action. That becomes the last straw for the son. Interactions of this sort are very common in situations with a live-in boyfriend or a new stepfather.

The early stage of remarriage introduces similar conflicts into the lives of children: competitive feelings toward the stepparent for the time and affection of the parent; conflicted loyalties between their positive feelings toward the stepparent and their own parent of the same sex; anger toward the parent and stepparent for interfering with the wish for a reconciliation between the parents; and, resentment over the stepparent's assigning chores or handing down discipline. In addition to these conflicts, which are common to parents dating, having a live-in partner, and remarriage, there are new potential stresses for children when the stepparent has children from a previous marriage or there are youngsters born in the new marriage. The presence of stepsiblings from the stepparent's former marriage or half-siblings from the new marriage creates new competitive possibilities for many children. Not only do they have to share their mother with her husband but they also have to share her with step- and/or half-siblings. What can make this especially hard for children is that acquiring these new siblings also usually means that they are partially losing a special place in the family. A boy who was the oldest child in the household may have a stepbrother who is now the eldest. Or the girl who was the youngest, the ''baby'' of the family, may be displaced by an even younger stepsister or the birth of a half-sister. The girl who had a brother and was the only girl in the family may now have a stepsister thus losing the unique feminine role in the sibship.

Stepsibling relationships also pose another potential problem besides competitive ones. A sixteen-year-old boy and his fifteen-year-old stepsister may find themselves attracted to one another. Living under the same roof, regularly or only when the stepsister is visiting on a weekend or during the summer, can stimulate exciting feelings that can cause great guilt in the youngsters or concern and uneasiness in the adults.

The number and serious nature of the potential stresses facing children whose parents choose to marry again can make it appear that it is easier to remain single. However, the stresses associated with remarriage, while real and perhaps partly responsible for the fact that approximately half of second marriages with minor children on the scene end in divorce, are also opportunities for enhanced emotional and social growth for children. The chance to observe a loving relationship between a man and a woman can serve as a new corrective model for intimate adult relationships. A close, caring relationship between a boy and his stepfather or a girl and her stepmother can facilitate the child's development of a solid sense of masculine or feminine identity. A warm, loving relationship between a boy and his stepmother or girl and her stepfather can build the youngster's self-esteem, increase confidence in feeling accepted by the opposite sex, and provide practice in relating comfortably to members of the opposite sex.

And there are numerous potential sources of stress for children who grow up in a single-parent household. Most one-parent households are mother-headed and have only one income, an income often substantially below that of a man, which frequently results in continuing economic distress; this means fewer opportunities for educational and extracurricular experiences. Reduced economic circumstances usually means living in a neighborhood in which the educational resources are not as good as they are elsewhere. The parent will also be less likely to afford extra music lessons and some athletic activities. Economic constraints may limit growth-enhancing experiences such as trips to museums and zoos, attending concerts and plays, or having a computer or set of encyclopedias right in the home. Even children whose fathers pay substantial child support are frequently faced either with not attending college or not going to the college of their choice, because many divorce agreements do not make provisions for this expense.

Economic factors are not the only source of possible stress for children who are raised in single-mother families. There is a great potential for mothers and children to form overly close, enmeshed relationships with each other. The tendencies in this direction, described earlier in the context of the pressures on parents associated with the short-term aftermath stage of divorce, can harden and become an ongoing life-style in the long-range phase of divorce. The child who is involved in an enmeshed relationship with mother has a more difficult time engaging fully in appropriate peer relationships. He may be immature, refusing to grow up or not being permitted to leave the mother–son dyad. Or she may be pseudomature, comfortable only with adults, as she becomes a parent or a peer and confidant to her mother, or a substitute mother to her siblings. Although the stresses of remarriage are avoided when a parent remains single, the opportunities for enhanced child development associated with remarriage are lost.

The stresses associated with each stage of the divorce process can be formidable even under the best of circumstances. Whether the side effects of the social surgery of divorce are better or worse than the impact on children of continuing a bad marriage is not the issue: either situation will create difficulties for youngsters of all ages. The question facing parents who do divorce is what can be done to minimize this stress for their children and thus facilitate healthy social, emotional, and cognitive growth. The very first thing parents—and other adults who hope to help youngsters cope effectively with divorce-related stresses—need to know is the critical importance of being able to communicate constructively with children. This is the cornerstone of assisting all children who are faced with stress.

3

►◄

Communicating With Children

When children are in emotional distress they either feel awful and know it or they find themselves involved in maladaptive, troublesome behaviors that serve as defenses against becoming directly aware of their inner pain. A youngster may feel frightened that a parent will get hurt in the course of an angry argument between parents or may ward off that fear by becoming angry and combative at school. He may be furious at the parent who leaves the family home when parents have separated, or he may preserve the loving feelings toward that parent by, instead, becoming provocative and disruptive at school. She may feel painfully torn in her loyalties toward each parent after divorce or actively take the side of one parent against the other in order to lay these loyalty conflicts to rest. Establishing a *communicational link* between an adult and the child serves several crucial functions that help reduce the youngster's emotional distress or the maladaptive behavioral defenses against feeling it.

Adult–child communication about emotional upset or problem behaviors gives children a sense that they are understood and are not alone with their troubles. This empathic bridging is itself a relief to children who can become overwhelmed by difficult feelings or the trouble they are getting into. To be frightened, sad, or feel behaviorally out of control is bad enough; to feel isolated in their distress is unbearable. The very fact that a child's troubles can be perceived and even possibly understood becomes a sustaining ray of hope.

When an adult opens a communicational channel with a child, it is a clear demonstration that the grown-up is not intimidated or repelled by the child's emotional or behavioral difficulties. The effect this has on children is to reduce the intensity of the upset. After all, if a parent, teacher, or some other responsible adult can voluntarily approach the problems, it must mean that they are not nearly as awful and need not be as overwhelming as they have seemed to the child. The adult's calm in the face of the child's emotional pain or behavior problems and the willingness to try to make sense of what is going on also provide the youngster with a model for confronting his or her troubles, and hope of resolving the underlying conflicts.

The process of communication affords insights into the nature of the emotional distress or interactional problems. A child can begin to understand why he or she feels sad, gets angry at school, worries about being hurt, feels unworthy, or has difficulty sleeping. Insight yields a dawning sense of mastery, new perspectives on events, and alternative options for behavior, all of which help relieve emotional pain or the need to act in ways that bring trouble to the child.

Adult–child communication can reveal a child's burdensome misconceptions and provide opportunities to correct them. The child who has believed himself to be the cause of a divorce and the youngster who has believed that a parent's failure to visit regularly was due to her own shortcomings are two common examples of misconceptions leading to internal pain or action defenses against it. Clarifying these misunderstandings is enormously relieving for children.

Finally, the communication process provides new, safe opportunities for expressing conflicted, worrisome feelings. This is more than catharsis, though that is helpful in its own right; it is a way to practice venting feelings that the child believes would be unacceptable to parents or other adults. The youngster who is furious at mother for beginning to date after divorce may worry that she will find that anger unacceptable and therefore reject the child for it. Or the child may become guilty or anxious about even feeling, let alone expressing, intense anger toward the mother whom he loves as well as, at least temporarily, hates for caring about someone else. Many children will inhibit powerfully conflicted feelings, such as rage at a loved parent, to the point of not even knowing that the anger is there. Instead they may seem depressed, disguise their anger by becoming uncooperative at home, or take their feelings out on someone else, such as a teacher or another youngster. Adult-child communication about these sorts of conflicted feelings can provide children with a safe arena for coming to know, accept, and therefore modulate them.

The great majority of parents are caring, well-intentioned people.

Many believe that it is important for their children to feel comfortable enough to tell them when they feel troubled or upset. Most parents also want to be open with their youngsters. Parents who are separating or who have divorced want to explain what has been happening and the implications of the divorce and the multitude of changes that usually accompany this important restructuring of the family. There is often an implicit belief that communicating with children about important family events which very much affect children's lives will help relieve their concerns and minimize potential negative effects on them.

However, the most common complaint child and family therapists hear from divorcing or already divorced parents is that it is difficult to talk with the children about important changes in the family. I have heard parents say: "He won't talk to me about his dad not living at home anymore," "I don't know what feelings she has about the divorce because she doesn't talk about it," "She must have questions about everything that's been happening, but she never asks me about what's going on," and, "I've tried to talk with him about the divorce, but he just clams up or walks away." Clinicians hear parents spontaneously mention the need to talk not only about divorce-related matters but also about topics such as death of a family member or pet, birth of a sibling, beginning to attend a new school, chronic physical illness of a child or a parent, a child's first piano recital, an adolescent's first romance, and peer pressures to drink and experiment with drugs and sex.

The fact is, however, that in a great many families parents rarely discuss emotionally charged topics with their children. Interested and involved parents ask their children about what happened at school that day, if they had a good time playing with friends at the park, whether they had fun at a friend's birthday party, whether a math test was hard, or what a concert was like. The responses from youngsters vary greatly: there are the open, rambling accounts given by preschoolers and early elementary school children; the often detailed, factual reports from boys and girls in later elementary school grades; and, the brief, unrevealing answers given by many adolescents. In most everyday efforts at parent–child communication, the topics addressed do not involve emotion-laden family transactions or relationships and require little if any self-disclosure of the child's private thoughts, concerns, or feelings. In short, they are "safe" subjects.

Other common forms of day-to-day parent–child communications are basically requests or directives—"What's for dinner?" "Will you play a game with me?" "Can I have an ice cream cone?" "Can I have the car this Saturday night?" "Can I have a friend sleep over this Friday?" "Will you drive me to a movie tomorrow night with my friends?" "Can I stay up to see the special on TV?" Parents direct (however gently) that youngsters set the dinner table, go to the bathroom, eat with utensils rather than their fingers, make their bed, stop hitting their brother, share their toys with friends, finish their homework, be home at a particular hour, and so forth. The responses of parents and children to requests and directives are usually brief and often are "answered" with behaviors rather than words alone. Conflicts surely arise, but these are typically handled with very brief discussion, negotiation, insistence, or discipline. Attention is rarely focused on anyone's private feelings, thoughts or concerns. Thus, it is not at all surprising that parents, no matter how well-motivated and caring, have trouble communicating with children about their personal reactions to important family events like divorce or other stressful life circumstances they encounter outside the home. They have virtually no experience at it!

Parents are not the only adults who are at sea when it comes to this type of communication with children. Teachers and pediatricians, who interact with children regularly, have remarkably little or no training in discussing the inner lives of children. Attorneys and judges, who often talk with children about highly upsetting issues such as custody and visiting schedules after divorce, or about injury and mistreatment arising from possible child abuse/neglect, are usually ill-equipped to communicate effectively with youngsters.

Adults are often hindered in their efforts to communicate with children by false assumptions about children's abilities to handle conversation about difficult issues. One powerful implicit expectation many adults have as they approach a child who is confronting a stressful life event is that the child will clearly and obviously welcome the opportunity to discuss his private reactions to the upsetting circumstances. Nothing could be farther from the truth! Children generally hate looking squarely at and talking about their emotional distress. The preferred modes for coping with internal turmoil are not to think about it, to act as if nothing were wrong, and to admit to no upset feelings. This can be enormously costly to the child, either burdening her with painful feelings or the consequences of getting into trouble as a result of the behavioral defenses against being in touch with

28

uncomfortable feelings. Most youngsters, even through adolescence, are reluctant to become consciously aware of, let alone discuss, their emotional upset.

Another false assumption many adults make is that children will be able to take a psychological step back from their emotional experience and observe what it is that they are feeling. This is a difficult process when it comes to painful feelings even for many adults. It requires a blend of cognitive and emotional maturity that is beyond most teenagers, let alone younger children. Even if a youngster is motivated to discuss private, upsetting feelings and concerns with an adult, the capacity to observe these internal states analytically usually does not appear until late adolescence.

Adults also often assume incorrectly that children can put their conflicted feelings into words. Even when youngsters are aware of being upset, it is usually experienced as a global, undifferentiated state of distress. Finding the appropriate language to express its specific nature requires a level of cognitive-affective integration well beyond the grasp of children until they reach their midteen years. It is far more likely for children under stress to translate their feelings into actions than words. These behaviors, which serve to protect youngsters from psychological pain, are precisely what often gets them into trouble with adults. The child who is sad about not seeing his father much after a divorce will rarely put that feeling into words. Instead he may withdraw from social interactions with friends or turn to compensatory ways of trying to feel good again, such as overeating, trying extra hard to do well at sports or academic subjects, or even using ''recreational'' drugs.

Finally, and perhaps most important of all, adults assume that they will find the child who is facing a difficult set of life circumstances poignantly appealing. Television programming and articles in the popular printed media often portray such children as silently suffering waifs. Our hearts go out to these children, and we are prepared to be understanding, empathic, and helpful. This seems to be a very popular, widely shared myth. In fact, when children are notably unresponsive to good-willed efforts to engage them and get them to talk about their troubles, adults then feel helpless and uncomfortable, two feelings that do not sustain an initial charitable perspective toward the child. This becomes even more problematic when the youngster has begun to ''act out'' feelings, that is, erect behavioral defenses against experiencing the emotional pain triggered by upsetting life events. The child who has become uncooperative at home, is overeating, picking on a brother or sister, in trouble at school for talking back to the teacher, has taken the family car without permission, or has come home from a party with alcohol on her breath rarely stimulates warm, nurturing, protective feelings in most adults. The task of understanding and keeping firmly in mind that the source of such behaviors is emotional distress, now rendered invisible because these behavioral defenses are in place and working to spare the child that pain, is formidable indeed!

Collectively, these false assumptions usually doom the well-intentioned efforts of parents, educators, pediatricians, and other professionals to communicate with children. Initial good intentions and caring feelings quickly give way to attempts at controlling or disciplining the youngster. Adults may feel resigned, defeated or angry about their failure to reach the child.

Even when adults are not encumbered by erroneous assumptions, their efforts to communicate may be hindered by uncertainty about how to talk to children. Thus, it is helpful to learn effective methods for initiating or enhancing communication about most problems. Communication between adults and children that helps youngsters cope adaptively with emotional distress and the behavioral defenses against its recognition is most effective from the preschool years through early adolescence. While some of the communication methods presented below can be used with older toddlers, infants and toddlers usually are best served in times of stress by adopting particular parenting styles and by altering the home atmosphere rather than by talking with them about their upset feelings. These supportive measures will be elaborated in subsequent chapters focused on infants and toddlers at each stage of the divorce process.

Communicating constructively with all youngsters around emotionally charged issues depends heavily on what are called *displacement techniques.* Displacement refers to the use of indirect forms of communication that are the stock and trade of child therapists. These include the use of hand puppets, dolls and dollhouses, action figures (soldiers, monsters, dinosaurs), and drawing. In short, many displacements capitalize on the kinds of activities and materials that are comfortable, appealing, and familiar to children. In addition there are verbal displacements such as reading a story together, making up a story that is tailor-made for a particular child and her life circumstances, and talking with the youngster about imaginary boys and girls or children in general.

Regardless of the specific displacement vehicle (hand puppets, draw-ing, talking about imaginary boys and girls), the aim is to represent in the displacement the nature of the child's emotional distress or the observable behavior problem, the likely source of the difficulty, alternative ways of coping, and, at times, a reassuring or positive outcome to the underlying difficulties. These displacement methods circumvent the need for a child to take a psychological step back from painful emotional experiences, observe them internally, and then put their feelings into words in order for effective communication to occur.

Displacement techniques will vary according to the youngster's level of development. What are familiar and pleasurable activities for preschool and many elementary school age children are experienced as babyish and silly by older elementary school children and adoles-cents.

Preschoolers and elementary school children enjoy many play activi-ties that lend themselves to displacement techniques. However, there are considerable differences among children. While some will find hand puppets great fun others will see them as childish or uninteresting. Some youngsters love playing with dollhouses while others are drawn to action figures, a distinction that often, but by no means always, falls along gender lines; girls typically prefer the former and boys the latter. The parent can use her knowledge of the child to make a good guess about what he will find engaging, and professionals who do not know the child well enough can ask the parent. Different activities and materials can be tried if the first does not capture the child's interest.

A professional (for example, day-care provider, therapist, pediatri-cian, educator, attorney, or judge) should always inform and obtain consent from parents if she plans to use these methods, as they are surprisingly powerful techniques. The basic strategy consists of several steps:

1. Represent in the displacement the observable signs of emotional distress. This can be crying, fighting, refusing favorite foods, being uncooperative at home, having trouble with schoolwork, demeaning or avoiding a parent, and so forth.

2. Comment about how upsetting the observable behavior is to the displacement figure who is used to represent the child.

3. Represent and verbalize the underlying emotional pain or internal distress that the displacement figure is experiencing.

4. Correct verbally by demonstrating in the displacement any misperceptions or misunderstandings (based on fantasies, beliefs,
or internal conflicts) the child may have that could be contributing
to the emotional distress.
5. Represent the acceptability of conflicted feelings.
6. Portray alternative ways of expressing and coping with conflicts.

After each step the child is invited to comment on what is going on,
what the displacement figure is thinking and feeling, and what might
happen next. However, the adult continues without pressing the child
for an answer if no comment is made by the youngster.

AMY is a bright, energetic four-and-a-half-year-old whose parents
separated six months earlier. She had no immediate observable
reaction at the time, but recently began showing signs of distress
just before going to her father's apartment every Wednesday and
Friday evening for overnight visits. She sobbed loudly and would
cling to her mother when it was time to leave for her father's.
Mrs. A was puzzled by Amy's distress. She described a good
relationship between Amy and her father. Mr. A was understandably
hurt and dumbfounded by his daughter's reaction. During
consultations with a psychologist, Mrs. A told of her new dating
relationship with a man she had met at work. Amy appeared cool
toward her mother's new friend.

Both Mr. and Mrs. A are caring, involved parents. Each had
tried discussing Amy's unhappiness with her. They asked what
was bothering Amy. Mrs. A also asked if everything was all right
at her father's house, and Mr. A asked if things were going well
at mother's. (It is common for parents to expect less than adequate
caretaking on the part of the other when this sort of problem presents
itself.) Each parent told Amy that she seemed scared and asked
her what she might be frightened about. These *direct approaches,*
which come so naturally to adults, shed no light on what was
troubling Amy.

The psychologist suggested that one parent, whichever felt more
comfortable beginning, start to represent Amy's conflicts using
displacement. Dolls and dollhouses were things Amy often played
with, so they were chosen by the parents as the specific vehicle
for the communication. Note, however, that this could have been
done just as effectively using other materials such as hand puppets

or drawings, depending on a child's interests. Mrs. A volunteered to try this first.

She was asked to select a relatively calm, quiet time on a day when no trip to father's was scheduled to introduce Amy to this indirect approach to communication. Mrs. A told her daughter that they would play a game about a girl who had not one but two houses. Mrs. A set up a scene in which there were two dollhouses. She said that a mother and daughter lived in one and the girl's father lived in the other. Amy was invited to give the family a name (she chose the "Two-House-Family") and to think up a name for the girl (she picked "Mandy"). Mrs. A then represented the observable problem in the displacement. She had Mandy and the mother doll playing together. Next she had the father doll come to the door and say, "It's time for you to come to my house now so we can be together and have fun." Then Mrs. A had the Mandy doll begin to cry and hold onto her mother.

Mrs. A then commented on how upset Mandy seemed to be. She asked Amy what might be upsetting the Mandy doll. Amy said she did not know but was watching the doll play with interest. Mrs. A accepted that readily and quickly moved to say that, "Mandy seems very scared about leaving her mom; look how she's holding onto her like she wants to stay with her mom." Here, Mrs. A represented and verbalized the emotional pain of the displacement figure.

Mrs. A had the Mandy doll go with her father to his house. When she got there, Mrs. A asked Amy, "What happens next?" Amy volunteered that the Mandy doll felt sad and missed her mother. When Mrs. A commented that Mandy's mother was home waiting for Mandy to come back the next day, Amy spontaneously and angrily said, "She's not at home, she's out with her boyfriend!" Mrs. A asked why Mandy did not seem to like that and Amy replied, "Because then she'll get married and go away." Mrs. A corrected this fantasy saying, "She wouldn't get married without talking to Mandy first, and besides even if she did get married some day, Mandy would still live with her mom no matter what. That's how it is between moms and their daughters." Amy replied that, "Mandy wouldn't want to live with that jerk anyway!" Mrs. A said that Mandy seemed angry at her mother for going on dates and not spending more time with her and suggested that if Mandy told her mom when she was angry about that maybe her mom would plan special times for her and Mandy. Here Mrs. A verbalized the acceptability of her daughter's anger and indicated a way to cope with it. Amy appeared to lose interest at that point and wanted to watch TV.

In this example Mrs. A followed the six steps to using displacement communication. She was able to elicit Amy's private worry that Mrs. A would get married and leave her. Amy's underlying anger about having to share her mother with Mrs. A's boyfriend was also revealed and then verbalized and accepted by Mrs. A. Mrs. A was able to reassure Amy within the context of the displacement, that is, by talking about Mandy, that boyfriends do not take mothers away from their daughters.

It is important to note that during the displacement activity neither mother nor daughter spoke directly about their own situation, thoughts, or feelings. Yet a great deal of communication occurred between them! It is crucial that the displacement be maintained and that the adult not give in to the temptation to begin addressing issues directly with the child as insights into the youngster's difficulties are achieved. Doing so disrupts the communication as children suddenly feel that the conversational spotlight is directly on them. It is equally important to permit the child to terminate the communication by going to a different activity such as watching television, getting a snack, or going outside to play. This is not a sign that displacement is not working but only that the child has had enough for the time being. The adult can return to the displacement at a later time. In fact, it is usually helpful to have the communication repeated several times over a period of weeks (or even months for older children). Mrs. A set up the same scenario with the two dollhouses approximately a dozen times over a three-week period before Amy's anguish at leaving her to spend the night with her father began to diminish. Repetitions of the communication at different times, sometimes using alternative displacements, such as hand puppets or drawing pictures to go over the same issues, are usually required for the communication to be maximally effective.

BRIAN is a usually quiet, somewhat shy, seven-and-a-half-year-old second grader. Yet recently he began fighting with other boys at school and taking their drawings and destroying them. His parents separated when he was six-and-a-half and are in the middle of a bitter divorce, in which the property settlement and level of child support are being fought out legally. His parents are furious at each other over these financial issues and are having loud arguments in Brian's presence. Even when Brian and his younger sister are with only one parent, they hear each say derogatory things about the other.

Guided by instructions from a psychologist they consulted, Brian's father began to set up an indirect means of communication. Because of Brian's interest in certain cartoons, animal hand puppets were chosen as the displacement figures. A tiger puppet was given the name "Tony" by Brian. A wolf puppet was used to represent Tony's father and a lion puppet his mother. A frog and a dog puppet were the other boys at Tony's school. Brian's father represented the observable signs of Brian's distress by having the tiger go to school and push the dog and frog puppet around. He had Tony say, "I don't like you, I'm going to take all your drawings and tear them up." Brian watched quietly. Brian's father then commented about how upsetting this all must be for Tony. "He really doesn't want to fight; it feels crummy to always be fighting instead of playing," he said. Brian was invited to decide what happened next. He said, "Tony's going to get into a lot of trouble," but would not elaborate on just what kind of difficulty this would be. Brian's father verbalized the tiger's underlying emotional pain by saying, "He must be so mad that he just gets himself into trouble day after day after day."

Brian's father then had Tony go home after school. He showed Tony's mother, the lion, having an argument over the telephone with the wolf puppet who represented Tony's father. The lion-mother said, "I want more money, you jerk," and the wolf-father replied, "You can't have any more, you double-jerk!" Brian's father asked Brian, "What happens now?" With considerable feeling Brian said, "Probably the two jerks will keep screaming and fighting like they always do!" His father then represented the acceptability of his son's angry feelings toward both his parents by having Tony say, to the wolf-father and lion-mother, "Why don't you two jerks just beat each other up; I hate it when you jerks fight all the time." Brian became very quiet. His father asked what the lion-mother and wolf-father would do, but Brian stayed silent. Finally Brian's father had each parent say how sorry they were that their arguing had upset Tony. He added, "Maybe that's why Tony fights so much in school. He's got mad feelings at his mom and dad but he carries those mad feelings to school with him instead of telling his parents how angry he gets at them.'' Then Brian's father provided an alternative way of coping with Brian's anger: "Maybe Tony should shout, 'time out' at his mom and dad when they start arguing." Brian took the tiger puppet and had him start hitting the lion-mother and wolf-father yelling, "Take that you jerk!." After several minutes, Brian's father asked if Tony wanted to put his angry feelings into words. Brian replied quietly, "He's just mad at them," and seemed to become restless. His father asked if his son would like to keep playing with the hand puppets or do something different. Brian opted for going to get an ice cream cone with his father.

In this interchange, Brian's father followed five of the six steps of displacement communication. Since there did not appear to be a misperception contributing to the difficulty, step number four was not enacted. Brian's attentiveness demonstrated his engagement in the puppet play. When he became actively involved, his anger at his parents became clear. Implicit in his problems is Brian's idea that he could not express his anger toward his parents for arguing nor did he feel empowered to do anything about it. His father accepted, in displacement, the son's anger at his parents and provided a way of both trying to stop it and expressing anger by suggesting that Tony yell, "Time out." Within six weeks Brian's provocative behavior at school was replaced by his usual quiet, somewhat shy style. This seemed due not only to the support he felt and the insights he achieved via the displacement communication but also to his parents gaining a fuller and more compelling understanding of how their fighting was at the root of their son's behavior problems and underlying emotional distress. They had substantially modified their style of arguing and were more careful to restrict their disagreements and shouting matches to times when Brian and his sister were not present. They had also begun trying to avoid cutting each other down when the children were within earshot.

The use of play materials (that is, dolls, dollhouses, and hand puppets) as the displacement vehicles is most effective from preschool through elementary school years though some young adolescents can still use drawings. For some teenagers and many older elementary school youngsters creative *verbal* displacements can be effective ways to initiate communication. These include talking about "other guys" (or girls) in general, or fashioning stories about specific, imaginary youngsters. But adolescents also need direct communication because they have a tendency to experience displacement methods as too circuitous and not relevant to them if they are overused.

CARL is a thirteen-year-old eighth grader who lives with his mother and two younger brothers ages ten and eight. Mr. and Mrs. C divorced three years ago when Carl was ten. He sees his father every other weekend, alternating between a Friday afternoon to Saturday afternoon and a Saturday afternoon to Sunday afternoon schedule. While Carl has shown some signs of irritability since his parents' divorce, until recently he has been doing reasonably well.

For the past six months, however, Carl has become increasingly resistant to listening to his mother. Requests for him to help out at home, as he had been doing, are now met with comments such as, "later," "not now," and "I'll do it in a few minutes." When he does not follow through and is reminded of what needs to be done, he becomes angry and tells his mother to leave him alone and not "bug" him. He seems to be getting more uncooperative, sullen, and angry as each week passes. This behavior does not appear when Carl is at his father's home. Mr. C feels his ex-wife must be doing something wrong. Mrs. C consulted a therapist about her mounting frustration with her son's behavior as well as her ex-husband's accusations that she is at fault for Carl's emerging difficulties at her home.

The clinician reassured Mrs. C that it is common for a child to have problems with the custodial parent and be on good behavior with the other parent and introduced her to the idea of displacement communication. She was given the six-step outline about how to implement this strategy and was told that with teenagers, unlike displacement communication using play materials with younger children in which all steps can be unfolded at a single time, the steps had to be done using very brief statements over a period of several days. The therapist suggested that Mrs. C begin the displacement statements at times when no conflict was evident and when she was not asking Carl to do a chore. Further, the clinician said that it would be best if her comments were made in a matter-of-fact tone with no expectation that Carl would respond to them.

On day one of this communicational program, Mrs. C mentioned to Carl, "I heard that after parents split up and get a divorce that a lot of times guys don't like to feel that they're taking orders from their mom, especially when they get to be teenagers like fourteen- or fifteen-years-old." Carl continued eating his afterschool snack. After a minute or two Mrs. C added, "I guess a guy can get pretty mad when he feels he's sort of being bossed around by his mother, and then he figures, 'she can't tell me what to do'." This was all that was said on the first day. Mrs. C had implemented step one by representing in a verbal displacement the observable signs of Carl's distress.

The next day Mrs. C said, "I was thinking about guys getting mad about feeling their mom is bossing them, and, you know, it must be hard for guys to start feeling upset with their mom. Especially if a mom and her son have been getting along pretty well and liking each other." Carl responded saying, "Well I'm not upset about anything." Mrs. C underscored her first comment; "Well it can't feel too good for a guy to feel like his mom is on his back all the time." Carl replied, "If you didn't bug me all the time, then I would be just fine!" Mrs. C concluded that day's communication saying, "It usually helps to try and figure things out and come up with a plan when you're feeling bugged. Let's think about it some more and see what we can do."

On the third day Mrs. C verbalized the underlying emotional distress saying, "I've thought some more about what we've been talking about and it seems to me that maybe guys feel their mom isn't respecting the fact that they're growing up when they keep asking him to do things. Maybe it feels like he'd be sort of a little kid if he did everything his mom said." Carl jumped in at that point and said, "I'm no wimp and I can think for myself!" Mrs. C moved quickly to correct his misperception; "I don't think a teenager is a wimp because he helps out around the house or respects his mom." Carl added, "He is if he just follows orders and gives in all the time." Mrs. C then accepted her son's conflicted feelings and suggested an alternative way of coping with them by saying, "I can see why a guy could want to be helpful to his mom and at the same time feel like a wimp by always doing what she asked. Maybe it would make more sense if a guy and his mom sat down and both of them made a list together of the things a guy could do around the house that would be a help." Carl said, "It would just be your list anyway." Mrs. C replied, "Then you make a list and we can talk about it. How about doing that this weekend?'' Carl agreed and drew up a more extensive list than Mrs. C had hoped for. They continued to communicate in these ways with Mrs. C implementing whichever steps in the communicational process seemed appropriate, as Carl had difficulty from time to time following through on the list he, himself, had developed.

This example illustrates a common problem in carrying out verbal displacements with teenagers: Carl frequently commented outside the displacement referring directly to himself and his mother; for example, ''*I'm* not upset'' and ''If *you* didn't bug me, then *I* would be just fine'' when responding to her displaced statements about ''guys.'' It is tempting for adults to respond in kind and immediately abandon the displacement by talking directly to the youngster about himself or their own role in the interaction. This is usually a mistake that adults must resist; adolescents may find this directness too threatening and retreat to uncommunicative shrugs or silence. After all steps in the process have been implemented, usually several times, a teenager may say something like, ''I'm talking about me and you keep talking about guys'' in an irritated way. The adult can try being more direct if the adolescent is clearly signalling that he is fed up with the roundabout quality of the indirect communication. But the adult should be prepared to return to the displacement method if the adolescent has difficulty communicating constructively in the more direct style.

Another difficulty in using verbal displacement with teenagers is the amount of restraint it takes on the adult's part to keep the steps brief and to space out the process over several days. There is an urge if the youngster is not responding much to the statements to push on further at that time. Conversely, if the adolescent is engaged in the process and revealing his or her thoughts and feelings, there is a tendency to try to capitalize immediately on the momentum of the communication. However, it is best to stick to the plan for a couple of weeks to avoid the possibility of the adolescent becoming skittish or overwhelmed by the conflicts that are being revealed.

In each of these three examples of displaced communication the parents have been calm and accepting of their children's responses. This is perhaps the most difficult part of implementing interventions of this sort. Parents are understandably and appropriately emotionally involved in their children's lives. They feel sad about problems their youngsters are having, angry about misbehavior, and defensive about their own possible contributions to their children's difficulties. Parents commonly feel on the spot when a child is showing signs of distress, and believe it reflects poorly on them (or worry that others will think so). No parent can completely put these feelings aside and remain fully emotionally neutral during all efforts at displaced communication with their youngster. But it is helpful for parents to keep in mind that they are doing something on behalf of their children when they talk to them in these ways and that if they do get upset and seem to "blow it," they can always try again later that day or even the following week. Children are so receptive to displaced communication that parents can return to it when they are feeling more calm and settled.

Finally, it may appear that these examples of parent–child communication depend on the parent intuitively knowing just the right thing to say. In these cases, a psychologist was carefully coaching the parents about what to say and anticipating, based on years of experience, the various possible ways a displaced communication might go. In subsequent chapters there will be many examples of how this type of parent–child interaction can unfold. The reader can find the script that best fits a particular child's age, behavioral difficulties, and/or distressed feelings for each stage of the divorce process. The very fact that displaced communication makes no direct references to the child permits adults to try out different kinds of displacement until one is found that works, without appearing inconsistent.

Communicating with children is centrally important to helping them cope with stress. But it is not the only ingredient in effective parenting. Subsequent chapters will describe other methods of alleviating divorce-related distress children experience and will illustrate communicational strategies tailored to children at different ages.

4

◄►

The Divorce Experience for Infants and Toddlers

The first stage of child development that we will examine is infancy and toddlerhood. It begins at birth and covers approximately the first two-and-a-half years of life. There are dramatic gains during this period in a youngster's cognitive and emotional growth. From being a baby who understands no verbal communication and without any language skills, the child progresses to the point where he can comprehend a great deal of what is said and is able to make himself understood much of the time. Motor development also proceeds at breakneck speed, with sitting up, crawling, walking, and running unfolding over this time.

These realistic accomplishments provide the basis for a shift from complete physical and emotional dependence to an emerging sense of independence from parents, especially the one who has been most centrally involved in the day-to-day care of the child. However, this newfound sense of freedom has not yet been consolidated. Infants and toddlers tend to become distressed when their primary caretaking parent leaves them, if only to go into another room in the home. Absences of several hours from this parent, even when left with a familiar caregiver, are stressful. The very young child is prone to develop powerful worries over being separated from a parent. The need for mothers to return to work quickly or increase their work hours after a marital separation can thus be especially stressful for infants and toddlers.

Infants and toddlers depend on parents for their emotional equilibrium as well as basic care. When young children are physically uncomfortable, hungry, tired, or frustrated, the calming influence of the

41

parent is essential. Without it, so-called "affect storms" in infancy and temper tantrums in toddlerhood tend to ensue and feel painfully disorganizing in these youngsters. Conversely, the feelings of an emotionally anguished or furious parent resonate within the very young child and result in great distress. This phenomenon of emotional resonance makes the children remarkably vulnerable to upset feelings parents frequently experience in the context of divorce.

Despite their tremendous strides in acquiring cognitive abilities, infants and toddlers are still quite limited in how much they can understand about their world. Thinking tends to be tied to concretely perceived objects and events with the capacity for abstract reasoning only minimally developed. The task of visualizing where a father's new apartment is and keeping in mind visiting schedules after the parents' marital separation is impossible. Yet these pale beside the conceptual task of understanding why a child's parents live apart and are "getting a divorce." The youngster's immature cognitive abilities make his life feel unpredictable, confusing, and at times frightening after his parents separate.

The young child's temperament has increasingly been recognized as a key factor influencing how she will respond to stress in her life.[1] Some children have an "easy" disposition that permits them to adapt to and even at times enjoy dramatic changes in their environment. Other youngsters with a "difficult" temperament become easily distressed when predictable routines are changed or loud noises (such as arguments between parents) are overheard. They are also hard to soothe once they become upset. These biologically determined, inborn factors, which we lump under the rubric of temperament, can play a significant role in how a young child adjusts to her parents' divorce.

These cognitive and emotional characteristics of infants and toddlers make them exquisitely vulnerable to the stresses of divorce. Pronounced changes in their routines, warfare between parents, and the emotional upsets of one or both parents are bewildering and painful life events for these very young children.

The Immediate Crisis Stage

As noted in chapter 2, the immediate crisis stage of divorce often consists of major changes in the life of the family, its structure and interactions. Parents separate, and usually it is the father who leaves the family residence. The parents' emotions can be intense with wounded pride and the anger and depression that so frequently accompany this psychological pain palpably in evidence. Guilt on the part of the parent who initiated or provoked the separation commonly results in depression or anger reflexively invoked to ward it off. Not only are there changes in the physical environment and usual day-to-day routines, but the emotional state of each parent also undergoes dramatic oscillations as they cope with their own reactions to the beginning of the end of their marriage.

The confusion that infants and toddlers feel is due in large measure to the cognitive limitations of early childhood. But these are not the only factors contributing to confusion and a more vague sense of disorientation. Day-care and baby-sitting arrangements may have to be altered as mother returns to or increases her involvement in work or school. New caregivers and new caregiving settings may be introduced into the lives of infants and toddlers, and along with these new arrangements come changes in schedules. All of these shifts can disrupt the smooth trajectory of childhood development, in part because very young children cannot organize them cognitively. As such, they cannot understand exactly what is happening to them or why their lives are changing so dramatically. This is especially upsetting to infants and toddlers, in part because they cannot anticipate significant events in their lives. Where they will be, what adult(s) will be there, how long they will be separated from a parent, and when and what they will be fed begin to feel totally unpredictable. The expectable sense of continuity in their lives is seriously disrupted by these major changes.

JASON's parents separated when he was fourteen months old. His mother had left her job as a salesperson in a women's clothing store one month before Jason's birth and had stayed at home full-time to care for her young son. Jason's father, a foreman for a large construction company, was not an involved father. He often drank with co-workers after quitting time and many times did not eat dinner at home. Both parents were nineteen years old when they married and now, at twenty-two, their relationship was distant, punctuated by loud arguments over minor irritations.

When Jason's mother filed for divorce, she moved out of the family apartment with Jason to another one. Within a month she realized she had to return to work full-time in order to help support herself and her son. Jason had enjoyed the full attention of his mother since his birth. She almost never left him with neighbors or baby-sitters and took him everywhere with her. But with her return to work, she had to arrange day care for him. On short notice she put together a patchwork pattern of day care. Mondays, Wednesdays, and Fridays, she dropped him off at a neighbor's house at 7:30 a.m. on her way to work. At 2:30 P.M. the neighbor returned Jason to his apartment where he was cared for by a high school girl who had just come home from school until 5:45 P.M., when his mother returned from work. Tuesdays and Thursdays Jason went to a different neighbor's home and was with the same high school student from 2:30 to 5:45 P.M. at his own home.

Jason cried and whimpered when his mother left him in the mornings. He began to suck his thumb after two weeks of this schedule. The two neighbors who provided lunch for Jason claimed that he often refused to eat. He spent most mornings watching television and cried plaintively when it was turned off. He seemed happier in the afternoons when he played with his own, familiar toys while being looked after by the high school sitter in his own apartment. However, he frequently would look up from some activity and ask "Momma?" and begin to cry. Jason's mother found him irritable and easily frustrated in the evenings. Though he had learned to walk before the parents separated, he had gone back to crawling and only walked occasionally. He protested when his mother began getting him ready for bed at night and sobbed when she left his room. Jason cried in a panicky way when his father came to pick him up for his every other week Friday evening to Saturday afternoon visit. He tried to hide behind his mother and clung to her desperately. In fact, Jason also acted this way whenever the doorbell rang; visits from mother's friends and the paperboy coming to collect money provoked the same response. Jason's mother occasionally began going out on dates several months later. He acted in a similarly frightened, upset way when the baby-sitter arrived, when his mother's date showed up, and again when she left to go out.

Though Jason's parents were both reacting well to their initial separation and were relieved by it, their young son was having great difficulty adjusting to the changes in his daily life. After spending his first fifteen months nearly always with his mother, he had to cope with repeated and prolonged separations from her. At the same time, he was confronted with the task of adapting to being with three new adults, two neighbors and a high school girl. In addition to obvious signs of upset, Jason also displayed more subtle indications of stress. His retreat from walking to crawling, his refusal of foods he had once liked, and his difficulty in going to sleep at night were evidence of significant interference in his general development. His life had changed dramatically, and he was not old enough to understand the changes or anticipate when he would be with his mother or separated from her. The basic sense of order and continuity in his life had been disrupted massively.

Infants and toddlers are extremely sensitive to the emotional states of their parents. Earlier the concept of emotional resonance was introduced to explain the young child's reactivity to emotions a parent is experiencing. Feeling unworthwhile, unlovable, abandoned, guilty, furious, anxious, and depressed is common in the immediate crisis stage of divorce. Not that a parent experiences all of these painful affects, but it is typical for parents to feel at least one and often to cycle back and forth between two or more of them. When a young child sees her parents angrily attacking one another (verbally or physically), privately enraged at the estranged spouse, depressed, or anxious, the child will feel overwhelmed and in great distress. The fact that the parent is "different" from her usual self causes infants to feel diffusely upset and toddlers to be frightened. Through emotional resonance, the young child also experiences an "affective flooding" as the pain the parent is wrestling with threatens to overwhelm the child's immature capacity to regulate reactions to powerful emotional stimuli and maintain his own equilibrium.

KELLY's parents separated when she was eighteen months old. Her parents fought bitterly for several months before the separation. Her mother was an elementary school teacher who had returned to work when Kelly was nearly a year old. Her father, an accountant, felt that his wife devoted her energies exclusively to her job and to their two daughters, Kelly and her older sister who was six. Kelly's mother accused her husband of being insensitive and controlling. He wanted his home to be meticulously neat, his laundry done on time, and his meals served punctually each evening. Each parent assailed the other and argued frequently and furiously over these issues.

Kelly's father moved out of the house at his wife's insistence.

He returned one afternoon when his wife was at work and took the stereo set, the television set, and all the pictures from the living room walls. His wife was enraged, accused him of stealing these items, and retaliated by prematurely cashing in a jointly held certificate of deposit worth several thousand dollars. Each filed complaints with the court and their legal fees were steadily mounting. Kelly's father was always late with support payments and his wife often did not have Kelly and her sister ready on time for the weekly Saturday afternoon visits with their father. When he picked them up and again when he returned them to their mother, he and his wife got into nasty, name-calling arguments. Occasionally these turned into physical fights with both parents shoving and at times slapping one another.

Kelly became increasingly fearful and angry. She withdrew from playing with the three other youngsters her age who were also in the care of a woman who ran a day-care service in her home. Kelly had been at this home for six months and had become comfortable with the woman and her other charges. She usually seemed happy and interacted well with the other children. Now she preferred watching television and playing by herself. When the other children tried to join her, Kelly pushed them away, pinched them, and yelled for them to go away. At home she became frightened when playing in her backyard. She frequently ran into the house in tears claiming she had seen a spider, a dog, or had heard a "funny noise." At night she worried about robbers who would break into the house and steal her favorite toys. Usually a sound sleeper, Kelly began waking several times a night and crying in a frightened way. She clung to her mother and insisted she be allowed to sleep in her mother's bed; this now occurred frequently and seemed to be the only way she would settle down and go back to sleep.

Kelly was responding to the warfare between her parents. Unlike Jason, Kelly had a regular, predictable schedule and was cared for by the same person each day for the whole day. Further, the day-care routine had been well established prior to her parents' separation and provided a sense of continuity she could count on amidst the changes in her family. However, the intense hostility she observed interfered with her previously good adjustment. Her fears seemed related to an idea that she or her parents would be badly hurt. She became hypervigilant so that many everyday occurrences, seeing a spider or hearing a noise, became a potential threat. As with many young children, these fears became intensified at night when fatigue and darkness make the monsters of the imagination appear more real and frightening. At the same time, Kelly was angry. Her physical attacks on children who tried to play with her or the toys she was using indicated how enraged she felt. Her interactions with her playmates seemed to mirror what she observed between her parents: hurtful pushing, possessiveness about material things, and a need for distance. Kelly was responding to the rage she saw and was also angry at her parents for acting in ways that disturbed and frightened her. Her relatively immature emotional equilibrium was upset by these powerful, angry feelings, and she was terrified that their explosiveness would hurt her or her parents.

Ninety percent of all minor children live with their mother after divorce regardless of the specific legal custody award. And it is likely that this number is even higher for infants and toddlers. Many courts still seem to follow implicitly the "tender years doctrine," in which it is simply assumed that very young children are best cared for by their mother. But much more frequently than courts favoring women in deciding on these living arrangements, divorcing couples often agree entirely on their own that infants and toddlers will be better off with their mother. Early socialization and child-rearing practices in the United States and most Western nations usually result in women being more comfortable with young children than are men. And our society seems more tolerant of men who leave their children in the primary care of their mother after divorce than the reverse. Still, there are instances in which divorcing men assume a primary caretaking role with their young children. Often these have been loving fathers who had been centrally involved in the day-to-day care of their youngsters.

MARK'S parents were married when both were in their mid-thirties. His mother was an account executive in a large advertising firm, and his father was a college professor. Both had pursued their careers single-mindedly and quite successfully. Mark was born after two years of marriage. His mother took a six-week maternity leave and then returned to work full-time. Her work schedule was hectic and she often came home late in the evening after a dinner meeting or an out-of-town presentation to prospective clients. Mark's father had a flexible schedule and was home most mornings as well as all late afternoons and evenings. He diapered and fed Mark regularly and spent many hours playing with him.

When Mark was sixteen months old his parents separated. Though there were some hurt feelings and arguments initially, both parents felt the divorce was a wise decision. Mark's mother felt tied down by her husband and son and longed for her previous life as a single career woman. Mark's father felt distant from his wife and resented her investment in her work. He suggested joint physical custody where Mark would spend half the week in each parent's home. However, Mark's mother's schedule was often unpredictable. During their first month of separation they tried to make a joint custody arrangement work, but Mark's mother frequently had to make last minute baby-sitting plans. With nearly no lead time or preparation, Mark would find himself at a neighbor's home for dinner or with a sixth-grade girl as a baby-sitter in the evening. Mark became upset by the unpredictability of his environment; not only was he moving back and forth between his parents and their homes but he had a changing cast of caretakers during the times that he was at his mother's home. He began to have temper tantrums, and his normally sunny disposition was replaced with general irritability. He pulled his cat's tail and "playfully" threw her across the room. Occasionally he pinched and bit his young grade-school baby-sitters while chortling gleefully.

His father thought Mark would be better off living with him full-time but was reluctant to suggest it to his wife, fearing she would become angry and vindictively seek and gain sole custody of their son. Mark's mother felt burdened by having to scramble to provide child care for him when her work schedule prevented her from coming home at the expected dinner hour. She began to feel frustrated and resentful of this interference in her career. She very much wished Mark could live with his father full-time; however, she imagined that then people would think she was a bad mother and did not really love her child. She felt overwhelmed by the guilt she experienced when she became angry at Mark or found herself resenting him.

Mark was reacting to the obvious disruptions in his daily routine as well as to the more subtle resentment he had begun to sense coming from his mother. His temper tantrums and mistreatment of his cat, and occasionally even his baby-sitters, were expressions of his anger over these issues and his feeling that his life was out of control. Despite being a bright youngster, his level of cognitive development did not permit a full understanding of the reasons for the chaos in his schedule. His life had become unpredictable and the emotional tone of his relationship with his mother had changed, due to her frustration and resentment. His developmentally appropriate needs for consistency in day-to-day activities, in caretakers, and in the quality of his relationship with his mother were not being met. It is difficult not to wonder how many other divorcing couples feel trapped by their own fears and guilt about departing from what they, or what they think others, believe is the "right" and proper living arrangement for their children after a marital separation. How many ongoing parental battles, difficult parent–child relationships, and children's problems are the result of an arrangement that is a poor fit with parents' personal strengths and life goals?

Changes in the environment of a young child (for example, new caregivers and caregiving settings, less time with father because he is no longer at home, decreased availability of mother as she increases her work or educational efforts) especially when they are unpredictable, warfare between parents, and the psychological disequilibrium of parents (for example, intense feelings of anger, sadness, anxiety, depression) can each constitute a powerfully stressful set of circumstances for infants and toddlers. These characteristics, which are so common in the early stage of the divorce process and may continue into subsequent stages, place enormous demands on young children to accommodate and adapt to multiple significant changes and upsetting events in their lives.

The Short-Term Aftermath Stage

Many children who are infants or toddlers during the initial stage of their parents' divorce will have become preschoolers or even older by the time the divorce process has moved into its second phase, the short-term aftermath. Since this chapter is devoted to infants and toddlers, we will address issues relevant to these early developmental periods where the divorce has proceeded to the second stage.

As the divorce process moves into its next stage, the multitude of changes in the child's daily routines become fixed elements of a new reality. Child care arrangements, the mother's work and/or educational schedule, and the pattern of time spent (or not spent) with the nonresidential father often become routine. The young child begins to experience a different but now predictable schedule. To the extent that these aspects of a youngster's day-to-day activities are still up in the air and have not become predictable, infants and toddlers will continue to be exposed to stresses associated with the initial, crisis period of divorce.

MARYLOU'S parents separated when she was four months old. Her father had begun a relationship with another woman while still married and this became the stated reason for the marital separation. During the initial crisis period her mother angrily and tearfully assailed her husband for his infidelity, while he furiously but with considerable underlying guilt defended himself. Marylou began awakening frequently several times a night, a change in the solid six-hour sleep pattern she had achieved. She often interrupted her bottle-feeding with intense crying for no apparent reason and refused the solid food she had taken to so well two months earlier. When she was six months old, her mother changed jobs from a previously held part-time position to a full-time one. Marylou spent mornings with her maternal grandmother and from 1 P.M. to 5:30 P.M. with a new baby-sitter in the sitter's home. Previously she had been looked after in the mornings in her home by her grandmother while her mother worked part-time. Both her grandmother and her baby-sitter reported that Marylou napped fitfully and briefly and seemed tense when held. She sucked hard and long when they bottle-fed her but then often "spit-up" and cried, as if in pain due to air-bubble-related cramps. Marylou also cried when awaking from afternoon naps and the baby-sitter found it hard to settle her down.

These difficulties persisted for nearly two months until Marylou was eight months old. Gradually, they began to lessen as Marylou's mother became less angry at her husband and more confident in her new full-time job. While the relationship between the parents was much less than cordial, it was no longer suffused with anger. By one year, Marylou was doing well on all developmental fronts. She ate and slept well, had begun to pull herself to a standing position and to try several tentative steps. Her face would light up when she saw her baby-sitter who reported that Marylou now seemed comfortable with her.

Marylou was able to adjust to her new caretaking arrangements, which had become a normal and expectable part of her day-to-day routine. The notable reduction in hostilities between her parents, her mother's emotional acceptance of her divorce, and her increasing confidence in herself at work and as a single parent served to reduce these sources of stress for Marylou.

What happens when daily routines continue to be unpredictable? The young child is then faced with feelings of ongoing uncertainty and a sense of discontinuity in his life. He cannot, even in the rudimentary and only ways infants and toddlers have available to them, experience a global feeling of predictability and safety. His most basic sense of security is shattered. Battles between parents also contribute to a very young child's sense of being overwhelmed, flooded by angry feelings he cannot modulate either through understanding or by distancing himself from the conflict. A majority of parents have reduced the frequency and intensity of overt warfare between them as well as their own private anger toward each other by the time they are past the initial crisis stage of divorce.

Most parents seem attentive to their children's need for predictable, secure child care arrangements and schedules. But a surprisingly large number of parents are genuinely unaware of how devastating to infants and toddlers are continued conflicts with their ex-spouse. It is as if parents assume that because the very young children cannot understand the nature of the arguments or even the meanings of the words being used that they will be unaffected by the battle. In a similar vein, many parents believe that they can mask the rage they feel toward an ex-spouse even when a fight has not occurred, so that their infant or toddler will not feel the effects of their anger. Neither is true. Even a bright toddler rarely understands the specifics of an angry exchange between parents but, nonetheless, is keenly aware of the emotions being felt and expressed. Infants and toddlers may not get the words, but they do indeed get the "music" through their tendency to emotionally resonate to feelings around them. They are thus painfully aware of a parent's continuing rage at the former spouse.

TIMMY was eight months old when his mother filed for divorce. She characterized her four-year marriage as unfulfilling and unhappy; she had made a mistake in her choice of marital partner. Deeply hurt by his wife's wish to divorce, Timmy's father became enraged at her instead of permitting himself to feel the loss of the relationship and the self-doubts it stirred up. They argued about child support, division of property, and visiting schedules. After a stormy ten-month separation, the divorce decree was granted. This legal resolution to the end of their marriage seemed to lower the level of overt conflict between them. However, when Timmy was twenty months old his mother began to date a man she had met through a church-based singles group. Timmy's father became enraged all over again. He berated his ex-wife for her dating relationship and accused her of being a "slut." He imagined that she had been involved with this man prior to their marital separation. This provided him with an explanation for his ex-wife's decision to leave their marriage. It was not due to any shortcomings in him as a husband and lover (as he unconsciously feared), it was because she was simply a promiscuous woman.

His newfound source of anger galvanized him into action. He filed a motion seeking custody of his son to remove him from the detrimental care of his ex-wife. At the same time, he frequently called his ex-wife late at night to harangue her with name-calling, to check up on whether her dating partner was still with her, and to threaten her with his plan to gain custody of Timmy. Timmy's mother was furious. She felt she had every right to date whomever she wished and have whatever kind of relationship, platonic or romantic, she chose. She also felt frightened and helpless by her ex-husband's telephone calls and his threat to take her son from her. As a young, somewhat naive mother with little formal education, she worried that her ex-husband just might convince a judge, who she expected would be a man taking a male perspective, that her home was in fact unsuitable for a young boy. Her attorney had told her that since her ex-husband was not threatening her physically, the police or courts would do nothing about the telephone calls. Her increasing sense of vulnerability fueled her anger at her ex-spouse. She "forgot" about arranged visiting times for Timmy to be with his father and counterattacked during telephone calls from him by stating angrily that her new partner was a better lover than Timmy's father had ever been and that he might just move into her home.

Timmy was panic-stricken by the palpable rage swirling around him. Though by temperament he had been an easygoing child from birth, he grew increasingly fearful and whiney. He had been at the same day-care center for four months and had become comfortable with the daily separations from his mother, who worked

part-time and attended junior college while pursuing a certificate
in practical nursing. At twenty-two months Timmy began crying
and clinging to his mother when she dropped him off in the mornings.
At the day-care center he could not begin using the toilet. The
day-care provider noted that Timmy was no longer able to sit still
for even short periods of time. Activities he had previously enjoyed
such as playing "dress-up," climbing on large wooden blocks,
and finger painting would now hold his attention for only a few
minutes at a time. He seemed to be in perpetual motion. He also
developed several "nervous habits." He twirled his hair around
his fingers incessantly and bit his fingernails. At twenty-five months
he began stuttering to the point that it was painful to listen to
him. At home he frequently whimpered at any noise, especially
the ringing of the telephone. He became fearful of strangers during
the day and worried about kidnappers coming into the house to
take him away at night.

Timmy was reacting to the prolonged, intense warfare between
his parents. His prior achievements of separating easily from his mother
at the day care center, developing large and small muscle skills by
climbing and finger painting, interacting socially with other children,
and sleeping comfortably through the night were all disrupted. Instead
he nervously wandered around the day-care center, twirled his hair,
and bit his nails. (These behaviors can be mistaken for "hyperactivity"
and result in inappropriate medication of young children.) At night,
he became fearful about being kidnapped, probably as a reaction to
the emerging custody dispute between his parents. Not only had Timmy
lost ground developmentally, he was also unable to move ahead and
start toilet training, a significant developmental accomplishment in
the lives of children. Timmy was flooded with chaotic feelings that
he could not possibly understand or organize cognitively or emotionally. He resonated to the rage he saw between his parents as well as
to the anger toward each other that even permeated their interactions
with him. They had become chronically angry, so that even when
they were not directly doing battle with one another they radiated
hostility in their tone of voice and general demeanor. Also, his mother
was fearful of losing Timmy to his father in a custody fight and
transmitted this worry to her son both subtly and overtly; he became
fearful of being kidnapped by a man and taken from his mother. At
the same time, Timmy had less contact with his mother. Her schedule

of work and school in combination with her emotional investment in her new dating partner created a global, diffuse feeling in Timmy of being less important to his mother and less central in her life. Not only was he being tossed about emotionally by the storms of rage between his parents he also felt that his home port was slipping away from him.

Though most of Timmy's difficulties were due to his being over-whelmed by the feelings created in him by the warfare between his parents and the chronic anger each experienced, in addition he had to contend with another formidable source of stress common to the second stage of divorce. His mother's laudable efforts to support herself and her son by working part-time and to improve her ability to earn a good living through further education and training took her away from Timmy for long periods of time. Even when she was at home, her involvement in school continued with reading and written assign-ments. At the same time, she was appropriately resuming a social life that included an intimate relationship with a new man. Her own adjustment to the divorce, though hampered by her ex-husband's angry intrusiveness and threats, was proceeding well. But as is so often the case, successful adaptation meant not only less time for her son but a feeling he began to develop of losing a top place in her priority list.

Single parents have many balls to keep in the air as they juggle their considerable responsibilities: work, school, friendships, dating, and parenting. Each demands her time and attention, and each provides its own special rewards. As she begins to put the pain and dislocation of divorce behind her, the single mother looks to her future, with some anxieties to be sure, but also with renewed enthusiasm, excite-ment, and hope. Her children, once a central part of her home and family focus, can be displaced despite her love for them as she sets sail toward a new life. And even very young children pick up on the fact of less time with her, less of her energies for them, and her loving feelings being in part directed toward someone new. Infants and toddlers sense these shifts in a mother's involvement with them and become uneasy. Normal separations from mother become painfully frightening, and youngsters are more readily frustrated and irritable.

Not all recently divorced women have the good fortune, opportunities and resources to become involved in work that helps support them and their children and/or education leading to jobs and careers that they might enjoy and profit from. Though these efforts can disrupt the child's feelings of continuity in his daily routines and of holding an important place in his mother's heart, both children and parents are likely to do well in the long run as mother reaches a new equilibrium in her life. The single mother understandably feels overwhelmed by the financial pressures of low-paying jobs, lack of skills to improve her economic situation, and haphazard (or no) child support payments. In some women this elicits anger toward the ex-spouse, toward men in general, and toward the courts. The considerable demands of caring for an infant or toddler, and in many instances, another child as well, can contribute to feelings of resentment toward children whom they also genuinely love. In turn this resentment spawns guilt. The infant or toddler then must try to adapt to life with a frightened, overwhelmed, and resentful parent.

The portrait just drawn is of a parent who is depressed. She may be mildly depressed and able to carry out her parenting responsibilities fairly well. Or she may be depressed to the point that she feels unable to cope with the real financial pressures and demands of parenting and holds lingering doubts about herself as an attractive, desirable woman. For the infant or toddler this is an acutely distressing situation. Mother is not off at work, school, or with a man. But she is not really "there" emotionally for the child. She may appear preoccupied, cry frequently, stare out the window, or spend a lot of time sleeping. For infants it feels in some sense that *their* mother is not there. The total configuration of behaviors and emotional tone is not the same as that of the mother the infant had become attached and bonded to. The infant may experience this "new person" as "not mother," to the point that she reacts as if her mother were not present and had been replaced by a stranger. The infant may begin to cry frequently, become difficult to console, seem distressed during feeding, and sleep fitfully. In extreme cases, she may lose interest in activities she used to enjoy such as watching a mobile over her crib, shaking a rattle, beginning to crawl or stand, and engaging in baby talk.

The toddler whose mother is depressed may also experience her as so different from her previous way of being that he feels he is with a near stranger. However, the toddler's more developed (than an infant's) capacity to recognize the continuity of a mother's identity, even across wide variations in her behavior and affect, will more likely lead him to become frightened by the changes in her. Toddlers in this situation try desperately to reengage their mother and bring back her mothering toward them. While this may appear as a sensitively

55

empathic attempt to draw mother out of her depression, it is actually a driven need to get her to resume her old ways of nurturing and playing with him so that he can again feel loved, protected, and supported.

CHRISTY'S parents separated when she was nearly a year old. They had been married for sixteen years and Christy was the youngest of their three children. Their two sons were in junior high school. Christy was an unplanned baby and may have represented an unwitting attempt on the part of her parents to save a failing marriage. Her mother had worked as a legal secretary for two years early in the marriage as she helped put her husband through law school. With the birth of her first son, she left her job and became a full-time homemaker. Her husband increasingly felt the marriage had become stale, that he no longer loved his wife, and was trapped in a meaningless relationship. He filed for divorce and moved to a house nearby.

Christy's mother was devastated by her husband's leaving her. She had felt that she had a relatively good marriage and was deeply wounded by the fact that her husband found her unappealing. She was frightened by the prospect of being single and having to return to work outside the home. But it was not simply that she anticipated feeling lonely and expected her standard of living to decline that worried her. Nor was it that after thirteen years she would need to return to working outside the home with rusty skills. It was the loss of life as she knew it that panicked her. Her basic identity as the upper-middle-class wife of a successful professional, hoped for and anticipated during her late adolescence and consolidated after sixteen years of marriage, was disintegrating. During the initial stage of the divorce she was shocked, bewildered, and hurt. She maintained some semblance of emotional equilibrium by becoming enraged at her husband and criticizing him to others at every chance. Her friends and parents rallied around her and joined her in derogating her husband.

However, after nearly a year, the full force of the reality of the divorce began to be felt. The divorce became final and joint legal custody was awarded to the parents. All three children continued to live in the family home and saw their father every week. A property settlement had been reached and child support payments established. Christy's mother became increasingly depressed. Her angry exchanges with her ex-husband became fewer and she spent less time furiously denouncing his actions and assailing his character to others. The anger-based defenses she had relied on and the emotional support they garnered her from her friends and relatives gave way to feelings of helplessness and hopelessness. She burst into tears frequently for no obvious reason and found it hard to get herself mobilized to care for her children or begin looking for a job. She spent more time watching television and interacted less with her children. Since she had lost interest in food she was less attentive to preparing meals for herself and the children.

Christy was almost two years old when her mother began sinking into this depression. Though she had been frightened and upset by her mother's anger during the first stage of the divorce, mother and daughter had spent a great deal of time in animated, pleasurable activities. Since the two were at home all the time, there were many opportunities for Christy's mother to read to her, talk and sing with her, and play games. She was an involved, caring mother and despite her rage toward her former husband was able to continue parenting reasonably well.

Christy experienced her mother's depression as an inexplicable and painful loss. She said, "Mommy sad" and "Mommy's tired a lot." Christy began making "happy pictures" for her mother, pastel-colored drawings with pretty flowers and a happy-face sun shining brightly overhead. She spent several hours a day in this activity. When her mother told her to go outside and play in the yard or at a friend's home, she refused and if her mother insisted, Christy cried and seemed panicked. She became a finicky eater. The television set became a baby-sitter, a replacement for her mother who slept late, napped frequently, and seemed lethargic and joyless when awake. Christy and her brothers went to their father's home each week, and she cried plaintively as she left her mother. Though she seemed lively and happy for the most part when she got to her father's house, she worried about her mother and asked to call her frequently as if to reassure herself that her mother was all right.

Her mother's depression disrupted Christy's general feelings of emotional well-being. At a time when youngsters are just beginning to venture forth into the wider world, she was preoccupied with her mother. Her life began to feel barren and empty. She had lost a feeling of pleasurable connectedness with her mother, and it was as if she were terribly alone. She did not have the cognitive wherewithal at age two to understand her mother's depression or to look forward with anticipated relief to times with her father. A toddler's sense of time is too underdeveloped for that. Instead each day, each hour with her mother felt interminable. Watching television distracted her from her painful loneliness. Drawing numerous pictures for her mother was an active and desperate attempt to pull her mother out of her depression and back to the way she had been, to restore, as it were, Christy's own feelings of pleasure and comfort. The seeds of future depression and anxiety over losing someone close were being sown in Christy's psyche.

Parental rage and depression have powerful effects on infants and toddlers. Their immature egos can neither understand nor gain emotional distance from these expressions of parental conflict and distress. Very young children feel overwhelmed and frightened as the adult feelings threaten to engulf them, blotting out any sense of joy or safety in their lives. When these stresses continue into the long-range period, the normal trajectory of child development can be seriously disrupted.

The Long-Range Period

It is difficult to speak of children being infants or toddlers as their parents' divorce moves into its long-range phase. By definition this third stage of divorce process usually does not begin until two to three years after the parents separate. By that time the child is well into the preschool years and beyond the focus of this chapter. Therefore, this section will be necessarily truncated and will address the experiences of older toddlers whose parents' divorce has proceeded quickly enough to have reached the long-term period within two years.

By the two-year point after the initial parental separation, toddlers frequently experience the loss of their father. Though at first many men maintain a visiting relationship with their young children, it is often the case that it gradually wanes over time.[2] There are several reasons for this change. Some men simply feel ill-at-ease with infants and toddlers. They feel awkward holding an infant and are not sure about what to say or do with toddlers. For them the discomfort of feeling inept as a father leads them to have less contact with their youngsters. Other men are so caught up in their angry, guilty, or sad feelings about the divorce that they feel they must distance themselves from all reminders of it, including their children. Mothers can contribute to this pattern by perpetuating conflict with their ex-husband. Arguing and criticizing him in front of the children when he picks them up or drops them off, conveniently "forgetting" visiting schedules so that he is left waiting for the children or does not ever get to be with them, and relitigating the visiting or child support agreements are all behaviors that can drive a powerful wedge between a man and his children.

For some fathers, pronounced feelings of being peripheral to the ebb and flow of their children's lives creates painful and poignant sadness. These men, who are committed to continuing their parental relationship with their youngsters, find the common visiting schedule of every other weekend insufficient to permit a sense of ongoing fatherhood. As one man put it, "It was too hard seeing my son and knowing, just knowing, we could never really be close. I didn't want to be like an uncle to him. I had to decide to cut my losses, so I moved to another state." This father was particularly insightful and introspective. But he gave voice to the underlying feelings of loss that beset other men after divorce.

Many men are not consciously aware of these reasons for letting go of the father–child relationship. They may be aware of being angry at their ex-wife, feeling jealous about a new romantic interest in her life, feeling harassed by her verbal assaults or legal actions, and a sense of personal awkwardness when with their children. But a large number of men do not make the connection between these feelings and their choice, consciously and decisively made or gradually and unwittingly unfolded, to essentially end the relationship with their youngsters. Instead they immerse themselves in their work, hobbies, dating relationships, or new marriage. They can no longer find the time to see their children, call or send birthday cards or presents. Frequently they are seen by their ex-wife, children, courts, and society as callously and selfishly uncaring. While some men do indeed fit this characterization, many others who appear to are in fact fleeing from a wearingly painful situation.

Having an infant or toddler substantially complicates the task of sustaining the father–child relationship. To begin with, many men are uncomfortable with very young children and feel at a loss about what to do with them. The same divorced man who could successfully maintain a mutually fulfilling relationship with an elementary school age or adolescent youngster may not be able to do so with an infant or toddler. The developmental needs of young children for consistency and stability in their environment also mitigate against a continuing father–child relationship. Infants and toddlers have difficulty being separated from their primary caretaker, usually their mother. As a result, weekend or longer visits with father are more difficult for the young child to manage. They become fearful, anxious, or even withdrawn during these separations and may want to avoid the pain that times with father brings. From a father's perspective, his young child appears reluctant to leave mother and be with him. Fathers begin to recognize this. Whether it is because they care about the well-being of their children or find so little personal gratification in having to cope with their distress, they begin to reduce the frequency of the visits. Both child and father are relieved, at least initially.

An even more subtle difficulty is posed by the young child's inability to maintain an internal sense of a relationship with an adult he is with infrequently. The toddler or infant who is in his father's care in the traditional every-other-weekend schedule, or who even sees his father weekly, will not be able to continue to attach to that man "father feelings." Young children cannot conceptualize the biological, or if adopted, the legal relationship described by the term "father." Their definition is guided by experiential criteria: the man who interacts with a child in fatherly ways (caring, limit setting, helping, playing) on a nearly daily basis is, by this experiential definition, his father. Men become distressed when they intuitively, and in a diffuse way they often cannot articulate, become aware of feeling as though they were no longer their child's father in a psychological sense. Though this feeling can arise as a result of a man's sadness in no longer being centrally involved in his child's life or from his awkward feelings about caring for an infant or toddler, it is frequently the case that he senses that his young child is no longer responding to him as "father."

BARRY'S parents had agreed to joint legal custody. He lived primarily with his mother and was in his father's care from noon every Saturday to Sunday morning. They thought that since Barry was only a year old when they separated, more than the usual biweekly contact was needed to maintain a viable father–child relationship. Their divorce proceeded smoothly and they remained on good terms. Each valued the other's parenting abilities and felt that their son would be best served if both parents continued to be involved in his life. By the time Barry was twenty-eight months old, their divorce had moved into the long-range period. The legal divorce had been granted and, more importantly, both parents had successfully resolved their feelings toward the other. They were not caught up in ongoing hostilities, nor were they enmeshed. Both had developed new romantic interests and were employed full-time in jobs they enjoyed. Barry's mother lived in a small, comfortable home and his father had bought a house only two miles away. They had adhered faithfully to the once-weekly schedule of Barry's time with his father but were appropriately flexible when necessary. Their son was a lively, robust youngster, who got along well with other children at the nursery school he had begun attending when he turned two. Now, at twenty-eight months, he was seen as a bright, well-liked child by the nursery school staff.

However, for the past two months Barry had been increasingly reluctant to go to his father's house. Toward the end of the week he would begin asking his mother, "Do I have to go see Daddy?" When his father arrived to pick him up, Barry cried and hugged his mother telling her over and over again that he loved her. At his father's home he seemed quiet and somewhat withdrawn. While he complied with his father's requests and did not cry once he was there, he seemed unhappy. His father described Barry's demeanor as that of a prisoner serving time and felt hurt and bewildered by this reaction. Barry's mother was equally puzzled. Both contrasted Barry's reluctance to go with his father to his comfort in separating from his mother to attend nursery school. His parents began discussing the possibility of less frequent visits and more planned, special activities when Barry was with his father in order to make those times more appealing to their son. Barry's father had already begun to cancel visits with his son claiming that his work schedule had become more time-consuming and that his relationship with his new dating partner occasionally involved social commitments that were difficult to break or reschedule. His contacts with his son became less regular and more infrequent.

Barry's father was wounded by his son's behavior. Not only did he find his own pleasure diminishing but he was genuinely concerned about his son's discomfort in coming to his home. He felt that Barry was acting as if he were a stranger rather than a loving father. He was a perceptive man and had put his finger right on the problem. Barry's age made it difficult for him to keep alive feelings reserved for a father. His father's two-fold hurt, his feelings of being rejected and his concern about causing his son discomfort, led him to consciously plan less frequent visits while finding "reasons" for informally reducing contacts with his son. This pattern can result in fathers drifting away from their young children after a divorce, as Barry's father was doing. Other men find themselves becoming defensively angry at their ex-spouse to rid themselves of just the sorts of wounded feelings Barry's father was able to permit himself to experience. These men interpret their child's reluctance to be with them as evidence of their ex-wife interfering in subtle or direct ways with the father–child relationship. This then results in an escalating conflict between parents or in fathers angrily distancing themselves from their ex-spouse and children. Some women do indeed vindictively try to poison their child's loving feelings toward his father as part of an ongoing war between parents. It is often difficult to know whether a child's reluctance or outright refusal to continue seeing his father is a product of enmity between parents or a developmentally based problem within the child.

An even more difficult issue to resolve arises when a mother begins to suspect that her young child's uneasiness about visiting with father is an indication that her ex-husband is in some way mistreating the youngster. At the extreme end of this spectrum of suspicion are allegations of physical or sexual abuse. While child abuse has traditionally been significantly underreported in the United States[3] and requires the protective attention of parents and professionals alike, the assessment of abuse in very young children when no physical or eyewitness evidence is available is an extremely difficult and uncertain procedure. The cognitive limitations of the toddlers, and even of preschoolers, requires the use of indirect and highly inferential methods of assessment. There are horror stories on both sides of the issue: instances of ongoing, even life-threatening abuse on the one hand; unnecessarily and irrevocably disrupted father–child relationships and damaged reputations on the other.

In an attempt to bring greater certainty to this serious problem, there has been an increase in the use of anatomically correct dolls of both sexes in child interviews. Unlike standardized tests (such as intelligence tests) that are based on established, quantified norms, these procedures depend heavily on the sensitivity, knowledge of child development, and clinical experience of the interviewer. Unfortunately, many professionals and parents look to the "results" of anatomically correct doll interviews to provide rigorous and clear-cut data on whether child abuse has in fact occurred. But many individuals conducting this type of interview have little or no formal knowledge of the accumulated research bearing on cognitive and social/emotional aspects of child development, have received little or no training in the use of projective tests or in play therapy, and have notably little experience interacting with children in the context of a clinical assessment or treatment relationship. To have such people making pronouncements about the probability that some form of child abuse has or has not taken place is foolhardy at best. At worst it may scar children emotionally, deprive them of a valued and developmentally critical relationship with their father, and seriously damage his reputation and life.

Suspicions or outright allegations of child abuse should never be taken lightly. But evaluations of potential abuse should be conducted only by mental health professionals who are well grounded in child development research and have extensive experience with both projective methods and conducting psychotherapy with children. Parents, attorneys, and judges ought to be properly and vigilantly skeptical when substantial expertise in (1) child development, (2) projective techniques, and (3) psychotherapy are not represented in the person(s) conducting this sort of assessment. Simply having done numerous child-abuse-related assessments without having all three types of expertise is never a substitute for these requirements. It is only testimony to the new and much needed visibility of this issue and the reluctance of well-trained, experienced child clinicians to become involved in an arduous, time-consuming, and highly uncertain task.

During the long-range period of divorce many children must cope with the parent establishing a new and significant intimate relationship. This may take the form of a monogamous, long-term dating relationship, a live-in partner, or remarriage.

MELISSA was a newborn infant when her parents separated. The initial crisis period lasted nearly a year as her parents coped with their hurt, angry feelings. The legal divorce became final when Melissa was a year old. Shortly after that her father moved to a distant state and remarried. She saw him infrequently after her parents separated. Her mother returned to school and eventually took and passed a state licensing examination to become a real estate agent and broker. She was enthusiastic about her work, enjoyed meeting her clients, and took pride in her ability to provide a solidly middle-class life for herself and her children. Melissa's mother began dating when her daughter was sixteen months old and her son was three. She met a man a few months later whom she cared for a great deal but was unsure of marrying at that point so quickly after her divorce. They dated for nearly a year, and when Melissa was twenty-six months old, he moved into the family home. He was a lively, happy-go-lucky man who despite never having been married or having had children quickly took to his partner's youngsters. He thoroughly enjoyed being with them and from the beginning of his dating relationship with their mother they often and comfortably did things together in a way that increasingly made them all feel they were a family. Melissa called him by his first name but frequently slipped "accidentally" and referred to him as "Daddy."

Melissa's mother was aware of the fact that children can worry about losing their mother's affections to a new man in her life. She and her partner discussed this and made sure that time alone with her children, together and individually, was planned. In this way she guarded against her youngsters feeling any loss of their mother's love and regarding her partner as a competitive threat. When he moved in, the children's emotional tie to him became stronger. They spontaneously called him Daddy more frequently and asked when he and their mother were going to get married. In fact, Melissa's mother was getting increasingly comfortable with that prospect, and the couple began planning a wedding after having lived together for two months. They openly discussed this with the children, who were excited by the idea of their mother getting married and were enthusiastic about participating in the ceremony. Melissa, and her brother, were doing well on all fronts developmentally. Not that everything was perfect: they squabbled and fought with one another as siblings often do, and Melissa occasionally had difficulty sleeping through the night. But overall the children seemed happily well adjusted.

Many children find the romantic involvement of the parent with whom they live stressful. Melissa's and her brother's ready acceptance of their mother's partner (and eventually new husband) and their emotional attachment to him were in part a response to his feelings of affection for them. He genuinely liked them and often included them in his time with their mother, so that he was not always in the position of taking her from them. Melissa's mother was appropriately sensitive to her children potentially experiencing her partner as a competitive threat and carefully continued to build in time with her youngsters without her partner present. Two key stressors were thus circumvented: Melissa and her brother did not have to worry about losing their mother, and they did not feel unwanted or excluded by their mother's partner. Developmentally, they were not old enough to contend with worries about loyalty or anxiety over sexual stimulation by their mother's romantic relationship, two conflictful issues that emerge for children of elementary school age and older. They also were not beset by ongoing parental conflict; a mother who was depressed, angry, or uncertain about her financial or social situation; or unpredictable daily routines. And they were at good ages for being receptive to a new, caring parenting person. Both felt secure in their feelings toward their mother and trusted her love for them. From this sturdy home base they were prepared to venture forth into the wider social world. And fathers, or their surrogates (that is, live-in partners, stepfathers, even grandfathers who live nearby or under the same roof), can be a natural developmental bridge between the close relationship young children typically have with their mother and relationships beyond the immediate family.[4]

Infants and toddlers do not have the cognitive resources to sort through and organize the stressful experiences so often (but by no means always) encountered as the divorce process continues across its three stages. Nor can they draw on a firm sense of emotional independence to distance themselves from the stormy and painful feelings their parents may be having. To the contrary, they resonate to them. Since very young children do not have well-established social relationships with adults other than their parents or with other youngsters, they do not have these potential social supports to serve as a buffer between the upheavals in their parents' lives and themselves. They are not able to escape to a neighbor's home to flee a battle between parents. They cannot talk over their upset with a teacher, a school counselor, or a best friend. They cannot even make it clear to their parents that they are distressed, frightened, angry, confused, or sad. Even older toddlers are not able to look inside themselves psychologically and articulate an awareness of being distraught.

Recognizing Distress in Infants and Toddlers

How do adults know that an infant or toddler is in distress psychologically? What are the behaviors or signs that a young child is being overwhelmed by environmental change or her parents' emotional pain? The examples in this chapter have illustrated a spectrum of expressions of distress that are common to infants and toddlers.

Perhaps the most common indicator that a young child is reacting to stressful life events is a *loss of developmental accomplishments*. This type of loss, which many mental health professionals call regression, can appear in any aspect of a child's life. An infant who has achieved a reliable sleep pattern of five to seven hours at night may revert to waking every two hours. The eight-month-old who has been crawling for a month may stop doing so. The year-old child who has been taking pleasure in trying new foods can begin refusing all but a few things she especially likes. The fifteen-month-old who has been walking with increasing confidence for two months may go back to crawling and actively resist attempts to have her try walking. The eighteen-month-old with clearly understandable language development who goes back to pointing, squealing, and using single syllables is giving up an important developmental achievement. A two-year-old who cries and clings to his mother when she leaves him to go from the kitchen to the bathroom is giving up his budding feelings of independence. The two-and-a-half-year-old who had begun using the toilet most of the time during the day may begin to wet and soil himself as he used to do a few months earlier.

The myriad of developmental accomplishments children achieve between birth and two-and-a-half years are too numerous to list completely. However, they can be grouped according to general domains so that parents and other concerned adults can be alert to issues that may signal a young child's distress. Examples assume that a developmental achievement has been attained and is being given up as the child reverts to an earlier pattern.

Domain	Examples
Sleeping	Reverting to earlier patterns of sleep (usually more frequent nighttime waking); refusing to go to sleep, struggling to delay going to sleep; having nightmares.

Eating	Refusing foods that have been enjoyed; restricting intake to a few types of foods; returning to using a bottle after having been weaned; returning to liquids after having eaten solids.
Motor Activity	Giving up the large motor achievements of crawling, standing, walking, or running in favor of earlier patterns; giving up small motor achievements such as feeding himself, picking up and examining blocks, building block towers, and beginning to draw in favor of earlier ones.
Language	Reverting to crying or pointing instead of trying to name an object; giving up clear words for earlier versions such as going back to using ''ba'' for ''ball''; giving up short sentences for single words; sounding ''babyish'' in tone of voice as she used to.
Toilet Training	Reverting to wetting or soiling instead of using the toilet; withholding stool; using places other than the bathroom, such as the living room, to relieve himself.
Emotional Independence	Reverting to crying or clinging when a parent leaves the room to go to another part of the house or leaves the child with a caregiver; becoming anxious and reticent with a caregiver instead of comfortably at ease; staying inside the house instead of playing in the yard or at a friend's house.

Another indicator of distress in early childhood is *emotional lability*. The youngster seems to become highly reactive to events in his environment. His emotional responses appear out of proportion to what is going on around him. A three-month-old may cry more intensely than usual when awakening for a feeding. A parent may sense her baby cannot wait as long as she used to for food or to be picked up and cuddled. A six-month-old who used to take great pleasure in being bathed may become greatly distressed during her bath for no apparent reason. The year-old infant engaged in a highly pleasurable activity, such as rolling a ball back and forth between himself and his older sister, may suddenly begin to screech and cry when his sister loses interest and interrupts the game to turn on television. An eighteen-month-old who is having great fun building with blocks may, in the next moment, knock them all down and begin crying. The two-year-old who is enjoying being read to may tell the parent, with increasing agitation, that he is not reading it right.

This quality of being on an emotional roller-coaster is often related to intense feelings of frustration. Becoming increasingly able to wait for some pleasurable activity and tolerate the temporary disruption or the end of it is something infants and toddlers get better at as they mature and, to some degree, start regulating their reactions to frustration. To the extent that there is chaos around them in the form of parental fighting, an emotionally distraught parent, or multiple changes in their daily routines, infants and toddlers can begin to feel more stressed generally and then less able to modulate their reactions to frustration.

Distress in infancy and toddlerhood can also be expressed with *anger*. Parents and other caregivers who spend a lot of time with young children and become sensitive to the emotional states of infants and toddlers begin to differentiate among cries of hunger, pain, fear, and anger. While an observer who does not know the child typically understands her crying at a particular moment as a response to some physical discomfort (for example, being cold or wet, having a cramp, being in an uncomfortable position against the side of a crib) or a need (for example, to be fed, held, cuddled), the caregiver is also aware of the possibility that the infant or toddler may be furious. Even an infant can be flooded with anger, for example, if a bottle or breast is withdrawn too quickly or he is put in his crib when he wants to be held or played with. A toddler's anger is usually more easily discerned; she may yell, bite, pinch, kick, or hit. He may deliberately urinate on the floor or wall, throw or break toys and other objects, or scream, "Hate you."

Young children become furious when their needs are repeatedly frustrated: when caretaking schedules are disrupted and become unpredictable; pleasurable activities are cut short or are less frequent; and when they must often wait for long periods to be fed, read to, cuddled, or played with. But in addition to anger being a response to prolonged or frequent frustration, it can be experienced by the child as he resonates to anger between parents or the rage one parent feels even when the other is not present. Older toddlers can become chronically angry, not only through this resonance mechanism but also as they identify with their angry parents. Children normally take in and make their own the emotions and behaviors they observe in their parents. To the extent that one or both parents are angry, children in the usual course of identifying with parents will incorporate into their own repertoire of feelings and actions the expressions of rage they see in mother or father.

Fearfulness is also an indicator of distress in infants and toddlers. Though it is difficult to discern the difference between fear and other kinds of distress (for example, frustration, physical discomfort, hunger) in very young infants, by six months a reasonably sensitive caregiver can observe clear-cut fright in infants. The six-month-old who cries intensely when a parent hands the child to an unfamiliar adult and the eight-month-old who cries and quickly crawls to the parent when a stranger enters the room are examples of normal fear in infancy. The fourteen-month-old who stops playing and wants desperately to be picked up by mother or father when a new adult approaches her is also exhibiting "stranger anxiety," which usually peaks at around eight months and again at about fourteen months.

Toddlers can become clearly frightened and upset about separations from parents: when the parent leaves the room to go to another part of the house (especially if the parent does not signal the departure), when a parent leaves for work, or drops the child at a day-care provider's house. Even when a toddler is happily playing at home with another youngster, it is common for her to try to catch sight of the parent from time to time. This visual base-touching is common in toddlerhood and the pleasure of play quickly gives way to fear when it cannot be done. Most toddlers are also intermittently frightened by the approach of animals and even small insects. The two-year-old who has been happily playing in his backyard may come running into the house screaming in panic because a strange dog has appeared or even a butterfly or moth has gotten too close.

In addition to fears about unfamiliar adults, separations, and animals/insects, toddlers are often frightened when they get hurt. An eighteen-month-old may trip and fall on the sidewalk and wail loudly even though he is not badly hurt. It is as if the youngster cannot calm the fear that he has sustained great and irreparable damage. Most parents know that minor falls and scrapes can be repaired by a reassuring hug, a kiss on the wound, or a medicinally unnecessary band-aid. With these actions the parent puts the child's fears to rest.

When an infant or toddler seems to become *withdrawn and listless,* it may indicate emotional distress. The young infant who eats less; who loses interest in a mobile over her crib; who seems unresponsive to the smiles, cooing, and hugs of a parent may be withdrawing from the overwhelming, painful feelings evoked by the chaotic events and powerful anger around her. Similarly, the older infant or toddler who appears listless and no longer takes pleasure in crawling, walking, or playing with previously enjoyed toys may be pulling back from the emotional pain of being with a depressed and unresponsive parent or an angry parent who handles him roughly and speaks harshly.

Withdrawal from an active engagement with caregivers, from pleasure in her own emerging abilities (for example, walking, talking), or from the joy of exploring the environment is often a last-ditch attempt on the part of an infant or toddler who is feeling flooded by the ongoing rage or depression of a parent. It amounts to a developmentally primitive way of shutting out the input from a markedly painful environment. In fact, young children whose parents are emotionally stable but who have painful physical conditions, such as digestive disorders or ear infections, manifest very similar kinds of withdrawal. Infants whose basic needs for relief from hunger or cold and to be held and cuddled are frustrated repeatedly and for prolonged periods will also display these same qualities of listlessness and withdrawal.[5]

The physiological, cognitive, and emotional immaturity of infants and toddlers in combination with the inherent and expectable unevenness of development in very young children will often result in *normal signs of distress* of the types we have presented here. Temporary loss of some developmental accomplishments, emotional lability, and expressions of anger and fearfulness are all commonly observed in healthy infants and toddlers who are not exposed to undue stress. The trajectory of child development is never perfectly smooth and uninterrupted. It is expected that developmental accomplishments, such as regular sleep patterns, food preferences, motor development, and language acquisition, will ebb and flow. New accomplishments frequently are briefly lost before they can be regained and fully consolidated. Previous achievements may be disrupted for short periods of time as an infant or toddler concentrates on attaining a new ability. The thirteen-month-old who is learning to walk and putting a great deal of her time and energy into that activity may begin waking in the middle of the night as she used to, or lose her ability to name some objects. A degree of emotional lability is part of the young child's immature system and is to be expected, especially in the face of frustration. Similarly, storms of anger over being frustrated are not uncommon, nor is stranger anxiety, to varying degrees. Fears of the sorts described above are well known to parents and can be the source of retrospectively humorous anecdotes about a particular child's early development.

These signs of distress take on special significance when they are evident for prolonged periods of time, when there are several signs present at once, or when they cannot be alleviated, at least temporarily, by the attention and efforts of a parent or regular adult caretaker. The youngster who shows some specific indicators of distress for over a month may be responding to the stresses of a sorely disrupted and unpredictable daily routine, overt battles (physical or verbal) between parents, an enraged or depressed parent, or perhaps an unrelated reason like a painful medical condition.

Though some parents mistakenly perceive the normal behavior and emotional style of an infant with a calm, placid temperament as signs of withdrawal, listlessness and withdrawal are not usually part of the expectable variations in child development. Unlike all of the other indicators of distress in infancy and toddlerhood, withdrawal from a personal engagement with adult caregivers and the absence of pleasure in exploring the environment and in emerging abilities are behaviors that should be of immediate concern.

5

►◄

Helping Infants and Toddlers Cope

When an infant or toddler has been showing signs of distress for longer than a month and parental efforts to alleviate them are not causing them to subside, it is wise to consult a pediatrician or family physician. Because very young children are usually unable to describe what they are feeling or "point to where it hurts," it is essential to make sure that a physical condition or disease process is not at the root of the child's prolonged distress. As noted earlier, digestive disorders and ear infections are but two particularly common physical problems that can cause ongoing distress in a young child. The possibility of an underlying physical condition requiring medical attention should be checked by a physician before an attempt at understanding the potential environmental and interpersonal causes of the distress.

In order to know how to help infants and toddlers cope with divorce-related distress, it is crucial to keep in mind fully the common sources of stress for children of this age. Unpredictable daily routines, hostilities between parents, and the emotional disequilibrium of a parent (especially the one primarily responsible for the day-to-day care of the youngster) are central causes of psychological distress in very young children across all three stages of the divorce process. Though they tend to be more common in the initial crisis phase of divorce, it is not at all unusual to see one or more of these problematic circumstances continue or even become exacerbated in the short-term aftermath stage. When they continue unabated even into the long-range period, their cumulative effects tend to take an even greater toll on youngsters.

Two potential sources of stress, usually associated with the long-range phase of divorce, are the primary parent's involvement in a romantic relationship (that is, taking a live-in partner or remarrying) and the gradual loss of the father–child relationship. The former, which can be so troubling to older children, appears to have considerably less impact on infants and toddlers. This is particularly true when a parent is sensitive to her child's worries over being displaced in her affections by the new man in her life and when he shows a genuine interest in them. The infant's or toddler's loss of the relationship with his father also seems to have surprisingly minimal impact on their well-being. Perhaps this is due to the fact that the majority of fathers seem to be considerably less involved in the lives of their very young children than are mothers. Infants and toddlers, because they do not conceptualize but instead experience relationships, will then sense the absence of their father as being only minimally different from his living at home.

Obviously this will not be the case when a father has been very centrally involved with his youngster. And it is not to say that developing a close, mutually pleasurable, ongoing relationship with father is unimportant. Both boys and girls can profit enormously from this sort of father–child relationship and keenly feel the lack of it as they move into subsequent stages of their development. Since it is notably difficult to first establish a significant father–child bond after years of little or no contact when the youngster is in elementary school or during adolescence, maintaining a continuous relationship from early on becomes especially important. In some ways it is akin to having a good investment. At first it may be relatively inconsequential compared to one's other sources of income and not much missed if it were not there. But over the years it grows into a substantial resource capable of providing needed reserves in times of trouble and great pleasure when things are going smoothly.

How can infants and toddlers be helped with the likely sources of divorce-induced stress in their lives? It is easy to say to parents, "Make sure that the daily routine of your young child's life is reasonably consistent." But what is "consistency," and how do you get it? To begin with, consistency means that the child has a regular, predictable daily schedule of where he will be and, even more urgent, who will care for him. In arranging for child care, it is most important to be sure that a particular person whom the parent believes is responsible and likes children will be regularly present during the caretaking hours. Well-equipped, attractive day-care centers with high rates of staff turnover (usually due to miserably low pay) are not nearly as desirable as a neighbor or two whom one can count on to be there regularly, or a woman who runs an in-home day-care service. Parents too often are swayed in making child care decisions by well-appointed physical surroundings, the number of interesting toys available, and professionally done brochures. On the other hand, parents may find that a nearby neighbor has too many children of widely different ages to provide good individual attention to each in her home-based day-care. She may be unpleasant to the children when their parents are not there or spend hours watching television rather than her charges.

How does a parent go about getting the information she needs to make an informed decision about day-care? Whether the care is provided in a private home or at a center there are several things to find out about.

1. How many children does a particular caregiver look after? In a day-care center with substantial physical space for children to move around or sit comfortably a ten-to-one child to caregiver ratio is appropriate. In a home-based service, a seven- or eight-to-one ratio is usually the maximum. Clearly, the fewer children per caregiver the better regardless of the setting.

2. How close in age are the children being attended to by a single person? Young children have enormously varied needs. An infant's care is quite different from that of a four-year-old. Further, satisfying peer interactions are less likely the more divergent the ages of the youngsters present. In a group of seven two- and three-year-olds there are many opportunities for learning about and enjoying social relationships. On the other hand, if there are three children under the age of one year, two between one and two years, one three-year-old and two four-year-olds, it will be difficult for peer interactions to develop and for the caregiver to attend to the markedly different needs represented by this age range. At the very least, two other children within a year of your child's age should be present.

3. How likely is it that the caregiver responsible for your child will be available throughout the day and is planning to be at the day-care center for at least the next six months? Infants and toddlers do best when there is consistency in who provides their care. A changing cast of characters leads to feelings of insecurity and unpredictability.

4. How comfortable with youngsters and knowledgeable about them is the caregiver? Does she have children of her own? Has she taught in schools? Ask her to tell you about the activities she uses with

children and about youngsters she currently has in her care. Does she seem to have a good feel for young children? Does she speak of children fondly? Children need to feel liked and valued as well as having a sense that their concerns will be responded to.

5. How well-equipped is the day-care or home setting? Age-appropriate toys and materials (from baby rattles and mobiles to climbing toys, paper, and crayons, and picture books) make it more likely that youngsters spend their time engaged in building skills or in social interactions as opposed to passively watching television or aimlessly wandering about. The availability of outdoor space and equipment (swings, tricycles) makes it possible to enjoy time outside the building as well.

6. How structured are the daily routines? Very young children require a great deal of guidance to have a successful day-care experience, with the flexibility to pursue their own interests within that structure. Does the day-care provider have a schedule of supervised activities? Is there a variety in her plans? Simply "looking after" children or "letting them decide" tends to lead to much sitting around and irritability born of boredom.

7. Does the provider have references whom you can contact? Several should be made readily available upon your request. Call them and get their sense of their youngsters' experience in the setting you are investigating. Would they send their next child to the center? Pleased parents are a good sign that the provider is doing well by children.

8. Cost and convenience of location are also clearly important. Given that the first seven questions are answered favorably, these practical and important considerations must be thought through.

These ways of checking on the suitability of child care arrangements focus on in-home and center-based day-care or nursery school settings. Many parents use baby-sitters instead. That is, a person comes to your home to look after your child or cares for your child and perhaps one or two others in her home. These are not licensed day-care providers. They are often chosen because of convenience of location, relatively low cost, and/or familiarity with the sitter. Nonetheless, the above points should still serve as guidelines for deciding whether a particular prospective sitter is likely to provide appropriate child care. Usually the small number of youngsters being cared for permits greater individual attention to each child but also reduces the availability of same-age playmates and the chances for peer relationships to develop.

A woman with a six-month infant and a four-year-old may baby-sit for a sixteen-month-old and a two-year-old. The wide age range is potentially offset by the low child–staff ratio. Still points three through eight of day-care criteria are relevant and should be looked into.

Once a day-care setting has been selected, it is up to the parent to maintain consistency in her schedule. The times of day the child is dropped off and picked up should be kept as regular as possible. Since very young children have insufficiently developed cognitive and verbal abilities to conceptualize, anticipate, and thereby organize a schedule in their minds, sameness of routine must be used to give an infant or toddler a sense of continuity and predictability in his life. Telling a young child what the schedule is will usually not help. But the sequence of morning routines, for example, can be kept constant: being awakened at the same time, then being picked up and hugged, diapered, washed, dressed, and fed in that sequence. The fixed order of morning activities creates an unspoken but convincing atmosphere of consistency. Similarly, activities after the child is picked up can be ordered as well. In the evening, mealtime and bedtime routines add to the feelings of predictability and security. It is tempting for many parents to do things spontaneously. While older children can take pleasure in a change in routine (for example, eating in a restaurant instead of at home on the spur of the moment, going to a friend's house after dinner with the child, having the youngster taken on a picnic by a neighbor instead of going to the regular daily caregiver), they are able to do so primarily because they are old enough to have a predictable schedule firmly conceptualized in their minds and thus can afford to depart from it. Infants and young toddlers are more likely be distressed than excited about such changes, especially if they occur nearly weekly or more often.

Maintaining highly consistent routines is an important method for building a sense of predictability and continuity into the lives of very young children. Another is to be sure that the infant or toddler has at least one, and possibly two or three, familiar objects she likes with her in the day-care setting. Some young children have a powerful attachment to a treasured possession such as a blanket, stuffed animal, or even a bottle and will make it clear that they want it with them. It is helpful for parents to not only tolerate these attachments but to facilitate them. They often represent being at home and especially being with mother, and therefore can serve as sources of reassurance and continuity from home/mother to day-care setting/daycare provider.

In fact, even if a youngster gives no obvious evidence of such an attachment (and many do not), a blanket sent with an infant or a stuffed animal, doll, or toy car a toddler takes to the day-care setting can be reassuring simply because they are familiar to the youngster.

WHEN JASON'S (see chapter 4) mother consulted a mental health professional about his distress, he was seventeen months old. His unpredictable child care routine and the newness of being separated from his mother each day had led to him to develop several symptoms: crying and whimpering when she dropped him off at each of the two neighbors' homes, thumb sucking, refusing lunch at the neighbors', retreating from walking to crawling, being frightened of strangers, and having difficulty going to sleep. Jason's developmentally appropriate and normal needs for consistency were explained to his mother. Jason's difficulties were described by the mental health professional as reactions to the stress of a new and unpredictable daily routine. His mother was relieved to know that there was not something terribly wrong with her son. She was encouraged to find a single setting in which Jason could stay for the whole day, each day of the work week. Using points one through eight, she selected an appropriate, nearby in-home setting. The mental health professional suggested that she send several favorite toys with Jason each day. Part of his bedtime routine was to choose two or three things he wanted to take with him the next day. He always included his bottle, which he used only to drink water. His mother had not let him take it to the neighbors' homes previously because she thought it was babyish and would lead to ''buck teeth.'' But once she understood its psychological significance to Jason, and many other children for that matter, she agreed to permit him to take it. She was also encouraged to write down morning, dinnertime, and bedtime routines that she would follow closely each day.

Within six weeks, Jason's mother reported that he seemed greatly relieved. Though he still had difficulty falling asleep at night, all of the other behaviors that had been symptomatic of distress had greatly lessened or completely vanished. She felt a new sense of competence as a mother as a result of being able to create such dramatic and positive changes in her son. This confidence subtly altered the tone of her interaction with Jason. She felt better about her parenting and became more relaxed and more playful with him.

Jason's mother had felt terrible about his difficulties and helpless to do anything about them. She feared that he was "emotionally disturbed." The process of putting his problem behaviors in an understandable developmental context and providing specific guidelines for what could be done to help Jason was itself enormously relieving. She had been given the tools, in the form of new understanding and of potentially helping actions she could take, to be the effective parent she was capable of being. Her renewed sense of effectiveness in turn added to Jason's sense of security and comfort.

Infants and toddlers also need help when parents are at war with each other. Adults often become so caught up in their hurt-angry feelings that they are not aware of the connection between their hostilities and the difficulties their children are having. The overwhelming feelings of fear and anger youngsters experience in response to their parents' fighting can create behaviors are symptomatic of distress. Some parents are capable of reining in their rage at one another, or at least containing it when the children are present, once they understand the connection between their warfare and their youngsters' difficulties.

KELLY (see chapter 4) had become fearful of spiders, dogs, and "funny noises," had begun waking several times a night clearly frightened, and had started to fight with children at her day-care center. Her parents were embroiled in a bitter divorce and frequently argued loudly in her presence. They consulted a mental health professional when Kelly was nearly two years old and her problematic behaviors had been going on for nearly six months. After taking a thorough history, it became clear that Kelly had been developing well prior to her parents' separation. The clinician explained to both parents that their daughter's difficulties were probably largely due to her feeling frightened and helpless in the face of their intense battles. The parents in turn pointed out that Kelly had never asked them to stop, did not seem especially worried during the fights, and could not possibly understand the nature of their arguments. The mental health professional described in considerable detail the concept of emotional resonance in children. He further explained that while they knew that no one was going to be physically injured during their fights, a young child observing loud parental arguments, which included at times shoving one another, could not possibly have such a sophisticated understanding of adult personalities, capacities for control of destructive impulses, and modes of expressing rage to be equally confident about everyone's safety. It was also pointed out that Kelly had begun adopting their emotional agenda of fighting over possessions when she angrily pushed children who wanted to join her in playing with a toy at the day-care center.

Though both parents were bright and well educated, their anger had blinded them to these connections between Kelly's problems and their hostilities toward each other. They soberly agreed to try to reduce the fighting in front of Kelly. Though they were successful at restraining themselves most of the time, when they saw one another at the times of picking up Kelly or dropping her off at one another's homes their time together was still difficult. It was suggested that these points of contact be minimized by having Kelly's father wait in his car in the driveway and Kelly's mother having her ready on time. This further helped reduce their open conflicts. Each parent was also encouraged to tell Kelly from time to time: "When Mommy and Daddy get very angry they sometimes yell at each other real loud. Girls sometimes get scared that these big angry feelings are going to hurt someone. Even big girls who are three or four years old can have worries about their mom and dad fighting. But no one is going to get hurt, and Mommy and Daddy are going to try to stop yelling so much because they don't want to scare anybody." Kelly's fearful, angry behavior gradually lessened over three months. This provided her parents with clear evidence that they could do something to help their daughter. They became even more motivated to curtail their anger and to work toward a more constructive resolution of their divorce through regular meetings with a mediator. Not that they developed a cordial relationship. Far from it. They continued to heartily dislike each other, but they had agreed to avoid going to war.

Kelly's parents were thoughtful, intelligent people who had the personal strength to reduce their conflict on behalf of their children. They had become so embroiled in their own angry feelings that they temporarily lost sight of what was in their youngster's best interests. Since children rarely can articulate how upset they are by their parents' actions, and those who are mature enough cognitively to put their concerns into words are often too frightened to do so, the parental hostilities continue unfettered by concerns about children. Becoming convinced of the effects their arguments are having on the youngsters serves as a brake to their runaway rage. They can begin to try to restrain themselves. And they can search for ways to avoid potential blow-ups, such as not interacting when a child is going from one parent's care to the other. They can also begin to reassure their child verbally, often using displacement methods of communication (see chapter 3), that despite the angry feelings between the parents no one will be hurt. Collectively this serves to reduce a child's distress over exposure to the raw conflicts that are part of so many divorces.

Not all parents are able to use the knowledge that their warfare is stressful for their youngsters and may be the primary cause of a child's problem behaviors. A minority of parents, probably under 10 percent, cannot put aside the tremendous anger they feel toward their former mate even temporarily. They are so wounded and defensively so bitterly enraged that they are preoccupied by their attempts to inflict psychological and at times even physical pain on their ex-spouse. Information about the effects their battles are having on their children are like frail straws in the face of a hurricane. They tear at each other unmercifully, unmindful of their youngsters' reactions. Harassment, intimidation, and protracted litigation are hallmarks of this sort of conflict.

TIMMY (see chapter 4) was nearly two-and-a-half years old when his mother sought the help of a mental health professional specializing in work with children. His father's fury over her dating relationship with a new man had driven him to call her at all hours of the night, berate her angrily, accuse her of promiscuity and infidelity during their marriage, and file a motion to obtain custody of their son. Timmy's mother had retaliated by comparing her ex-husband unfavorably to her current lover and disrupting Timmy's schedule of being with his father. Timmy had become fearful about separating from his mother, worried about kidnappers at night, had trouble engaging in previously pleasurable activities at his day-care center, and had developed several nervous habits. His mother had a vague sense of the possibility that her son's troubles were in some way related to the hostility between herself and her former husband. The clinician confirmed this for her, spelling out the concept of emotional resonance. He also noted that Timmy's separation fears and worries about being kidnapped could very well be a response to his father's threat to sue for custody and thereby take him from his mother.

Timmy's mother was receptive to these explanations. They made

sense to her and confirmed her suspicions that Timmy's problems
were a sign of his distress over the parental warfare. However,
she was at a loss about what to do about it. Though she readily
agreed to keep in check her own tendencies to retaliate against
her ex-husband, she felt helpless about getting him to change his
behavior. Simply restraining herself would only make her feel more
helpless and angry and not significantly alter the conflict. She was
right. Her ex-husband continued his harassment and verbal assaults
both on the telephone and in person when picking Timmy up and
dropping him off, despite his ex-wife's having reduced her role in
the battles. If anything, her new calmness infuriated him further.
Her attempts to get her former husband to come to an appointment
with the mental health professional, with her or by himself, were
unproductive. He refused to have anything to do with "shrinks."
A call from the clinician was greeted with monosyllabic replies
and vague statements that he and his ex-wife "can work things
out on our own." Though not openly belligerent during two
telephone conversations initiated by the mental health professional,
it was clear that Timmy's father was unable to make use of the
help that was being offered.

In the meantime Timmy's condition worsened. His mother was
counseled to take the following actions. First, she was to change
her telephone number and keep it unlisted. She carefully instructed
the day-care center and close friends and relatives to whom she
gave the new number to give it to no one, especially not her ex-
husband. Second, with the help of her attorney she drafted a letter
that outlined the conditions of the visiting arrangement between
Timmy and his father: the schedule set down in their divorce decree
would be strictly adhered to with no variations; when he picked
Timmy up and dropped him off he was to remain out of her home
and entirely off her property; she would send Timmy out when
she saw his car; and all further communication between them was
to be exclusively in written form. At first Timmy's father refused
to accept these plans. Though he could no longer reach his ex-
wife by telephone, he continued to come to her door when picking
up Timmy and dropping him off. During these times he loudly
assaulted her with obscenities.

Timmy's mother, her attorney, and the clinician agreed to send
a letter from the attorney informing Timmy's father that a legal
restraining order would be sought to keep him off his ex-wife's

property and away from her. The letter also stated an intent to seek a court-ordered reassessment of the current visiting arrangement with the aim of modifying the divorce decree so that Timmy's father would be able to see his son only during the day and only if the visits were supervised by a third party. In fact both the restraining order and the modification of the visiting arrangement became necessary as this process unfolded over a six-month period. By that time Timmy was nearly three years old and had begun seeing a therapist for his continuing problems. Shortly after the legal orders took effect, Timmy's father found a job in a city several hundred miles away and moved out of the area. He rarely saw Timmy. Whether it was due to this change of circumstances or the therapy, or perhaps a bit of both, Timmy's problems began dissipating when he was three-and-one-half years old.

For those minority of times that insight and understanding are insufficient to motivate and guide appropriate parental behavior, it is helpful to take decisive actions of the sort Timmy's mother was helped to do. Hoping the situation will change with time, that the storm will blow over so to speak, rarely works when intense battles have been ongoing for over a year and a parent cannot be engaged in a constructive process aimed at quieting the conflict. Often a parent gets frightened about stirring up more conflict by taking appropriate steps to reduce the level of warfare or may not be aware of what actions are possible. It is likely that Timmy's father was suffering from a mental illness known as a narcissistic personality disorder in which his own hurt and rage took precedence over any concern for others. Many parents, especially during the initial crisis stage of divorce, are prone to experiencing problems that temporarily look somewhat like this sort of narcissistic pathology. The key word is "temporarily." Usually within six months or so of the marital separation, the intensity of feelings of damaged pride and hurt and the vindictive single-minded rage they may defensively evoke spontaneously reduce to manageable levels. The feelings may still be there and pleasurable fantasies of getting even or seeing something awful befall one's ex-spouse may continue to be intense. But the behavior of the adults comes under the control of reason and self-expectations for constructive parenting. And with time the hurt tends to fade, and along with it the rage over feeling so deeply wounded.

The emotional equilibrium of the parents, especially of the parent primarily responsible for the care of the youngster, is an important component of a child's good adjustment to his parents' divorce. When a parent feels overwhelmed by her fear of returning to work, her anxiety over reentering the dating scene, or her depression over the loss of her marital relationship and/or the status it brought, a child feels unprotected, insecure, and fearful. In addition to fear, he may evidence other signs of distress such as loss of developmental accomplishments, irritability, or anger. The center of his world, which protects and sustains him, seems to be crumbling before his eyes. An experience in adulthood approximating this painful situation for very young children is suddenly to develop a disease that interferes with mental or physical functioning. When a digestive disorder causes eating to be painful, when a paralysis makes certain movements impossible, an adult experiences the fear, frustration, anger, and even depression of no longer being able to count on a part of himself to automatically, without his thinking, serve his basic needs. That is somewhat how young children feel when a parent is emotionally paralyzed and can no longer provide the kind of care they need. The main difference is that adults can be helped to understand what is happening, are able to hope for or look toward some possibility of relief, can think of ways to compensate for their infirmity, and take solace in past accomplishments or other abilities they still possess. A young child has none of these to call on; his whole world is disintegrating.

CHRISTY (see chapter 4) was two years old at the time her mother felt overcome by depression. It was as if she had become a different person. In place of her active, imaginative ways of engaging her daughter throughout the day, Christy saw a woman who often cried and even more frequently slept. When awake she moved around the house like a zombie, nearly oblivious to her daughter's needs for meals, play, and comfort.

Christy's father consulted a child psychologist about his daughter's panic over leaving her mother to come to his house, her poignant attempts to pull her mother out of her depression, and her listless television watching. He was deeply and appropriately concerned about the kind of care Christy was getting at her mother's house. He worried about his daughter's safety because of the minimal supervision she was receiving as a result of her mother sleeping so much. Christy's mother agreed to see the child psychologist. The extent of her depression was immediately apparent. The clinician helped Christy's mother find a therapist who would work with her to resolve her depression. Though it seemed to be a reactive depression, rather than biologically based, antidepressant medication was prescribed to help alleviate the acuteness of her condition immediately and thereby permit her to enter into a therapeutic relationship with a social worker she had begun seeing regularly for psychotherapy. At the same time, the child psychologist urged both parents to arrange temporarily for Christy to spend late afternoons and evenings with her grandparents who lived an hour away. Her mother was told that this would relieve her of the burden of having to take care of Christy when she really felt unable to do so. Knowing she would have time to herself might also make it possible to mobilize herself for the several hours each day that Christy would be with her.

Christy's mother was simultaneously relieved by this plan and guilty over not being able to care fully for her daughter. However, after a month of this less difficult schedule and with the help of her medication and therapy, Christy's mother was able to resume being primarily responsible for her daughter. The parents, on their own, decided that Christy would spend every Wednesday with her grandparents as well as Saturdays with her father. With the predictable and loving relationships with her grandparents and father readily available to her, and her mother's reduced depression, Christy again became a happy, active youngster.

While the loss of a very young child's relationship with his father typically (when he has not been a primary caretaker) does not cause a youngster great immediate distress, it can be devastating to the man and may preclude the development of a sound, developmentally valuable father–child relationship in the future. We have discussed a range of reasons fathers may have for retreating from a relationship with their child and have noted realistic difficulties in sustaining and nurturing a father–child bond when infants and toddlers are involved. Special consideration must be given to a young child's needs in order to guard against unnecessarily losing what has a good chance of becoming a treasured relationship for both father and child.

BARRY (see chapter 4) was not distressed about the decreasing frequency of time with his father. To the contrary, he seemed genuinely relieved! Despite the fact that he had a regular and familiar day-care routine and two parents who loved him a great deal and coparented well together, he was fearful about leaving his mother to be with his father. When he was with his father, he was compliant but somewhat withdrawn and joyless. What complicated this picture was Barry's ease and comfort in separating from his mother each day to attend a day-care center. This contributed to his father's pain over Barry's distress about going with him. The mental health worker whom his parents consulted was able to put Barry's reactions into a developmentally understandable context. A toddler's difficulty in sustaining a loving bond with a parent he sees only once a week was emphasized. The fact that infants and toddlers define parenthood experientially rather than through intellectual awareness of biological and legal ties was explained. Further, a father who occasionally "helps out" diapering or feeding a young child and playing with him for brief periods of time does not elicit the kind of emotional attachment reserved for the parent (usually the mother) who is primarily responsible for the care of the youngster. That his son reacted to him as if he had become a stranger was no reflection on Barry's father, but rather was a consequence of Barry's age, the schedule of their time together, and the absence of a primary parenting role for his father before the divorce.

Barry's immediate relief when he did not have to go with his father was contrasted with the kind of mutually pleasurable relationship that could develop as Barry got older, assuming the father–child relationship was not permitted to wither away now. With that educational preface, Barry's parents were encouraged to increase rather than decrease the contacts between father and son. It was suggested that Barry's father see him every other day for an hour or so in the early evening after dinner. They could play in the yard or walk to a nearby park. Each week Barry would also spend one weekend day with his father but return to his mother's home to sleep. Both parents were asked to firmly support and adhere to this schedule for three months. The clinician suggested that Barry's mother mention from time to time: "It's nice when guys can see their dad and know he cares about them. It makes a guy feel special. And when a boy gets older he can play ball with his dad and go on fishing trips and campouts with him too." In this way Barry's mother was implicitly both holding out an expectation that he see his father regularly, that it was something she believed was a good thing, that fathers were important to boys, and that the future promised even more good times with father.

After three months the parents reported that Barry was comfortably and easily spending time with his father as planned. They wondered about introducing the idea of Barry's father taking him to dinner one night a week (rather than seeing him after dinner) and having Barry sleep over on the one weekend day he was with his father. They were counseled to talk with Barry about these possible changes before suggesting to him that he try it. Barry readily accepted the notion of dinner with his father (at a popular fast-food chain, of course) and within a month indicated that he would like to sleep over "sometimes" on the weekend.

This father–child relationship was saved largely because both parents cared deeply about their son, respected each other's parenting abilities, valued the contribution each could make to their son's life, and were not at war with one another. The difficulties in this case were primarily those posed by the developmental characteristics of young children not by an inconsistent or painful environment. Parents like Barry's can make excellent use of knowledge about child development and the needs as well as limitations of very young children. They can implement suggestions for alleviating a child's distress or come up with such strategies on their own.

Barry's situation raises the question of whether joint physical custody would have been helpful. In this arrangement the child lives with each parent part of the time, usually at no more unbalanced a ratio than 70 percent to 30 percent. The fact that Barry had already lapsed into a somewhat distant relationship with his father soon after the marital separation would suggest that joint physical custody would have placed a great amount of stress on this particular boy. The regular, often prolonged separations (two to three days) of a joint physical custody arrangement would have been too hard for Barry.

What are the indicators that joint physical custody would be a desirable arrangement for an infant or toddler? First, it is essential that each parent be in a position to provide the consistent nurturing environment that is so important for young children. Parents need to be in sufficiently good health, physically and emotionally, to parent effectively. A seriously debilitated parent cannot meet the needs of a child. This is not to say that adults with physical handicaps or emotional problems cannot care properly for youngsters. There are many examples of parents with physical infirmities or limitations who are nonetheless competent parents. Similarly, adults may suffer from emotional upsets and still continue to be appropriately attentive and caring parents.

The issue is not whether a parent is in perfect physical and emotional condition. Rather the question is whether an adult's difficulties specifically interfere with his or her parenting. An adult who is confined to a wheelchair or who is plagued by anxieties over intimate relationships with other adults can still be a loving, effective parent. On the other hand, a substance abusing, impulse-ridden, abusive, or otherwise seriously disordered adult cannot fulfill the needs of a child. To the contrary, such a parent may constitute a source of considerable distress for children.

In addition to both parents being able to provide adequate care for a young child in their own right, it is crucial that parents not be at war with one another and be capable of effectively coparenting on behalf of the youngster. It is not necessary that parents love or even like one another. They may continue to have hurt feelings and harbor resentments toward each other, but they need to be capable of putting aside these residues of their intimate relationship in order to parent together. When parents genuinely believe that their child will be served best by having an ongoing relationship with both parents and when they respect each other's capacities to parent, it is more likely that joint physical custody will work. And they must be able to put aside their less than cordial feelings toward each other so that they can communicate about their child. It is enormously helpful for parents to fill in each other about how the child seems to be feeling and behaving, what their recent interactions with the youngster have been like, and about any special and noteworthy events that have occurred. This permits both parents to have a full sense of the ebb and flow of their child's life. Both halves of the picture, the mother's and the father's, are necessary so that they can, together, provide the child with a sense of continuity in his life.

It is not necessary for parents to be in complete agreement about how a child should be raised. Especially for infants and toddlers, religious beliefs, views about a child's household responsibilities, rules about nighttime curfews, and disciplinary styles need not be consonant. While these differences can become points of friction between parents as the child grows older, they are of little consequence to infants and toddlers. If parents of older children do not agree about these sorts of issues, a good coparenting relationship, mutual respect for each other's parenting, and the belief that the child profits developmentally from her contacts with both parents, can collectively provide the materials to build an effective bridge for communication between the parents. This kind of bridge makes it possible to resolve different opinions or to learn to help the child and each other live with them.

Another key ingredient of a successful joint custody arrangement is the physical proximity of the parents' homes. Extended car travel is not comfortable for many infants and toddlers especially if the only adult in the car is driving. While being in the car is not by itself unsettling to young children (few suffer motion sickness, for example), it does mean that the parent-driver cannot respond as effectively to a child's needs. A crying infant cannot readily be picked up, fed and comforted. A toddler who wants his father's attention must put up with the frustration of not having it fully or immediately. Both infants and toddlers cannot move around in a car. Each will be (or certainly should be) riding in a car seat. They cannot crawl, walk, or otherwise explore their environment. They are in a position of an enforced passivity during the ride. Parents who must drive long distances with their child, whether in a joint physical custody arrangement or simply for weekly or biweekly visits with the parent they see least, can do some things to ease the stress of a prolonged car ride. Interesting toys can be brought and frequent stops made. If another adult, besides the parent, (a dating partner, a child's grandparent) can come along, the young child can have her needs responded to more readily without distracting and irritating the driver or causing frequent stops. Joint physical custody can work up to a distance of an hour or two driving time, but it is less stressful for all concerned if the parents live less than an hour from each other.

Finally, but as important as any of the other conditions for successful joint physical custody, the parents must be aware and respectful of an infant's and toddler's developmental needs. Very young children find long separations from a primary parent highly distressing. Though some parents have shared equally in the day-to-day routines of child care (in which case the youngster will be uneasy about separations from each), it is more typical that the mother has been the parent most actively involved with a young child. At the same time, an infant's and toddler's experiential definition of parenthood means that less than frequent contact with one parent will result in their losing their tenuous sense of that person as "parent." When one adds to these considerations the fact that very young children require consistency in their environment, it begins to make joint physical custody for infants and toddlers look like a very difficult proposition. And indeed it is. However, it is not impossible.

A young child could live in his mother's home for four days a week, but see his father nearly every day for an hour or two, and during the remaining three days live with his father and see his mother for an hour or two nearly daily. This would enable him to achieve an interpersonal consistency. Environmental consistency could be sought by having the same kind of crib and blankets in both houses, both parents using the same type of bottle (even down to the same shaped nipple) for feeding, and having several objects such as stuffed animals and toys regularly moved back and forth with the child. Assuming both parents are committed to this kind of arrangement, the young child, through the same mechanism of emotional resonance that may cause problems, can derive a sense of comfort. It is also helpful if the young child's temperament is easygoing so that he can respond well to all of these changes.

Some parents seem oblivious to the developmental needs of young children. Instead, in decidedly anti-Solomonesque fashion, they indeed divide the child in half. Schedules of having an infant or toddler on alternate weeks or alternate months in each parent's home with little or no contact between the child and the parent he is not living with is a travesty of joint physical custody. One set of divorced parents had an arrangement in which their fifteen-month-old had begun spending alternate six month periods with each parent and was to have no contact with the other parent during those times. A year-old child whose parents lived over a thousand miles apart was put on a plane every other week by himself to shuttle between his parents' homes. Such examples of joint custody may serve the needs of the adults but are entirely unmindful of a young child's developmental requirements. While a particular youngster may not display obvious symptoms of distress under these conditions, the emotional bonding with both parents will be considerably less than optimal. Sometimes children who have a good disposition and sturdy ego will tolerate this kind of disregard for their needs, but then become highly problematic youngsters when they reach elementary school or adolescence.

Overview

The young child's developmentally based requirements for a consistent daily routine, for parents who are sufficiently stable emotionally to provide for his physical and emotional needs, and for relative tranquility between his parents is clear. Though the illustrations in this chapter often involve youngsters who are having difficulties and whose parents consulted a mental health professional, none were emotionally disturbed or atypical children. They were in distress because one or more of their key needs were not being met. What differentiates them from children in general is not the circumstances of their parents' divorce, or even the intensity or extent of their distress. The only characteristic which distinguishes them from nearly all other very young children of divorce is that each had at least one parent who recognized that his or her child was having trouble and was able to bring himself or herself to seek the advice of a professional. Parents of infants or toddlers can use these examples and the issues they illustrate to sensitize themselves to their children's needs, to possible signs of their distress, and to ways of correcting or avoiding stressful circumstances for their children arising from parental divorce.

6

►◄

The Divorce Experience for Preschool Children

The second stage of development is the preschool years from ages three to five. During this period, gains in the areas of cognitive, emotional, and social development bring children from the relatively narrow world of toddlerhood to a readiness to begin elementary school. Despite their considerable developmental achievements, preschoolers have notable limitations that contribute to their experiences of divorce. Causal relationships are understood in egocentric terms. Here "egocentric" does not mean being inappropriately self-absorbed. Rather, it refers to a normal characteristic of young children to ascribe the cause of certain events to themselves. Even adults do this, though usually in a joking way, as they carry the childhood tendency forward. Adults will say, "It rained because I washed my car," or "The Yankees lost because I didn't go to the game." What adults say in jest, preschoolers earnestly believe. A child can believe that a parent's emotional distress or anger, and even the divorce, is his fault.

Children between the ages of three and five also have a great deal of difficulty distinguishing what they imagine from what is real. A fantasy that a strange dog will bite them, that there is a monster in their closet, or that they will fall off a swing can become so compelling that a youngster feels and acts as if it were really about to happen. For children of divorce, this means that fantasies of being abandoned by their mother, unloved by their father, or punished for an angry feeling can create a great deal of distress.

The preschool years are also a time of increased struggles for independence. Attending a day-care center and/or nursery school is common. These experiences provide new opportunities to be separate from parents and become more involved in the social world of peers. Yet a preschool child's sense of social and emotional independence is still tenuous. She must continue to rely on a secure home base in order to consolidate her independence. When a youngster's parents divorce, this security is threatened. Venturing forth into the wider world of day-care centers and nursery schools then becomes more taxing and anxiety arousing.

Preschoolers make another important step developmentally; they develop an attachment to their father which is qualitatively different from the one they have toward their mother and is special in its own right.[1] Boys begin to look to their father as a model for their emerging masculine identity, and girls turn to their father for confirmation of the value and acceptability of their femininity. A father provides a potentially pleasurable alternative relationship to the one with mother and becomes an ally in the child's efforts to emotionally separate from her. Clearly, when divorce makes a father peripheral to the lives of his children, these important contributions are lost or diminished.

Temperament continues to be a major factor in child development during the preschool years. This biologically determined predisposition to respond to the environment in particular ways affects the youngster's experience of events in his life. The preschooler who has an "easy" temperament adapts quickly and comfortably to changes in his world and is not dramatically affected by strong feelings from his parents. On the other hand, the youngster who has a "difficult" temperament is vulnerable to feeling greatly distressed over even minor changes or conflict in his environment. Divorce often means that there will be significant alterations in children's daily routines and child-care arrangements, as well as considerable conflict between parents. Temperament thus plays an important role in the youngster's experience of divorce and his adaptation to it.

The greatest developmental achievement of preschool-age children is a new capacity for abstract thinking. Heightened efforts to understand and master the environment lead preschool youngsters to be more curious about the divorce process and to actively attempt to understand the changes in their lives set in motion by their parents' separation. Not only do preschoolers ask "Why?" and "How come?" and "What if?" questions, but they now have the wherewithal to try to find answers themselves when adults do not provide them. Though they are still limited in their capacity to understand the social, emotional, legal, and financial complexities of divorce, they try to make sense of the new developments they see around them. When they do, they make much use of a newly available cognitive resource—the capacity to produce organized, clear-cut fantasies. These are based on concerns that all preschoolers must cope with: separation from home and parents, their role in causing events in their lives, and how good and lovable they are. When these developmentally appropriate concerns are mixed with a child's bewilderment and distress over the multitude of changes in his life that divorce brings, the result is fantasies that often frighten a youngster and make him sad. It is ironic that the very cognitive capacities which potentially permit preschool-age children to gain a greater understanding of the events in their lives become significant contributors toward psychological pain for them. Rather than reacting solely to having their basic needs unmet and experiencing global, diffuse feelings of anguish, as infants and toddlers do, these youngsters create new and internally driven sources of emotional distress.

The Immediate Crisis Stage

The environmental characteristics of the immediate crisis stage of divorce do not change substantially as a function of the child's age. Whether a youngster is an infant, toddler, preschooler, or even older, many of the family dynamics and events, such as the dislocation of daily routines, hostilities between parents, and emotional upheaval in parents are much the same.

Many youngsters between the ages of three and five are already used to being in day-care or nursery school. It is more likely that mother has returned to work outside the home by the time children reach this age. In fact, the majority of preschoolers in the United States have mothers who are employed part- or full-time outside the home. These children have become accustomed to being in the care of adults other than their parents. The routine of being dropped off at a day-care center, nursery school, or baby-sitter's house and being picked up at least several hours later is familiar and predictable. Preschoolers have had the opportunity to form pleasurable attachments to their adult caregivers and friendships with children their age.

It is extremely helpful for parents to keep the child-care arrangements intact at least during the initial crisis stage of divorce. The predictability and familiarity of the schedule and the daily activities and social interactions defining this experience create a feeling of continuity and consistency in a preschooler's life. Amid all the changes that divorce brings—in schedules of time with each parent, how parents act toward each other, how each parent feels, and possibly less time with mother as she increases her work or educational efforts—the out-of-home caregiving setting can provide a reassuring sense of consistency. When this schedule is disrupted, preschoolers can be expected to show signs of distress in much the same ways that we saw for toddlers whose daily routines became unpredictable. Despite being more advanced developmentally, preschoolers still require a firm sense of consistency in their lives. When changes in the child's routine are unavoidable, it is necessary to recognize that she will need special help in adjusting successfully to them.

ALLISON was nearly four years old when her parents separated. She had been attending the same day-care/nursery school since she was two-and-one-half years old. For her first year she went half-days for five days a week. When she was three-and-a-half, her mother returned to work full-time as an elementary school teacher and Allison became a full-time nursery school student. She enjoyed her longer hours in this familiar setting and had made an excellent adjustment to the change.

Allison's mother initiated the marital separation and filed for divorce. Her husband refused to leave the family residence on the advice of his attorney. The attorney claimed that Allison's father would be in a better bargaining position regarding the financial elements of the divorce settlement if he were not the one who left the family home. Allison's mother moved out with her. Unfortunately, the apartment she could afford was at a significant distance from the day-care center. Further, the center had become too costly with the parents now maintaining two separate residences. Allison had to leave her old day-care providers for a new, less costly, and more conveniently located home-based center.

Allison's mother was empathically aware of how hard this would be for her daughter. As a teacher of young elementary school children, she had seen how distressing family moves and attending a new school could be for youngsters. She followed the advice she used to give to parents whose children were changing schools. Three weeks before making the shift to the new center, she explained to Allison that she would be going to a new place each day and would have to say goodbye to everyone at her day-care center. She truthfully told her daughter why this was necessary and that the day-care center would have a going away party for her (something she had arranged for with the staff). Allison was understandably upset initially and cried. She claimed she did not want to go anywhere else. Her mother gently reiterated the reasons for the change and told Allison that the new place was very nice, that the woman who would be there liked girls a lot, and that she would meet new friends there.

Two weeks before the change, she scheduled several visits at the new center. She introduced her daughter to the woman who provided the care, and together they explored the house. Allison had a chance to see the toys and play materials and was told about the activities that were planned each day. She met the six other youngsters who attended the center. Each visit lasted about an hour. Allison, an adaptable girl with an easygoing temperament, quickly found things she liked about the new place. There were neat toys, special magic markers for drawing, and a great tire swing that hung from a large oak tree in the backyard. Two girls were close to her age, and she began playing with them during the visits. The woman she had met also had seemed very nice. The goodbye party at her old center went well, and each of the children in her play group drew pictures for Allison to take with her. When it came time for her to begin going to the new center, Allison had some difficulty separating from her mother. But within two weeks she was comfortable there and had begun to settle into her new surroundings.

The sensitive preparation by Allison's mother, and the fact that she, herself, was managing her separation from her husband well contributed to her daughter's good adjustment. The farewell party to mark the end of Allison's tie to the old center, her mother's careful explanations of the reasons for the change, holding out to her daughter a confident expectation that she would do well at the new center, and going with her daughter for brief visits to the new center collectively formed a sturdy bridge from one setting to the other. Clearly Allison's easygoing nature and her previous positive experiences of being separated from her mother and in the care of other adults also contributed to the smoothness of the transition. Without all of these factors, we would expect Allison to have the sorts of difficulties created by disruptions in daily routines which were described in chapter 4.

The continuation of predictable and positive daily routines does not always result in good child adjustment during the initial crisis stage of divorce. Preschoolers develop fantasies about the divorce and imbue old, familiar routines with new and unpleasant meanings. Whereas the external, environmental parameters of a child's life are paramount for infants and toddlers, and are still very important for preschoolers, the preschool-age child also brings his own private agenda to situations. The nearly certain connection between pleasurable, non-stressful environmental conditions (for example, consistent daily routines, minimal hostilities between parents, emotionally stable parents, good parent–child relationships) and the infant's and toddler's successful adaptation to parental divorce, is not quite so close or automatic for preschoolers. The preschool youngster's own thoughts and understandings of events in his life come into play and can be decisive factors in his adjustment.

FRANK was four years old when his parents separated. They had developed a distant and loveless relationship over their six years of marriage. As they moved into their early thirties, they both wanted to end the marriage and seek other partners. Frank's father managed a small restaurant and his mother had begun working full-time as a bank teller when Frank was two-and-one-half years old. Since that time he had been attending a day-care center/nursery school component.

Frank was able to continue at that center when his parents separated. Three months after his father had moved out of the family residence to an apartment, Frank began having trouble when he was dropped off at the center. He cried, whimpered, and clung to his mother. When she attempted to leave, he tried to hang on to her and stop her. The center staff encouraged Frank's mother to leave quickly so as not to prolong these painful interactions. This sort of advice, aimed at preventing the point of separation from being unnecessarily drawn out and therefore unduly stressful for the child, did not seem to reduce Frank's discomfort. Each day the same scene was repeated. Frank did not demonstrate the usual preschooler's tendency to settle down and become happily engaged in activities once mother has left and the immediacy of the separation experience is no longer present. The day-care personnel reported that he seemed sad and withdrawn for most of the time, a dramatic change from his previous active and pleasurable involvement.

At home, Frank displayed similar fearfulness when his mother left him with a baby-sitter to go out with friends occasionally. He also seemed somewhat sad at home. His mother tried talking to him and asking him what was wrong. She pointed out that Frank had always liked going to the day-care center, especially since he had begun the nursery school part of it. After several attempts to get Frank to tell her what was bothering him, he blurted out, "You're gonna go away and leave me!" His mother reminded him that she always had taken Frank to the day-care center and that he liked the people there and enjoyed playing with the toys as well as with other children. Frank said, "You're gonna leave me and go far away to live." His mother was puzzled by this worry but reassured her son that she was not going to move away from him. Her efforts seemed ineffective. Her son continued to be frightened when she dropped him off at the day-care center and generally sad at the center as well as at home.

Frank's daily schedule had been unaffected by his parents' separation. In reality, the routine of being taken to the same day-care center at the same time each day and being picked up at a regular time had not changed. This is why his mother was so surprised by his fears. But the meaning of going to the center had changed as had his trust in consistent parenting. Being left at the day-care center no longer meant that he would be playing with other children and being cared for by an adult other than one of his parents until his mother came for him in the late afternoon. At the very least, being left at the center came to represent, in Frank's mind, the first step to his mother abandoning him forever.

His mother had not been able to understand her four-year-old's private logic. She assumed, as many parents do, that her son would immediately know and fully believe that she would, of course, continue to raise her son in her home after the marital separation. Frank was trying in his own way to understand the divorce. He had seen and heard his parents argue and knew that his father had moved out of the home and now lived "far away" (actually about ten miles). He saw his father every two to three weeks. Frank's way of conceptualizing divorce was that it was a process: first the parents argue and then the father moves out of the house; next the father has little to do with his children; and, finally, the mother moves away after arranging for the children to be looked after in a day-care center. He was a precociously bright four-year-old and his logic was very reasonable.

Frank's sadness was not only a result of his anticipation of being lonely after his mother left him for good. He also was feeling like an unlovable little boy. If your father has left you, and your mother is planning to leave you, you must be an awful person. Though Frank could not articulate this reasoning, he experienced the results of it by becoming sad. Notice the preschooler's normal tendency to organize events in an egocentric manner: his father left *him* (not the family residence, not his wife, not his marriage). And his mother was preparing to leave him, too. What a terrible boy he must be!

Disrupted routines, whether due to realistic changes or to the new meanings a youngster gives them, can be a source of distress for preschool-age children. Parents are usually aware of the fact that an unpredictable or new schedule can cause preschool children to become upset. Allison's mother was especially well-attuned to this issue. It is the private, most often unspoken, meanings that children attach to their routines that make it so difficult at times for parents to understand why their child is so upset. Without knowing what is disturbing a youngster, parents feel helpless about what to do.

Hostilities between parents are another source of stress for preschoolers, as well as both older and younger children. Just as was the case for infants and toddlers, preschool-age youngsters resonate to strong feelings around them, especially those coming from their parents. Because preschoolers are more advanced developmentally than their younger counterparts, they are even more aware of and thus more sensitive to parental battles than infants or toddlers. A relatively brief, sharp exchange between parents is experienced by the preschooler as a "big fight." A protracted, angry shouting match accompanied by some pushing or slapping is devastating to the preschooler who observes it. He must not only contend with the powerful reverberations that this anger sets up in his psyche through the mechanism of emotional resonance, but he is also faced with the meaning he attributes to the argument and his fantasies about what will happen next.

Infants and toddlers resonate strongly to parental warfare and are too cognitively immature to anticipate relief when it ends. Preschoolers also resonate to the rage swirling around them. Though they can anticipate a time of relief, they can also imagine it becoming much worse. In fact, the latter is a far more common use of a preschooler's newly acquired cognitive ability to abstract and go beyond the actual events that are occurring. Anyone who is familiar with children in the three-to-five-year-old range knows of their fondness for listening

100

to and creating their own tall tales. Even as they are relating some occurrence on the playground or at nursery school they tend to embellish and exaggerate. And then they are notably given to believing the version of reality they have just constructed! As long as parents know this about preschoolers (and even early elementary school youngsters) and do not confuse it with lying, it can be a source of entertainment for parents and children alike as well as a vehicle for gently reminding youngsters of the difference between fantasies and wishes on the one hand and reality on the other. Thus, while infants and toddlers are trapped in the immediacy of a parental war because they cannot cognitively project themselves beyond it to anticipate relief, preschoolers are terribly burdened by their capacity to imagine what might happen next and then anticipate that.

ALBERT was a high-strung youngster from birth. He had colic for the first five months of his life and had to be held a great deal to prevent him from crying in pain. His mother was a calm, caring woman who appropriately had ignored the advice of friends and neighbors to "let him just cry it out." She intuitively had recognized her infant's pain and comforted him for hours on end. He progressed well developmentally after his colic subsided but continued to be sensitive to noises, changes in his environment, and smells. His parents swore that he could smell pizza when they were still a block away from the carry-out store. Albert's temperament could be classified as "difficult" because of his acute sensitivity to his environment. It was as if his environment intruded upon him easily and upset him. His mother was aware of his needs and articulated them by referring to him as "high-strung."

When Albert turned three his parents began him in a half-day nursery school. Not surprisingly, he cried at first and seemed overwhelmed by his new environment. But with the patient understanding of his teacher and mother, he soon was enjoying his new world outside the home.

Albert's father, an engineer with a large automobile company, had developed a serious drinking problem. Though he could contain the effects of his alcoholism on his work performance (he never drank during the day), he headed straight for the liquor cabinet on arriving home. Within an hour he was feeling the effects of the alcohol. He loudly complained about his wife's poor cooking and the messy house. He also angrily accused her of babying Albert and having done so since his birth. While Albert's mother took her husband's complaints about her housekeeping and cooking rather stoically, she became enraged when he assailed her mothering. She defended her care of Albert by referring to his colic and his being high-strung. Her husband would retaliate by claiming that she was turning Albert into a sissy. She occasionally responded by saying, "A sissy huh, well he gave up the bottle when he was fourteen months old, which is a lot more than I can say for you!" These arguments had become more frequent and intense and often lasted for up to two hours. Though Albert's father never struck his wife or son, nor threw objects about, the atmosphere was so charged with rage that Albert's mother began to worry about her husband becoming physically violent.

As she began to realize how untenable the marriage was, Albert's mother carefully made plans to leave. She began working outside the home as a secretary-receptionist at a physician's office two months before she filed for divorce. Albert began attending the afternoon, day-care session of his nursery school when his mother began her job. As with all new things in Albert's life, the change to being away from home all day instead of half-days elicited upset feelings at first. But again with the help of the day-care staff and his mother he soon settled into his new routine.

When Albert was three years and eight months, his mother filed for divorce and his father moved out of the home. However, their angry arguments did not stop with their separation. Albert's father would frequently come back to the house because he had "forgotten" something; a shirt, a jacket, a tool he needed, a book he had left behind were all reasons to return to the family residence. Each time he came back, a fight took place. He entered the house like an inspector general, imperiously finding fault with his wife's housekeeping. At other times he berated his wife, accusing her and her attorney of proposing outlandish settlements which he claimed would "bleed me dry." Every visit resulted in a rage-filled argument. Albert most often left the room in which the fighting was taking place. He went outside to the yard or to his room. He almost never cried or spoke when his parents were engaged in a battle. His distress manifested itself in other ways. He began wetting his pants nearly every day at nursery school and also wet his bed every night. This high-strung, somewhat shy boy began picking fights with children at his nursery school. The staff at the school reported his pushing and hitting other youngsters with no apparent provocation. He angrily shouted at these youngsters, "I'm gonna kill you!"

In addition to wetting his bed at home, he had great difficulty going to sleep at night. He wanted his mother to stay with him until he fell asleep, something he had not asked for since he was two and a half. During the night he awoke in a panic with nightmares. He dreamt monsters and "bad guys" were chasing him and wanting to kill him. In the evenings, before going to bed, he played for hours with his G.I. Joe action figures. There was little organization to his play, which consisted largely of his having the figures angrily shoot each other while yelling, "You're gonna die," and having army trucks crash into one another repetitively. His mother's attempts to draw him away from this play were met with stubborn resistance. When he was not watching television or playing with his army men, he laid on the sofa staring at the ceiling. Sometimes he went outside and stared off into space. During these times he looked sad and lost.

The preseparation fights between Albert's parents, which continued when they began living apart, were taking their toll on him. Though he tried to distance himself physically from the warfare in his home by going outside or to his room, he could not escape it entirely. Powerful feelings of rage were being stimulated in Albert as he resonated to his parents' fury. He was also angry at them for making life so miserable for him. At the same time, he was frightened about becoming angry at his parents directly. Instead he expressed his angry feelings toward other children at nursery school and in his solitary play with action figures and trucks. But it was not diffuse anger alone that Albert was wrestling with. He had become preoccupied with ideas of killing and death.

Resonating to parental anger can be seen in infants and toddlers as well as preschoolers. Albert had gone beyond resonating. He elaborated in his imagination both the likely final outcome of the angry exchanges he witnessed between his parents as well as what the final result of his own anger might be. Though Albert was not fearful during the day, the anxiety he felt over the potentially catastrophic results of the anger between his parents as well as the rage he felt welling up within him became clear at night. His uneasiness about going to sleep alone, his nightmares, and his bed wetting were all testimony to Albert's fears. The content of his frightening dreams as well as his sadness suggested not only the ideas of anger and death but punishment as well. In his nightmares he was in danger. Such dreams often indicate feelings of guilt which a youngster believes might lead to punishment. Albert had heard his parents repetitively argue over how his mother had raised him. In the normally egocentric manner of young children, he put two and two together and got five; he was the cause of his parents' fights and therefore their divorce. He felt guilty and sad about the role he was convinced he had in his parents' troubled relationship.

Changes in daily routines and parental warfare are key stressors for preschoolers in the immediate crisis stage of divorce. They are the first shock waves of the initial marital separation to reach the youngster. Global feelings of distress over the upsetting events are compounded by the preschooler's tendency to give them special and disconcerting private meanings. Parents must not only contend with the obvious connections between disrupted schedules and parental hostilities and the distress they so frequently cause preschoolers. They must also be on the lookout for likely meanings a youngster attaches to these facets of the divorce process. Achieving consistent daily schedules and reducing the fights between parents are still critically important to the well-being of preschoolers. But parents often must go beyond this to understand the child's internal realities as well.

The Short-Term Aftermath Stage

The initial divorce shock waves of disrupted daily schedules and parental warfare frequently continue and at times intensify during this phase of the divorce process. Even separations that began in a low-key manner can become suffused with defensive rage in response to emerging feelings of loss, loneliness, rejection, damaged self-esteem, guilt, and/or anxiety over financial or social circumstances which often crystallize in one or both parents as the reality of the divorce begins to sink in. Battles over property settlements, child support, custody, and/or visiting schedules provide the flash points during this period.

TOMMY was four-and-one-half-years old when his father filed for divorce and moved out of the family residence. His parents had been married for nearly eight years and were in their late twenties at the time they separated. Tommy's mother had returned to school when he was nearly two in order to pursue a graduate degree in social work. She was about to complete her studies, when her husband left the family residence. Tommy's father was an investment broker with a large brokerage house. He was a somewhat distant, aloof man who had great difficulty with intimate adult relationships. He had no close friends and treasured time alone to pursue his greatest source of enjoyment, collecting rare coins. He experienced his wife as an irritating interference in the time he wished to devote to his more-than-casual hobby.

Tommy's mother had become increasingly upset by her husband's gradual withdrawal from the marital relationship. She resented the time he spent with coin dealers as he sought to add to his already substantial collection. She described herself as a "people-oriented person" and could not understand someone who valued material things over interpersonal relationships. She became more irritated with her husband and they constantly squabbled over minor household tasks. Tommy's father felt that his wife was increasingly intruding into his private, personal "space." They discussed the possibility of separating, and though each had misgivings about bringing their marriage to an end, they also both began to experience a sense of relief at this prospect.

The initial crisis stage of divorce had more an air of calm than crisis. Tommy and his mother continued to live in the family home and he kept attending the day-care center/nursery school he had been going to for the past two years. Tommy's father had moved into a comfortable apartment and very much enjoyed the peace and quiet of living alone. Despite his problems with adult intimacy, he felt devoted to his son. Although he had been peripheral to Tommy's care when he was an infant and young toddler, he had become more involved with him as Tommy became more verbal. He frequently had taken his son with him on trips to coin dealers and was sharing his hobby with him. The parents agreed on a once weekly schedule of time for Tommy to be with his father. This alternated between Friday evening to Saturday afternoon and Saturday evening to Sunday afternoon.

The first several months of the marital separation went smoothly, and Tommy continued to do well at nursery school and with each parent. As the divorce moved into the short-term aftermath stage,

Tommy's mother began dating a man who worked in the same school system where she had found a position as a school social worker. This angered Tommy's father on several grounds. First, it seemed "too soon" for her to date. And second, he resented the fact that Tommy seemed to like this man who often included him in activities with Tommy's mother. At the same time, his attorney had been receiving proposals from his wife's attorney outlining financial settlements that he felt were unfair. Tommy's father had expected that the family house would be sold and the cash balance after the mortgage deduction would be divided equally. He also anticipated paying considerably less in child support than was being proposed, since his wife now had a full-time job with excellent fringe benefits. He angrily instructed his attorney to make a counterproposal incorporating these wishes.

Tommy's mother was furious when she heard about this offer from her attorney. She believed that her husband was being totally insensitive to Tommy's need for consistency by suggesting the family home be sold. That would require a change of residence for her and her son, probably to a less expensive and less desirable neighborhood. Tommy would lose the reassuring familiarity of his home and neighborhood friends. She also felt that the higher level of child support was indicated in part because her husband earned a substantial salary and in part because her income was as yet insufficient to maintain the life style she and her son currently had.

The conflict escalated: Tommy's mother adamantly refused her husband's counterproposal; he vindictively began being late with the support checks he was sending as part of the predivorce, interim court order; she instructed her attorney to include the value of her husband's coin collection in the process of arriving at a property settlement; he asked his attorney to begin exploring the possibility of seeking joint legal custody of Tommy. They began having intense arguments over these issues. They called each other on the phone and what would begin as reasoned attempts to settle the matters at hand quickly became bitter, acrimonious, accusation-filled battles. When they saw each other on the days Tommy's father picked up and then dropped off his son, they sniped at each other sarcastically. He asked her how her love life was going; she answered by saying it was a lot better than fondling coins. He asked her if she thought about Tommy's welfare or if she was only preoccupied in indulging herself. She pointed out that he was really the self-indulgent one, spending great amounts of time and money on his coins while refusing to send enough money to help support his son. At times these verbal jousting matches went on for nearly half an hour while Tommy looked on silently. The two rarely became explosively angry, except during their telephone calls. But their venom and mutual derogation was palpable.

Tommy began "sassing" his teacher at school. When she asked him to do something, he at first pretended he did not hear her. He referred to her and other day-care personnel as "dopes" and "dumb heads" loudly enough for them to hear him as he talked to other children. When they asked him why he was saying those things, he replied: "Don't you know? It's your job to know. Boy, are you dumb!" He had also begun teasing some of the younger children at the day-care center/nursery school. He laughed at their efforts to do things that he already could do well. He mimicked their crying or whining when they were distressed. When they completed a drawing or finished building something with blocks, Tommy belittled them and derogated what they had accomplished. He would engage a younger child in a competitive game and laugh derisively when he won. Tommy was becoming a thoroughly unlikable little boy. At home he was irritable. He complained when his mother asked him to put a toy away or come to the dinner table. He whined when he could not have his way about what to have for dessert, which television program was on, and what time he was to go to bed. However, with his father he was quietly obedient. Although his behavior at home had become less pleasant than it had been, the main site of his difficulties was his nursery school.

Tommy was reacting to the hostilities that had sprung up between his parents. He loved them both, so it hurt and angered him to see them tear at one another, insult each other, and generally be mutually demeaning. Essentially he took his complaints to school with him instead of directly to his parents. His derogation of his teachers was an expression of his anger toward his parents for being so nasty to each other. In addition to his anger toward his parents, impulses to demean and derogate others were being stirred up in him. Through emotional resonance to his parents' mutual derogation, and the model of antagonistic interactions they presented, Tommy began to take on their feelings and also act as they had. He found convenient and safe foils for these impulses in younger children at school whom he could successfully control and belittle.

Unlike infants and young toddlers, boys and girls of preschool age usually have formed a valued relationship with their father even when he has not been centrally involved in their day-to-day care. It is still very much the case that mothers are the primary parent in the lives of infants and toddlers. "Modern" fathers in an egalitarian marriage tend to help out in diapering, feeding, holding, and cuddling very young children. But "helping out" itself implies the secondary role of these fathers in child care. Such fathers may spend more time playing with their infants and toddlers than has been the case traditionally, but this does not lead to the kind of attachment a primary parent receives from her very young child. While there clearly are exceptions to this situation, the vast majority of infants and toddlers form their earliest emotional attachments to their mother.

As a toddler of two years begins the psychological task of emotionally separating himself from his mother, he naturally begins to look to other relationships. Feeling separate from mother does not lead to feeling fully independent. Instead, new opportunities for different kinds of relationships are explored. Fathers are good candidates for a child's partner as the youngster begins to widen his social-emotional world. Fathers can be fun! They play; often permit the child a wider latitude of freedom; are less likely to be overly concerned with protecting and thereby, to some degree, inhibiting the child's explorations of his environment; introduce new activities; and do not usually restrain a youngster inadvertently by frequently trying to hold and cuddle him. Fathers' interactions with their young children have been characterized as being more "distal" and more playful than a mother's.[2] That is, the physical distance between them is greater than that between a mother and child, which has the effect of permitting and encouraging greater physical freedom and independence.

In these ways fathers come to be experienced by children as a developmentally progressive force in their lives. A mother's nurturance continues to be crucial to a youngster's sense of consistency and general well-being. But a father's relationship fits the developmental needs of an older toddler and especially a preschooler for separation from mother and independence. Fathers begin to become psychologically central in the lives of preschoolers. A disruption of that relationship means more than a loss, partial or complete depending on the schedule of postdivorce father–child contacts, of a loved parent. It may undermine the preschooler's efforts to consolidate her newfound emotional independence.

The father–child relationship has other special meanings for preschoolers in addition to emotional separation and independence of mother. A difference in how boys and girls relate to their father begins to emerge. It has been long recognized that fathers serve as role models for their sons.[3] Boys begin to consolidate their budding sense of masculinity through identifications with their father. They increasingly see themselves as being like their father and want to do what he does and even look like him. Preschool-age boys will frequently try on their father's shoes, draw or "write" (actually scribble) with his pen, try foods he eats, and share in his interests in music or sports. Boys begin to develop, often without even being aware of it, their father's mannerisms of speech, gait, and attitudes as their identifications with him take hold.

Until very recently, the role fathers play in their daughters' early development was seen as minimal. We now know better.[4] Preschool-age girls become very emotionally attached to their father. Because girls share the same gender as the mother and, therefore, are like her and appropriately identify with her femininity, the task of separating from her is more difficult than it is for boys. There are two opposing psychological forces at work: a girl's need to separate emotionally from her mother and gain independence, and the simultaneous press to model herself after mother in order to consolidate her own sense of femininity. An attachment to father facilitates the emotional separation while providing a safe base from which she can partially return to her mother emotionally by identifying with her. While girls clearly do not look to their father as a model for femininity, they do gain from him a confirmation of the value of their femininity to males. When these father–daughter bonds are weakened the developmental costs can be great.

GAIL HAD ENJOYED an increasingly close, loving relationship with her father. Her parents were traditional in their approach to child-rearing. Gail's mother had been nearly exclusively responsible for her early care. Her father, a big, burly construction worker had begun playing with her more when she left infancy and became a toddler. He carried her around on his shoulders, gave her piggy-back rides, and wrestled on the living room floor with her. As she moved into her preschool years, they began playing catch with footballs or tennis balls, depending on the season of the year. With the help of this relationship, Gail was becoming an assertive, feisty girl. She adapted well to a nursery school that she had begun shortly after turning three, and was seen by her teacher as a leader. Socially outgoing, physically fearless, curiously questioning were phrases her teacher used to describe her.

When Gail was just over four years old, her parents separated. Her father had been twenty and her mother eighteen when they married nearly six years before. Now, in her midtwenties, Gail's mother found her husband "unloving." She felt they were drifting apart. She wanted very much to be told she was loved and to feel that she was in a romantic relationship. Her husband was a caring man but was undemonstrative about expressing affection verbally. She felt put off by his somewhat gruff, physical approach to life in general and to her in particular. She came to the conclusion that she wanted to leave the relationship and pursue a college education. Gail's mother yearned for a life beyond her blue-collar roots and for a relationship with an open, emotionally expressive man. She felt stuck on all fronts. Their sexual relationship had deteriorated with neither finding it pleasurable any longer. Gail's father realized his wife had been upset and dissatisfied for a long time but did not know what to do about it. He had rejected her suggestion to see a marriage counselor a year earlier. Opening up emotionally and talking about his private feelings was not something he was comfortable with. Even the thought of doing that in the presence of a stranger was intolerable. At the same time, he was deeply wounded by his wife's wish to end their marriage. He felt that his work, his interests, and his whole manner of being intimate had been judged and found wanting.

He met this crisis as he had dealt with all other important issues in his life, by trying to take charge. He stoically accepted his wife's wishes, moved out of their house, and he, himself, filed for divorce. He offered a fair level of child support and division of property and also agreed to have his wife and daughter continue living in the family residence. The parents arranged a mutually satisfactory child custody and visitation plan; mother would have sole legal custody and father would see his daughter every other weekend and once a week for dinner. The initial stage of their separation went well. Gail and her mother lived at home, Gail continued attending the same nursery school/day-care center, and her mother began college on a nearly full-time basis. Though Gail's mother felt sad and somewhat guilty about her decision to separate from her husband, she looked forward to the possibility of a bright, exciting new future.

Gail's father, on the other hand, was suffering. Unable to express or cope with his grief over losing his wife, he began a wildly careening social life. He went to singles bars nearly every night, drank too much, and had numerous one-night stands. When not at these bars, he went to sporting events with buddies from work. The single, consistently bright spot in his life was his daughter. He looked forward to their being together on alternate weekends and weekly Tuesday dinners. But within four months this too, began to depress him. The quality of several brief spontaneous interactions during each evening gave way to planned, more formal-feeling time together. He took Gail to her favorite fast-food restaurant every Tuesday night, but he could not comfortably pick her up, carry her around on his shoulders, or fall to the floor playfully wrestling with her there. He began to feel awkward with his own daughter. His feeling ill-at-ease carried over to the weekends they spent together. He had been comfortable with and used to an easy give-and-take style of relating, not only to his daughter, but to all people. He began to sense that his style worked only when he had frequent contact with Gail. He made valiant attempts to recreate this atmosphere every other weekend but felt it was falling flat. So he made plans. He took his daughter to the movies, the zoo, a nearby park, and out to restaurants for meals. Their interaction became a set piece with no room for spontaneity. He felt his daughter slipping away from him. His sadness was overwhelming to him. He was an action-oriented man, had been so all his life. He applied for and got a job in another state where construction was booming and left.

Gail adapted well during the initial crisis stage of her parents' divorce. Her daily routine remained intact, her mother was adjusting well and able to continue her thoughtful and loving parenting, and she saw her father regularly and fairly frequently. As she neared her fifth birthday, her parents' divorce became final. She wanted to bring a copy of the decree to her nursery school to show her classmates what "divorcing papers" looked like.

It was just after the divorce was legally granted that Gail's father moved out of state. Gail did not weep or ask to see her father.

She seemed to accept this loss in a nearly matter-of-fact way, but her demeanor changed both at her nursery school and at home. Many of these shifts were subtle and her mother paid little attention to them. Her teacher, however, was sensitively aware of the changes in Gail. She rarely volunteered to share her ideas and feelings or be among the first to participate in a new game. Her daring physical style gave way to a lack of interest in climbing, jumping, and riding the tricycles at the center. She appeared almost timid compared to her previous approach to these activities. She also became less inclined to play with the other children, preferring instead to draw or color by herself. Though her behaviors were within normal limits for a child her age, they were markedly subdued when contrasted with how she had looked a few months earlier.

At home Gail began asking her mother frequently where her father was, what his apartment looked like, whether he had enough food, and if his job was safe. Her mother answered factually that he lived in a particular state, she had no idea what his apartment looked like, and she was sure he had enough to eat and that his job was just fine. But a day or two later Gail worriedly asked her mother the same questions all over again. In the evenings and on weekends Gail began following her mother from room to room in the house. She seemed to want to be near her mother most of the time. She colored in her coloring books and drew pictures to send to her father. She stopped playing outside, and when neighborhood children came to the door to invite her to play, she usually refused claiming that she was busy. At her nursery school she began telling the teacher and other children that her father was working ''far away'' in order to make a lot of money. When he had enough money he was going to come back and take Gail to Hawaii to live in a huge mansion. It would have a swimming pool and they would own seven horses, so she could ride a different one each day of the week. She also said that her father was sending her fancy dresses and jewelry, but she could not bring them in to show everyone because they were too expensive and ''they might get wrecked or lost.'' Gail's teacher became increasingly concerned about her retreat from a robust involvement in daily activities, her withdrawal from playing with the other children, and the tall tales she was telling.

The changes in Gail signalled the onset of a depressive reaction. She could no longer take pleasure in activities that had been great fun previously. Her withdrawal from social activities at nursery school and in her neighborhood was a sign that she was retreating from the place she had made for herself in the world beyond her home. Instead, she acted more like a young toddler who prefers to be close to her mother rather than venturing into the wider world of peer relationships and activities. She was giving up her assertiveness and independence, in part because the relationship with her father that had sustained these efforts was no longer available and also because she was preoccupied by having lost him. She was worried about his well-being, probably because she had sensed his mounting depression just prior to his leaving. It is possible that she was also responding emotionally to that depression, which contributed to her experiencing similar feelings.

Gail's tall tales about her father are an example of the preschooler's tendency to use a psychological defense called "denial in fantasy" to ward off painful feelings. In her imagination he had gone away for her sake. He would make a great deal of money, return for her, and take her to a special place where she could live like a queen. Why did this fantasy develop and what purpose did it serve for Gail? It is likely that Gail had understood her father's departure in the preschooler's egocentric terms. He had moved far away because she was not lovable or important enough for him to stay. Her fantasy was an attempt to ward off the pain this "understanding" created. In her imagination he indeed left because of her, but it was out of love for her not because she was unimportant to him. Though there was no dramatic evidence that Gail was in distress, her social-emotional development had been disrupted and her self-esteem dealt a serious blow.

A preschooler's developmental thrust toward greater emotional separation and independence from the primary parent, the one who has been centrally involved in his early care (typically mother), can also be interfered with by too much closeness with mother. When Gail's father left, she lost his support for the progressive forces in her psychological life. Other youngsters must cope with the other side of this coin, namely an emotional pull from mother to remain a toddler-like child by being close to her.

Many parents become overwhelmed by feelings of loneliness as the reality of the divorce begins to be felt more keenly in the short-term aftermath stage. As difficult as their marital relationship may have been, and as much as a parent was committed to ending the marriage, feeling alone and burdened by the role of being a single-parent can be painful. It is not that the parent begins to believe that the divorce was a mistake. Nor is it that she wants her former spouse back. She usually realizes that the divorce was a necessary and desirable action to end a loveless and/or tension-ridden relationship. The ex-spouse's shortcomings are still clearly seen, and he continues to be experienced as an undesirable partner. There is no wish to undo the separation and reconcile. The parent is firmly committed to the divorce process continuing. But the social surgery of severing the marital bonds between two people can elicit similar reactions to that of physical surgery; it may have been necessary, but it is painful in the short run.

There are multiple sources of this emotional pain. Many newly divorced parents feel anxious about re-entering the work force or moving from part-time to full-time employment. Can they hold down a new or full-time job successfully? Feeling socially isolated is also a common complaint of men and women in the short-term aftermath stage of divorce. Single persons tend to be invited to participate less frequently with people they knew when they were part of a married couple. Once outside the marital relationship, previous social relationships seem to wither away or end abruptly. Even in bad marriages, there is a sense of, if not companionship, at least a feeling that one is not entirely alone.

Under these stresses some parents turn to their children as a source of comfort. This creates a shift in the parent–child relationship. The specific nature of the change depends on the youngster's age. For preschoolers it usually means greater physical and emotional closeness with the parent. She may become overly protective of her preschooler, engage him in play to the near exclusion of opportunities for interacting with other children, hold and cuddle him frequently as if he were a much younger child, or take him into her bed as if he were a soft teddy bear whose presence was comforting and reassuring.

SARAH's parents separated when she was three-and-one-half years old. Her parents had been married for nine years and had a son seven years old as well as Sarah. Sarah's mother was eighteen when she married her husband. He was ten years her senior. She had looked up to him, was grateful for his attention and at first experienced her marriage as a rescue from her unpleasant, combative relationship with her own parents with whom she was living. Her husband had shared this rescue image and had felt like a knight on a white horse who could do no wrong in his young wife's eyes. As the realities of marriage settled in, each became increasingly disillusioned and dissatisfied. They bickered frequently and became acutely aware of their perceptions of each other's shortcomings. He began spending longer hours at his office where he worked as a draftsman for an engineering firm. She attended junior college, obtained a two-year certificate in retailing, and began working part-time in a large department store. Each felt that their marriage was going nowhere and had openly discussed the possibility of a trial separation for a year before acting on it.

Sarah's mother filed for divorce, and her husband moved out of the family residence. Their divorce proceeded in a relatively amicable way with brief, but intense, conflicts over some of the financial aspects of the final settlement. Sarah's father had not been substantially involved in the rearing of her or her brother. He was a somewhat emotionally distant father. The parents initially agreed to an every other weekend schedule of visitation, which gradually became once a day every three to four weeks. Sarah continued attending the nursery school she had begun a few months before her parents' separation. Though Sarah's mother was relieved during the initial phase of the divorce process and enthusiastically devoted more energy to her work, after six months she felt increasingly burdened by the rigors of single-parenting. Her son had become uncooperative at home and was not doing well in school. He argued with her over nearly everything: washing his hands before coming to the dinner table; picking up his toys; whether he had to drink his milk; and the time he was supposed to go to bed. She felt worn down and resentful by his disagreeable behavior. She became fatigued by the demands of her job as well. Socially she did very little. Between her work and single-parenting, she felt she had no time for herself. Her only adult companionship consisted of lunch with co-workers.

Sarah, a good-natured youngster, became her primary source of pleasure as the divorce moved into its short-term aftermath stage. Sarah willingly helped out in the kitchen when her mother prepared meals. She spontaneously hugged her mother and told her she loved her. After dinner they sat on the couch nestled in each other's arms, watching television until both fell asleep late at night. When they got up to go to bed, Sarah sleepily and automatically followed her mother into her bedroom and climbed into bed with her. They slept together in mother's bed nearly every night. On weekends,

Sarah accompanied her mother on all her errands. They went shopping together at the food market, browsed in clothing stores, and sometimes ate lunch together at a fast-food restaurant. Sarah's brother had no interest in participating in these activities and spent these times playing outside with neighborhood friends or going to their houses. Sarah and her mother were left to be together by themselves. Their relationship continued to grow closer in these ways during the year of the short-term aftermath period of the divorce.

At four and a-half, Sarah was doing well at nursery school. She was liked by her teachers who saw her as always ready to be helpful and to please them. Her intellectual development had proceeded apace. She knew her alphabet, could identify colors accurately, and counted to 100. She had begun to be able to recognize many written words and could even read in a preprimer book. She also drew extremely well and spent a lot of time at nursery school making pictures for her teachers and to take home to her mother. She was never discourteous to her teachers and rarely got into arguments with other children. She was a teacher's delight! However, they did feel that her social relationships and her large motor development were lagging behind her other achievements. She quietly refused to play running games or to use the climbing equipment, opting instead to sit on a swing. When her class played "Duck-Duck-Goose," a competitive running game, she participated awkwardly and seemed uncoordinated. She did not like riding the big wheel tricycles and appeared inhibited and unsure of what to do when she was on one. During free play times, Sarah chose to talk to her teachers in a pseudo-adult manner discussing the lunch selections for the day, the weather, and the rowdy behavior of some of the boys. She avoided this unstructured opportunity to interact with her age-mates. Though her teachers genuinely liked her, they grew concerned about her uneasiness with other children and the inhibited quality of her play.

Sarah was a bright, engaging youngster whose mother was inadvertently interfering with the developmentally age-appropriate need to become socially and emotionally engaged with peers and to gain a sense of independence from the mother–child dyad. Out of her own needs, she physically, emotionally and socially held her daughter close to her. The unspoken message was clear and powerful: I need you, be with me, stay close to me, devote yourself to me. Below the level of her conscious awareness, Sarah responded to her mother's pleas. She was staying a very little girl for her mother's sake.

Sarah's mother did not ask her to try to do things that are initially uncomfortable for many preschoolers, such as going on her own to a nearby friend's house, staying with a baby-sitter at night while she went out, being at a neighbor's house while she shopped, and sleeping alone in her own bed. Though older preschoolers have usually mastered these developmental accomplishments, they are achievements not easily won. But once these abilities are firmly within a preschooler's repertoire, she feels more confident, more sure of herself in new situations, and generally more independent.

Sarah's quiet, less troublesome (to parents and teachers alike) problems rarely come to the attention of mental health professionals. Few parents or teachers recognize this sort of disruption in child development. The emotionally enmeshed relationship illustrated here can continue for years, especially between mothers and daughters, as independence and self-assurance are eschewed in favor of the pleasures this closeness brings. The developmental costs are hidden at first and often do not become clear until later stages of development, especially in adolescence.

The most common sources of divorce-related stresses for preschoolers during the short-term aftermath phase are continued parental hostilities, the emotional disequilibrium of a parent, and the loss (partial or complete) of the child's relationship with his father. The ways in which these stresses manifest themselves can vary widely. Parental warfare may involve constant, corrosive sniping or explosive verbal or physical aggression. The emotional upset of a parent may take the forms of depression, anxiety, loneliness, or general irritability and anger. And the child's relationship with his noncustodial parent may abruptly cease or gradually become more distant.

The Long-Range Period

The stress on children due to disruption in routines in the initial stage of divorce is considerably less common in the long-range period. By this time schedules are usually firmly in place. A preschooler's fantasy that just as his father moved away and left him, his mother might follow suit, tends to lose its force over time with sensitive parental attention and the accumulating evidence that he can count on her to continue to live with him. However, the long-range period can result in changes of residence as the custodial parent finds she can no longer financially maintain her previous home, she pursues educational or work opportunities arising in a different location, or she remarries and then moves to a new house. When these moves occur, it is important for parents to be sensitive to their preschooler's anxieties over what the change will bring as well as feelings of loss of the familiarity and comfort of his home, neighborhood, and, to a lesser extent, his friends and playmates.

The efforts Allison's mother made can be used effectively to help smooth a child's transitions to a new home, neighborhood, and school. Clear explanations of the reasons for the move help keep a preschooler's potential, worrisome fantasies in check. Appropriate recognition of the sadness over losing the comfort of his familiar environment can ease the pain of these losses. Holding out expectations for good adjustment and accompanying the child to a new day-care center or school a few times help reduce the anxieties of the unknown. When these actions are taken with sufficient lead time (at least two or three weeks before the change and even longer if a big move is being planned and discussed), the chances of the youngster making a good adjustment are maximized.

The parental warfare that may have erupted in the first two stages of the divorce process is less likely to continue or begin anew in the long-range period. Parents may dislike each other intensely, have little respect for each other, or continue to harbor strong angry feelings left over from the marital relationship, per se, or from their interactions during the first stages of their divorce. But most parents are able to put their open conflicts to rest during the first year or two of being separated. A substantial percentage, perhaps as high as 25 percent, have developed a cordial relationship by the long-range phase. They often do not feel extremely close, but each continues to be interested in the other's welfare and how each other's life is progressing. They ask after each other's health, work, and personal relationships in thoughtful and nonintrusive ways. Both have come to terms with the end of their marital relationship without having to annihilate each other. They are free to get on with their separate lives.

Parents who are unable to resolve their hurt-angry feelings over the end of their marriage are likely to be embroiled in continuing hostilities. To the extent that this is the case, preschoolers suffer.

They may become generally fearful and develop a timid approach to physical activities and social relationships. Or their parents' anger may resonate within them and cause them to become combative with peers. Developmental achievements may be lost to anxiety or a preoccupation with fighting. Timmy (see chapter 4) was faced with intense parental warfare during late toddlerhood as was Albert (see preceding section of this chapter). Preschoolers exposed to the cumulative stresses of parental fighting into the long-range period of divorce can be expected to display the sorts of fearfulness of a Timmy or the anxiety and anger of an Albert.

A more common stressor facing preschool age children whose parents' divorce has evolved to the long-range phase is the absence of the noncustodial father. It is not the sadness and grief over the loss of the father-child relationship characterizing the early stages of divorce that is troublesome in this phase. Rather, it is the chronically distant nature of the father–child relationship that can create problems.

STEVE'S parents separated when he was six months old and the divorce became legally final within a year. Sole custody was granted to Steve's mother, and modest child support payments were agreed to. His mother, a computer programmer, had worked full-time since Steve was two years old and part-time for a year before that. She earned more money than her ex-husband and was proud of her ability to provide for herself and her son. She also found her work gratifying and interesting. Her social life was minimal, and she was comfortable with having no romantic interests. Her former husband was a high school English teacher who had moved to a city several hundred miles away when the divorce was granted. Up until that time he had seen his young son for a few hours one day a week at his (the father's) parents' home. Steve's father did not know what to do with him when he was an infant and young toddler. When Steve was with his father, it was his paternal grandmother who interacted with him most, changing his diapers, feeding him, and playing with him.

From eighteen months to nearly four years of age, Steve had no contact with his father other than afternoons at the zoo and dinner at a fast-food restaurant the three or four times a year his father came into town. However, when Steve turned four, his father developed more of an interest in him. He suggested to his ex-wife that Steve come to his house for half of the Christmas holidays and for three weeks over the summer. Steve's mother was surprised by her ex-husband's wishes to see him more often and for such extended periods of time. She was not sure that he could provide appropriate emotional care for their son, given his minimal involvement in Steve's life. However, her former husband was adamant, and the schedule of visits he wanted was even less than what was spelled out in the divorce agreement. (Their decree called for biweekly visits in addition to the Christmas and summer periods.) Feeling uneasy, but at a loss about what to do other than comply, Steve's mother assented to the proposed schedule.

Steve had progressed fairly well in his development. He was a somewhat shy, serious youngster who tried hard to please adults. He also had a pseudomature air about him. Intellectually, he was precocious, but physically he hung back from mixing with other boys at his nursery school as they played tag, climbed on playground equipment, and jostled one another for seats during snack times. He loved to look at picture books, especially ones that had to do with space exploration, his favorite major league baseball team, or dinosaurs. His interests were decidedly like those of many other boys, but he seemed inhibited about physical interactions with boys his age. He appeared unsure of how to act or what to do when with them. At home he was a cooperative youngster who was strikingly sensitive to his mother's moods and feelings. Though she was often in good spirits, she experienced the usual ups and downs of everyday life. It was as if Steve was always tuned in to her broadcasting frequency and was quick to pick up on her state of mind. His mother was delighted with this characteristic and described her son as a caring, sensitive boy.

When he began the new visiting schedule with his father Steve was reluctant to go. He told his mother that he would rather stay with her. She explained that his father had a right to see him and that the divorce papers said he had to visit him. On his return from his first week-long Christmas vacation visit, Steve was irritable. He was less cooperative at home and seemed somewhat withdrawn as he spent more time than usual watching television and in his room looking at his baseball cards. However, within a week or so he was back to his old style. His father had told Steve's mother that their son had been quiet and shy during the visit; Steve's father felt disappointed. When Steve came home from his three-week stay with his father the following summer, he seemed not only irritable and withdrawn but sullen as well.

He had begun to pick on a younger child who lived a few houses from him, and at nursery school that fall he appeared angry. He pushed small children out of his way and was less cooperative with the teachers. His mother noticed that Steve was more on edge when he was with her as well. He snapped, "I don't feel like it," when she told him it was time for bed. When she asked him what he would like for dinner, he replied, "Anything. What do you care?" with considerable irritability. That phrase and others like it, "What do you care?" "What difference does it make?" became a common refrain at home. His mother was distressed and puzzled by the changes she saw in her son. She was not sure whether he was just asserting his independence or whether the initiation of visits with his father was stirring up unpleasant feelings in her son.

Steve's development up to the time of his new visiting schedule with his father had been reasonably good, if a bit one-sided. He had developed a capacity for caring about other people and being sensitive to their wishes and concerns. His cognitive development had been very good as well. However, as is so often the case with boys growing up without a man they can feel close to (father, grandfather, stepfather), he was uneasy and felt awkward interacting with other males. This personality and behavioral style has often been confused, in the professional literature and by the general public, with being effeminate. Steve was not at all effeminate; rather, he had had many opportunities to interact closely with women (his mother, his paternal grandmother, his day-care center and nursery school staff). He felt comfortable with them, knew their expectations, and to some degree identified with their personality characteristics such as interpersonal warmth, sensitivity to others, and discomfort with aggressive physical activities. But he felt ill-at-ease with other boys. Not because he was effeminate but because he had no experience, no practice, in how to act around other males. He had no emotional bond with a male to serve as a model for how males relate to one another. This contributed to his shyness and awkwardness during the visits with his father.

Further, he did not experience his father psychologically as "father" with the special qualities and feelings of attachment that relationship implies. As we saw earlier (see chapter 4), young children do not define parent–child relationships in the intellectual terms of a biological or (if adopted) a legal connection. Their definition is experiential and rests on regular and frequent contacts with an adult who acts in parental ways—providing care and affection, setting behavioral limits, and helping the youngster learn about his world. Steve's father was not his psychological father. At some level of awareness both knew that. It accounted in part for Steve's uneasiness with him, because the boy felt he was going away from his mother to be with a stranger, a difficult task for children. It also produced feelings of disappointment in his father because his expectations for a father–son relationship were not being met. Instead of permitting himself to feel his disappointment and help himself cope with it by understanding why Steve could not possibly act like a loving son given his developmental stage and the history of their nonrelationship, he became subtly critical of his son.

Steve's increasing general irritability, his anger toward younger children, and the bitterness he began to express towards his mother were reactions to visits with his father. He could not fully understand why his mother was sending him away for what felt to him like extremely long periods of time to be with a stranger. Though an intelligent youngster, he was not sufficiently advanced cognitively to understand why his father had the right to have him for those times. Abstract ideas such as parental rights and legal court orders are well beyond the grasp of even intellectually precocious preschoolers. This age-appropriate limitation led Steve to call on his fantasies to provide the reason for these visits.

In normally egocentric preschool fashion, Steve imagined that rather than his mother complying with his father's parental rights and the letter of the divorce decree by permitting him to visit his father, she was sending him away. Perhaps it was because she was displeased with him or maybe she just did not love him anymore. His bitter comments of "What do you care?" and "What difference does it make to you?" suggest that Steve felt he had become unimportant to his mother. This perceived withdrawal of affection by his mother in combination with the subtle criticisms he felt from his father, due to the latter's disappointment in the visits, made Steve angry. His becoming nasty with younger children was both an expression of this anger and an attempt to make himself feel better by lording it over other children, so he could feel big and powerful.

Steve's problem in feeling comfortable with other boys and taking pleasure playing with them was the result of a long-term absence of a relationship with his father or some father surrogate such as a stepfather or grandfather. Though not a sign of emotional disturbance, it is a common limitation for boys raised from early childhood in single-mother households. Children whose parents are not divorced but who have an emotionally distant relationship with their father exhibit similar difficulties in developing close, mutually rewarding male friendships.

Girls who are raised nearly exclusively by their mother and have little or no contact with their father tend to develop an overly close, enmeshed relationship with their mother (see the discussion of Sarah in this chapter). They may have a difficult time establishing their emotional independence from mother and carving out their own identity apart from her. Since girls and boys do not interact extensively prior to adolescence, a girl's nascent discomfort with males causes few if any difficulties prior to that time. As we shall see in the chapter on adolescence, a girl who has not established an emotional bond with a man, and therefore has not had the chance to practice being comfortable with and accepted by a male, will have a harder time relating to boys in her adolescence.

Preschoolers whose custodial mother remarries in the long-range period of the divorce process can experience other difficulties. Preschoolers, much like infants and toddlers, are generally far more receptive to a new stepfather than are older children. However, the preschooler whose parents' divorce has reached the long-range phase must have been very young at the time his parents separated. The vast majority of infants and toddlers live with their mother rather than in joint physical custody or with their father when their parents separate. By the time a child reaches preschool age, he will have spent a large fraction of his life living primarily with his mother. Having to adjust to a household that includes his mother's love relationship with her new husband can create a feeling of being displaced from center stage in her affections. In a way similar to the birth of a new sibling, the introduction of a new husband who is loved and who takes a great deal of mother's time can provoke feelings of rivalry, fears of being unloved by mother, and ensuing anger in preschool children.

MEREDITH's parents separated when she was a year old. They had been married three years and she was their only child. Her mother had begun working part-time as a billing clerk for an automobile dealer when her daughter was six months old and had increased her job to full-time shortly after the marital separation. The marriage had been brief and both parents were able to let go of it emotionally in a relatively short period of time. Though they argued frequently during the initial crisis stage of their divorce, usually over his drinking and verbal abuse of her, by the short-term aftermath phase they had very much gone their separate ways. Meredith's father had moved to a town fifty miles away and saw his daughter infrequently. By the long-range period he had reduced his contacts with her to a few visits of less than two hours each in a given year. Usually these occurred around her birthday, Christmas, and Easter. Though he brought her presents, he spent very little time with her. He was behind in his child support payments, which he had continued to make sporadically. Meredith's father was gradually dropping out of her life not because of parental warfare but probably due to the considerable difficulties inherent in maintaining a parent–child relationship with very young children.

Meredith's development had progressed uneventfully. She was cared for by her maternal grandmother during the days until she was two and one-half when she began attending an in-home day-care center. At four, she changed to a nursery school/day-care center. She was a fairly easygoing youngster of average intelligence who adapted well to new situations and had begun making friends at her new nursery school.

Meredith and her mother had a close, loving relationship. As an only child, she received a great deal of her mother's time and attention. Her mother dated frequently from the time Meredith was two years old but rarely brought her male friends home. She sensed her daughter's mild uneasiness around the ones she had invited for dinner and saw no reason to burden her by entertaining her dates at home. She also was a religious woman who felt it was inappropriate to engage in any sexual intimacies under the same roof that her daughter lived. Though she had several affairs, they were conducted exclusively at her dating partner's residence and she always returned home the same evening she had gone out.

When Meredith was nearly four years old, her mother began dating the man she would marry. Their relationship grew closer and deeper. He had begun working as a salesman at the automobile dealership where she worked. His personality was much the same as hers, and they each felt they had found a kindred soul. They were relaxed individuals who were comfortable with themselves and enjoyed being in the company of other people. Both loved to socialize. They liked going to parties, attending sporting events, and going to movies, usually with another couple or two. They shared the same religious beliefs and had begun going regularly to religious services together. He had also been married once before, for two years, but had no children from that marriage. Each agreed that they would want one or two children together. After dating for six months, they decided to get married and set the date a few months into the future.

Meredith had sensed that her mother was becoming involved in an important relationship. Her mother went out more frequently in the evenings, even during the week, and had begun to spend weekends away with her dating partner leaving Meredith in the care of her maternal grandmother who lived a few miles away. Her daughter was almost four-and-a-half when Meredith's mother told her of her plans to marry Dave. Meredith's initial reaction was minimal. She asked where they would live, and her mother told her that Dave was going to move into their house. Her mother and Dave were married when Meredith was three months short of turning five.

At first Meredith seemed curious about Dave. Though she had met him many times, especially since her mother had announced her marriage plans, she had not spent much time with them. They had taken Meredith to dinner and to movies, but that had been the extent of her being with Dave. However, within a month after Dave moved in, Meredith began to be unusually demanding with her mother. She insisted on having certain foods for dinner, constantly asked her mother to play her favorite games (Go-Fish, Hungry-Hungry Hippo, and Hi-Ho Cherry-O) with her, and pleaded with her mother to read story after story to her at bedtime. She complained when her mother told her she and Dave were going out for the evening and cried when the baby-sitter arrived. When her mother and Dave cuddled together on the couch while watching television, Meredith whined for her mother to get her a drink, a snack, or to come play a game with her. Sometimes, Meredith plopped herself down on the couch between them and curled up in her mother's lap with a contented smile on her face.

At school, Meredith had begun pinching other youngsters. In a typical scenario two or three children would be engaged in some activity, such as playing house or taking turns using a slide. Meredith would stand by watching for a few minutes and then ask one of the children to play a different game with her. If the youngster refused, Meredith pinched her. She had also become possessive of her teacher. She always wanted to sit next to her during quiet activities such as stringing beads for necklaces and bracelets, drawing, and fingerpainting. When she was told by the teacher that she had to take turns with other children in sitting close to her, Meredith pouted and refused to participate in the activity. Meredith's mother and Dave were surprised by these changes in her, found themselves becoming increasingly irritated by her behavior at home, and were upset by her difficulties at nursery school.

Meredith had tranquilly accepted her mother's marriage plans only because she could not anticipate cognitively the changes it would bring. When Dave and her mother married and began living together, Meredith was confronted by the loss of her cherished position of being the only person her mother loved and thought was important. In response to coming face-to-face with the reality that her mother's emotional life did not revolve around her, Meredith became angry at her mother and jealous of her relationship with Dave. At home she competed with Dave in the ways available to a preschooler by trying to pull her mother's involvement with him toward her instead. Her insistence that her mother play games with her and read several stories to her at bedtime was aimed at drawing her mother back into her orbit and out of Dave's. At times she literally and physically came between her mother and Dave as when she sat down between them on the couch and lay in her mother's lap.

At school these family dynamics were being repeated. The script was the same even though the cast of characters was different. She was competitive with other children for the female teacher's attention and tried to break up any personal closeness she observed even among other children. Her anger was expressed at home through her competitive and controlling behavior and at school by her controlling behaviors toward the teacher and her pinching other children and disrupting their play. She was struggling with having been partially displaced in her mother's affections by Dave. This triggered feelings of being unimportant and unloved by her mother. To defend herself from having to experience the emotional pain this blow to her pride and sense of self-worth brought, Meredith tried to recapture the centrally important place in her mother's life while simultaneously venting her anger

126

over being hurt. This emotional and behavioral agenda was so compelling for Meredith that she brought it with her to school regularly.

Preschoolers are considerably more advanced cognitively, emotionally, and socially than infants and toddlers. Children make great strides in each of these areas between the ages of three and five. But preschool age youngsters are still quite limited in their intellectual understanding of complex events such as divorce. They are notably dependent emotionally on key adults in their lives, especially parents, for their sense of well-being. And though they have widened their world considerably through involvement in play groups in their neighborhoods, and day care/nursery school, the centrally important social relationships in their lives are still within their families, with parents, grandparents, stepparents, and siblings. They cannot easily escape and distance themselves from the upheavals created by their parents' divorce. Disrupted daily routines, parental warfare, a parent's emotional disequilibrium, and the loss of a relationship with a parent are sources of powerful distress in preschoolers. The newfound ability to use their imagination often leads to further, internally created stress, as frightening fantasies arise unbidden. The preschooler's tendency to organize explanations for events in egocentric terms provides another source of distress through ideas of self-blame. The preschooler thus confronts more sources of stress than infants or toddlers.

Recognizing Distress in Preschoolers

It is generally easier for parents and other adult caregivers to recognize signs of distress in preschoolers than in infants or toddlers. To begin with, preschoolers are more verbal and are more likely at times to express their feelings and concerns in words. However, many youngsters express their distress behaviorally. But adults have clearer ideas of what constitutes normal, healthy behavior in preschoolers than they do for infants or toddlers. Though the range of ''normal'' encompasses great diversity, parents and caregivers involved with preschoolers develop a sense of the outer limits of this range and therefore are more likely to notice when a youngster is exhibiting behaviors that are inappropriate. Furthermore, the parent of a preschooler has spent more time with him than the parent of an infant or toddler. Based on this longer experience, parents of preschoolers have had the opportunity to develop clear expectations for how their children act from day-to-day across different situations. Therefore, the parent is more likely to take note of out-of-the-ordinary behaviors or emotional reactions in their children.

Still it is useful to keep in mind the different ways in which preschool youngsters manifest signs of emotional distress. There are several broad categories of reactions that are indicative of a young child's distress. These are loss of developmental accomplishments, failure to achieve appropriate developmental accomplishments, emotional lability, anger, fear, anxiety, sadness, and withdrawal. Within each of these categories there are many forms that distress may take.

Loss of developmental accomplishments can occur in domains of sleep, eating, motor activity, language, toilet-training, emotional independence, and social relationships. The table below lists the kinds of losses preschoolers may commonly experience in response to stress within these eight domains. Examples given assume that a developmental achievement has been attained and is being given up.

Domain	**Examples**
Sleeping	Attempting to delay bedtime; insisting on sleeping with a parent in the same room or bed; having nightmares.
Eating	Restricting intake to a few types of foods; trying to return to using a baby bottle; eating less or more than usual.
Motor Activity	Refusing to ride a tricycle or use a swing; giving up an interest in finger painting, drawing or coloring.
Language	Going back to using "me" instead of "I" in referring to self; giving up smooth speech and beginning to stutter; giving up complex sentence constructions for simpler ones; sounding "babyish" in tone of voice.
Toilet Training	Reverting to wetting or soiling instead of using the toilet; withhold-

	ing stool; using places other than the bathroom such as the living room to relieve herself.
Emotional Independence	Reverting to crying or clinging when a parent leaves the child to go to another part of the house or leaves the child with a caregiver; staying inside the house instead of playing outdoors or at a playmate's house; nearly exclusively preferring to be in a parent's company as opposed to playing with friends.
Social Relationships	Refusing to participate in previously enjoyed peer group activities; having trouble taking turns while playing with peers; strongly preferring the company of adults over being with age-mates; having to decide what and how games will be played.

It is also important to assess whether the child has failed to progress in these domains regardless of whether certain accomplishments had been previously attained. Examples include: a four-year-old who has never been toilet trained and continues to wet and soil his pants; a three-year-old who always has cried when left with a baby-sitter or other caregiver; a five-year-old who has never been able to take turns while playing with other children; a four-year-old who has always crawled into bed with his parents and always resisted sleeping alone. These are illustrations not of loss of developmental accomplishments, but a failure to achieve them at all. These youngsters are not regressing to earlier levels of development in the face of stress. Instead they may be stuck at an earlier stage of development because of being so distressed and then appear unable to progress to expectable preschool accomplishments.

A preschooler may also display *emotional lability* in response to feeling distressed, oscillating between very different feelings in a brief period of time. The three-year-old who is quietly watching television may whine and complain when called for dinner, be delighted and hug his mother for fixing his favorite meal, and run from the room crying when his favorite dessert is not available. A four-year-old may be telling her mother about her day at nursery school and fly into a rage when her older brother interrupts briefly to ask when he should be home for dinner. A five-year-old enjoying a game of tag with playmates may burst into tears when he is caught, run to his mother, and after a hug be happily on his way back to the game. Though emotional gear-shifting of these sorts are not unusual in pre-schoolers, they may indicate that the child is feeling particularly stressed if they occur frequently and with considerable intensity.

Expressions of *anger* are among the most common ways that pre-school-age youngsters show that they are distressed. While it is often difficult to discern anger in an infant, and young toddlers are less likely to use this avenue to discharge feelings of distress, preschoolers usually leave little doubt in the minds of adults that they are angry. Since preschoolers are considerably more involved with peers than are infants or toddlers, playmates become convenient and compara-tively safe targets for their fury. They rarely have to worry about being hurt in return, as they fear they might if they attack the parent at whom they are enraged. Nor do parents, day-care center staff, or nursery school teachers tend to discipline preschoolers severely. Though these young children hardly think it through in these ways, they seem to know the facts intuitively. Physical aggression toward peers such as hitting, shoving, kicking, grabbing a toy away, pinching, and spitting are common ways that young children attack their peers. Older or precociously advanced preschoolers engage in verbal aggres-sion as well. This takes such forms as name-calling, teasing, belittling, and criticizing. It is important to keep in mind that expressions of anger toward peers, and often siblings as well, represent the child's rage primarily at a parent. Some preschoolers will infrequently lash out, physically or verbally, at another youngster because the other child has hit first, taken a toy away, or called him a name. But persistent aggression at peers, usually unprovoked, is nearly always anger meant for a parent. It is being let out at someone the child feels is a safe and/or convenient whipping boy.

Preschoolers will also get angry directly at parents, though it is more common to see anger toward peers or siblings. They may hit, kick, pinch, or even bite a parent at whom they are enraged. They may call her names or swear at her as well. However, preschoolers are much more likely to inhibit these more direct expressions of anger toward parents in favor of their disguised forms. The child may cry angrily, be deliberately disobedient, or scream that a parent does not care about them. In these instances the youngster knows she is angry, but her rage automatically comes out in ways that, irritating as they may be, are considerably more acceptable to parents than are physical attacks, swearing, and name-calling. At times a preschooler expresses anger in even more disguised ways, so that he and his parents may not even recognize his anger. Attempts to control a parent, intrude on her time with other adults or spent in quiet reading, and frequent accidents that break household items or lead to messes a parent must then clean up are often the result of hostility directed at the parent. And at some level many parents know that. They find themselves being irritated, annoyed, or downright furious at their child. This is more than parental upset due to being inconvenienced by intrusions or having to clean up a spilled drink. The parent's anger is often a response to knowing they have just been on the receiving end of a masterfully disguised but nonetheless angry assault.

Fear is also an indicator of distress in preschoolers especially when it is in response to events or circumstances with which the youngster previously felt comfortable. The four-year-old who begins to cry when being left at his familiar nursery school, the three-year-old who pleads anxiously for his mother not to go out that night even when a well-liked baby-sitter is going to be there, and the five-year-old who is frightened of being in his bedroom alone at night are examples of fear one would not necessarily expect in a nondistressed preschool-age youngster. In addition to fear over being separated from the primary parent, preschoolers often become frightened of certain aspects of their environment. Fears of loud noises, animals, heights, and the dark are common examples of normal phobias during this stage of development. The youngster who startles and clings to his mother while hearing a car horn, a child who is uneasy about climbing the height of a slide in a park, and the preschooler who runs into the house when seeing a strange dog is not necessarily reacting to stressful life events. However, if these phobias persist and begin to interfere substantially in a child's day-to-day activities, they may be reflections of undue distress.

Uneasiness in social situations is another way that preschoolers show fear. Feeling frightened about playing games with peers or hanging back from joining a play group may indicate an underlying worry about social interactions. These often are manifestations of fear over being separated from a primary caretaker or her substitute (for example, a day-care center staff member or baby-sitter) or a concern about being physically hurt.

General, diffuse nervousness, sometimes referred to by mental health professionals as *anxiety* can be due to less obvious worries. In the examples of fear just given, there is usually a clear object or situation in the environment that triggers the fearful response in a youngster, fear of being separated from mother, fear of heights or loud noises, and fear of being involved in a social interaction. But preschoolers can now internally generate, through frightening fantasies or unconscious conflicts, private, more hidden anxieties. Wetting or soiling one's pants or bed and "nervous habits" such as repetitive hair twirling, throat clearing, tugging at one's clothing, and stuttering are manifestations of this global anxiety. It is often difficult to discover the private sources of distress, which the youngster herself usually is not aware of, that give rise to these anxieties.

Sadness is another form that preschoolers' distress may take. A youngster may look sad, cry plaintively, or even say that he is unhappy. The child appears subdued and joyless. When a preschooler becomes *withdrawn and listless* it is likely that he is experiencing emotional distress. Usually this is a child's version of adult depression and it can share some of the same characteristics. Loss of interest in previously pleasurable activities, lethargically spending long periods of time watching television, aimless wandering about the house, lack of interest in food or even candy, claiming to be bad or ugly, and derogating his own efforts such as drawings or tricycle riding are ways in which this depressive withdrawal can be manifested.

As with signs of distress for infants and toddlers, many of these indicators of distress in preschoolers are *normal, appropriate reactions* to the hard work of growing up. This is true for all of the examples just given with the exception of depressed withdrawal. It is not the mere presence of these behaviors and feelings that bespeaks a youngster's distress but rather their intensity, duration, and the degree to which they interfere in a child's life. If these signs continue for over two months and interfere in the preschooler's capacity to move forward developmentally on cognitive, emotional, and/or social fronts, it is likely that he is burdened by undue distress.

7

►◄

Helping Preschoolers Cope

In helping preschoolers cope with divorce-related distress, it is essential to be aware of the likely sources of stress for children in the three- to five-year-old range. Disruption in the youngster's daily routine, warfare between parents, the emotional upset of the custodial parent, and the loss of the relationship with the noncustodial parent are centrally important facets of the divorce experience that contribute to a preschooler's distress. As noted earlier, the main way divorcing parents can help their young children adapt well to their separation is to eliminate or reduce the environmental sources of distress.

Ensuring that the child's daily schedule is consistent and predictable, reducing parental hostilities, and getting help for an emotionally distraught parent, as well as providing added help for her with child care are methods parents can use to remove ongoing stresses in their youngsters' lives. Note that these actions do not involve the child directly. They are ways parents can *alter the divorce environment* in accordance with the child's developmental needs for reasonable consistency, tranquility, and the availability of an emotionally stable parent. When parents recognize and correct these problems, preschoolers usually experience a rapid and enormous sense of relief, freeing them to get on with the developmental tasks at hand.

Parents of preschoolers also need to be aware of possible internal sources of distress as well as environmental ones. The preschool-age youngster's newly acquired cognitive abilities now make it possible for him to develop clear, organized fantasies and to "understand" his environment using the egocentric logic common to this stage of

133

development. Private, internal sources of distress in the forms of frightening fantasies and burdensome self-blaming beliefs must be attended to in addition to the more obvious environmental stressors. This requires parents to listen more closely to their preschoolers and observe their behaviors with an eye toward discerning the potential presence of these internal contributions to a youngster's emotional upset. In addition to altering the divorce environment, parents will often need to communicate directly with their child in order to alleviate her distress.

An important action parents can take right from the beginning of a marital separation is to carefully tell the preschool-age youngster about divorce. With about a week or two lead time, at least one parent and preferably both of them, can inform the child that "Mommy and Daddy are going to get a divorce." It is essential that what this will mean for the preschooler be spelled out clearly. He should be told which parent will be moving out, where that parent will be living, when the child will see him, and whether there will be any changes in his daily routine. Hopefully this can be done relatively calmly. This first talk should be kept brief.

It is also helpful for the parents to explain the reasons for the divorce a day or two after the first talk. The preschooler's tendency to develop egocentric, self-blaming beliefs about divorce and self-derogating beliefs about why a parent is leaving to live elsewhere can be short-circuited with realistic explanations. This is not to say that parents should tell the child the adult details of their disagreements. Explanations should be tailored to the child's developmental level. Placing before the youngster issues of infidelity, alcoholism, financial problems, or sexual incompatibilities only burdens and confuses a child unnecessarily. It is reminiscent of the story about the preschooler who asked his parents where he came from. His parents quickly launched into a discussion of reproductive biology and lovemaking between a married couple. When they concluded their lengthy and complex explanation, the child asked in bewilderment, "But did I come from Cincinnati or have I lived here all my life, I mean, where was I born?" The parents should explain that the divorce is happening because: "We aren't getting along anymore. When grown-ups who are married can't get along and don't love each other anymore, they need to stop being married and live in different homes." Parents should emphasize that "Divorce stuff is grown-up business. It's the mom and dad who can't get along anymore. But parents keep loving their children after the divorce. Your mom and dad will always love you. Dads and moms live in different places after divorce, so your dad (or mom) won't be living with you anymore. He (she) doesn't want to live away from you, but divorce means that the parents can't keep living together. One of them has to move away.'' (Clearly if the parents are planning a joint physical custody arrangement this explanation will be somewhat different.) If the noncustodial parent will be seeing the youngster regularly that should also be told to the child.

Even when parents invite questions from a preschooler, there are likely to be few, if any. It is helpful for the parents to tell the preschooler a day or two after the second talk that ''Lots of kids whose parents are getting divorced have some questions about it. Like how come the parents are getting the divorce, who the kids will live with, where their dad [mom] is going to live, and when they're going to see their dad [mom].'' Raising and then answering these questions provides the parents with an opportunity to follow up on their initial explanations to the child. It also lets the preschooler know that these are questions many other children have and that it is all right to have them.

The process of explaining the upcoming marital separation to a preschooler takes place over several talks each spaced a day or two apart. This paces the flow of information to the preschool-age child so as not to overwhelm him. Even if a preschooler pushes to discuss it further at any one time, the parent can answer briefly and then suggest that they continue talking about it the next day.

Just as it is essential for parents to be aware of the specific environmental sources of distress for young children, it is equally crucial for parents to be alert to the kinds of stress that arise for preschoolers internally. Earlier we divided these into beliefs acquired through egocentric logic and fantasies. There is overlap between these two categories. As used here, fantasies refer to anticipated events or feelings while beliefs are explanations of past occurrences. In either case, they represent distortions of what reality will likely bring or what has already occurred. Together they provide a useful distinction in the types of internally generated distress with which preschoolers often must cope. The table below gives examples of these two internal sources of distress.

Source	Examples
Fantasies	The custodial parent will abandon the child; the child will be kidnapped; the parents will hurt or kill one another while fighting; the child will be hurt or killed by enraged parents; a parent will stop loving the child; the parent will love his/her new dating partner or spouse more than the child.
Beliefs	The child caused the arguing between the parents; the child could have stopped the fights and thus prevented the divorce; the parent who left the home did so because he did not love the child enough to stay; the noncustodial parent has not visited much (or at all) because the child is unlovable (that is, not pretty, not smart, not nice).

These fantasies and beliefs, often unspoken and sometimes not even consciously available to a preschooler, can cause any of the indicators of stress presented earlier.

An inconsistent daily schedule can cause distress in preschool-age children in much the same way as it does in infants and toddlers. Being able to count on where he will be and who will take care of him provides a preschooler with the necessary feelings of stability and security that constitute a firm base from which he can conduct the business of growing up. Selecting a regular care-giving setting, sending familiar objects such as stuffed animals, a prized blanket, or toys with the child, and maintaining a regular schedule for dropping off and picking up the youngster at the day-care setting are key elements in achieving daily consistency in the child's life. Similarly, introducing consistent early morning, dinnertime, and bedtime routines contributes to a child's sense of predictability in the environment. For example, having a preschooler get up in the morning, wash, get dressed, have breakfast, brush his teeth, and then be taken to the day-care setting, all in that order, creates an atmosphere of sameness. Having a fixed sequence of activities provides a convincing sense of consistency.

When changes in the youngster's daily schedule are necessary, parents can be helpful in a variety of ways. Explaining the reasons for the changes to a preschooler, holding out expectations for good adjustment in the new setting, and accompanying the child to the new day-care site can help a youngster cope with the transition from one routine or setting to another. The excellent efforts of Allison's mother can serve as an example of this kind of parental help (see chapter 6).

At times this sort of careful attention to providing realistically consistent daily routines does not entirely allay the preschooler's distress. Or the youngster may become upset over familiar and quite predictable routines. If none of the other environmental sources of stress (that is, parental warfare, an emotionally distraught parent, loss of the noncustodial parent) is present, it is likely that the child is responding to some new meaning she has attached to her schedule. In fact, even if other environmental stresses are at play, it still may be some fantasy or belief that is causing the preschooler's distress.

FRANK (see chapter 6) was four-and-a-half-years old when his mother first made an appointment with a social worker at a child guidance clinic to discuss her son's problems. His intense fearfulness when his mother dropped him off at his nursery school/day-care center and his inability to participate in the activities there had continued for three months. Despite the fact that he was familiar with the center and had a regular, consistent daily routine, he became panicked when his mother left him there. The social worker and mother agreed that there did not seem to be stressful events prominent in Frank's life and that his predivorce adjustment at the center had been good. His mother reported that Frank had told her, ''You're gonna leave me and go far away to live,'' and that her reassurances did not seem to be helpful. She was worried about her son and was very much relieved when the social worker told her that fears over being separated from mother were not at all rare in very young children whose parents had divorced. She explained to Frank's mother that preschoolers sometime develop a fantasy that their mother will leave them to live in another home because they have already seen one parent do just that. In those instances mother must go beyond her helpful efforts to keep a realistically consistent schedule. Consistency is important, but a mother needs to correct the child's fantasy or misperception that she will act as the child's father has and leave the home.

The social worker suggested that Frank's mother pick relatively calm times when she and Frank were together to begin the process of dispelling Frank's frightening fantasy. These should be times that the threat of being separated from her by going off to nursery school or being left with a baby-sitter was not imminent. She suggested that Frank's mother begin making statements that followed the first four steps in the outline for using displacement methods of communication (see chapter 3): represent the observable signs of the child's distress in the displacement; comment about how upsetting these behaviors are for the child; verbalize the underlying emotional pain of the child; and correct the child's misperceptions (fantasies, beliefs) that are contributing to the youngster's distress. The social worker explained how much easier it was for children to confront and resolve their worries using this indirect approach. She coached Frank's mother to represent his distress by saying, "Sometimes boys get real upset when their mom leaves them at their nursery school and then they cry and don't feel like doing any of the fun things there that they used to." Next she commented on how upsetting this was: "You know, when boys cry like that and feel so upset, they really hate it. Boys don't like having to cry and worry, and they also don't like not being able to have any fun at their nursery school." Then the underlying pain, the frightening fantasy, was addressed: "Sometimes the reason a guy cries when his mom leaves him at his nursery school is because he has a big worry that she's going to move away and leave him all alone. He's seen his dad move away to a new apartment, and he starts worrying that his mom might do the same thing and move away from him."

These comments, which represent the first three steps in the displacement communication process, took Frank's mother under a minute to verbalize. She was cautioned to keep her statements as brief as possible. The preschooler's relatively short attention span, especially in the face of upsetting topics, and his unhappiness about being lectured underscore the need to have communication be short. Frank's mother was asked to make these comments casually while she was partly engaged in some other activity such as preparing dinner, watching television, or washing the dishes. Children respond best when they feel that they are not in the parental spotlight. Frank's mother wanted to sit her youngster down for a serious heart-to-heart talk. She was told that this tends to make preschoolers uneasy and less receptive to the messages in the displacement statements. The social worker also said that it would be helpful to pause briefly between each step of this process to allow Frank a chance to ask questions or make comments. However, she was to make no attempt to get her child to talk. Following any one of these statements with questions like, "What do you think about that?" or "Isn't that sort of what you've been feeling, Frank?" would be unhelpful. They would put him on the spot and thus partly undo the indirectness of the communication.

The final element in this four-step process is to correct the child's internal sources of distress (fantasies, beliefs, conflicts). Frank's mother was helped to put this into words by saying: "Divorce is real confusing to most boys. Even five- and six-year-olds get the idea that their mom might go away and live somewhere else just like their dad did. But this is not how divorce works. Moms and their boys stay together until a guy gets real old, like eighteen or nineteen years old, and then if he wants to he can go to college." Here the troubling fantasy is restated and corrected with the reality.

Frank's mother went through these four steps about every other day. After nearly two weeks, Frank asked, "Are you going to move away? Who would take care of me? Grandma?" Frank had become comfortable enough to put his worry into the form of a direct question, and he did so with apparently minimal anxiety. His mother's displacement communications had begun taking effect. She could now answer him directly: "I'm never going to leave you. Your dad moved out because he and I are getting divorced. That means we will live in different places. But I will keep living with you no matter what. Moms don't leave their boys." These forceful statements in combination with the correction of Frank's fantasy via the displacement statements finally reassured him. His fear when being dropped off at the day-care center quickly vanished. His sadness also disappeared and he was able to once again enjoy his time there.

Frank's mother had been helped to find a way of ridding her son of the frightening fantasy that she would abandon him. Her use of the outline for displacement communication and coaching by the social worker about specifically what to say permitted her to establish a communicational link with her son. Though Frank did not respond to the communication directly for two weeks, he was already being gradually reassured by the statements she had been making. His worst fear was being put into words in a calm manner. Several underlying messages could thus become clear: many boys feel as you do, so you are not bad or unusual for being frightened; I know what you are feeling, so you are not alone with your fears; I am unafraid of your worries, so they are really not as overwhelming as they feel to you; and, your fears can be removed so you can feel good again. Though statements of this sort are never made explicitly, they are conveyed implicitly as part of the displacement communication process. They make it possible for a youngster to confront his fears more directly and then be reassured by his parent. The main reason the direct reassurance Frank's mother gave him earlier did not work is that he was too overcome by fear to really hear it. Without the crucially important implicit messages in displacement communication (that is, you are not unusual, you are not alone with your fears). Frank was unprepared to hear and make use of his mother's reassurance.

Parental warfare is a potent source of distress for preschoolers throughout the entire divorce process. The young child's tendency to automatically resonate to his parents' rage and his anger at them for attacking one another produce intense and overwhelming feelings of anger in young children. Preschoolers, like infants and young toddlers, tend to respond to these powerful feelings of rage by becoming globally and diffusely distressed as well as fearful. Toddlers and preschoolers alike will also at times adopt the style of conflict resolution modeled by their parents and become aggressive with peers at a daycare center or in their neighborhood.

Preschoolers are greatly upset by warfare between their parents for other reasons, too. Not only do they resonate to their parent's rage and become angry at their parents for causing them distress, they also are likely to develop frightening fantasies of what these battles will bring and burdensome beliefs about their cause.

WHEN ALBERT (see chapter 6) was four years old, his nursery school teacher suggested that his mother talk with a mental health professional about his difficulties. He had continued wetting his pants at school and his bed at night, picking fights with other youngsters, and having nightmares for nearly four months. His mother asked her employer, a physician, to recommend someone to see. The physician referred Albert's mother to a child psychiatrist. The psychiatrist met with Albert's mother twice and with Albert once. He concluded that Albert was reacting to the parental warfare. His reactions were particularly intense because of his own "difficult" temperament and the worries he had seemed to develop about his parents' rage, as well as his own anger getting explosively out of control. The psychiatrist explained the concept of emotional resonance to Albert's mother. He also confirmed for her that Albert was indeed high-strung and that was due to his biologically given temperament. He noted Albert's preoccupation with death, which was being expressed in the boy's repetitive play with toy soldiers. The psychiatrist carefully explained how preschoolers develop frightening fantasies based on parental battles they observe. He outlined a two-pronged plan for Albert's mother to implement.

First, she was to do all she could to reduce the open conflicts with her husband. This included restraining her own impulses to attack him verbally, and insisting that he come to her home only in order to pick up and drop off Albert while remaining in his car rather than coming to the door during these times. She was also asked to have her husband call to set up an appointment with the child psychiatrist. Albert's mother followed through on these suggestions.

Her husband then came in to see the psychiatrist and received the same explanation of Albert's difficulties. The importance of limiting his son's exposure to the conflicts between parents was emphasized. Albert's father found this first meeting with the psychiatrist relieving. It was as though he were being given a reason to withdraw from the field of battle. He came for several more appointments. During these the psychiatrist empathized with the tensions Albert's father had been living with. He gently acknowledged Albert's father's struggles with alcohol and pointed to the ability to cope that he had displayed by continuing to perform well at his demanding job despite his drinking and the upheaval in his life the marital separation and its attendant conflicts were causing.

Albert's father was helped to make a commitment to begin attending meetings of Alcoholics Anonymous and was invited to consult the psychiatrist from time to time about his son or about

141

his own adjustment to the divorce. Albert's father was able to begin going to AA meetings and within a month had become "dry." He participated effectively in the plan to establish a truce between himself and his wife. While neither parent had much in the way of positive or respectful feelings toward each other, they were able to initiate a halt to their hostilities. In doing so, they each began to reap the benefits of this new scenario. Albert's mother was relieved to have her husband stop coming to her house and verbally assaulting her; his father felt more in control of his life and on a more even keel emotionally; and, both felt good about getting on with their new lives.

The second prong of the plan involved Albert's mother using displacement communication with her son to alleviate his private worries. Using the toy soldiers he liked to play with, she began this process following the first five steps of the outline in chapter 3: representing in the displacement the overt signs of the youngster's emotional distress; commenting on how upsetting this is to the displacement figure who represents the child; verbalizing the underlying emotional pain (that is, fantasies, beliefs, conflicts); correcting in the displacement the child's misunderstandings or misperceptions; and, representing the acceptability of the child's conflicted feelings. She was instructed to pick a quiet, calm time to begin this communication.

One evening after dinner, she told Albert that she would like to show him something with his G.I. Joes (favorite action figures for boys). She picked out three figures and told her son that two of them were generals and one was a sergeant who usually took orders from the generals. They were all in the same army. She represented the observable signs of her son's conflict by having the generals argue over what the sergeant had to do. One wanted him to go on a march and the other said he had to be a lookout and watch for the enemy. She had them argue back and forth, become angry, and call each other names. Then she said that "The sergeant got so upset about the generals arguing that he wet his pants." Albert laughed. She had the sergeant go to two other soldiers and start pushing them around. Next his mother commented on how upset the sergeant was about his own behavior: "The sergeant felt awful about wetting his pants and picking on his own soldiers. Big guys feel terrible when they do those things." Albert's mother implemented the third step, showing the underlying distress of the sergeant who represented her son, by saying, "The sergeant is mad at his generals for fighting. He's also scared that they might get so angry that they will start beating each other up and hurting each other. Sometimes he even worries that he started them getting mad at each other because they're arguing about what he should do."

The fourth step of correcting these troublesome misperceptions was accomplished by Albert's mother telling him: "But you know, generals are sort of like parents. Sometimes they get along together, and sometimes they don't. When generals fight it isn't because of the other soldiers and when parents fight it isn't because of their kids. Even when parents call each other names and get real mad at each other no one gets hurt. They just yell and say bad things but everyone is very safe. And after a while the fighting stops." She concluded, representing the acceptability of her son's feelings, by saying: "All boys, even five- and six-year-olds who are big and brave, get very scared when their parents fight. They worry about someone getting hurt and feel real bad that maybe they caused the fighting. But boys don't cause fights between grown-ups and no one will be hurt." Albert's mother showed him this play several times a week. Sometimes she reintroduced it by saying, "Let's see what happens when generals can't get along," or "Let's see how a sergeant feels when his generals fight." Albert rarely said anything during these brief plays. They usually lasted for less than three minutes. Occasionally, he picked up one of the generals and had him knock the other one down and jump on him. Albert's mother then said, "No, generals really don't hurt each other, that's what the sergeant is worried about but it doesn't really happen." Sometimes she said, "That's a big worry that the sergeant has in his imagination, that the generals will hit each other, but it really doesn't happen that way."

After nearly five weeks, Albert became bored with this communication, but he had also stopped picking on other children and no longer wet his pants at school. His nightmares had become less frequent, as had his bed wetting. His mother continued with this play once a week or so for another few months. Within six months, all of Albert's signs of distress had abated.

It is likely that Albert's good adjustment was due both to his parents reducing their conflict and the reassurance he was receiving via the displacement communications. But not all parents are able to be as responsive as Albert's had been. Their commitment to healthy parenting cannot be mobilized in the service of helping their youngsters. Instead they continue to do battle with one another and lose sight of the needs of their children.

TOMMY's (see chapter 6) parents consulted a child psychologist together when he was nearly five years old. Tommy's nursery school teacher had become concerned about his derogation of teachers and his verbally picking on younger children and teasing them. Though his parents came ostensibly seeking help for Tommy, they spent nearly the entire time in their first three sessions hurling accusations at each other while defending their own positions. The psychologist pointed out how enraged they were with each other and suggested that she meet with each parent separately to facilitate an assessment of Tommy's difficulties and to develop a plan to help him. In the sessions with Tommy's father, he insisted that Tommy was fine when he was with him. He attributed the irritable and whiney behavior Tommy's mother reported to his wife's poor parenting, especially her inability to set appropriate behavioral limits for her son. She should punish Tommy for these behaviors. Similarly, he claimed that Tommy's problems at nursery school were also due to his wife's not setting limits and disciplining their son for his inappropriate behavior at school. Attempts to explain how upsetting it is for preschoolers to see their parents at war cut no ice with Tommy's father. He claimed he was protecting his legal rights. He also angrily pointed to his wife's beginning to date even before the divorce was final.

The sessions with Tommy's mother were equally unproductive. Though these meetings were to be focused on how to help her son, she spent the entire time derogating her husband. She, too, claimed that she was pursuing her legal rights and was not about to let her husband take advantage of her either in the financial settlement or the custody arrangement. In a final meeting with both parents present, they rejected the suggestion that they seek a mediator to help them resolve their disagreements and dismissed as ''silly'' the idea that they talk with their son about the divorce and the feelings he had using a displacement communication. When Tommy began kindergarten, his problems intensified and his parents began him in twice-a-week psychotherapy. However, they continued their bitter legal battles and acrimonious interactions. After a year of individual therapy, Tommy's difficulties remained firmly in place and the public school recommended placement in a classroom for emotionally disturbed children.

Tommy's parents could not begin the process of emotionally disengaging from each other. They retained a close relationship of sorts through their intense conflicts. Neither could put their marital relationship in the past and get on with their lives. Their single-minded commitment to this warfare never wavered as they poured enormous amounts of time, energy, emotional resources, and money into it. They could not empathize with their son nor even intellectually appreciate their contribution to his difficulties. Meanwhile, Tommy's problems continued. His behavioral reactions to being upset gradually became a part of his personality style. He began to be seen not as a reasonably healthy youngster who is in distress, but as a child suffering from an emotional disturbance.

Preschool-age youngsters can also develop stress reactions to the loss of the relationship with their noncustodial father. The attachment many children develop to their father by the preschool years makes them sensitive to changes in the amount of time they spend with him and to shifts in the nature of their interactions with him. Preschoolers not only feel the pain of losing a father they have grown close to and love but may also suffer disruptions in their development, because they no longer have their father present to facilitate their achievement of emotional independence and a valued, positive self-image.

GAIL (see chapter 6) had begun to cling to her mother, withdraw from physical games and other social activities at her nursery school, and tell fanciful stories about her father shortly after he left the area to take a job in another state. The mounting concern of Gail's nursery school teacher prompted her to suggest that Gail's mother consult a child therapist about her daughter's difficulties. The mental health professional met twice with Gail and three times with her mother. She then met with Gail's mother and took the time to explain to her the important role an involved father has in his daughter's development. She said that Gail was grieving, in the way preschoolers do, over the loss of her father. The therapist pointed to Gail's excellent developmental progress prior to her father's leaving and noted her retreat from these accomplishments, which the loss of her father had precipitated.

After gaining Gail's mother's permission, the therapist had several extensive telephone conversations with Gail's father. She empathized with his obvious sadness over no longer feeling close to his daughter and described her difficulties to him. The therapist explained how important Gail's father was to her and suggested that he resume seeing her. Though he lived in another state, he could still come back for weekends with her every other month and have her spend a week or two with him at his home over the summer. In between visits, the importance of regular telephone calls and writing to her was underscored. He was told that if he could bring himself to tolerate his sadness over losing the closeness of their relationship and maintain a connection with his daughter, it was likely that his own distress would subside over time. They would then have a foundation on which to build their relationship.

Gail's father was able to respond well to these conversations. He followed through fully on the clinician's suggestions. The therapist also elected to have several weekly sessions with Gail. Using displacement communication, she was able to talk with Gail about her sadness over having her father move far away. They played with a dollhouse during the sessions. The therapist showed the father and mother dolls getting a divorce and had the father doll move far away. She had the girl doll stop playing with other children at her nursery school and wanting to stay close to the mother doll at home. The therapist said, ''The girl doll is sad about her dad going away and she doesn't feel anything is fun anymore. She wishes she could play with her friends at nursery school and feel like a big girl as she used to, but she's too sad to feel good.'' In these ways the therapist implemented steps one and two of displacement communication: representing the observable signs of the youngster's emotional distress, and noting how upsetting this was to the figure who represented the child.

Gail entered into the play and had the girl doll cry. She said, ''The girl doll wants her daddy back.'' The therapist empathized with the girl doll's feelings saying, ''Girls love their dads a lot and it feels awful when they can't see him anymore.'' Gail solemnly nodded her agreement. The therapist represented Gail's underlying belief of being responsible for her father's moving away by stating, ''The girl doll feels sad about not seeing her dad, but she also feels especially awful because she thinks the reason he left was because he didn't love her enough. A lot of girls have that idea. They figure that if they were only pretty enough or nice enough then their dad wouldn't have gone away.'' Gail responded by saying, ''He (the father doll) just doesn't love her anymore.'' When asked how come, Gail quietly replied, ''She can't even throw a ball or climb up a slide; who would want her?''

This permitted the therapist to proceed naturally to the fourth step of displacement communication, correcting Gail's misunderstanding of her father's departure. She told Gail: ''The father doll didn't go away because he didn't like the girl doll. He loved her so much that it made him sad that he couldn't be with her all the time. He left because he was so sad, but he loves his daughter and thinks that she's really a neat kid.'' Gail looked dubious about this and asked, ''Why doesn't he keep seeing her if he loves her?'' She could not really understand how fathers, especially a big, strong father like hers (and nearly all young children see their father in this way regardless of what he is like) could feel that upset. The therapist recast her statement: ''Grown-ups sometimes have grown-up worries and grown-up upsets about divorce. Even dads can get real sad and upset about grown-up stuff.'' Gail seemed to grasp this way of stating the issue. After several repetitions of this sort of play, interspersed with their having talks about Gail's pet cat, her favorite television programs, and her beginning kindergarten soon, Gail began to act more like her old self at nursery school and at home. She had found a place to grieve, in displacement, and was also beginning to be able to understand that her father leaving did not mean that he did not love her or that there was something unlovable about her.

In her sixth session, Gail excitedly told her therapist about a telephone call she had received from her father the other day and proudly showed her a postcard that she had received from him the day before. The therapist acknowledged these renewed contacts and reminded Gail that, ''Fathers really do keep loving their girls after a divorce; it just sometimes takes them a while to show it.'' Gail seemed back on track developmentally and her therapy sessions were discontinued after another month.

Gail's therapist was able to empathize with her distress and correct her belief that her father no longer cared about her. She was also able to explain to Gail that she had not been responsible for her father leaving. Even before her father began implementing the suggestions of the therapist to reestablish contact with his daughter, Gail was experiencing a great deal of relief through displacement communication. She seemed less sad, had become more involved in activities at her nursery school, and was spending less time at home following her mother from room to room. When Gail's father called and sent her a postcard, this progress was greatly accelerated.

Though Gail's therapist chose to see her in a brief psychotherapy, it is likely that Gail's mother could have carried out the displacement communication herself. With explanations about the value and nature of this type of communication, and with coaching about how to implement it, many parents can effectively use this method, even using the same words, to alleviate their child's distress. However, it is also of enormous help to have the environmental sources of distress eliminated or at least greatly reduced. The reality of her father reaching out to her was extremely valuable to Gail.

There are also stresses children experience that are not so much the result of losing their relationship with their father but instead stem from distressing circumstances surrounding their visiting relationship with him. It is striking to observe how many parents, mothers and fathers alike, assume that their preschool age or even younger child will naturally be comfortable leaving his mother for long periods of time to visit his father. Even if the youngster has had a good relationship with his father, it is difficult for older toddlers and young preschoolers to be separated from their mother (assuming of course she has been the primary parent) for as long as a week. When the father–child relationship has been a distant one, this kind of visitation-induced separation is even more problematic for toddlers and preschoolers. The child feels as though he were being sent away by his mother to be with a near stranger, someone he knows but certainly does not experience emotionally as his father.

STEVE'S (see chapter 6) relationship with his father had never been close. He had minimal contact with him from the time his parents separated when he was six months old. While their brief contacts may have been sufficient to sustain his father's tie to his son, Steve was too young to develop an emotional relationship with his father in the context of such infrequent contacts. He was also too young to understand the legal rights his father had to see him. When his mother sent him on these visits, Steve was bewildered. Steve's mother had felt uneasy about the visits to begin with and was concerned about her son's having become aggressive at nursery school and bitter towards her.

Steven's mother talked with a mental health professional who explained the difficulties preschoolers have in maintaining the sense of a father–child relationship when there has been little contact between them. He also pointed out how anxious young children can become when they are separated from their primary parent for as long as a week. The likelihood that preschoolers will develop fantasies that the parent does not care about them anymore or is displeased with them as they try to explain to themselves the reasons for their being sent away on visits was presented to Steve's mother. The clinician advised her to discuss these matters with her ex-husband and try to find, together, an alternative visiting plan.

It was recommended that Steve's father come back into town at least one weekend a month and see his son during the day. At the same time, a visit to father's home over Christmas vacation should be kept to three days and the summer visit to a week. It was hoped that the greater frequency of contacts between times at his father's home and his not having to leave the security of his own home for overnight stays during these weekends would gradually increase Steve's comfort in leaving home to be with his father. Further, the reduction in the length of the Christmas and summer visits would be expected to minimize Steve's uneasiness about them. The mental health professional also suggested that Steve's mother send familiar objects such as toys and a favorite stuffed animal or his pillow and blanket with him on these trips.

At first Steve's father balked at the proposal for a revised visiting schedule. He claimed it would decrease his time with his son. Steve's mother pointed out that what the mental health professional had suggested would actually mean more frequent visits and that their total time together might actually be even greater, especially if father came to town more than one weekend per month. She encouraged her ex-husband to discuss it with the mental health professional. Accordingly, he made an appointment and traveled from his home to keep it. The mental health professional acknowledged and elaborated upon the important role fathers can play in the lives of their sons. He supported Steve's father's wishes to develop a good relationship with his son. However, he also

149

pointed out Steven's distress. The issue was not whether or not Steve's father should continue seeing his son but how to tailor their times together to Steve's developmental needs. His father could appreciate the logic of what he was told. He agreed to try the new schedule for a year to see how it might work. He reserved the right to go back to the current arrangement if the new one did not seem to be helpful. The mental health worker thought that this acceptance of the proposed schedule on a trial basis was reasonable.

In addition to implementing the new visiting plan, Steve's mother was encouraged to use displacement communication to help him with his worry (and defensive bitterness) that his mother was sending him away on visits because she did not love him anymore and was annoyed with him. First, she represented Steve's overt signs of distress and empathized with his discomfort over them. She said: "I know that sometimes boys get upset about having to go away to visit their dad. They get angry and start feeling that their mom doesn't care about them anymore. Some guys even start taking their angry feelings out on younger kids at their nursery school. It sure feels crummy for guys to be so upset." She continued by addressing her son's underlying concern: "You know, lots of boys get to feeling that their mom is sending them to their dad because she wants to get rid of him for a while. Almost like she doesn't really love him anymore. That idea makes most boys feel worried and mad." She added the final step in this four-part communication, correcting his belief that she no longer cared about him, by saying: "But when a guy's mom sends him to visit his dad, she's doing it because it's the law and also because she hopes that a guy will get to like being with his dad and have a good time. She still loves him a lot." Steve's mother made these comments casually, often as she was looking up from the newspaper she was reading or while she and Steve were clearing the dinner dishes. She had been told that it was important to keep her statements brief and not to give them the formal quality of a parental lecture.

Steve listened closely to what his mother said but did not respond verbally. He seemed interested, but when she was finished, he just began to draw or watch television as if he had not heard her. Steve's mother was careful not to try to get him to talk about his feelings and ideas about what she had said. This would have undone the indirectness of the displacement communication. After going through this process several times over a two-week period, Steve seemed to become less edgy at home. His nursery school teacher reported that his picking on younger children had subsided. Occasionally, Steve still responded to his mother's asking him what he would like for dinner or what he would prefer doing on a particular weekend day by again saying, "What do you care?" His mother took these opportunities to underscore the fact that her cooperating in his visits with his father did not mean that she did not care about him. She said: "I care a lot. I love you. Just because a mom doesn't stop a guy from visiting his dad doesn't mean that she doesn't love him anymore. Sometimes the law says the visits have to happen and besides a boy might have a good time with his dad." Once Steve said, "I hate going to dad's! I want to be here with you." His mother accepted his feelings and told him of the new visiting arrangement that was to start the following month. Steve seemed relieved. He was also somewhat surprised that his concerns had been heard so well.

The essential ingredient in this sort of success story is the willingness of divorcing adults to adopt effective parenting strategies. Steve's mother and father were able to do just that. They changed the visiting schedule, and his mother implemented the displacement communication method. It might not have gone this way, however. There are many instances in which a mother in the position Steve's mother was in digs in her heels and refuses to permit visiting to continue. Under the guise of protecting their children, these mothers frequently are actually using them consciously or unwittingly, to punish their ex-husband by withholding contact with the youngster. There are also fathers who, when they are in the position Steve's father was in, insist that their rights must be preserved. The right of their children to be free of distress assumes a lower priority than their own rights for visitation. When parents abdicate their parenting responsibilities in these ways, the outcome is considerably less happy than it was for Steve.

The anxiety, sadness, or loneliness of a parent, especially of a custodial parent, can lead that adult to turn to her child for comfort. She frequently hugs and cuddles her youngster as if the child were much younger. Her subtle air of desperation and her disregard for whether the child wants to be hugged indicates that she is taking comfort from the child, not giving affection. She unnecessarily includes the youngster in nearly all of her daily activities; they prepare and eat breakfast and dinner together, clear and wash the dishes, and run errands. In the evening they play games, curl up on the couch to watch television, and even sleep in the same bed. On weekends (when the child is not with his father), they putter about the house, work in the yard, go shopping, or take in a movie. Except for any child care that must be provided during times mother is at work or perhaps taking educational classes, these preschoolers and their mother are nearly never out of each other's sight. Like psychological Siamese twins they seem joined by a powerful, if invisible, bond that keeps them together far more than is healthy or natural.

While all young children are vulnerable to becoming enmeshed in this sort of sticky parent–child relationship, it is mothers and daughters who seem most prone to developing one. As boys move into the preschool years, they are less comfortable than girls with being overly close with their mother. The socially enforced sanctions imposed on being a "momma's boy" come into effect and, along with the internal developmental push for independence, propel boys away from their mother. At the same time, mothers are more likely to turn to their more cooperative, interpersonally oriented daughters for comfort. Further, girls do not tend to remind mothers of their ex-husband, whereas boys may be seen as a "chip off the old block" and thus less likely to be a source of comfort to their mother.

SARAH'S (see chapter 6) nursery school teachers were becoming increasingly concerned about her lack of involvement with peers, inhibitions about participating in physical activities, relatively slow development in large muscle coordination, and the pseudomature quality of her style of relating to adults. They had observed Sarah and her mother interact briefly in the mornings and late afternoons during drop-off and pick-up times. The closeness between mother and daughter struck them as more appropriate between a mother and young toddler than in a mother–preschooler relationship. The teachers had begun pointing out Sarah's difficulties to her mother while also noting her considerable developmental progress in many cognitive skills. They also praised her general cooperativeness at nursery school. The teachers urged Sarah's mother to discuss these issues with a mental health professional.

Sarah's mother was uninterested in pursuing this recommendation. Even after the teachers provided her with the name and telephone number of the psychologist who consulted at the nursery school, she remained reluctant. She did agree to have the psychologist unobtrusively observe Sarah and gave the teachers permission to share their concerns with him. After the psychologist had discussed the teachers' concerns with them and had watched Sarah's style of interacting at the nursery school several times, he met with the nursery school staff and told them what he concluded. He said that Sarah's development in the areas of emotional independence from her mother and the subsequent move to peer relationships was being interfered with by being in an enmeshed mother–daughter relationship. He counseled the teachers to explain to Sarah's mother the need preschoolers have to carve out their own identity apart from their parents. This requires a great deal of practice in interacting with peers as well as their parents' permission and encouragement to emotionally invest in relationships outside the home. When a lonely or anxious mother spends a great deal of time with her daughter, she is sending the message that she needs her daughter to stay closely involved with her.

The teachers gently conveyed this to Sarah's mother. However, rather than being receptive to the information, she became miffed. She pointed to Sarah's true developmental achievements, noted her willingness to have Sarah attend nursery school rather than stay at home with a baby-sitter, and reminded the teachers of how cooperative and pleasant her daughter was. She refused to meet with their consultant or any other mental health professional. Sarah's quiet expressions of difficulty persisted. The following year she began attending kindergarten half days. Her mother selected another day-care center for Sarah to go to for the other half days.

Sarah's mother was not prepared to give up the comfort and gratification she was receiving from the close relationship between herself and her daughter. The teachers' efforts to bring to her attention the early signs of Sarah's development not being fully on track were experienced as a criticism of her and her daughter. She was too emotionally vulnerable to hear what the teachers were trying to tell her. Her capacity to parent her daughter was being interfered with by her own needs. Because her daughter was meeting these so effectively and was not having very obvious problems, her mother could continue to keep herself unaware of the developmental costs that were beginning to accrue for Sarah.

153

Had she been able to see the enmeshed quality of their relationship and the ways it had begun to impede Sarah's progress, she could have done several things to facilitate her daughter's development. As a first step, she could have begun seeking other sources of personal gratification and emotional support. Community services and religious institutions offer a variety of discussion and social groups for single parents. These can provide a supportive function as well as be a place to develop new friendships. Recently divorced adults can also reach out to friends and relatives for understanding, to serve as a sounding board, and for companionship in social activities. These adult-focused resources can permit distressed divorced parents to have their needs met outside of their relationship with their children. In doing so, they can continue parenting effectively without burdening the parent–child relationship with their own emotional needs.

A parent who is anxious, lonely, or sad cannot afford to encourage her preschool age child to become emotionally independent. Finding other ways to meet their needs can free parents to help their children become independent. They can leave their youngster at a home of a neighbor who has a child of about the same age when they do errands on the weekend. This sends the preschooler the message that the parent is comfortable being apart from the youngster. It also gives children a chance to practice their social relationships with peers. In the early evenings, a mother can help her child learn to play on her own or with a sibling rather than always interacting with her. She can sometimes clear and wash the dishes herself and read or listen to music afterwards while her preschooler draws, plays with her brother, or watches television. The mother who does this is implicitly telling her child that she expects them occasionally to have separate emotional time even when they are in the same room. They can be together but have their attention focused elsewhere than on each other. A parent can insist on a youngster sleeping in her own bed. She can encourage her child by pointing out that, "Big girls sleep in their own big bed" and "Big girls feel better about being able to sleep all by themselves" and "Girls feel bigger and better the next day when they've been able to sleep by themselves." Fears can be handled by gentle support and the promise to check on the youngster every five minutes until she falls asleep.

In these ways a mother accomplishes several things at once. She makes it clear that her own emotional well-being is not tied to having a close relationship with her youngster. She simultaneously holds out clear expectations for the child to be independent and appropriately separate from her. The youngster then must seek at least some pleasures in relationships with peers and in her own emerging feelings of independence.

While a lonely single parent can turn to her preschooler for comfort and thus increase the likelihood of developing an enmeshed parent–child relationship, dating and remarriage can precipitously disrupt a close relationship between the parent and youngster, as we saw in the case of Meredith.

MEREDITH (see chapter 6) had progressed well developmentally until her mother remarried. She had been an infant when her parents separated and was their only child. Though she attended a day-care center/nursery school and her mother had worked and had an active social life, Meredith was convinced that she was the center of her mother's emotional universe. This changed dramatically when her mother married Dave and he moved in with them.

Her mother and stepfather met with a social worker at a local child guidance clinic to try to figure out what to do. The social worker had several meetings with Meredith's mother and stepfather, one session with Meredith, and a session with all three members of the family together. He then shared the results of his evaluation with mother and stepfather. Meredith's hurt and anger over feeling displaced in her mother's affections were explained. He pointed out that Meredith had not had to share her mother before nor had she had a chance to develop a significant, close relationship with anyone other than her mother. Her father had been distant and uninvolved, so that her primary parent was also, in effect, her only psychological parent. The tendency of children in this situation to develop an overly close, exclusive relationship with their mother was underscored.

The social worker recommended a three-step approach to helping Meredith. First, the importance of special time for mother and Meredith to be together without Dave was noted. He recommended that they resume doing some of the things they used to do before mother remarried. Mother and daughter could take in a movie and garden together occasionally without Dave present. In this way, some of the appropriate mother–daughter closeness could be preserved. Second, the social worker recommended that Dave also spend more one-on-one time with his new stepdaughter. They needed to get to know each other. Meredith could accompany Dave on some of his errands and be left at home with him while mother met a friend for lunch. Though children will often resist being left with a new stepparent, it provides an opportunity for each to gain a better sense of the other and begin to develop their own relationship. These two steps also provided Meredith with chances to be with her mother and her stepfather in a noncompetitive context. When all three were together, her competitive agenda took precedence over the more constructive elements in her relationship with each. Finally, the social worker suggested that her mother begin to use displacement communication with Meredith in order to get at her feelings of being cast aside in favor of Dave. He explained the greater receptivity of preschoolers to indirect communications when conflicted issues were being discussed and outlined the first four steps in this process.

Meredith's mother chose to use her daughter's collection of "My Pretty Pony" horse figures as the vehicle for the displacement communication. She invited her daughter to watch a play she would present using three of the figures: one to represent a girl pony, one to be the girl pony's mother, and one to be the stepfather. Meredith's mother constructed a play in which the girl pony and her mother lived together. They ate hay together and ran in the fields. They loved each other a lot. Then Meredith's mother had the mother pony meet a new man pony and get married. After setting the stage in this way, she implemented step one of the displacement communication (representing the youngster's signs of observable distress) by having the girl pony feel left out of the new marital relationship. The girl pony angrily tried to get the mother pony to come run in the fields and jump fences with her: "Neigh, neigh, come with me mommy. Let's run and jump fences like we used to." Meredith's mother had the girl pony angrily shove the stepfather pony aside to be close to her mother. Meredith was delighted. She picked up the girl pony and had her jump on the stepfather pony and kick him repetitively. Her mother said, "It looks like she doesn't like her stepdad." Meredith replied vehemently, "Who needs stepdads? They just get in the way and eat up all the hay." Meredith's mother said, "But the mom pony likes the stepdad." Her daughter dismissed this saying, "Who cares."

Then Meredith's mother went on to step two of the displacement communication and demonstrated the girl pony's being upset by her own actions and feelings: "The girl pony doesn't really like having to try to get her mom away from her stepfather pony. She wishes she didn't have to feel worried about not getting her mom's attention and she wants to stop being angry at the stepdad pony." Meredith responded by saying, "No she doesn't. She likes being mad at him." Meredith's mother went on to the third step and verbalized the underlying emotional pain that was giving rise to her daughter's distress: "It sort of looks like the girl pony feels that her mom doesn't love her anymore. She feels the mom pony is giving a lot of her love to the stepdad pony, and she doesn't like that at all." Meredith quickly said, "Yeah, who needs him anyway."

Going on to the fourth step, Meredith's mother corrected this misperception: "I think the girl pony feels like her mom only has one love pie, so if she gives the stepdad a big, huge piece there just isn't as much left over for the girl as there used to be. But that's not how it works. Moms have two love pies, one for their kids and one for other grown-ups. They can give their whole grown-up love pie to their new husband, and that still leaves the whole kids' pie for their daughter." She went on to explain that "When a mom gets married it's like she just got a new love pie and she gives it to her husband. But the love pie she gave to her daughter is still there. Moms keep loving their daughters just as much after they get married." Meredith seemed taken aback by this. It was a new idea. Her mother noticed her confusion and drew a picture of two love pies. She drew a girl near one and a man near the other one. She also made a thick line down the middle of the paper to show that the girl's love pie was all for her and the stepfather's love pie was only for him.

Meredith's mother repeated this play numerous times over a month-long period. She reintroduced it by saying things like, "Let's see how the My Pretty Pony family is doing today" and "I wonder how the My Pretty Pony girl is feeling today." Sometimes Meredith seemed uninterested and her mother did not insist. At the same time, the first two parts of the overall plan were being implemented. Meredith took great pleasure in having some of the times alone with her mother restored. Though she seemed uneasy at first at being alone with Dave, she gradually warmed up to him. He was not especially psychologically minded. However, with the new knowledge about Meredith's needs and concerns he had gained in the meetings with the social worker, he became a more sensitive, involved stepparent. He showed Meredith magic tricks and then taught her how they worked. He bought a riddle book appropriate for older preschoolers and read to her from it. They seemed to be on the way to forming a good relationship. Meredith's demanding and angrily controlling behavior began to subside at home and at her nursery school.

Meredith's mother and stepfather were able to use the information given them by the social worker and implement his recommendations. The blow to Meredith's self-esteem that the marriage had brought was softened, and the damage it had been doing was repaired. Meredith learned that her mother could continue to love her just as much as she had before the marriage. The concept of "two love pies" concretized for this preschooler, and thus made more understandable to her, the difference between love in adult relationships and the love a parent has for her child. The times alone with mother showed Meredith that she could continue to enjoy some measure of exclusivity in her relationship with her mother. And the one-on-one times with Dave permitted them to begin to develop their own relationship. This overall approach served to greatly reduce the sources of stress in Meredith's life. Accordingly, her problem behaviors began to dissipate.

At times parents avoid talking directly to the preschooler or even their elementary school age child about the marital separation. Some parents believe the child cannot understand the divorce issues. Others feel that they are protecting their young children from a painful reality. In most instances it is the parent who feels awkward, anxious, or guilty and wants to avoid discussing the divorce with the child directly. The preschooler's cognitive limitations and need to keep himself unaware of disturbing parental conflict lead him to ask few if any questions about the fact that his father is not at home at night anymore or that he has to move with his mother to an apartment. It is important to remember that preschoolers do observe what is going on around them and are far more likely to develop frightening fantasies and burdensome, erroneous beliefs about the changes in their lives that divorce brings when explanations from parents are not available.

Overview

The centrally important sources of environmental stress for preschool age children are inconsistent daily routines, parental warfare, the emotional upset of a parent (especially the custodial parent), the loss or continued absence of the relationship with the noncustodial parent, and the remarriage of the custodial parent. Because preschoolers have the capacity to develop organized fantasies and construct egocentric beliefs about divorce, there are also internal sources of stress. Fantasies about being abandoned or of someone being seriously hurt are common as are beliefs that the child has been responsible for the divorce or the lack of contact with the noncustodial parent. Children can be helped to cope with distress by avoiding or removing its environmental sources and by using displacement communication to alleviate internally based upset.

8

▶◀

The Divorce Experience for Early Elementary School Children

Early elementary school is the third stage of child development. It covers the ages of six to eight years, which typically span a youngster's movement from kindergarten through most or all of the second grade. There is considerable growth in all areas of development during this period. Teachers and parents alike are struck by great leaps in cognitive, emotional, and social maturity.

Children in early elementary school gain an increased capacity for abstract thinking, which permits them to go beyond their concrete perceptions and experience. This results in the ability to conceptualize alternative, future realities. They develop clear, coherent fantasies of what could happen. For youngsters whose parents divorce, this means that frightening fantasies, such as being abandoned by the remaining custodial parent or of parents being hurt as a result of their rage at one another, are more likely to arise. These fantasies burden children and heighten their distress over divorce.

Advances in cognitive development make a physical joint custody arrangement more viable than it is for younger children. The ability to anticipate when they will be with each parent allows children to accommodate more readily to a schedule of moving back and forth between two households. Increased knowledge of temporal and spatial relationships makes separations from each parent (to be with the other) more tolerable; time away from a parent no longer seems interminable; and the physical location of the two homes relative to one another is more clear. They can keep the sense of being at each household firmly in mind even when they are not there so that an experience of continuity can be maintained in their lives.

However, the early elementary school child is by no means fully adept in his capacity for abstract thought. The complex legal, interpersonal, and emotional parameters of divorce are still beyond his grasp. Therefore, explanations of what divorce is and why it happens must be kept simple. And the tendency to develop egocentric causal explanations is still notably present as it is for preschoolers (see discussion in chapter 6). Thus, early elementary school children are prone to "understand" divorce-related events as being caused by themselves.

Emotional independence blossoms during this stage of development. Greater cognitive and physical competence lead to enhanced self-confidence. The early elementary school child attends "real" school (not just nursery school) and learns to read and write. But emotional independence is not the same as emotional self-sufficiency. The youngster in early elementary school still depends a great deal on parents for feelings of safety, security, and positive self-esteem. In much the same way that a toddler has to touch base with a parent, visually or physically, to maintain an emerging sense of separateness, the early elementary school child requires an internal kind of base touching with her image of a stable home in order to continue to feel confidently independent. When this mental image of a dependable family home base is disrupted by divorce, the child is likely to experience a disturbance in her overall sense of well-being. Her efforts in the wider world of school and peers can therefore be undermined.

Boys and girls continue to strengthen their emotional attachments to their father. Boys further consolidate their masculine identity through regular, ongoing interactions with father, sharing his interests and participating in activities with him. Playful competition arises in their relationship as boys test newfound abilities against the yardstick of their father. Girls, too, make use of their relationship with father to further their own sex-role development. Though they identify with and model themselves after their mother, girls look to their father for acceptance and validation of their femininity. He also continues to serve as a bridge between the mother–daughter relationship and the world beyond it. When parents divorce, these valuable, developmentally progressive characteristics of the father–child relationship may be lost or become significantly unavailable. The sex-role development of boys and girls can be interfered with and their pride and self-esteem damaged.[1]

The young elementary school child has made powerful attachments to both his parents. Despite being more emotionally and socially independent than his preschool counterparts, the early elementary school youngster usually loves his parents very much. Perhaps because he has consolidated his own sense of independence, he can now afford to accept and take pleasure in his emotional involvement with them. It is not that early elementary school children love their parents more than younger children do; rather, they are more self-aware of this love and less ambivalent about it. The struggles for emotional independence give way to a less conflicted and more idealized bond of love with the parents.

Early elementary school children also have developed a sense of family. Not only are their separate relationships with each parent centrally important but a love of and trust in their family unit begins to emerge. The considerable gains in cognitive, emotional, and social development make for more complexity in their interpersonal experiences and in thoughts they have about them. They move from an exclusively dyadic to a broader familial sense of relationships. How it feels to be at home, at a park, or out to dinner with one's family is comprised of a mosaic of family interactions and feelings.

When children reach elementary school, they also become more attuned to interactions between people that do not directly involve them. They are more aware of how mother relates to their brother and the quality of the relationship between their parents. These perceptions also contribute to the gestalt of their overall sense of family. Dramatic changes in the spousal relationship brought about by marital discord and separation, therefore, disturb the young elementary school child's overall sense of family.

These focuses on the family make the theme of loss and its attendant sadness the primary features of the divorce experience for young elementary school children. Each of the key environmental sources of stress are experienced most frequently as forms of loss. The loss of harmony in the household due to parental strife; the loss of a particular quality of parent–child relationship when a parent becomes distraught; the partial or complete loss of a relationship with the parent who moves out of the home; and the partial loss of a close relationship with the custodial parent who increases her work efforts, becomes involved in a serious dating relationship, or remarries are the multiple threads of loss, which together constitute the fabric of the divorce experience for early elementary school age children.

The Immediate Crisis Stage

We have seen the considerable effects of parental warfare on the lives of infants, toddlers, and preschoolers. The presence of intense or prolonged hostilities between parents is also a pivotal source of environmental stress for early elementary school children. However, unlike very young children, elementary school children do not resonate primarily to their parents' rage or even become angry about the disconcerting battles they observe. Instead, they typically feel overwhelmed by sadness over losing their familiar and cherished sense of family cohesiveness. Youngsters at this stage of development also are especially vulnerable to frightening fantasies about what might happen when parents become so enraged and are frequently burdened by egocentric beliefs about their role in their parents' marital troubles. The costs in terms of loss of developmental accomplishments; failure to progress on cognitive, emotional, and/or social fronts; and painful sadness, fearfulness, and guilt can be considerable.

ALEX HAD JUST TURNED SIX when his parents separated after nearly a year of escalating, bitter conflict. Successful real estate sales people, earning over $25,000 a year each, they were both in their early thirties and had been married for seven years. Alex's father and mother battled over numerous issues. His tendency to spend money freely, make major purchases without consulting his wife, drink too much, and not help out with household chores enraged Alex's mother. She felt that she was being treated as a housekeeper and baby-sitter. Her feeling that she was always put in a position of being inferior to her husband infuriated her. Alex's father had his own complaints. He thought his wife was controlling and competitive. She wanted to decide how to spend their money, try to get him to change his spending habits, and was constantly reminding him that her ability to earn money was just as good, if not better, than his. He also experienced his wife as unaffectionate and uninterested in their sexual relationship. He had begun an affair, which became the final straw for his wife when she found out.

She filed for divorce and insisted that he move out of the family home. After he had moved to an apartment several miles away, they continued to have frequent angry telephone conversations. They also saw each other several times a week. Even though Alex visited him only every other weekend, his father often dropped by the family house. He had kept his keys, claiming that it was still his house, too. He would appear unannounced, let himself into the house, prepare a snack, putter in his basement workshop, or pick up a video or audiotape to take back to his apartment. At times he was already in the house when his wife returned home from work. Alex's mother found this intolerable. They accused each other of being controlling and unreasonable, swore at one another, and occasionally pushed or physically threatened each other.

Two months into the separation, Alex's mother changed the locks at the house. Her husband became enraged when he first discovered this. He stood at the front door angrily shouting that he was going to break it down. He cursed at her and pounded the door. His wife felt both frightened by his anger and delighted that she had been able to get to him. She taunted him from an upstairs window and told him to go back to his "whore" and leave her alone. This scene repeated itself many times though Alex's father never did any damage to the property nor did he become physically assaultive. When they were not doing battle, they constantly derogated one another in front of Alex. His father made comments such as, "I wonder if the ice-bitch has made any sales this week?" and "What she needs is someone to give her a good slapping around," when Alex was with him. Alex's mother directly and sarcastically asked him questions such as, "How's your father's lady friend? Oh, I forgot, she's really not a lady is she?" and "Is your father still drinking? One of these days he's going to lose his job."

Alex was overwhelmed by the rage that seemed to suffuse his whole world. No place felt safe anymore. His parents fought all the time. Even when he was alone with each of them, they were chronically angry and said awful things about each other. He began crying easily at home and at school. His first-grade teacher noticed how forlorn and sad Alex looked during the day. He was having difficulty completing assignments at his desk, such as printing a sentence or adding two numbers. He never volunteered to run errands for the teacher or participate during daily show-and-tell time. At recess he stood watching other children play and sometimes started to cry for no apparent reason. He ate his lunch by himself but usually did not finish the sandwich and fruit he had brought from home or the milk he bought in the school cafeteria. When his class drew pictures about a topic being studied, Alex rarely finished.

His drawings had a barren, lifeless quality often consisting of a single tree or flower with a black sky overhead. When his teacher said that one such drawing looked sad, he silently began to cry.

At home he spent a great deal of time lying on the floor watching television. He stopped playing with neighborhood friends and stayed in his house nearly all the time. When his mother was putting away freshly laundered clothing in his chest of drawers, she found cookies, half a jar of peanut butter, and some crackers. Alex claimed he had taken them from the kitchen and kept them in his room in case he got hungry. At night he had begun having trouble going to sleep. He cried when his mother left the bedroom and claimed that he did not want to be all alone.

Alex was overcome by sadness. Though some elementary school age children grapple actively with their distress over parental warfare by becoming obstinate, angry, or aggressive (with parents and/or peers) as preschoolers do, Alex felt flooded by sad feelings. He cried frequently and was preoccupied with his grief to the point that he could not learn effectively in school or participate in social relationships with peers. His cognitive and social development were being interfered with significantly. His emerging feelings of mastery and independence were being undermined by the loss of a secure home base from which he could venture forth into the wider world. He listlessly withdrew to his house and passively whiled away the time on the floor watching television. His fears of being alone at bedtime and hoarding food are common reactions when early elementary school children feel they can no longer trust their parents to care and provide for them in an ongoing, consistent manner.

This constellation consisting of overt sadness, an inability to continue learning in school, withdrawal from pleasurable activities with neighborhood friends and classmates, and worries about having to care for oneself entirely constitutes a depressive reaction in young elementary school children. The child may display all or only one or two of these symptoms, which may be intense and pervasive or relatively mild and confined to certain situations. But whether severe or mild, it is important for these depressive reactions to be recognized by parents as well as teachers and other professionals (for example, school-based mental health professionals, pediatricians, family physicians) who have the opportunity to observe and hear about the youngster. If unrecognized and left unattended to, a depressive reaction can harden and crystallize into a full-blown depression requiring treatment by a mental health professional.

The early elementary school child's tendency to experience a depressive reaction, or some elements of one, in the face of parental hostilities rather than primarily becoming fearful or angry, as younger as well as older children do, is noteworthy. Many early elementary school children do indeed respond to parental warfare by becoming frightened and reflexively may try to ward off feelings of sadness by becoming angry and aggressive. However, these feelings and behaviors tend to occur in the context of grief over their parents' enmity. Why are young elementary school children so prone to depressive reactions? It is likely that they experience their parents' fighting as proof that their family will never be the same.

The combination of the marital separation and parental hostilities makes the youngster painfully aware that he is losing forever his treasured sense of family. Not only is he worried about who will take care of him and whether the parental rage he sees will get out of control, he has lost his niche in the world. He is also often burdened by the belief that he caused the divorce and that his father has left because of him. These egocentrically arrived-at beliefs batter the child's self-esteem. He has lost his family, and in large part it was because he was bad. We know that two important contributing factors to depression both in children and adults are serious losses and dramatically lowered self-esteem. The young elementary school child suffers both because of how he encodes, interprets, and experiences the dissolution of his family. For a child of this age, parental warfare underscores and makes more certain the fact that his family had ceased to exist.

The loss of the feeling of family as it is restructured through the divorce process is not the only loss a child experiences when her parents separate. The father–child relationship also is frequently disrupted by divorce. Youngsters usually have become very attached to their father during the preschool years. Whether the relationship is in fact close and characterized by frequent pleasurable interactions or is more distant and rests on the fantasies, idealizations, and wishes of the youngster, it has become a centrally important psychological factor in the lives of early elementary school children.

When parents separate, a child of this age nearly always resides primarily with her mother. Sometimes mothers leave the family home with their children, but more typically it is the father who moves out and finds another place to live. In either case, elementary school age and younger boys and girls usually see considerably less of their father when parents separate. The incidence of joint physical custody, where the youngster lives part of each week or alternate weeks with each parent, is still relatively uncommon. A recent survey of a large socioeconomically diverse Michigan county revealed that joint physical custody awards involved fewer than 5 percent of children whose parents divorce. This figure dropped to under 3 percent for preadolescent children. Michigan has among the most receptive attitudes among the states toward joint physical custody, and the county surveyed was populous and cosmopolitan. The number of young children in the primary custody of their father is also generally quite low. It was about the same as for joint physical custody in the Michigan survey.

Even when there are frequent and regular contacts between a noncustodial father and his children, the quality of the father–child relationship is dramatically altered. The everyday brief, often spontaneous, interactions between father and child are replaced by planned, more structured time together. And the father's ongoing participation in the ebb and flow of his youngster's life is disrupted. The child telling her father about what happened at school that day, his observing her pleasure and occasional upsets when she plays in the yard with friends, insisting that she give her Barbie dolls a rest and come to dinner, helping her learn her list of spelling words for school the next day, listening to a song she made up for him, and reading her a bedtime story, tucking her in, and giving her a goodnight kiss are no longer part of either of their daily lives. A great majority of children see their father every other week or less when their parents separate.[2] But even the father who spends one weekend day, including an overnight stay, with his child and takes her to dinner one night a week (a highly frequent visiting schedule), is often relegated to the role of ''Disneyland Dad'' by this arrangement. He cannot be centrally involved in the day-to-day aspects of his child's life. The normally smooth, brief interactions within the context of family life are extremely difficult to duplicate in time-limited, one-to-one visits. Well-meaning, loving fathers find themselves planning fun-filled activities in part to make up for having less time together and to some degree to alleviate feelings of mutual awkwardness over the formal character of visits. Children eagerly await these times together. Their expectations for a marvelous time contributes to father and child engaging in special activities. The weekends with father become high points for the child, while everyday life with mother is sometimes experienced as a valley by contrast.

Nevertheless, as exciting and pleasurable as these visits can be, the child is still faced with the loss of the particular quality of her relationship with her father when he lived at home. This is not to say that ongoing, regular father–child contacts are unimportant. They contribute to the youngster's crucial sense of still being important to her father and loved by him. Though it does not have the same feel as the in-home relationship had, it still can be close and emotionally rewarding for fathers and their children.

A more common scenario during the immediate crisis stage of divorce is for the father and child to be together for one weekend out of two or three. At times, this may not include the full weekend or involve overnight stays. In these instances the changes in the quality of the father-child relationship described above become more pronounced. The young elementary school child has difficulty sustaining an emotional bond with a parent he sees so infrequently. In much the same way as we observed in younger children, the early elementary school youngster depends on very frequent interactions with a man who clearly functions in the father role (helping, comforting, limit setting, playing) in order to maintain "father feelings" toward him. Unlike much younger children, however, the child who has begun elementary school cognitively understands who his father is. It does not feel as if he were with a near stranger, but it still is not the same as it used to be.

Whether fathers see their children regularly and frequently, not at all, or somewhere in between, youngsters experience some loss of the relationship with him. It may consist of a shift in the character of their time together. This often puzzles the parents who note that a father may be paying more attention to his child or spending more time with him than he did before the separation. But it is not the amount of time or attention that is at issue; it is the changes in feeling tone and in the overall nature of their relationship that alters it and thus creates a sense of having lost, to some degree, what the child previously had. Or the loss may be greater and more obvious, as it is for the strikingly large number of youngsters who see their father only a few times a year (or even less). In either case, the bottom line still adds up to a feeling of loss for the child.

MOLLY WAS NEARLY SEVEN YEARS OLD when her parents separated. She had just begun second grade and was a lively, intelligent youngster. Her father was a carpenter employed by a large construction company and her mother was a nurse who worked at a small, private hospital. In addition to Molly, they had another daughter who was four years old. Molly's parents' marital relationship had been a distant one with each vaguely dissatisfied for several years. They liked each other and rarely argued. However, they both felt that something was missing in their marriage. Molly's mother had begun a romantic relationship with a young physician-in-training whom she had met at the hospital. They spent a great deal of time together and their work relationship gradually had progressed to their falling in love. Molly's mother had not set out to have an extramarital relationship. Her feelings of emotional emptiness in her marriage set the stage for it. She told her husband that she wanted a divorce and planned to marry her lover when the divorce became final.

Molly's father felt hurt and angry, but his reaction had the quality of what a man is "supposed to" feel in this situation rather than genuine outrage. He, too, had begun to think of leaving the marriage as his long-standing feelings of dissatisfaction crystallized. His wife's unfaithfulness rankled and also raised doubts in him about his sexual prowess. But he quickly began a relationship of his own with an old high school sweetheart whose own divorce had recently become final. The blow to his masculine pride and self-esteem was greatly softened by their gratifying intimacy.

Molly's father moved out of the family residence and into an apartment only two miles away. He very much wanted to continue his relationship with his daughters, and that led to his remaining nearby. With each parent involved in a new love relationship, the initial stages of their separation proceeded relatively smoothly. While they had their disagreements as their attorneys helped them work toward a financial settlement, these were relatively minor. They also thought well of each other's parenting abilities and believed that the children still needed both of them. They mutually agreed on sole maternal custody with liberal visitation for father.

Two weeks after Molly's father moved out, her parents agreed to sit down together and tell their daughters of their separation. They told the children that they had fallen out of love with each other and were not happy being married anymore. They were careful to emphasize that they both still loved the children and would always love them. Even though they were getting a divorce and would no longer be living together, their love for the girls would not change. As is so often the case, even with children considerably

170

older than Molly and her sister, the girls reacted with shock and disbelief. They cried and asked repetitively why their parents were divorcing. They asked no other questions. The parents had established a visiting schedule that included the children spending every Saturday from noon until Sunday at noon with their father. In addition, he took them to dinner regularly, sometimes at his apartment and other times out to a restaurant, on two weekday evenings. The girls were with their father for about two hours when they had dinner together.

Molly and her father had a warm, caring relationship. Since she was a toddler, he had played a major role in her bedtime routine, making sure that she washed up and brushed her teeth, reading a story to her, and tucking her in for the night. They both treasured these times. Molly's father also frequently took her with him when he had errands to do and showed her the construction sites of jobs he had worked on. She had her own hard hat with "MOLLY" stamped on the front of it. The fact that her father would not be living at home anymore saddened her immensely. Though she saw her father with considerably greater frequency than most youngsters do following a marital separation, she missed his ongoing presence in the household. She frequently burst into tears at dinnertime without her father. Going to bed at night provoked quiet tears, and she began taking her hard hat to bed with her.

On the days she was to have dinner with her father, she seemed on edge. Her teacher reported that Molly was "wound up" and had difficulty concentrating on her schoolwork on those days. The teacher tried empathizing with Molly's upset, saying, "I know this is a hard time for you with your parents getting divorced." Much to her surprise, Molly vehemently denied that her parents were in the process of divorcing. She stated, "My mom and dad aren't getting a divorce, it's just that I'm sad because he has to work so hard that he's not home a lot like he used to be." Molly's teacher tried to dismiss this by going on to reassure her that everything would work out fine and that she was sure Molly's parents both loved her very much. Molly became furious at her teacher. She cried, angrily tore up the math assignment she was working on and frantically insisted that her parents were not getting a divorce. Molly shouted, "You don't understand at all! It's just my dad is working a lot. He's building a big, new office building. That's why he isn't home."

Molly's teacher was shaken by this uncharacteristic outburst and by the child's persuasive statements that the divorce was not occurring. The teacher called Molly's mother who confirmed that she and her husband had indeed separated and that Molly had been carefully told about it. She confronted her daughter about what Molly had said to her teacher and reiterated the fact that she and her husband were getting a divorce. Molly put her hands over her ears and screamed, ''You are not getting a divorce!'' She added, ''Dad's gonna move back home soon. Everything's going to be just like it was.''

Despite these assertions, Molly continued to appear painfully sad most days. She began staying indoors after school rather than playing with friends in the neighborhood. During these times and in the evenings after dinner, she spent hours looking at old family photographs. Pictures of the family when they vacationed at a cottage in the northern part of the state and snapshots taken at her birthday parties over the years were her favorites. She sadly sorted them and resorted them over and over again into different piles; photographs of her and her father, pictures of her father and mother, and those of the entire family were the categories she used most often. Though she perked up briefly when she was with her father, she also asked him frequently when he was coming back home. He gently told her that when mothers and fathers get divorced they keep living apart. Molly would then become agitated and insist he had to come home. She promised to be especially good when he did. Her father, not wanting to upset his daughter further and hoping the reality of the divorce would gradually sink in for her, did not usually pursue these kinds of conversations further.

After four months, both parents had become concerned about Molly. She had continued to insist to classmates and to her teacher that her parents were not getting divorced. Her teacher reported that Molly often seemed sad and that it was interfering with her completing written work as well as participating in class discussions. She seemed preoccupied. At home, Molly continued to let both of her parents know that she was fully expecting and awaiting the day that they would get back together again. She also cried easily, had little to do with her friends, and had trouble falling asleep at night. Although she looked forward to her frequent and regular visits with her father, she nearly always seemed irritable and withdrawn beforehand as well as when she returned home.

172

Molly's depressive reaction to her parents' separation was clear. She seemed to be responding simultaneously to the loss of her family as a unit and the loss of the closeness in her relationship with her father. The sadness that flooded her emotional life had submerged her interest in learning in school and her pleasure in being with friends. Her comment about being "especially good" provided a clue to an internal source of her distress as well. She had apparently constructed the developmentally understandable, egocentric belief that her father had left the family home because she had not been a good-enough girl. It was not only the real losses of her family's togetherness and her closeness to her father that had led to her depressive reactions; she also took her father's leaving as an indication that she was in some vague, undefined way not a good-enough girl. This internally rooted source of stress had precipitated a painful loss of self-esteem and self-worth that compounded the observable losses she was experiencing.

When she was not feeling sad, Molly was engaged in trying to actively cope with her distress by using the defenses available to her developmentally. She tried to ward off her emotional pain primarily through the use of denial. On first hearing of her parents' plan to separate, Molly was disbelieving as well as shocked. Her disbelief was an automatic denial of the upsetting reality her parents had told her about. Molly was also using the defense of denial when she insisted to her teacher and classmates that her parents were not really separated; it was only that her father was working long hours. The time she spent pouring over old family photographs was also an example of denial. She immersed herself in representations of past family togetherness and closeness with her father in an attempt to counter the current reality of the marital separation and the partial loss of her father it had brought. Finally, Molly's steadfast belief that her parents would resolve whatever differences had caused them to separate and that her father would then come home was a further instance of her use of denial. Here she was trying to undo the reality of the permanence of their separation. This reconciliation wish is common throughout the elementary school years[3] and even on into adolescence.

Molly's use of denial in these several ways is quite typical of how younger elementary school children try to cope with their sadness over the losses that divorce brings. Sometimes early elementary school children become angry and begin picking on siblings or classmates, or they may become obstinate and uncooperative at home. These, too, are attempts to cope actively with their sadness rather than passively permitting themselves to be engulfed by it. Unfortunately, neither denial nor anger are effective defenses in the long run. Denial leads to distortions of, and failures to accept, obvious realities, while becoming aggressive only gets the youngster into trouble and makes it less likely that he will receive empathic support from his parents and teacher. Further, these defenses are usually not able to fully contain the child's sadness; crying, trouble concentrating in school, and withdrawal from peer relationships often continue and are not substantially ameliorated by these defenses.

The Short-Term Aftermath Stage

The early elementary school child often comes to this second stage in the divorce process still filled with sadness over the losses described in the preceding section. Valiant attempts to deny that the end of family life as they have known it is real and final usually, though not always, have given way in face of the ongoing restructured household. Many children handle their sadness over these losses by simply trying not to think about the divorce. Frightening fantasies of being completely abandoned and painful beliefs that they might have caused their parents' divorce or are responsible for their father not visiting them much are dealt with in much the same way. During this stage of divorce, these young elementary school children can do well at school, play with friends, and be delightful at home. As long as they are not persistently reminded of their parents' divorce, they can put this reality away much of the time and go on with their lives.

A major reason that parental warfare continuing into this stage is so upsetting to early elementary school children is that it is a painful reminder of the fact of the divorce. Similarly, many parents report that their child is doing fine in general but becomes noticeably sad, irritable, and/or uncooperative just before a visit with the noncustodial parent, as well as on returning from such a visit. Maintaining an ongoing relationship between the youngster and his noncustodial father is of potentially great value to children. Children can continue to feel loved and appreciated. Boys can benefit from the opportunity to consolidate their masculine identity further by modeling themselves after their father. Girls are able to consolidate their sense of emotional independence from their mother as well as deepen the feeling that

174

their femininity is cherished by a man. It is somewhat paradoxical that these important developmental gains exist side-by-side with the heightened sadness and distress that visits with father tend to provoke.

A major source of environmental stress for young elementary school children is having a parent, especially the primary custodial parent, unable to regain her emotional equilibrium. A youngster's capacity to continue the developmental task of shifting increasing amounts of time and emotional investment from parents and home to the wider world of peers and teachers depends on having a trusted home base. It is only from this position of safety and security that the early elementary school child can turn his attentions outward. The loss-related disruptions so prominent in the first stage of divorce for young elementary school children usually subside gradually. Though their sadness can be easily triggered by reminders of the divorce, such as parental hostilities and the schedule of visits, children in early elementary school grades can usually put this out of their mind sufficiently to carry on with their normal developmental agenda.

An overly anxious, lonely, or depressed custodial parent endangers the early elementary school child's sense of having a supportive, trusting home base. The confidence he needs to go forth and learn in school, look up to and even love his teacher, increase his social skills, and take pleasure in budding friendships is seriously undermined when his custodial parent is in emotional distress. A parent absorbed in her own pain is less available to the child. She may be less able to notice his accomplishments, praise his efforts, or provide a sympathetic ear when he is troubled by not finishing an assignment in school, losing a game, or having an argument with a friend. An emotionally upset parent may not only be less sensitive to her youngster's everyday needs, psychological as well as physical, and thus less supportive, she may also begin to turn to the youngster to have her own needs met.

Early elementary school children are quick to become engaged in helping their distressed parent. To begin with, it makes them feel very big, important, and well loved to be needed by a parent. They experience it, though they cannot possibly articulate it quite this way, as a vote of confidence in their emerging and ever-increasing abilities. It also can provide children with an opportunity to act out favorite and potentially very gratifying wishes. The youngster who feels that by helping a parent he is becoming the head of the household is putting into action the fantasy of being the one in charge. Rather than always being in the position of seeking permission and trying to influence a parent about what will be served for dinner or how late he can stay up at night, he becomes the one who needs no one's permission and who often makes the final decision. Children also have another, quite different, vested interested in being helpful to a distressed parent. As satisfying as it is to feel big, important, and in charge, they want desperately to restore the parent to her previous level of functioning so that she can resume praising and supporting their efforts to grow up and empathizing with the bumps in that process. Though this is a motive the child is not consciously aware of, it is as powerful as the feelings of self-importance and being in charge that the youngster is cognizant of directly.

MICHAEL'S MOTHER had become increasingly immobilized by the anxiety her marital separation had stimulated. Michael was seven and his sister three when his father abruptly decided to move out of the house and leave his position as an emergency room physician to become the director of a prestigious private hospital in a distant city. Though she had been aware of mounting tensions in their marriage and had even suggested that they see a marriage counselor a year earlier, Michael's mother felt entirely unprepared for her husband's sudden departure. She had been employed by an art dealer after receiving a master's degree in fine arts at the age of twenty-three. Two years later she met her husband and they were married a year thereafter. She reduced her work hours to half-time and settled comfortably into the role of a new homemaker. Michael was born two weeks after her thirtieth birthday. She and her husband had wanted their first child to be a boy, and she was delighted for herself and for her husband. She left her job to become a full-time mother and wife. Her husband's career was on the rise. Being an emergency room physician meant that he frequently spent long hours, often late into the evening, at work. Their marital relationship grew more distant. Michael's mother immersed herself in being a new mother and in keeping the household running smoothly while her husband devoted longer and longer hours to his career.

She tried talking to him about her need for more closeness and her wish to have another child. Michael's father was an uncommunicative man who found it difficult to discuss almost anything other than his work. The three people he was closest with were also physicians who shared his speciality area of emergency room medicine. They frequently discussed cases, ate together, and played doubles tennis twice a week. He felt increasingly bored at home and found his wife uninteresting. He could not discuss his patients with her, and she showed little curiosity about his work. After nearly eleven years of marriage, he could not recapture the feelings that first attracted him to his wife. When an opportunity for new and exciting professional challenges presented itself, he quickly took it. He told his wife that their marriage had become unworkable and announced his plan to accept the new position and move away.

His wife was stunned. She was in a daze during much of the initial crisis stage of the divorce. Her husband said goodbye to his children, but did not explain that he and his wife were going to be divorced. As with nearly every other aspect of child-rearing, he left it to his wife to tell the children what was happening. But she was too shocked to carry out this painful task. When the youngsters began asking where their father was, all she said was that he was working in a different city and that he was not coming home. It was testimony to the distance in the father–child relationships and his arduous work schedule that it was not until several weeks had gone by after their father left that they began to wonder where he was. In addition, the daily household routine had not changed much. Michael's father regularly sent ample support checks to his wife. She was able to continue being a full-time homemaker.

However, after several months, her initial shock began to wear off. Her fantasy that her husband would have second thoughts about leaving his family and send for them to join him was giving way to an increasing realization that she was in the midst of an irreversible divorce process. He rarely called home and was abrupt with her on the telephone. Her attorney told her that her husband had filed for divorce and that his attorney was moving forward with a comprehensive proposal for the divorce settlement. Her attorney advised her to accept what seemed to be a fair and reasonable financial arrangement along with her having sole custody of the children.

Eight months after they had separated, the divorce became final. This legal event and the concrete details of the settlement seemed to move Michael's mother from feeling stunned while hoping for a reconciliation to a full recognition of the reality of the divorce.

As the divorce process continued into the short-term aftermath stage, Michael's mother became increasingly anxious. She began worrying about whether the next support check would arrive on time. She wondered if the checks would continue coming. The idea that her ex-husband would meet someone and remarry began to loom larger in her mind. She became preoccupied with the fear that after her ex-husband remarried, the support checks would become less frequent, be unilaterally reduced, or just stop coming completely. She had heard (and it is often true) from friends who had been divorced that after a while men, especially after they remarry, are less committed to supporting their former wife and their children from that marriage.

The prospect of being responsible for supporting herself and her two children was frightening. How could she earn enough money to do that? Who would hire her? She had been out of the work force for eight years and felt overwhelmed by the prospect of going back. She imagined having to move from the comfortable, upper-middle-class neighborhood she had lived in for a decade. She conjured up scenarios of having to sell her house and going to a lower-middle-class area across town. Perhaps she would have to go on welfare. These images not only frightened her; she experienced intense feelings of humiliation over the prospect of losing her status as the wife of a well-to-do professional. She began voicing her worries in front of her children. She wondered aloud about where they would live and how she could afford to buy the children clothing.

Michael was keenly aware of his mother's distress. He tried to reassure her by saying, "Everything will be okay, Mom." He also told her that he did not need a lot of clothes and that he could even get a job delivering newspapers or passing out advertising circulars in the neighborhood. He hugged his mother to comfort her and stayed with her as she went over the monthly bills. He also became more cooperative and spontaneously helpful at home. He set the dinner table, cleared the dishes after the meal was done, and took out the garbage without being asked. He waited patiently for his mother to finish putting his little sister to bed, so he could sit with her later in the evening as she ruminated about her financial situation and watched television.

Michael's mother was aware of her son's efforts to comfort her and allay her anxieties. She vaguely knew that he was acting too grown-up. Yet she found a great deal of solace in his attentiveness.

She felt she could count on him to love and care about her. He made her feel less alone with her worries and was genuinely helpful around the house. She was not aware, however, of the gradual erosion of the appropriate generational boundary between her and her son. She was becoming less parental with him in a variety of ways. She discussed with him adult matters such as finances and her need to find a job. She did not discourage her son's promises to get a paper route by pointing out the reality of his being so young. His firm bedtime had disappeared as they stayed up late together after his sister was asleep. There was also the physical intimacy of his giving his mother long, comforting back rubs during these times.

Michael was nearly eight years old and just completing second grade. His teacher reported that Michael was becoming a behavior problem at school. He had begun asking her why he had to do some of the assignments she gave the class. Why did he have to practice his printing when he could already write cursively? Why did he have to ask permission to go to the bathroom? How come she called on another youngster to answer a question when he had his hand up first?

Michael was also having trouble with other boys on the playground during recess. He often insisted that they play a particular game or that he get an extra turn. When his classmates refused, he angrily left the game. Increasingly he spent more time by himself at recess. After school he rarely played with neighborhood children anymore. He claimed that their games were boring and that he was "too old for little kids' stuff." He frequently looked after his sister and became a disciplinarian with her. He told her she could have no dessert unless she helped pick up her toys from the family room floor. Although he was often helpful around the house without being asked, he bridled when his mother told him what to do. Requests that he take a bath or practice his spelling list were met with a stubborn refusal accompanied by long, involved explanations of why it was really not necessary for him to do whatever it was that his mother had asked.

In spite of his precocious maturity, Michael began having terrifying nightmares. He frequently awakened in the middle of the night frightened that a giant was coming to kill him. His mother was becoming increasingly concerned about her son's willfulness at home and at school. She confided in a friend that in some ways

Michael seemed more like an adult than a little boy. She was also worried about her son's unwillingness to play with his friends during the day and his frightening dreams at night. Things did not seem to be going right for her son.

Michael was responding to his mother's clear calls for help and reassurance. She had largely abdicated her parental role vis-à-vis her son in the face of her anxieties. She found his willingness to listen to her concerns and his efforts to soothe and comfort her a warming ray of pleasure in what she feared might become a very bleak situation. In many ways Michael had become a "little man of the house."[4] And he took great pleasure in being elevated to this new adult-like status. He enjoyed giving rein to his developmentally normal wishes to be free of adult restrictions and controls. He relished his position as a seeming co-adult in the household who had no set bedtime, could discipline his sister, and have a determining voice in what would be served for dinner. At a deeper psychological level, he also experienced his closeness with his mother as exciting. Their emotional and even physical intimacy contributed to his sense of being his mother's equal.

However, Michael was paying dearly for these pleasures. His feelings of being like an adult, which were being inadvertently cultivated and strongly reinforced at home, brought him into conflict with his peers and his teacher. The latter, unlike his mother, did not accord Michael the position of being an adult. He was not free to choose what he wanted to do in the classroom. And she expected him to follow her directions and obey the rules. His classmates did not accede to his wishes as his younger sister had to do at home. They were unwilling to have Michael decide what games to play or how they should be played. These realities challenged and frustrated Michael's growing sense of omnipotence, of being the person in charge of any given situation. He responded by becoming argumentative with his teacher and his peers and finally withdrew from participating in activities with the other boys.

The smooth developmental progress he had been making was disrupted. At the same time, he found himself greatly upset by his nightmares of a giant coming to kill him. Dreams of this sort can represent many kinds of psychological conflicts. One possibility here is that Michael's nightmares were expressions of his unconscious fear of punishment for having forbidden feelings. When a boy feels very close to his mother and experiences his position in the postdivorce household as taking his father's place, he can begin to feel guilty. Though this guilt is often below the level of conscious awareness for the child, the punishment he then expects can manifest itself in the disguised form of recurring nightmares. Michael was in the position of having fantasies that many boys entertain come true; he was growing up quickly and enjoying the pleasures of his new adult-like status. Unfortunately, when these commonly held wishes are translated into reality, the psychological costs are usually considerable.

When a divorced parent begins to fashion a new work or social life, the early elementary school child is confronted by another kind of stress. Rather than feeling centrally important to his parent and experiencing the pleasures of being treated almost like an adult as Michael did, the youngster can feel peripheral in her parent's life. This is most upsetting to the child when it is the primary, custodial parent (typically mother) who is creating a new life for herself. It is ironic that at the same time that a mother is making a realistically good adjustment to the divorce, her child may feel that she is losing her. As a woman appropriately invests her time, energy, and interests in her work and perhaps in new social relationships, her youngster in fact usually sees less of her. But it is not simply that the child and mother interact less. A mother who is genuinely interested in her job or career is emotionally involved in it. Similarly, a mother who has a serious dating relationship is emotionally occupied with it. Youngsters often sense these emotional investments and begin to feel comparatively less important to their mother.

At times a custodial parent's work and social commitments take on the quality of defensively escaping from a painful situation. Her job and her romantic relationship(s) become especially important to her because they are being used to ward off intense feelings of loneliness, anger, depression, or anxiety. She throws herself into these activities not so much, or only, because she values them in their own right, but to keep herself from feeling miserable. Her work and/ or dating serve as ballast to keep herself on an even keel in the face of powerful and distressing feelings about the divorce.

Young elementary school children's difficulties adjusting to the emotional shifts they sense in the mother–child relationship as mother becomes more involved in work or social activities differ from those of younger children. Now it is not that unpredictable changes in daily routines are upsetting the youngster. Nor is it that she is unaccustomed to being apart from her mother most of the day; children in elementary school are used to that. By elementary school most children have also become confident of their emotional independence from mother, so it is not necessarily the case that an enmeshed mother–child relationship is being threatened by mother's new emotional commitments. For young elementary school children, it is more likely that feelings of being unimportant and less loved by mother are being stimulated. She begins to feel that she simply does not count as much as she used to, and her self-esteem and feelings of self-worth are correspondingly shaken.

LAURA was five years old when her parents separated. Her mother had become increasingly dissatisfied with her traditional role as the wife of a successful businessman. She had been a secretary in the company her future husband worked for at that time. She was dazzled by his charm and intellect and impressed by clear early signs of his success. She fell in love with him and married when she was twenty-four. She was happy staying at home full-time when their first child, a son, was born four years later. Laura's mother returned to work on a part-time basis when her son was three years old. Laura was born five years after her brother, and her mother again decided to be at home full-time. But she felt herself becoming restless and vaguely dissatisfied with being a full-time wife and mother.

When Laura was two years old, her mother began to work part-time for a firm responsible for setting up conventions for professional societies and businesses. A bright, personable, and well-organized individual, she soon became successful in her new position. She earned a handsome salary even while working only part-time. However, even more important, she delighted in feeling successful in her own right. Success in parenting and running a household were not how she measured her worth. It was the pleasure in having her work recognized that she found enormously gratifying. Being told how competent she was by her supervisor as well as by the people for whom she planned and orchestrated conventions and conferences made her glow with pride.

When she was given more responsibilities for organizing even bigger meetings, and healthy salary increases to go with them, she felt that she was validating her sense of self-worth. She also enjoyed the fringe benefits that came with her work. Traveling to interesting cities, staying at fine hotels, and eating at top-notch restaurants were fun in their own right as well as contributing to her sense of being important. She felt she had outgrown her traditional roles as wife and homemaker. At the same time, she liked the attentions of the men she met in the course of her work, though she had not developed a specific romantic interest. She began to view her marriage as confining and as an unpleasant reminder of her previous identity.

There were no overt conflicts in her marriage and for the most part she had a friendly, if somewhat distant and not particularly loving, relationship with her husband. Laura's father was a prominent businessman in his community. He had become a senior vice-president at his large firm, and earned a substantial income. He was a man with traditional values and was increasingly unhappy with his wife spending long hours away from home. It was her lack of time with the children, he complained, that bothered him the most. But he was also dismayed by the lack of emotional and physical intimacy in his marriage. Laura's father recognized his wife's desire to have a career and said that he supported her in her efforts to achieve fulfillment in that domain. He reluctantly came to terms with the fact that his wife's serious commitment to her work and the corresponding reduction it led to in the extent of her availability to her children and husband would have to be accepted if their marriage was to continue.

He was a sensitive and caring father who began to arrange to spend more time with his son and daughter as his wife was home less often. When his wife began to raise the possibility of divorce, he was flabbergasted. He had thought that their relationship was cordial, and the atmosphere at home was pleasant most of the time. He felt he had acceded to and had even become somewhat supportive of his wife's wishes to pursue her career. He could not fathom why she wanted a divorce. However, he realized that she was serious about separating and began to make arrangements to move out of the family residence. He planned to buy a home close by enough to make joint physical custody easier to implement.

His wife did not pressure him to leave quickly and was in full agreement with their sharing custody of the children. She valued her husband's parenting abilities and wanted the excellent relationship he had with the children to continue. She also thought that split week custody (three and a half days at each parent's home) would fit well with her plan to increase her work schedule to full-time. Laura's father had found a suitable house about a mile and a half from his former home. A month before he was to move, he and his wife told the children about their plan to separate and divorce. After he left the family home, the joint physical custody agreement was immediately put into effect. He arranged for a female college student to be in his house from the time the children returned from school until he came home at dinnertime.

The immediate crisis stage of the divorce proceeded with minimal hostilities between the parents. Ten months after they separated, the divorce became final. Laura's parents remained on reasonably comfortable terms with each other and were able to communicate well. They were both flexible about the joint custody schedule and kept each other apprised of how the children were doing as they moved back and forth between the two homes.

Laura's initial reaction to her parents' separation was one of surprise and disbelief. She had known other children at school whose parents had gotten divorced but had never thought her parents would split up. They hardly ever argued! For several months after the separation, Laura kept asking each parent why they were getting a divorce. Her mother had told her that she and Laura's father just were not in love anymore. She said she did not want to be married and would be a lot happier living her own life without her husband. She told her daughter openly that she had been the one to ask for the divorce. Laura's father shared his confusion about the divorce with his daughter. He pointed out that he had not been unhappy being married but that Laura's mother was. He thoughtfully was able to add several months later that when one person was unhappy being married, pretty soon the whole family gets unhappy, too. Both parents emphasized their love for their children and the fact that the children would still be living part of the time with each parent even though the parents were not together anymore.

Laura's struggles to deny the reality and permanence of her parents' separation and her driven need to question them about it subsided after four months. A deep feeling of sadness took their place. However, she continued to do well at school and was able to stay involved with her peers. By the short-term aftermath stage of the divorce, Laura had become accustomed to the shared custody arrangement, which involved she and her brother living with each parent for half the week. However, she found her mother's increased work hours and greater frequency of out-of-town travel quite difficult. She had trouble falling asleep for two or three nights before these nearly monthly trips. She also returned to feeling intensely sad during the three to four days her mother was gone. Although she was at her father's home at these times and enjoyed a close and loving relationship with him, she felt the absence of her mother acutely.

When Laura was six years old, a year after her parents had separated, her mother became involved in a serious dating relationship with a man whom she had met through work. Though she had no plans to remarry, and in fact was quite committed to staying single, the relationship grew more close. Her partner was over for dinner frequently and occasionally spent the night at her home. Though Laura was unfailingly polite to him, she often left the room he and her mother were in to play in her bedroom by herself. In addition to looking sad a great deal of the time, Laura began to be quietly demanding of her mother when her dating partner was not visiting. She poignantly asked her mother to play tic-tac-toe, go for a bicycle ride, or cook her favorite dinner. When her mother told her that she was busy and could not do what her daughter was asking, Laura sadly went off to her room to play with her Barbie dolls. She almost never got angry nor did she cry or persist in trying to get her mother to do what she wanted. She did, however, develop frequent stomachaches, which at times kept her home from school and other times made her feel she had to stay in her house and rest rather than go out to play with her friends. These episodes often coincided with one of her mother's out-of-town business trips. Laura's teacher had no complaints about her schoolwork, however, or her peer relations. She did decide to contact both of Laura's parents about their daughter's obvious and constant sadness. Sometimes Laura expressed her feelings by writing short poems or drawing pictures. Her poems were about girls who were all alone with nothing to eat and no one to take care of them. She made drawings in which a girl lived all alone in a big house. It was dark and snowy outside, and the girl huddled near the fireplace to get warm. Laura's parents and her teacher grew increasingly concerned about her unremitting sadness.

Laura is the kind of youngster who usually does not provoke a worried or concerned reaction in adults. Her academic progress and her peer relationships were developmentally on course. She was not a behavior problem in school or at home. For the most part she suffered quietly and made few complaints. Her comparatively silent depressive reaction could easily have been dismissed as shyness or a lack of assertiveness. Girls in both early and later elementary school grades are more likely than boys to display this kind of stress response. The absence of obvious disruption in their development and the fact that they do not tax the patience of parents or teachers through irritating or aggressive behaviors make it unlikely that their emotional pain will be recognized.

However, Laura's pervasive sadness and her difficulty falling asleep along with intermittent stomachaches especially before her mother's trips were indicative of a depressive reaction. Laura felt increasingly unimportant to her mother. Her neediness was expressed in her pleas for her mother to do things with her. The poems and drawings she did at school were vehicles for expressing her intense loneliness and feelings of emotional deprivation. Many different kinds of conflicts can be at the root of physical complaints such as headaches and stomachaches when there is no medical reason for them. It is likely that Laura's stomachaches were a reflection of the hunger she felt for her mother's affection as well as an underlying anger toward her for not fulfilling this need.

This combination of a powerful wish to be emotionally close to a parent and anger over not having this desire met can create serious conflicts within a youngster. Because the feelings at play are in opposition to one another (that is, the wish to be close versus the urge to express anger), the child frequently buries an awareness of the conflict deep in his mind. Usually only one part of the conflict is expressed directly while the child remains unaware of the other part. The latter is hidden from view but surfaces in disguised forms. Such a conflict can also result in the anger being felt while the wishes for affection are kept out of awareness. In this case, the child appears obstinate, irritable, or even enraged while the underlying desire to feel close to the parent is not obvious. This form of the conflict is more typical of boys and comes to the attention of mental health professionals more readily.

The short-term aftermath stage of divorce often brings disruption of parent–child relationships. They may be of the sort Michael experienced where a youngster's normal wishes to be grown-up dovetail all too well with a distressed parent's own need to escape painful feelings of loneliness or anxiety. The result is a skewed and enmeshed parent–child–relationship that interrupts the child's progress by preoc-cupying him and distracting him from his developmental agenda. Rather than being overly close to a parent who is upset, the child may begin to feel peripheral to the emotional life of her parent as Laura did. The youngster loses a sense of being valued and loved, and depressive reactions can occur.

These difficulties always take place in the larger context of the loss experience that divorce represents for early elementary school children. The loss of the sense of the family as a unit and the partial or complete loss of the relationship between the child and his noncusto-dial parent are always at issue. Though youngsters tend to be most vulnerable to these losses during the immediate crisis stage of the divorce process, the reactions are also frequently in evidence, directly or as a backdrop, in the short-term aftermath stage as well.

The Long-Range Period

The picture of the long-range period of the divorce process can be quite varied for early elementary school children. The youngster who was an older preschooler or had just begun elementary school when his parents separated may still recall and continue to live with the pain of the multiple losses divorce brings for children of this age. They may miss their father and yearn for the family to be together again. With the separation only two years or so in the past, they are likely to be living in a single-mother household with all the opportunities it provides for an enmeshed parent–child relationship. For these young-sters, the divorce experience and its attendant sources of stress is still very much alive and real.

However, in some cases the marital separation may have occurred during the child's infancy so that the youngster has no conscious memories of life when his parents were married. He does not experience feelings of loss over the dissolution of the family unit or the quality of his relationship with father, when he used to live at home. Similarly, having to give up a particularly close relationship that a child and single-parent formed when the latter begins to date or remarries may not be a source of stress. The early elementary school child whose parents separated when he was an infant and whose mother remarried when he was a young preschooler usually does not have the opportunity to become significantly enmeshed with his custodial mother. Whatever disruption that remarriage might have caused at the time it occurred (see chapter 7) often has been handled by the parent and stepparent and has faded into the recesses of the child's barely recollected experiences. For the early elementary school child in this situation, things as they currently are seem always to have been that way.

BARBARA's parents separated when she was almost a year old. They had been married for three years. Her father had been an immature, impulsive man who had great difficulty holding a job. He had blamed these problems on his co-workers and his bosses and had taken out most of his frustration and anger on his wife. He had criticized her constantly and at times had become physically abusive, pushing and slapping her. He did not want a child and found Barbara's normal infant crying annoying. He also resented his wife's attention to their young daughter.

Barbara's mother was frightened by her husband's violent temper and his abuse of her. When she was twenty-three she moved out of the family apartment to live with her parents. She felt she needed their financial support, the child care they could help provide for Barbara, and safety from her husband. She returned to school and pursued an accounting certificate at a junior college. She also worked part-time at an all-night convenience store. During the immediate crisis stage of the divorce, Barbara's father angrily harassed his wife with frequent telephone calls. He had begun drinking heavily and could not hold any sort of job. With her parents' support, Barbara's mother retained an attorney. Her main goal was to prevent any harm coming to herself or her daughter. Since there had been no property and nearly no money that the couple had shared, the only thing of concern to Barbara's mother was obtaining sole custody and monitoring any visiting arrangements between father and daughter. She and her attorney offered Barbara's father supervised weekly visits that were to take place in the home of Barbara's parents. He angrily refused and increased his telephone harassment of his wife. Barbara's parents changed the telephone number and kept it unlisted. After several months, Barbara's father moved to another city and had no further contact with his wife or daughter.

The second stage of the divorce process was calm and pleasurable for Barbara and her mother. Barbara was in the care of a loving grandmother while her mother was at school or at work. She had a grandfather who played with her frequently after he came home from work. Barbara's mother was adjusting well to the divorce, too. She felt very much supported by her parents and was grateful to them for all of their help. She was comfortable in the knowledge that her daughter was receiving excellent care during the day and was able to parent Barbara effectively after she came home in the late afternoons. There were, however, the sorts of tensions one can expect from this arrangement. Barbara's mother and grandmother disagreed at times about how long the baby should be left to cry, how warmly she needed to be dressed, and what foods she should eat. Barbara's mother chafed under the burden of knowing that she was living in her parents' home rather than in her own. And old adolescent conflicts erupted from time to time between Barbara's mother and her parents, especially over how late she should stay out with friends or on a date.

Barbara's mother looked forward to finishing her schooling, getting a full-time job, and moving to her own apartment. When Barbara was three, her mother completed her schoolwork and received an accounting certificate. She immediately found a good job at a large accounting firm and three months later moved to her own apartment with Barbara. She started her daughter in nursery school half-days when Barbara turned four. During the afternoons, Barbara's grandmother continued to care for her. Barbara's mother began dating a man she had met through the church's singles activities. After they had known each other a year, they married and bought a house soon afterwards. Barbara was nearly four years old when they married. As is the case for many very young children, Barbara had accepted her mother's marriage fairly easily and began to develop her own relationship with her new stepfather. The divorce process was in its long-range period before Barbara had even begun elementary school.

When Barbara was six and in first grade, her little brother was born. Her mother and stepfather had prepared her well for her role as a big sister. That and the fact that she was old enough to realistically become her mother's big helper made it possible to participate pleasurably in her brother's entry into the family. While she had some feelings of rivalry, she was also sufficiently older than her baby brother so that competitiveness between them was not especially problematic. Although Barbara knew that she had a "dad" living far away, she never heard from him and rarely asked any questions about him. When she was five she spontaneously and naturally began calling her stepfather "Daddy." Given her age at the time her parents separated, the lack of contact with her biological father, and her acquiring a caring stepfather while still very young, he was in fact her real psychological daddy. Barbara progressed well developmentally.

Barbara was not subject to any prolonged divorce-related stresses. Her mother's move back home provided her with a consistent as well as loving daily routine. She was sheltered from her parents' hostilities by living in her grandparents' home, and her father's moving out of town made Barbara's mother more comfortable as well. Her mother was not flooded with painful feelings nor was she overwhelmed by being a single parent; she had the support and help of her parents. Nor did Barbara and her mother form an enmeshed relationship. Barbara's mother pursued her own preparation for a career, and she dated. The presence and involvement of Barbara's grandparents also made it less likely for an overly close mother–daughter relationship to develop. All of these factors smoothed the way for Barbara to accept sharing her mother with a new man and to build her own very daughter-like relationship with him.

Children who are very young when their parents separate tend to have the fewest difficulties in the long-run.[5] In Barbara's case, her mother was able to cushion the stresses that could have been problematic (such as inconsistent caretaking, parental warfare) by making use of the support her parents could give. Some divorced mothers do not have the sort of relationship with their parents that would permit this kind of arrangement. Others feel it would be too humiliating to "go home" or are worried about stirring up their own adolescent conflicts with their parents over control and autonomy. In fact, the appropriate temporary use of such extended family arrangements is often valuable and serves to protect children and their custodial parent from unnecessary and potentially debilitating divorce distress.

While Barbara was spared the multiple stresses that the divorce process can bring for young children, others must endure the accumulation of these stresses over the long-range period. Among the most corrosive sources of long-term environmental stress for children is parental warfare. When parents fight during the early stage of their divorce, early elementary school children often experience it as underscoring the demise of their family unit. It therefore provokes feelings of intense sadness. However, as hostilities between parents continues, children frequently become fearful and combative. They develop frightening fantasies of a parent's or even their own anger getting out of control and hurting someone. They also express their anger and try to cope with it actively by becoming aggressive with peers, siblings, and/or parents. Youngsters resent their parents' attacks on each other and, at the same time, learn by observing them that the direct expression of anger is an acceptable way to behave. This brings them into ever-increasing conflict with parents, teachers, and other children.

LARRY was two years old when his parents separated. His mother worked as a paralegal assistant before his birth and returned to work full-time shortly after the marital separation. Larry's father was an assistant superintendent of a large public school system. He was a demanding, self-centered man who had not been able to come to terms with sharing his wife's time and affection with their young son. He became increasingly critical of her shortly after Larry's birth and frequently derogated her for not meeting his needs. His wife found this behavior intolerable but hoped that he would eventually adjust to the addition of a child to their relationship. She was twenty-four when they were married and twenty-seven when they separated; her husband was three years older than she. Larry's father became more unhappy with their marriage and felt that his wife was too immersed in her care of their son, too inattentive to his desires, and maddeningly disorganized in how she planned her time. She, on the other hand, found her husband immature, self-absorbed, and critical. She was miserable in her marriage. She was also concerned that if she and her husband continued to stay together, Larry would turn out just like his father.

She filed for divorce and asked her husband to move out of their house. He was relieved by her decision but was also infuriated by her wish that he leave. He liked his home and had spent a great deal of time making it just the way he wanted it; he had set up a workshop in the basement, built a study for himself down there, and constructed an elaborate wooden deck off the family room glass door-wall. He had been the one to select the paint and wallpaper for nearly every room in the house. He did not like the idea of renting an apartment, which could not possibly duplicate his comfortable home. Paying rent also seemed a ridiculous, added expense. He insisted on staying in the home, setting up a bed in the basement, and living there. His attorney supported his remaining at home to strengthen his bargaining position in coming to a financial settlement. Larry's mother was enraged by her husband's plan and felt helpless to get him to leave. Their home became like an armed camp. She slept in her second-floor bedroom, her husband lived in the basement, and they saw each other on the first floor as they took turns using the kitchen and watching television or listening to music in the family room.

The first floor of the house became the battleground. They argued frequently and bitterly whenever they saw each other there. They called each other names, derogated one another, and occasionally pushed or slapped each other. This living arrangement continued for nearly a year. Larry's mother finally could no longer tolerate it, and after obtaining several concessions through her attorney, she moved to an apartment with her son. The divorce became final when Larry was four years old. His parents had joint legal custody. Larry lived with his mother and saw his father every other weekend for the full weekend and one weekend day on the alternate weekends.

Larry began attending a nursery school/day-care center full-time when he was two and a half, and continued there half-days after starting kindergarten (which was only in the mornings) at age five. His schedule and daily routines were consistent, and his mother was doing well at her job. However, his parents continued to argue and bitterly assail one another even as the divorce moved into the short-term aftermath stage ushered in by the legal divorce decree, and when each of their schedules stabilized. Larry's father was frequently late with his support checks. Larry's mother would wait for a few days after it was due and then angrily telephone him asking where the check was. These calls quickly deteriorated into venomous mutual name-calling and faultfinding. When Larry's father came to pick up his son, he waited in his car as he and his ex-wife agreed. However, he blew the horn furiously if his son was more than a few minutes late coming out of the house. Larry's mother took great pleasure in antagonizing her former husband by not having Larry ready exactly on time. However, she became enraged when he blew the car horn and made obscene gestures at him from the front door as Larry walked to his father's car.

When Larry was six, his mother began a serious dating relationship with a man she had met at a friend's party. A few months later they agreed that Al should move in with her and her son. He was an executive with a large chemical producing company and had an ex-wife and a daughter about Larry's age. Larry's father was enraged by his ex-wife taking a live-in partner. He claimed it was bad for Larry's emotional development and would demonstrate to a young, impressionable boy that "promiscuity" was an acceptable life style.

When Larry was seven, his father reopened the issue of his son living with his ex-wife and filed a motion to have Larry live with him and see his mother every other weekend. His ex-wife was furious. She saw her former husband's legal action as harassment and attributed it to his enduring wish to hurt her and deprive her of any happiness. She countered legally by asking the court to restrict her son's time with his father, claiming that his father's anger was having a negative effect on Larry. Both parents talked about this conflict, as well as previous ones, in the presence of their son. They openly and angrily derogated one another in front of Larry, each describing the other as a miserable human being and an awful parent.

It is not surprising that in light of the stress of his parents' ongoing warfare Larry was having many difficulties. The hostilities between his parents had been going on with great intensity for five years, ever since he was two. And since their separation, they had been all too comfortable disregarding the effects of their rage on Larry and frequently using him to vent their anger at each other. Even the current legal battle placed Larry squarely in the middle of his warring parents.

During Larry's late toddler and preschool years, which were during the first two stages of the divorce, he became a fearful, timid child. He worried about kidnappers and about the apartment in which he and his mother lived burning down and killing her. He was frightened by the loud noises trucks and buses made and cried easily when he fell or scraped a knee or hand. He was often somewhat shy and withdrawn with other children at his day-care center. Shortly after his mother's partner moved in with them, he started wetting his bed several times a week.

Now, as a second grader, he had become increasingly angry and aggressive at school. He used magic markers to scribble on other children's clothes, pushed smaller youngsters to the ground, and occasionally took an article of clothing from them, such as a glove or hat, and refused to give it back. When he was not physically hostile in these ways, he used his excellent intellect as a weapon to verbally attack, tease, and belittle his classmates. At home, he criticized his mother's cooking, demanded that she buy certain kinds of cookies and that she order pizza twice a week, and told her that her live-in partner was a slob. When he was not attacking his mother with these specific complaints and demands, he sarcastically criticized her for forgetting to pick up milk on the way home from work, making a wrong turn while driving, watching "dumb" television programs, wearing ugly clothes, and so on. His mother felt she was constantly being barraged with criticisms. Al tried on several occasions to get Larry to stop his angry attacks on his mother, but this only led to Larry sullenly withdrawing to his room muttering, "Who does he think he is? I don't have to listen to him." His mother openly talked to Al, with Larry in earshot, about how much like her ex-husband Larry had become. She found herself beginning to dislike her son at times and knew that something was going terribly wrong in his development.

The continuing stress of bitter parental warfare was taking its toll on Larry. During his preschool years he had reacted to the hostilities between his parents by becoming fearful and withdrawing from active involvement in peer relationships at his nursery school/day-care center. After Al moved in with his mother and him, Larry had begun to wet his bed. Though bed wetting has many causes, including physical ones, in this case it seemed to be a way of expressing his conflicts over partially losing his mother's attention and their closeness when she became involved in a serious, live-in love relationship. As he moved through the early elementary school grades, Larry became more active in his attempts to cope with these reactions to the parental rage that continued to suffuse his world. Rather than being fearful and withdrawn, he went on the offensive both at school and at home. He adopted his father's bitingly sarcastic and critical style vis-à-vis his mother. He used his classmates as whipping boys for the anger he felt toward both of his parents. He had become a chronically angry, hostile little boy.

Larry's hostility was a defense against underlying feelings of sadness and fear. He had openly displayed his distress when he was a preschooler, but as a second grader, he could no longer tolerate the passive, helpless position of being always frightened and unhappy. He became assertive to the point of being combative both verbally and physically. He identified with what looked like, through his young eyes, his father's strength. His father never looked sad or worried. Instead he was always on the offensive, verbally attacking his ex-wife, angrily derogating her in Larry's presence, and occasionally pushing and slapping her when they were in the immediate crisis stage of their divorce. Modeling himself after his father alleviated Larry's painful feelings of fear and helplessness. It also made him feel close to his father and more masculine. Unfortunately this style of coping with his fears and sadness brought him into serious conflicts with his classmates, school authorities, and his mother.

Many boys can become like their father as the normal process of identifying with him proceeds during elementary school and on into adolescence. It also helps a boy feel close to his somewhat distant (emotionally and/or physically) father. However, these identifications can drive a wedge between a boy and his mother when he displays some of the behaviors she found unacceptable in her former husband. At times mothers are vigilantly on the lookout for these sorts of identifications and may even magnify them in their own minds. The result can be that she then loses sight of her love for her son and becomes more distant from him or critical of him, which adds to the youngster's distress.

Young elementary school girls whose parents' divorce has reached the long-range period are usually among the children best adjusted to marital disruption. The divorce occurred early enough in their lives for feelings of loss of the family unit or of a close relationship with father not to be remembered; or they might never have existed in the very young child's experience. Therefore, a distant visiting relationship with father can seem like the natural order of things. And the great majority of custodial mothers have made good adjustments to their divorce by the time it has entered its long-range phase. However, ongoing parental warfare can cause girls great emotional distress. If hostilities between parents are present in the long-range period, a girl of this age, whose parents separated years before, may cry easily, look very sad, withdraw from peer relationships, and/or have trouble sleeping. Their distress takes the form of a depressive reaction rather than the angry picture Larry presented.

A more common problem for early elementary school girls is a major disruption in their close relationship with mother when she remarries. Girls generally have a more difficult time than boys achieving the necessary degree of emotional separation from their mother during the preschool years, especially when a loving relationship with father or a father-substitute is unavailable. Girls and mothers can easily gravitate toward one another and begin to establish an overly close relationship, as each seeks protection from the stresses of divorce. This closeness is supported by society's valuing a strong emotional bond between mothers and daughters and is further buttressed by the normal processes of a girl's identification with her mother. Without a caring relationship between father and daughter or a loving marital relationship between a woman and her husband, the typical factors modulating this mother–daughter closeness are not present. The relief from divorce stresses that each can obtain from their close relationship drives mothers and daughters even further together.

JAN and her mother lived by themselves in what had been the family home from the time her parents separated. She was an eighteen-month-old toddler at that time. Her mother was twenty-four and her father twenty-eight when they married. Two years later they decided to divorce. Her father initiated the separation shortly after receiving his master's degree in business administration. He had returned to school to pursue an advanced degree after having worked as a computer programmer for several years following graduation from college. Jan's mother was an administrative assistant in the staff benefits office of a large university. She was a somewhat shy, inhibited woman who had little dating or sexual experience when she met her future husband. She had become pregnant after they had dated for six months. They were married three months later. Neither really wanted to get married, but Jan's mother could not tolerate the idea of obtaining an abortion. Jan's father reluctantly went through with the marriage, but it was soon clear to both of them that it would not work out. Rather than spending their lives in an empty, loveless marriage, they decided to divorce.

Jan's father moved to the West Coast shortly after the separation to take a lucrative position with a rapidly expanding computer software company. Jan's mother continued working full-time at the university. She earned nearly $20,000 a year and had excellent fringe benefits. The immediate crisis and short-term aftermath stages of their divorce were relatively stress-free. They quickly reached a divorce settlement that consisted of Jan being in her mother's custody, her father coming into town and renting a hotel room once a year for a week-long visit with his young daughter, and quite modest child support from Jan's father. In return for the relatively low child support (given his high starting salary), Jan's father agreed to give up his share of the equity in the house they co-owned.

Jan's mother was delighted to be out of a dead-end marriage. She earned a good income with prospects for advancement to more senior and even better paying administrative positions, and was quite confident of being able to support and raise her daughter on her own. Her love for her daughter gave her a full feeling of emotional satisfaction. She proudly noted each new accomplishment her daughter achieved and spent hours playing with her, teaching her, and taking her to museums, plays, and out for dinner. Jan's mother felt comfortably independent and was in no hurry to become involved in a romantic relationship. She was emotionally stable and did not need to use her daughter for special support.

They had settled into the long-range period of divorce easily. Jan was an assertive, outgoing girl who was comfortable both with adults and youngsters her own age. Her teachers from nursery school on had reported that she was an engaging, bubbly youngster who could work independently or follow directions with equal ease. This began to change, however, midway through second grade. Her mother had begun a serious dating relationship toward the end of Jan's year in first grade. Jim worked as a laboratory technician at the hospital affiliated with the university. He and Jan's mother met while taking sailing lessons through the university's sailing club. Though Jan's mother had not been looking for a husband, she was thrilled with her relationship with Jim. He was a thoughtful, considerate man, who seemed to be deeply in love with her and was genuinely fond of Jan. They married in the late fall when Jan was in second grade.

Jan had just turned eight and had become uncharacteristically sullen at home. Her cheerful, cooperative disposition was replaced by a critical attitude toward her mother. Jan snapped at her when dinner was a bit later than usual or a favorite pair of jeans had not been washed yet. She complained regularly about being asked to set the dinner table, make her bed, or help out with the gardening. Minor irritations led her to yell at her mother, angrily stomp to her bedroom, and slam the door. This occurred when her mother did not hear exactly what Jan was saying and asked her to repeat it or was a bit slow in answering some questions her daughter had asked because she was thinking of what to say. On the other hand,

Jan continued to do well in school, got along splendidly with her teacher, and played frequently with her friends. Her mother had expected to hear from Jan's teacher that she had also become edgy and uncooperative at school, but her teacher had noticed no changes at all. Their parent-teacher conference revealed that Jan had continued to do very well both academically and socially.

It became clear to Jan's mother that something was bothering her daughter. She planned a serious discussion with Jan to try to get at the root of what was upsetting her. She told Jan that she had noticed her acting irritable and angry. She said that she wanted to find out what was going on so that she could help Jan feel better. Her daughter denied being upset about anything and fidgeted uneasily during their talk. Her mother calmly gave her examples of how Jan had acted as though something were bothering her. Jan responded by blaming her mother for not listening to her and giving her too many chores. When her mother pointed out, logically, that she was not asking Jan to do any more than she usually did, her daughter insisted that she had. She tried several other times to have this kind of open discussion with Jan, but they were unproductive. Jan sat sullenly staring at the floor or out the window, and steadfastly denied that anything was wrong. Jan's mother became increasingly worried about the changes she observed in her daughter and felt frustrated in her efforts to help her.

Jan had traversed the first two stages of her parents' divorce with no disturbances in her development. These periods had been relatively quiescent. Her parents had not gone to war with one another, and her mother had adjusted well to their separation. She was able to arrange for consistent child care and she provided a comfortable, loving atmosphere at home because she, herself, was feeling good about her place in life. Jan had been only a year and a half old when her parents separated so that she was not burdened with feelings that she had lost the sense of her family being together. Nor did she have to cope with sadness over losing her relationship with her father. As a preschooler and then later as an early elementary school child, Jan's experience of her family, her daily routines, her relationship with her father, and her relationship with her mother were all exactly as they had always been in her recorded memory.

However, her mother's marriage was a big change for Jan. She and her mother had grown very close over the six years when there had been just the two of them living together. Jan's mother had a good job that she enjoyed and had not turned to her daughter out of her own need to cope with painful feelings about the divorce. She did not feel burdened by her single-parent role, and in fact, took great pleasure in raising her daughter. Instead, Jan felt overly close to her mother in subtle ways. First, she was used to having her mother's undivided attention when they were together. There was an exclusivity about their relationship, at least from Jan's young perspective. Second, Jan had not been able to modulate her feelings of closeness to her mother because there was no other adult whom she loved. All her emotional investment was in her feelings for her mother. It was not that she was a dependent little girl who could not separate from her mother or form relationships with other children and her teachers. To the contrary, she was an outgoing, socially accomplished youngster. However, her secure home base consisted entirely of her exclusive relationship with her mother.

When Jan's mother married, the mother–daughter relationship was altered. She no longer was the focal point of her mother's attentions at home. Their day-to-day interactions became different in many small but cumulatively important ways. Conversations at mealtimes, evening hours, and weekend activities now all involved Jan sharing her mother's attention and affections with her stepfather. There was less one-on-one mother–daughter time. Jan's preferences for what to have for dinner, which television programs to watch, or what to do on weekends were less likely to be fulfilled as there was now another person's wishes to be taken into account. Each of these issues seemed trivial, yet collectively they added up to a major change in the character of the mother–daughter relationship. And Jan resented these changes. She became irritable and angry, but she was unaware of why she had those feelings. Her mother was still loving and attentive, her stepfather was caring and unintrusive with her, and no one was acting inappropriately. There was no obvious reason for Jan to feel as she did. No one could put their finger on what was upsetting her.

The trajectory of child development in the long-range period of divorce is quite varied. Many youngsters have made an excellent adjustment to their parents' divorce. However, other early elementary school children are burdened by cumulative divorce-related stresses that take their toll on developmental progress. Some children achieve a good adaptation temporarily only to be distressed by events, such as remarriage, in the long-range period.

Recognizing Distress in Early Elementary School Children

Early elementary school children can display signs of distress similar to those observed in preschoolers. Loss of developmental accomplishments or failure to achieve them, emotional lability, anger, fear, anxiety, sadness, and withdrawal are all possible manifestations of distress in young elementary school children. However, there are several signs of emotional upset that are especially common among them.

Sadness is by far the most common stress reaction to divorce among children in the early elementary school grades. It can be displayed in obvious ways such as crying, looking sad, and saying that they feel sad or lonely. But sadness can take more disguised forms as well. A child may become overly quiet, draw pictures with figures crying or being all alone, or talk wistfully about pleasant memories of previous family vacations or times with his father. The overall impression one gets is that the child seems unusually subdued or unhappy.

Sometimes sadness is hidden from view as children try to protect themselves from feeling it directly. The youngster may deny that the divorce is occurring or believe firmly that the parents will eventually reconcile and get back together. Children of this age also can become combative or provocative with peers, teachers, and parents as ways of warding off underlying feelings of sadness. These defenses may at times be the only clear indication that the child is wrestling with feelings of sadness. However, these defenses rarely work perfectly. The parent who recognizes that denial and anger are common defenses against sadness can usually spot overt expressions of this unhappiness that surface from time to time.

Depressive reactions are also a typical response of early elementary school children to their parents' divorce. Sadness, or the defenses against it, is one prominent component of this phenomenon. It also includes being preoccupied by sad thoughts that can interfere with schoolwork, a withdrawal from previously pleasurable activities such as playing with peers and pursuing special interests (for example, playing with certain toys or following a sports team), and a loss of self-esteem that can show up in self-deprecating attitudes and comments. A child who is experiencing a depressive reaction is more than sad; he is feeling awful about everything, including himself, and can find little joy in his life.

Anger is also an indicator of distress in early elementary school children. It may be a defense against sadness or it can reflect the child's rage from other sources as well: anger over one parent being hurtful toward the other, resentment toward a parent for not giving the child "enough" undivided attention, and anger as a style of interacting learned by seeing the parents fight. Children can express their anger directly and clearly at a parent by yelling, criticizing, or name-calling. However, more frequently an angry youngster will retarget his rage toward a safer object such as a classmate or a neighborhood child. At times the anger is manifested more covertly through whining, complaining, "accidentally" spilling drinks repetitively, "forgetting" not to draw with crayons on their bedroom walls, and the like. Or the child may become uncooperative, sullen, and obstinate.

A youngster's own anger, especially towards parents whom he also loves, is not only a sign of ongoing distress. In addition, it exacerbates it. To become angry at a parent may in the child's mind result in the parent being hurt, physical punishment, abandonment, or a loss of parental love. Youngsters of this age are quite capable of producing frightening fantasies of what the consequences of their rage might be. This is why children "choose" (not consciously or by plan) disguised ways of expressing anger toward a parent. Picking on another child, complaining, becoming uncooperative at home, having "accidents" are nearly always indirect manifestations of a child's anger toward a parent. Headaches and stomachaches without a medical cause can be the result of such underlying anger. The child experiences fear and/or guilt about his anger toward a loved parent that cannot be expressed directly. Instead it is automatically held in, and the resulting tension produces physical symptoms.

General anxiety is also a sign of distress in early elementary school children. As noted earlier, this is often reflected in frequent nervous habits rather than a fear of some specific event or object. Instead of being frightened of the dark or being separated from one's mother, the youngster may bite her fingernails, frequently tug at an article of clothing, scratch herself repetitively, or chew on strands of her hair. These behaviors often are not in response to a particular situation, though they can become more frequent and obvious at certain times. Getting ready to leave home for school, preparing to visit the noncustodial parent, or bedtime can exacerbate these signs of anxiety. The anxiety is often due to private, internal conflicts of which the child herself is usually unaware. They are below the level of consciousness and are difficult for parents to figure out without the help of a mental health professional.

Fear is a less common form of distress in early elementary school children than it is for preschoolers or toddlers. It is nearly always based on the youngster's fantasies (exceptions include a realistically dangerous environment due to intense and impulse-ridden parental warfare or neighborhood crime). Some fears continue to be part of the "normal phobias" of early childhood discussed in chapter 6. These include fears of the dark, of heights, and of sudden loud noises. However, children of divorce, when fearful at all, are apt to worry about other things as well, such as a parent being hurt in a car accident, someone coming to kidnap them, being left alone briefly when a parent goes outside to mow the lawn or chat with a next-door neighbor, or not having enough to eat. These are not normal phobias and usually emerge as the result of divorce-induced fantasies based on parental hostilities (leading to fear of someone being hurt), custody battles (leading to fear of being kidnapped), and the fact that one parent has already left the home (leading to fears of being abandoned by the other parent or not having enough to eat).

The *loss of developmental accomplishments or the failure to achieve them* are less typical signs of distress for early elementary school children than for infants, toddlers, and preschoolers. By elementary school many earlier achievements have been consolidated. And the child has emotionally made a partial shift in his investment from home to friends and school. Nonetheless, young elementary school children are still vulnerable to regressions in several of the domains listed in chapter 6. The child may lose accomplishments in the areas of sleeping, eating, toilet-training, and social relationships. A youngster may begin having trouble sleeping without a parent nearby, restrict the food he will eat to the few things he liked as a preschooler, or begin wetting his bed again at night. In addition to loss of developmental achievements, a child may be unable to progress to new ones. An early elementary school child who cannot become comfortable being away from home all day at school, nearly always prefers to be with adults than with other youngsters, is unable to develop stable friendships, or has trouble interacting with more than one youngster at a time is having difficulty attaining appropriate developmental accomplishments. Often sadness, a depressive reaction, anger, and/or anxiety may be contributing to these problems.

Unlike the signs of distress for infants, toddlers, and preschoolers, these indicators (that is, sadness, depressive reactions) are rarely manifestations of the normal ups and downs of child development. They may be transient and disappear spontaneously after a month or two, come and go intermittently, or persist, become more intense, and interfere increasingly with a child's developmental progress and sense of emotional well-being. But regardless of their course, they are nearly always signs of undue distress. When they have lasted for over three months or are clearly compromising the child's capacity to get on with his developmental agenda and feel good, they warrant a parent's special attention and help.

9

►◄

Helping Early Elementary School Children Cope

Parents and other adults who have contact with early elementary school children can be helpful when they are aware of the nature of the divorce stresses that children confront. Parental warfare, the emotional upset of a parent (especially the primary, custodial parent), the loss (partial or complete) of the child's relationship with the noncustodial parent, and the custodial parent's becoming involved in a serious dating relationship or remarrying are the major environmental sources of stress for children of this age. Whenever possible (with the obvious exception of dating and marriage), it is in the child's best interest for parents to avoid or minimize these stressful circumstances.

Internal sources of stress are also important. The child's increased cognitive capacities permit him to construct frightening fantasies. These include fantasies of someone being hurt by a parent's or his own anger, or being abandoned with no one to care for him. A child may also worry about his custodial mother having enough money for groceries and to pay the rent or mortgage. These are frequently fueled by her own, often obvious, distress about financial matters. However, even more common to the early elementary school years are egocentric beliefs about aspects of the divorce that result in the child feeling bad, unlovable, or unimportant. The developmentally normal tendency to ascribe to oneself the reason for events happening (or not happening) can cause great emotional distress. Youngsters of this age often blame themselves for their parents' marital strife, experience their father not living at home with them as an "understandable" rejection of an unlovable child, believe a noncustodial father does not visit frequently or regularly because they are bad or not worthwhile enough for him to see, and feel that a custodial mother's affection for a new man in her life are evidence of their not being important or lovable enough for her to spend all of her time with them. These normal egocentric beliefs undermine a child's self-esteem; he no longer feels valuable, lovable, and good. The result is often a painful depressive reaction.

In addition to the specific sources of external and internal stress, it is important to bear in mind that early elementary school children have reached a point in their development when they are aware of a sense of family. Children of this age have come to expect and take for granted that family life, as tension-filled and unpleasant as it may be, will have an enduring continuity. It has always been there as a base from which to grow and stretch cognitively, emotionally, and socially. It will, of course, always be there. Forever. The news that their parents are separating therefore stuns young elementary school children and gives rise to an acute sense of the loss of their family unit. While preseparation tensions and problems within the family surely affect children, this sense of shock and loss is the first clear divorce-related stress children experience.

The first step parents can take in aiding their early elementary school youngster cope with the initial separation is to explain as calmly as possible that, ''Mommy and Daddy are going to get a divorce.'' This is best done one or two weeks before the parent who will be leaving in fact moves out. If there are children who are much younger or older than the early elementary school child, he should be told separately. However, young elementary school children can be told with other siblings who are also in elementary school or are older preschoolers. It is important for parents to spell out exactly what ''divorce'' will mean for them. In this first talk children should be told which parent is leaving the home and when that will take place. If it is known where that parent will be living, the child should be told and soon thereafter shown where it is. The child should also be told where he will be living; if it is other than the family residence, this will take additional explanations later.

In addition to this factual information, parents can tell the child very briefly why the divorce is occurring. There are several explanations appropriate for youngsters of this age. Parents may say: ''Mommy and Daddy are not getting along anymore. We argue a lot and we are very unhappy. When parents argue a lot, things are not very much fun at home. We've tried to get along better but it's not working.

Getting divorced means that moms and dads don't live together anymore so that they won't have to keep not getting along, arguing, and being unhappy.'' If only one parent wants the divorce, it is reasonable to be honest about that, since the child will eventually piece it together and may even possibly distort what is really happening. The parent who wants the divorce can say, in addition to the above statement, ''I know that your mom [dad] would like to keep trying to get along, but I think it won't work, so I think we need to get a divorce.'' The other parent can say, ''I know that your mom [dad] wants to get a divorce, but I want to keep trying to get along. She [he] doesn't think it can work, so we won't be living together anymore.'' If there has not been any obvious fighting, parents can omit the references to arguing in the above statement and stick to ''not getting along'' and ''being unhappy together'' kinds of phrases. However the parents decide to explain the divorce, their final statements in this talk should emphasize that the parents still love the child and that ''divorce is grown-up business which happens only because a mom and dad are having trouble getting along [or being happy together or loving each other].'' Children need to be reassured that they are loved and that they had no hand in the divorce.

Parents are often reluctant to have this kind of first talk with their children. Some worry that they will make the child unnecessarily sad, frightened, or otherwise upset. Others feel that young children, even those who already have started attending elementary school, will not be able to understand what they have to tell them. Many parents find themselves too angry, worried, or depressed to bring themselves to talk about the separation with their children. Nevertheless, it is extremely important that they try. Children will not be ''unnecessarily'' sad or distressed, they will be *normally* sad and distressed. But if a parent is with them and is reaching out to them, explaining things, and reassuring them with continued parental love, it becomes more manageable than finding out through overhearing angry plans to separate, noticing one parent no longer at home, or hearing of it from an older sibling or classmate. When parents use the kind of language suggested earlier, children can understand what they need to know about what is happening. Finally, parents must work to overcome their own distress sufficiently to be able to have this sort of brief first talk with their children. The wording provided here has helped many parents reduce their painful feelings enough to help their children about the divorce. It is also useful for parents to know that this will take less than five minutes so that they need to "keep it together" for only that brief period of time.

The elements of the first talk should be repeated again a day or two later. The fact of the upcoming separation, what it will mean to the child in the immediate future, brief explanations appropriate to a young child's level of understanding about why the divorce is happening, and reassurance of the parents' love for the child and that divorce is caused only by adults are the topics to be repeated in the second talk. This, too, will be very brief, lasting not longer than five minutes.

A few days after the second talk, and again throughout the immediate crisis stage of divorce, it is helpful if at least one parent can empathize with the sadness and loss a child is likely to be feeling soon after the separation. The realities of the divorce should first be reiterated. What it means to the child can be spelled out again: he lives with one parent (except in cases of joint physical custody); he sees the other parent from time to time or regularly (or does not have contact with that parent); and, he continues to live in his home (or has to move). The explanations for why the divorce is happening can also be recapitulated in terms of parental fighting, arguing, being unhappy, not loving each other anymore, and that the parents are doing something about that. They are choosing to live in separate places, so they do not have to be so upset anymore. The child can be reassured again about divorce being "grown-up business" that happens because adults are having trouble making their marriage work. Repeating this sequence of defining what divorce will mean for the child, explaining its necessity, and reassuring the child further clarifies the youngster's views of the divorce. It also sets the stage for the parent to empathize with feelings the child may have about the marital separation.

Displacement communication (see chapter 3) works particularly well in the process of empathizing with the child's sadness and sense of loss. After the above sequence has been reiterated, a parent might say, "Lots of kids have sad feelings when their parents split up. They feel sad that their mom and dad don't live together anymore and that the whole family isn't together like it used to be. Usually guys [girls] feel sad for a while, but you know, it gets better. Kids start feeling less sad and they get used to their parents being divorced." If a parent has noticed the youngster crying from time to time, she may say: "Most kids have real sad feelings when their parents split up. They feel like crying a lot of the time and sometimes they do cry. Even big kids like fourth and fifth graders cry, too. It's sad for guys [girls] to not have the whole family living together and to see their dad only every other week [once a month, very little]. But after a while kids get used to the divorce and start feeling better."

These one-step-removed sorts of displaced communications accomplish several things at once. They let the child know that his feelings are recognized and understood; he is not alone to deal with his misery; his feelings do not frighten or repel the parent; he is not weak or babyish for having these feelings, in fact many youngsters share them, even older ones; and, there is an expectation that things will get better in the future. At times children respond to these displacement messages by denying any sadness or upset feelings and/or insisting that the parents reconcile their differences. It is not helpful to bludgeon the youngster with the reality of his painful feelings by doggedly trying to convince him that he does indeed miss his family being together and is, of course, sad. Instead, a parent can gently empathize with the child's underlying, if not admitted, distress by saying, "Most kids hate feeling sad when their parents are getting a divorce. It feels awful. But it does get better." If the child persists in denying feeling sad, the parent can then accept the statement and just hug the child briefly before going about her business.

It is not useful to extract verbal confessions of sadness (or any other feeling) for displacement communication to work. If the child expresses his conviction that the divorce will not really occur because the parents will reconcile, the parent can say, "Most kids want their moms and dads to get back together and live happily ever after. But that's sort of a divorce fairy tale, and when parents get divorced, they stay divorced." If the child insists that they should or will reconcile, the parent can just pat or hug the child briefly. Young children sometimes need to hold onto a little bit of their denial of the reality or finality of the divorce for a while. It gives them some breathing room to begin to accept the divorce and come to terms with their feelings about it. The above sorts of displacement statements acknowledge the child's wish as one that is widely shared by children, clearly places it outside the realm of reality, yet does not try to rip it away from the child prematurely.

A common loss for boys and girls is the disruption in the father–child relationship. After most marital separations, children live with their mother and see their father considerably less than they used to. Parents can help their youngsters deal with the emotional pain of this situation in several ways. Arranging for frequent and predictable times to be with the noncustodial parent, or establishing joint physical custody, reduces the child's feeling of the loss of his father. Further, one or both parents can use displacement communication to empathize with their youngster's expectable sadness and to correct self-blaming beliefs about the divorce or a lack of frequent contact with the noncustodial parent.

MOLLY (see chapter 8) was overwhelmed by sadness when her parents separated. She appeared grief-stricken at home and at school. She cried easily and frequently, had withdrawn substantially from playing with friends, had trouble falling asleep at night, and seemed preoccupied to the point that she could not concentrate on her schoolwork. This depressive reaction and her unsuccessful attempts to cope with it by trying to completely deny the reality of her parents' divorce, had continued for four months. Her parents had become increasingly concerned about her. They had expected her difficulties to subside over time.

Molly's mother and father met with a therapist who specialized in working with children. She put Molly's reaction into an understandable context emphasizing the ways early elementary school youngsters react to their parents' divorce. The therapist pointed out that Molly was suffering from two kinds of losses: the loss of her sense of family and the partial loss of her loving relationship with her father. Molly's defensive use of denial, which her parents found odd and disturbing, was explained as a normal attempt to stem her sadness. She further noted that children are often especially shocked and pained by divorce when parents have not fought. They are typically unaware of marital problems that do not manifest themselves in open conflict. Though parental warfare is difficult for youngsters, its absence makes the divorce more of a surprise and less immediately understandable.

As is so often the case, Molly's parents were relieved to learn that their daughter's reactions were common and were by no means a sign of her being emotionally disturbed. They could begin to conceptualize Molly's feelings and behaviors as a response to the stress of the marital separation. The parents were also complimented for not going to war with one another, for coping well with the divorce so that they each could continue parenting effectively, and for the excellent relationship each had with Molly. The therapist told Molly's parents that they had been successful in avoiding several of the sources of stress for children when parents decide to part. At the same time, she began to explore their decision to have a sole custody arrangement.

The therapist pointed out that the fact that they were getting along reasonably well, believed that Molly needed both of them, respected each other's parenting abilities, communicated well about Molly and her sister, and lived near one another were precisely the conditions that made joint physical custody potentially workable. Molly and her sister were old enough to understand and adapt to a shared custody arrangement, which would involve splitting their time each week between their parents' households. While this would not significantly reduce Molly's sense of losing her family unit, it could alleviate her feelings of having lost a close, caring relationship with her father. With the therapist's help, Molly's parents agreed to a schedule according to which the girls would live with their mother Saturday afternoon through Tuesday evening and with their father from Wednesday after school through Saturday morning. This would permit each parent to be with the children both during part of the school week and for part of the weekend.

The therapist also helped them to use displacement communication to address Molly's feelings that she had lost her family and her painfully burdensome belief that her father had left because she had not been good. The therapist advised Molly's parents to use the first five steps of displacement communication to get at both of these issues. She provided them with the following model communication with respect to their daughter's feelings of having lost her family: "Most girls feel very sad when their parents stop living together and get divorced. A lot of girls cry sometimes and don't feel like playing with their friends or paying attention in school. They wish it wasn't really happening at all." With these statements, the parents were representing the observable signs of Molly's upset. Then the youngster's unhappiness with her own distress was represented by saying: "Girls hate to feel so sad. They don't want to cry and they miss playing with their friends and having a good time at school. They wish they could feel better." The third step, representing the underlying emotional pain, involved verbalizing for Molly her feeling of having lost her family unit. The therapist suggested this might be done in the following way: "When a girl's parents split up, she feels like she's sort of lost her family. Even fourth and fifth graders feel as though they don't have a family anymore. All the good times the family used to have together seem gone forever. Most girls have real sad feelings when they think that they've lost their family.'' Then Molly's parents could go on to change this perception to some degree by saying: ''You know, it's true that the whole family doesn't live together after parents get divorced. But, in a way, it's like there's a new kind of family. The dad and mom live in different places and don't eat dinner together or take vacations together. But they both keep loving their kids. The kids see each parent a lot and sometimes they even live part of the time with their mom and part of the time with their dad. It's like they have two homes instead of one, and there can be lots of good family feelings in each home.''

In this way the idea that the sense of family can continue with each parent can gradually be added to and can partially offset the feeling of having lost ''the family.'' It underscores the restructuring of family relationships that divorce brings. However, it cannot completely assuage the realistic feeling of having lost the original family; the fifth step of accepting the child's feelings (grief in this case) is important. This was explained to Molly's parents, and it was suggested that they add: ''But even when there are good family feelings at each parent's home, most kids still miss their whole family being together like it used to be. For a while it makes a lot of kids feel sad and wish that their parents would get back together again. But after a while those sad feelings start to go away because girls see that both parents love them and there are good family feelings when they're with each parent.''

In the course of explaining displacement communication to Molly's parents, the therapist was careful to alert them to some of the common pitfalls they needed to avoid. She told them that the statements should be made casually and kept brief so that the child does not feel as though she were being lectured and that they should use the third person form of speech (''kids,'' ''most girls,'' and so forth) and not ask Molly to respond directly to what they were saying so as not to undo the indirect nature of the communication.

When Molly's mother used this displacement communication, Molly at first continued trying to persuade her to get back together with her father. She frequently cried and then angrily told her mother to be quiet. Molly's mother would finish this five-step cycle, which took under two minutes, and then go about her business. She did not press Molly about any of these issues. She also did not depart from the sequence by trying to point out the finality of the decision to divorce, nor did she talk with Molly directly about her becoming upset during these statements. She did, however, hug her daughter and told her, "Things will get better; you'll see." Molly just listened quietly when her father went through the same five steps. Occasionally, she pleaded with him to "come back home." This gave her father a chance to underscore the fact that Molly and her sister had "two homes now and you're both loved very much in each one."

Molly was excited about living with each of her parents. She became involved, with her father's encouragement, in picking out a pillow, blanket, bedspread, and a stuffed animal for her new bedroom in her father's house. The reality of being able to live with him part of every week and with her mother four days a week along with the displacement communications each parent presented to her every third or fourth day began to reduce her feelings of sadness. Both parents also used the displacement method of communication to help Molly with her belief that she was in some way responsible for the marital break by not having been a good girl. Her mother used hand puppets for this task. She showed Molly a play in which a girl cat was very sad about her parents getting a divorce. She cried sometimes and did not feel like playing with the other girl cats anymore. She kept thinking of the divorce and it made her sad. Molly's mother had the girl cat say, "I hate feeling sad. I wish my parents would just get back together so everything would be like it used to." In this way, the first two steps of the displacement process were accomplished; Molly's overt signs of being upset and her distress over feeling so bad were represented.

Molly's mother went on to articulate her daughter's underlying emotional pain, "I bet this girl cat thinks that maybe she did something to make her parents divorce happen. A lot of girls think that if they had been nicer and had been a really good girl, then their parents wouldn't get a divorce." Molly entered the play at this point: "She (the girl cat) probably wasn't being nice to her dad. She didn't listen to him when he told her it was time to get ready for bed and he got sick of her wanting to have more stories." Molly's mother took this idea and added it to the story. She had the girl cat puppet say, "Maybe if I promise to be real good and go to bed right on time, my dad will come back." Molly agreed and wanted to pretend that had happened. Molly's mother took this opportunity to go on to correct this belief, "The girl cat has the same idea that a lot of girls have. She thinks that the divorce was happening because she did something wrong. Sometimes girls even think that when their dad moves out of the house it's because he doesn't love them anymore. But that's not why parents get divorced and dads move out. Divorce is always grown-up business. Kids never make the divorce happen. It's always because the mom and dad can't get along or because they just don't love each other anymore and don't want to be married anymore."

Molly's father was not comfortable with this way of using hand puppets, but he felt at ease telling stories. The nights Molly was at his home, he added what he called a "special story" after he finished reading her usual bedtime stories to her. He made up tales of girls who lived long ago or in other countries. Using these displacement vehicles, he went through the same steps Molly's mother did using the cat puppet. One such story was the following: "There was once a girl named Lucy who lived a long time ago in England. She lived with her mom, her dad, her little sister, and a dog. One day Lucy's parents told her they were going to live in different houses. They had stopped loving each other and didn't want to live together. So they went to the King and told him that they wanted him to sign the divorce papers. The King knew that sometimes moms and dads really do stop loving each other and that they'll be happier if they get a divorce, so he signed the papers. But Lucy felt awful. She cried and didn't even want to teach her dog any new tricks or play with the other girls in her village. She hated feeling so bad and kept trying to get her parents to get back together. But they didn't want to get back together and besides the King thought the divorce would be best for everyone. That was why he signed the divorce papers. Deep down in her mind Lucy felt especially sad. She thought that if she'd been a nicer girl and hadn't given her dad a hard time by not listening to him sometimes that her parents wouldn't have gotten divorced. Lucy didn't know exactly why parents got divorced. So her parents took her to the King. He explained that parents only get divorced because they fight or because they stop loving each other. Kids never cause divorce. He was a wise old King and he knew that kids don't make divorce happen. Divorce is only grown-up business. So Lucy started to feel better after a while. She stopped crying, except once in a while, and started to teach her dog how to roll over. She also started playing with the other kids again. It felt so good to know that she didn't make the divorce happen and that her mom and dad still loved her very much.''

Molly found these stories very enjoyable. She loved hearing them and often asked questions about the stories that had nothing to do with the divorce theme. She wanted to know what kinds of clothes the girls wore, whether they had to go to school, if they traveled on horseback instead of in cars, and so on. The messages were being heard. After three months of the change to joint physical custody and of having her sad feelings over losing her previous family circumstances and her self-blaming belief about the cause for the separation alleviated via displacement communications from both her parents, Molly was doing well again. Occasional sadness was the only remnant of her depressive reaction.

For early elementary school children, who are especially vulnerable to feelings of loss and are also given to egocentrically derived perceptions of their world, a custodial mother's normal work and social activities can precipitate a depressive reaction. These youngsters are already wrestling with the pain over having lost their sense of a family unit. Many have also experienced the loss of the preseparation quality in their relationship with their father (as Molly did). Thus sensitized to loss, they become acutely aware of any shifts in their mother's attention to them and in time spent together. Their tendency toward egocentrism results in their "explaining" even relatively minor and benign changes in the feeling tone and the relationship with their mother as a sign that they are no longer lovable or worthy of their mother's affections.

A custodial mother can help her child cope with this distress by structuring special time for her and her youngster. Taking this action demonstrates clearly and concretely that the parent still loves the child. In addition, parents can use the indirect methods of displacement communication to acknowledge their child's worries about being unimportant to her mother and explain that a mother's investment in her work, friendships, and dating relationships is not an indication of lack of love for her youngster.

IN TERMS OF environmental sources of stress, Laura (see chapter 8) could have been expected to be doing very well. Her parents were on reasonably good terms, each believed that the other was a good parent and was important to her, and they had arranged a flexible, effective shared custody arrangement. In fact Laura was progressing well in many ways; she continued to learn at school, had several good friends with whom she played regularly, and was not a behavior problem. However, her pervasive sadness and frequent stomachaches led her parents to consult a mental health professional when she was six-and-a-half, nearly a year-and-a-half after they had separated.

The mental health worker met twice with each parent separately, twice with both parents together, and twice with Laura. He assessed Laura's difficulties as being a reaction to feeling unimportant to her mother. He explained to her parents that Laura was not emotionally disturbed but was experiencing her mother's increased involvement in work and her new romantic relationship as "evidence" that Laura was comparatively unimportant. The mental health professional emphasized the fact that Laura's mother was doing nothing wrong; her daughter's reaction was not at all unusual for an early elementary school child in her position. He also underscored the fact that Laura's parents had handled their divorce in a mature, thoughtful manner. Their daughter's continued good adjustment in school and with friends was testimony to how well they had managed the divorce and to their good relationship with Laura. He outlined for them the ways young elementary school children feel and think about divorce. A sense of losing the family unit and the tendency toward egocentric thinking was described. Laura's initial attempts to deny the reality of her parents' separation were seen as a way of warding off feelings of loss of the family unit. At the same time, Laura's intense sadness and her stomachaches, both of which became worse just before mother's out-of-town trips, were linked to the egocentric belief that her mother no longer cared for her as much as she used to.

Laura's mother was surprised by this. She felt she loved her daughter every bit as much as she had before the marital separation. Her greater work involvement and her dating relationship made her feel more fulfilled and happier than she had ever been. The mental health professional noted the realistically good adjustment both parents had made. That was beneficial to Laura and would continue to be so. But the sensitivity of young elementary school children to any sort of loss and their readiness to interpret changes in a parent–child relationship egocentrically as proof that they were less lovable was reiterated.

He suggested a three-step approach to helping Laura. First, the very useful joint physical custody arrangement should be continued. Frequent and regular contact with each parent had been helpful and could be expected to continue to serve Laura's developmental needs. Second, Laura's mother was encouraged to be alert to opportunities to do things with her daughter as they had prior to the separation. This might include activities they used to share such as bicycle riding, walking in a nearby park, and reading stories together. However, the mental health worker also noted the value of more brief, spontaneous interactions: inviting Laura to play a game of cards, watching television together for a few minutes, and building something with her Lego set. These occasions had become less frequent because Laura's mother felt that whenever she did things with Laura, she had to plan for fairly large blocks of time. She had unwittingly reduced the frequency of brief interactions because she felt they would not satisfy her daughter. She had not recognized the value of doing things with Laura for only a few minutes at a time. The mental health worker also suggested that Laura's mother use displacement communication to alleviate her daughter's private worry that she was not loved or valued as much as she had been. It was felt that Laura's father ought not be the one to do this, since it might inadvertently seem to Laura that her father was being critical of her mother's new life style.

Laura's mother thought that the drawings her daughter had been bringing home from school would be a natural vehicle for the displacement communication. Laura's mother told her daughter that they could make up a story about the pictures she had been drawing of a girl who lived all alone in a big house. She took one of Laura's pictures and said, "Let's make up a name for this girl." Laura suggested "Judy." Her mother continued, "Judy looks very sad and lonely. She's all alone and it's cold and snowy outside. Let's make believe that Judy's parents got divorced, and in the picture she's feeling all alone. She misses her family being all together. She's at her mom's house and her mom isn't home. Judy misses her a lot and feels very sad." Laura added, "Her mom's away on a business trip." Laura's mother represented her daughter's distress through the displacement figure by saying, "Judy wishes she could feel happy just like she used to. She really hates feeling sad and lonely.'' Then Laura's mother verbalized her daughter's underlying emotional pain, ''Judy feels sad and lonely, mostly because she has the idea that her mother works a lot and goes on out-of-town trips because she just doesn't love Judy as much as she used to. Judy figures that if her mom still loved her a lot, then she wouldn't spend so much time working and going on trips.'' Laura elaborated the story by sadly saying: ''Her mom just doesn't like playing with her anymore. She doesn't want to cook dinners either.'' Laura's mother empathized with her: ''That would make any girl feel very sad and lonely. Even bigger kids, like fourth graders, would feel sad about their mom not playing with them or cooking dinner for them.''

Laura's mother then corrected her daughter's underlying painful belief that she was not as important to her mother as she had been, ''When a girl's mom starts working more and even going away on business trips, a girl can start believing that her mom just doesn't love her as much anymore. I bet Judy thought that. But Judy's mom still loves her just as much as before the divorce happened. She likes her job and the business trips are something she has to do. She even likes going on them sometimes. But I'm sure she misses Judy when she's working and when she's away on those trips. Moms think their girls are very, very important and they keep loving them a whole lot even though their job takes a lot of time.'' Laura's mother repeated this four-step displacement communication using her daughter's dollhouse and doll figures to address similar feelings about her dating relationship. These interactions occurred once or twice a week. Laura watched them attentively and occasionally contributed to the stories and doll play. She enjoyed them in part because they gave her more time with her mother; they were doing something together.

After several weeks, Laura asked, ''Why can't Judy go with her mom on some of her trips?'' This possibility had not occurred to her mother. She consulted the mental health professional about Laura accompanying her on trips from time-to-time even though she would miss some school days. They agreed that since Laura was doing well academically, this should not be a problem. Laura went on one trip to San Francisco and another to Dallas. But she declined subsequent invitations. Despite her excitement about going on the first trip, she in fact found both journeys boring, and she missed her friends. Laura no longer felt excluded from her mother's travels, but she had no wish to give up school and friends to take these trips. At the same time, Laura and her mother were doing more together. Planned activities such as bicycle riding and more brief interactions of the sort recommended by the mental health professional gave mother and daughter more time with each other. The displacement communications served to bring to the surface and then correct Laura's sense of being less important to her mother. Within two months, her sadness had been reduced and her stomachaches were gone. After another four months, only a trace of her sadness remained. It no longer seemed necessary to continue the displacement communication.

Rather than feeling peripheral to a parent's new postdivorce life, and therefore relatively unimportant and unvalued, some children are faced with the opposite. A custodial parent who is depressed or anxious may enlist the aid of her child in order to try to cope with her own feelings of helplessness and vulnerability. In order to address and alleviate a child's distress in these cases, the parent must be willing and able to examine her own behavior, separate her child's needs from her own, and respond to them appropriately.

MICHAEL'S (see chapter 8) mother made an appointment to see a social worker who specialized in working with children experiencing stressful life events such as divorce, remarriage, and the physical illness of a family member. She told the social worker about Michael's difficulties with his teacher, his problems getting along with boys in his class at school, and his nightmares. In the course of the first three meetings with Michael's mother, the social worker saw that this youngster's difficulties were a natural outgrowth of his adult-like role within the postdivorce household. She shared this view with Michael's mother and explained how much boys of this age want to feel very close to their mother and helpful to her. She empathized with his mother's anxieties over finances and about going back to work. The social worker noted the sudden and unexpected nature of the marital separation and told Michael's mother that women who experience that kind of shock can profit from sessions with a professional. She gently explained to Michael's mother that it is not at all unusual for a mother to turn to a son or daughter for help in these times of stress, but that she and her children would do well if she could resolve her anxieties and return to being the effective parent she had been before the divorce. They agreed to meet on a weekly basis for a few months.

During those sessions Michael's mother was helped to confront her anxieties directly. Her worries about her ex-husband deciding to stop sending support checks, her fears about being unable to support herself and her two children, and her fantasies about having to move to a particularly undesirable neighborhood were explored openly. She began to work on the underlying feelings of her inability to be on her own that were the source of these anxieties. The social worker also underscored several facts: Michael's mother was an intelligent, capable woman who learned quickly and got along well with people, and she had enough equity in her home to be able to move to a smaller house in the very same neighborhood, if necessary, rather than having to go to a less desirable area. Within a month Michael's mother found a job working at an interior decorating store. Her previous education in the arts and experience working for an art dealer had fostered excellent abilities to visualize in ways that allowed her to be an effective consultant on home furnishing. She enjoyed her new position and was gratified by the income she was able to earn.

As she gained confidence in herself, she was able to begin focusing on the problems her son was having. The social worker explained that Michael's mother would have to restructure her relationship with her son and begin to insist that his role in the household be that of a child and not a small version of an adult. As she implemented these changes, it would also be important to tell Michael why they were occurring, using displacement communication. The first task was to change how she interacted with her son. This consisted of several straightforward shifts in her behavior. To begin with, it was suggested that she refrain from discussing finances or her new job with her son. These talks only made Michael feel that he was privy to grown-up matters. If her son asked about these issues, she could say, "I've got a good job, I've taken a careful look at the money situation, and I've decided that I'll be able to handle all of that. Things are looking good." The emphasis on "I" rather "we" highlights the fact that finances are solely the province of adults. Any offers Michael might continue to make about getting a paper route or not needing any more clothing could be met with his mother telling him, "That's very thoughtful Michael. But it isn't really necessary. You're a good kid for wanting to help, but

I've got the money stuff under control. Your job is to go to school, learn and have fun with your friends. The best way you can help me is by listening to me when I ask you to do something, like go to bed on time or not boss your sister around.''

Second, it was important for Michael's mother to reintroduce an appropriate physical-emotional distance between them. His giving her back rubs as they stayed up late at night together needed to come to a halt. She could stop asking for them, and if Michael volunteered, she could say, ''No thanks, Michael. It's nice of you to want to do that, but I'm feeling fine.'' By reducing these requests for help from her son in the form of asking him to listen to her adult worries, accepting his offer to work or forgo new clothing, and encouraging the physical intimacy of late evening back rubs, Michael's mother was communicating her own sense of competence and self-sufficiency as well as maintaining an appropriate generational boundary between them. She was the parent and he was the child. Her comments needed to be gentle in order to avoid unnecessarily bruising her son's young ego.

Michael's mother also had to begin making it clear to him in other ways as well that she had expectations for him to be her child not her adult-like partner. A regular bedtime and several routine, age-appropriate chores were instituted. His attempts to discipline his younger sister were met with firm statements that, ''That's my job. You're her brother not her parent. I'll tell her when to pick up her toys, when to wash up for dinner, and when to go to bed. You can help me by being her big brother. If she needs help with something, you can give it to her. But don't tell her what to do.'' It was equally important to express expectations for Michael to behave well at school. His mother told him, ''Your teacher is the grown-up in the classroom. You and all the other kids need to listen to her. You're a big, smart boy. I'm sure that you can understand what are the right things for you to do at school. Only little kids give their teachers a hard time and try to get their teacher and their friends to do what they want to do.'' In these ways Michael's mother was not only curtailing her requests for him to be her adult-like partner, she was making it clear that she expected him to act like a big boy, not a grown-up, at home, with his teacher, and with his friends.

Not surprisingly, Michael heartily resented these changes. He had been taking great pleasure in being his mother's confidant and in feeling close to her in adult-like ways. Suddenly, he was being asked to give up these newfound gratifications and return to being ''just'' an eight-year-old boy. He nagged his mother about finances. When she insisted she had everything in hand, he asked, ''Could I have a TV for my bedroom?'' and ''Can we go to Disney World this winter?'' in subtle efforts to get her to talk with him about ''their'' financial status. His mother wisely answered directly (it was no to both questions) without discussing them beyond saying, ''I don't think that would fit the way I see how money should be spent in the family.'' He bridled about having to go to bed on time and thus give up the cosy late-night back rubs he gave his mother, and the times they spent curled up on the couch watching television until midnight. He insisted he would decide when he should go to bed. He also claimed that he should be the one to tell his sister what to do because he was older. When his mother told him she expected him to behave properly at school, Michael referred to his teacher's assignments and rules as ''stupid.'' He argued that he did not have to do what his teacher asked since she only told him to do ''dumb things.''

Michael's reluctance to go back to being an eight-year-old prompted his mother to use a mixture of direct and displacement communication to help him understand these changes. She told him directly, ''I know you've gotten used to my treating you sort of like you are a grown-up. I used to tell you how worried I was about not having enough money and I was glad you listened and even thought of getting a paper route. When I got real upset, you used to give me nice back rubs. And you kept me company by staying up late with me even though you had school the next day. You used to try and help me out by taking care of your sister, too. But all those jobs are really too big for a guy your age. Besides, I've got a job now and I'm feeling good about things. I'm not nervous about money stuff any more. It's time for you to go back to being my big boy.''

In addition to this direct acknowledgement of the changes that she was implementing in her relationship with her son and in his role in the household, she also used displacement communication to help Michael accept giving up the pleasures of having an adult-like position at home. She told Michael that she had heard about a boy who was a little older (in order to facilitate the ''big boy'' quality she was hoping to convey) than he who lived on a farm.

She said, "James lived with his mother and his brother. His parents had gotten a divorce, and his mother was very worried about who would plant the corn and pick it when it was ripe. She was also worried about who would milk the cows. She thought they might have to sell the farm and move away because the money from selling their corn and milk was how they paid their bills. James wanted to help his mom, so he stopped going to school and instead he planted corn in the fields and got up very early every morning to milk all the cows. He was a big help to his mom, but he was missing out on going to school and playing with his friends. James thought that was all right because he was a good boy and he liked helping his mom so she wouldn't have to worry about money. James sort of got used to doing all that work and not going to school. He felt like he was a grown-up and that he was helping his mom a lot. But after a while James's mom got a job. She was able to buy new milking machines. She just put them on the cows and they milked them real fast. His mom used some of her money from the new job to hire a neighbor to plant and pick the corn. Pretty soon she wasn't worried. So she told James he didn't have to do his planting and milking chores anymore. He could go back to school and learn and he could also play with his friends. When James found out he didn't have to do all the work around the farm, something sort of funny happened. He wasn't happy! He got mad at his mom and told her he wanted to keep doing the planting and milking. He didn't want to go back to school or even play with his friends. He said that going to school and playing was silly and it was only for little kids. He just wanted to keep helping his mom.''

Michael's mother then accounted for her son's discomfort with his own distress, "James didn't want to argue with his mom. Deep down in his feelings he really wanted to go to school with the other guys and play with his friends. He hated arguing with his mom.'' Michael appeared bored. He looked out the window and fidgeted, but he stayed and listened. His mother moved to step three of displacement communication and verbalized her son's underlying emotional upset, "James had gotten used to feeling like a grown-up. He was doing grown-up work and was helping his mom. They even talked together about how much money they'd get for the corn and milk they sold. When his mom said that her new job made things okay and that he could go back to school, he felt bad. Instead of feeling happy to be able to go back to being a third grader and not having to help his mom with such hard jobs, he sort of felt like he had to go back to being a little kid. And he thought that he wasn't important to his mom anymore. He said, 'You don't need me anymore and you want me to be a baby.' That's how it felt to James.''

This twin burden, feeling he was going back to being a "little kid" and believing he was now unimportant to his mother, was addressed in the fourth step of the displacement communication, "James just figured he was going to be an unimportant little kid now, but what James didn't know was that his mom still loved him a lot and wanted him to be a *big* boy. Big boys are very important to their mom because they can help out in lots of ways. They can also learn things in school and grow up to have good jobs. And big boys, even fourth and fifth graders, need to have time to play with their friends instead of spending all of their time at home with their mommy.'' The fifth and final step in accepting difficult feelings was accomplished by Michael's mother saying, "I know that most guys would feel like James did. They'd be mad about having to be a big boy instead of being like a grown-up. But after a while the mad feelings start to go away.''

Michael's mother repeated this story, with only minor variations, about twice a week. She would reintroduce the story by saying that something had reminded her that day about how James felt or by claiming that she had heard about another boy who was sort of like James. Then she went over the same steps with reference to the "other boy." Occasionally, when her son became angry about having to go to bed on time or her refusing to discuss finances with him, Michael's mother would say, "Sounds to me like some James kind of feelings." At other times she would say: "Going to bed on time isn't being a little kid. Big guys go to bed on time because they know it's important to get enough rest to be able to learn in school the next day and play with their friends. Gee, even teenagers do that. It helps a mom a lot to see her son be a big boy.'' She made similar comments when Michael resisted doing homework assignments or wanted to stay at home on a weekend day instead of playing with his friends. After four months Michael had reinvested himself in being a boy. While some of his old trouble surfaced from time to time, he was doing well at school, both with his teacher and his friends. The relationship with his mother had become appropriately that of a mother and son rather than mother and live-in adult partner.

The combination of Michael's mother regaining her own emotional equilibrium, reducing her requests for him to be in an adult-like relationship with her, firmly insisting that he assume the role of an eight-year-old boy rather than a mini-adult, and holding out clear expectations for age-appropriate behavior at home and at school permitted Michael to return to childhood. The pain this reentry caused Michael, in terms of no longer feeling important or big in his mother's eyes as well as his own, was substantially alleviated by the use of displacement messages. It is crucial that the underlying meanings these changes can have for a youngster be addressed. Children can resist parents' well-intentioned efforts to reinstitute the appropriate generational boundary between themselves and their children out of a sense of humiliation as well as the understandable reluctance to give up the pleasures of being in an adult-like position in their family. Michael was able to achieve reentry into childhood successfully because his mother paid attention to these sources of resistance that were interfering with her efforts to redefine his role in his relationships with her, his sister, his teacher, and his classmates. Both environmental and internal sources of stress must be reduced to help children continue to progress in healthy, adaptive ways.

Parental warfare is perhaps the most damaging environmental source of stress that can undermine their successful adaptation to divorce. In the short-run, hostilities between parents, so common in the first and second stages of the divorce process, tend to intensify the young elementary school child's feelings of sadness and loss. And some youngsters, especially boys, may engage in troublesome aggressive behaviors when their anger is stimulated by parental warfare. However, it is not only sadness and anger that can burden early elementary school children whose parents are embroiled in an anger-filled, bitter divorce. As noted earlier, these children are also prone to developing depressive reactions. Difficulty concentrating in school, withdrawing from previously pleasurable peer relationships, and trouble sleeping are not at all unusual reactions to parental warfare. Fantasies of being left to care for themselves on their own and beliefs that they are responsible for their parents' marital separation add an internal dimension to the stress of parental hostilities. But as in cases where a parent is enmeshing the child in an overly close relationship to fulfill her own needs, here too the first step toward alleviating the child's distress is for parents to take stock of their own behavior and its impact on their youngster.

ALEX (see chapter 8) had been displaying all the signs of a depressive reaction when his parents separated. In addition, he had begun hoarding food at home in his room and was fearful of being alone in his bedroom when it was time for him to go to sleep. His teacher and the school psychologist met with each parent and reported their concerns about Alex. They recommended that the parents consult a psychologist at a local child guidance clinic. Both parents were skeptical but followed the school's advice.

In their first meeting with the psychologist, they described their marital conflicts and ongoing battles. During the session they angrily interrupted one another and often spoke sarcastically about each other's perceived shortcomings. When the psychologist asked them about the problems their youngster was having, they repeatedly lapsed back into arguing about each other's antagonistic behaviors. Alex's difficulties were given short shrift. The psychologist suggested that he meet separately with each parent to try to understand how their son was experiencing the marital separation. Both reluctantly agreed.

In the course of several meetings with Alex's mother the psychologist was able to bring the boy's problems more sharply into focus for her. He showed Alex's mother that the difficulties her son was having were not simply a collection of isolated behaviors and feelings having little to do with one another. She had tried to dismiss these as unrelated events that, viewed singly in this way, could be discounted as only part of the normal ups and downs children have. This view permitted her to avoid coming to grips with her son's difficulties. When the psychologist described them as being part of an overall picture of a depressive reaction to the divorce process, Alex's mother was able to begin to see how distressed her son was.

The psychologist explained to her that young elementary school children often experience their parents' divorce as a loss; the child's sense of family togetherness comes to an end. He emphasized that warfare between divorcing parents can increase this feeling of loss, because children begin to believe that they can no longer count on their home to be a secure, trusted base for support. This was

226

put into the developmental context of youngsters needing to feel that they will be cared for and protected by parents as they go about the task of expanding their world beyond the family to school and friends. The psychologist noted how hard it was for children to feel they had that sort of support when parents are devoting a great deal of time, energy, and attention to battling each other. Alex's crying easily, having trouble finishing schoolwork, withdrawing from interactions with other boys, and feeling lonely at bedtime were pulled together and presented as signs of his depressive reaction. The psychologist empathized with the anger Alex's mother felt toward her husband but also urged her to see things from her son's point of view.

Over several weekly meetings with the psychologist, Alex's mother became sensitized to her son's emotional distress and was able to begin recognizing that the animosity between her and her husband was contributing to it. Unfortunately, Alex's father was unable to do the same. He frequently cancelled his sessions with the psychologist, and when he came he could not put himself in his son's shoes to see how he might be feeling. He claimed that Alex was probably having some trouble with another boy at school. Alex's emotional distress was attributed to his being fearful of a possible physical confrontation with this "other boy." That was why Alex cried easily, could not concentrate on his schoolwork, and did not want to go outside to play. He was just scared of a fight. While the psychologist continued to make himself available to Alex's father, it was clear that this was probably not going to be productive. The psychologist candidly told Alex's mother that if her son was going to be helped, it would depend on her ability to reduce, if not put an end to, the parental hostilities and begin to talk with Alex about the divorce.

Since the parents had been unable to enter into a constructive dialogue and each consistently triggered resentment in the other, the psychologist suggested that Alex's mother limit her contacts with her husband. Negotiations around the divorce settlement were to be conducted exclusively through their respective attorneys. She could maintain this distance when Alex's father picked him up and dropped him off at her house by refusing to enter into any discussions at those times. The importance of her doing this in as neutral and matter-of-fact a way as possible was emphasized. It would be unhelpful to Alex if she implemented this part of the plan in a smug or provocative manner. Alex's mother agreed to try this but had difficulty accepting the idea of limiting her negative comments about her husband in front of her son. The psychologist explained that children hate it when parents criticize each other. This sort of indirect warfare only perpetuates the hostile atmosphere of the child's world and makes him feel worse. Alex's mother said: "What should I say? That he's a great guy and Alex should grow up to be just like him? You want me to praise him and say good things about him? That would be dishonest. I'd be lying to my son and giving him the wrong ideas about his father."

The psychologist carefully distinguished between praising someone and painting them in extremely negative ways. It was not at all untruthful to simply refrain from saying derogatory things about her husband. She certainly need not tell her son that his father is a terrific fellow with numerous wonderful attributes. That would feel to her like lying. But on the other hand, she could keep her opinions about her husband to herself rather than voicing them in the presence of her son. Her questions about Alex's visits with his father were identified as not-so-subtle efforts to demean her husband in her son's eyes. When she asked Alex, "How's your father's drinking?" it was neither for information purposes nor rhetorical. It was a chance to put her husband in a negative light, to show her son that his father was a bad man. Alex's mother was able to see her role in creating an atmosphere of hostility. Though she continued to feel angry at her husband and think of him as a "complete ass hole," she was able to keep these opinions to herself instead of insisting on sharing them with her young son.

The psychologist also suggested that she try talking with her son about the divorce and about the feelings he was having about it. Her attempts at discussing this directly had been met with silence. The psychologist explained displacement methods of communicating with children and began to help her implement this approach. He told her that it could be used to address Alex's feelings of loss of the family unit, his apparent fantasies that she would abandon him so that he would be left to fend for himself (revealed in his hoarding food and fears of being "all alone" at bedtime), and the belief that he was in some way responsible for the divorce. Though there was no clear evidence for the latter, it is such a common way for young elementary school children to "understand" divorce that it made sense to reassure Alex on that score. The importance of choosing a quiet time and not following up displacement messages with direct questions was emphasized.

Alex's mother was skeptical of this style of talking with her son. She insisted that he would "see right through it" and therefore would not be able to benefit from it. The psychologist assured her that most parents thought that any reasonably intelligent youngster would "see through" displacement methods. He added, "It seems obvious and transparent to us but not to the great majority of children. Even older elementary school kids and some teenagers will often be able to make use of this sort of one-step-removed talking because it gives them a chance to see their difficulties more clearly and hear helpful things. They're more comfortable because they don't feel like the spotlight is on them. It's like a psychological mirror that gives children a chance to see themselves more clearly." Alex's mother was nonetheless uneasy about using these methods. The psychologist recommended that she begin to get a feel for how this might work with Alex by reading children's books about divorce to him. He recommended *Divorce is a Grown-Up Problem* and *The Dinosaurs' Divorce*.[1] Alex's mother was much more comfortable taking this tack. She was used to reading to her son and this seemed more natural to her.

She began by reading each of the books every second or third evening before Alex got into bed. Thus, these were additional stories rather than taking the place of the usual bedtime reading. His mother introduced them by saying: "Sometimes guys get sort of curious about how other kids feel about divorce and what other guys think about when their parents get divorced. All kids have ideas and feelings about divorce, and it's helpful to see what they are." Alex enjoyed hearing these stories but occasionally asked his mother to read "regular" stories when she began one of the divorce books. She agreed and at those times did not read the divorce stories.

As she became more comfortable reading these two divorce books to Alex, the psychologist was able to help her implement the five step displacement communication in the context of the stories. On one page of *Divorce is a Grown Up Problem* the child says, "I wish my parents hadn't gotten divorced. I wish they would just be happy again and we could all live together." Alex's mother was able to use this as a way to begin to address her son's feelings of loss of the family unit. When she read that page she added, "Most guys feel real sad when their parents decide to get a divorce.

A lot of guys cry, even big kids like third and fourth graders. They feel so sad that they don't even care about their schoolwork or playing with friends anymore. And when their parents fight or say bad things about each other then kids feel even more sad. They wish they could feel happy again, but it's so hard to feel good when you feel so sad.'' Then she verbalized the underlying emotional pain by saying: "When kids get so sad about divorce it's partly because their family just isn't all together anymore. They miss having everyone together, mom, dad, and the kids all living in the same place. It feels like their family is ending and that's very sad for most guys.'' She went on to partially correct this belief: "But when parents get divorced and live in different places, a guy can still feel like he and his mom are a family, and when he's with his dad then he and his dad are a family. Kids still love their mom and dad and the parents both still love their kids. And that's what families are all about. Parents and kids loving each other, and moms and dads helping their kids to grow up.''

However, because the loss of the original family unit is indeed real, the fifth step of displacement communication, accepting the child's feelings, is important, too. Alex's mother told him, "It's sad for guys to have their family of mom, dad, and the kids all living together come to an end. But those sad feelings get better after a while. Guys start to feel good about living with their mom and being with their dad and the sad feelings start going away.'' On the very next page of this book, the child character's feelings begin to be portrayed. This begins with, "Sometimes I really feel scared. I worry about who's going to keep me safe.'' Alex's mother built on this using, the first four steps of displacement communication. After reading that page she mused aloud: "Yeah, I can see that. Guys can get real worried when their parents get divorced. A lot of guys get scared of going to bed at night. Some kids want their mom to stay with them until they fall asleep. Sometimes guys even worry about whether their mom will keep taking care of them, like fixing meals and stuff like that. Kids hate to feel so scared. They want to feel good and safe.'' She went on to acknowledge and correct Alex's frightening fantasies, "Most guys start to worry about how maybe their mom will move out of the house just like dad did. Then they would be all alone. They'd have to fix their own meals, wash their clothes, and all that kind of stuff. And they'd be all alone at bedtime when it was dark outside. That's a real scary idea even for big kids. But, you know, parents don't leave kids to live alone. Parents decide which one will live with the kids because both parents know that all kids need to be taken care of. When the mom lives with her kids, she just isn't going to leave and move away no matter what.''

Alex usually listened quietly when his mother read the divorce books. Sometimes he nodded his agreement at various parts and occasionally became teary. His mother could comfort him directly at that time by hugging him and reminding him that, ''The feelings get better after a while.'' When his mother told him that ''Moms don't move away no matter what,'' Alex asked, ''Even if a boy is real bad?'' His mother tried to get him to elaborate that idea: ''Like what? How would a guy be bad?'' Alex shrugged, but a few minutes later said, ''What if a kid broke his mom's favorite coffee cup or spilled grape juice on the couch?'' His mother replied: ''Moms wouldn't like that. They might even get mad. But they would never leave no matter what.'' As Alex felt increasingly reassured, he began to play a ''what if'' game. He asked directly, ''What if I was hungry and came home from school and ate all the food in the house? Would you go away?'' His mother could playfully continue to be supportive, ''Even if you ate the whole refrigerator and then ate your bed, I'd still be here.'' Because Alex had become comfortable, he had shifted to direct questions about himself and his mother rather than talking about ''guys'' or ''kids.'' Since this repartee had a humorous and imaginary quality, Alex's mother also responded directly rather than using displacement.

The use of displacement communication also took place around the possible belief Alex may have had regarding his role in the divorce. Within the context of reading to her son, Alex's mother was able to verbalize and then correct the idea children often have that they might have caused the divorce. After two months of these sorts of interactions, coupled with the reduced air of parental hostility, Alex's depressive reaction began to lose its intensity. He rarely cried, became interested again in his school activities, played more with friends, and was more comfortable going to bed at night. Though remnants of his sadness were still clearly in evidence at times, he was adapting well to his parents' divorce and was regaining his developmental stride.

The uneasiness and skepticism Alex's mother felt about displacement communication are not uncommon. Reading books to children can be very useful in helping a parent who feels awkward talking to her child in this alien way become familiar with this process. Reading stories about another youngster and her parents' divorce is actually a displacement communication, though not closely tailored to a specific child's situation. Nor does it usually follow the sequence given in chapter 3 for displacement communication. Nonetheless it is a way for parents to begin raising divorce issues with their children. Parents can then select the relevant sections of the book upon which to build. Key themes can be elaborated via the steps of displacement communication. Statements such as "most kids" or "a lot of guys [girls]" serve to underscore the normality and acceptability of the youngster's circumstances, feelings, and concerns. Specific underlying feelings—including sadness, rage, fantasies, beliefs, and conflicts—also can be acknowledged and corrected. Relief from both external and internal sources of distress then often results in a diminution of difficulties.

However, at times parental warfare becomes so chronic and lasts for so long that what began as a child's reactions to this external source of stress and the internal stresses it stimulates becomes incorporated into the youngster's personality development. Early elementary school children, like preschoolers, can suffer serious long-term effects due to the parents' unremitting, and long-standing hostilities. When this is the case, the individual efforts of parents are usually not able to correct the problems. Even if parents are able to call a full truce to their fighting, the child has already been changed substantially by his reactions to the anger he has lived with for years. Psychotherapy is often required to aid the youngster's return to a healthy developmental path.

LARRY (see chapter 8) pushed younger children, destroyed his classmates' property and belittled them. He criticized his mother in ways strongly reminiscent of and eerily like his father. Larry's mother had become increasingly aware of the serious nature of her son's difficulties. School personnel were also concerned about Larry and urged his parents to have him evaluated by a mental health professional. Larry's mother made contact with a child psychiatrist in private practice. The psychiatrist saw Larry's mother three times, Larry twice, and Larry and his mother together once. The psychiatrist called Larry's father and asked him to participate in the evaluation process. She emphasized the importance of fathers to their sons and told him that children could be helped best when two caring parents were involved. Larry's father agreed to several sessions with the psychiatrist but told her he would not meet together with his ex-wife. The intractability of the parental hostilities and the entrenched nature of Larry's problems led the psychiatrist to recommend twice weekly psychotherapy for this boy and once a week, separate guidance sessions with each parent.

The bulk of the work in the parent meetings was focused on the ways in which their warfare had been affecting their son. The psychiatrist explained how toddlers, preschoolers, and elementary school children normally react to divorce and the complications caused by parental battles. The fearfulness Larry had exhibited as a toddler and preschooler was tied to his worries over one or both parents being injured or even killed as a result of their angry exchanges. She tried to construct a fully elaborated image of the ways divorce is perceived and felt by youngsters, highlighting the helpless and sad feelings very young children experience when parents fight and divorce. In educating Larry's parents and providing them with numerous examples, past and current, of the toll their divorce was taking on their son, the psychiatrist was able to show them the importance of their reducing the hostilities between them. She provided suggestions about how to minimize contact with one another, such as communicating via notes rather than by telephone or in person, and staying out of each other's home when Larry was being picked up or dropped off. She often mediated their disputes, even without seeing them together, always maintaining her role as an advocate for the child's best interests.

The sessions with Larry involved efforts to help him give up his combativeness and hostility, which were serving as defenses against the frightened, sad, and helpless feelings he had experienced during the first two stages of his parents' divorce and which continued at an underlying psychological level. The psychiatrist used a variety of displacement vehicles including puppet play, toy soldiers, games (including Wheel of Fortune and Life), and dollhouses. These helped Larry begin to become more aware of what he was feeling and doing, rather than just having painful feelings and getting into trouble at school. She could empathize with how difficult it had been for him to grow up with the people he had loved most hating each other and treating each other with such anger and contempt. Over the course of the two-year therapy, Larry was gradually able to give up his defensive anger and come to terms with his sadness and fear. His therapist became his ally, an adult who did not fight while accepting and understanding his most private feelings. The rule of confidentiality (which ensures privacy between therapist and child) permitted him to express and explore thoughts and feelings that could only be warded off and left to fester before. Therapy was concluded when Larry's signs of distress were gone.

At the beginning of fifth grade, which entailed a change from elementary school to middle school, Larry's parents agreed not to mention his past problems to his new teacher. School records from his elementary school generally were not forwarded to the middle school. The parents met, separately, with Larry's fifth-grade teacher. They were gratified to learn that she perceived him as a bright youngster who was doing fine academically and was getting on well with classmates.

Among all the potential environmental stresses confronting children whose parents divorce, remarriage is perhaps the most common. The great majority of divorced mothers and fathers do marry again.[2] They often enter these second (or subsequent) marriages with a mixture of excitement and trepidation. These adults know that even marriages that begin with love can end painfully and disrupt their lives. Many parents are also generally aware of the stresses inherent in so-called "blended families." These include rivalry between the child and the new spouse for the parent's time and affection; tensions in the stepparent–stepchild relationship; loyalty conflicts the child experiences between his feelings toward his stepparent and his own parent of the same sex; competitive feelings between step- and half-siblings, and so on.

It is this writer's impression that these sorts of "blended family" conflicts can be substantially reduced if the following conditions are met. First, it is important for the parent not to surprise a child with a remarriage. Divorce is typically a shock most youngsters do not anticipate regardless of the warning signs that may have been present. They are not prepared to cope with another wrenching surprise that will seriously affect their lives. Children need to be assured that before a big change such as remarriage occurs, they will be told clearly and well in advance. Second, a child will adjust better to a new marriage if the relationship between a divorced single-parent and her child has not been an exclusive or an enmeshed one. Barbara (see chapter 8) did well when her mother remarried in part because mother and daughter had not been overly close. Barbara had other adults (her grandparents) in her life whom she saw regularly and who loved her. Her mother was involved in work and a social life. The bonds between them, while strong, had not become sticky. Single parents who have clear emotional investments outside the home (that is, a job and social activities) are less likely to be enmeshed with their children. And children who have adults other than their custodial parent whom they see frequently and love will not have all their emotional eggs in the one basket of their relationship with that parent. The ongoing involvement of the other parent, the child's grandparents, and/or other close relatives can provide alternative loving interactions with adults other than a custodial parent. Baby-sitters, day-care providers, and nursery/elementary school teachers cannot create this kind of emotional counterweight to balance an exclusive parent–child relationship. This requires the love of an adult who will be in the child's life regularly, frequently, and for the foreseeable future. Other caring adults appropriately feel both emotionally peripheral and transient to the child.

A child's successful adaptation to remarriage also depends on factors within the newly formed family rather than on premarriage issues. The parent's continued efforts to make time for interactions with her children that do not include her new spouse is one essential factor. Another is the role the new stepparent adopts toward the children. If he competes with them for his new wife's attention or seeks to exclude them from interactions with her, they will tend to resent him. If he quickly becomes too "parental" by giving out chores and handing down discipline, they will also resent him. On the other hand, if he likes the children, includes them in some of the adults' weekend plans, and behaves initially in somewhat of a Dutch uncle manner, early elementary school children will usually begin to accept and often come to love him. Children of this age are less accepting, on the average, of a new stepparent than preschoolers and younger children tend to be. However, they will often get over their uneasiness when they are appropriately prepared for the marriage and when parents and stepparents are sensitive to these issues.

If one or both premarriage conditions are not met, it is more difficult for the child to be receptive to a new stepparent. The parent who surprises a youngster with remarriage undermines the trusting relationship between them and does not give the child a chance to get used to the idea before the reality is upon him. And the parent who has had an exclusive relationship with her child, who is the sole loving adult in the child's emotional life, must grapple with powerful feelings of loss and competition that remarriage will frequently stir up in the child.

JAN (see chapter 8) had been progressing very well on all developmental fronts until her mother remarried. However, her mother's new marriage had precipitated angry reactions. Attempts by Jan's mother to talk with her daughter about these changes had been fruitless. Mother and stepfather consulted a child psychologist about Jan's difficulties. After two meetings with Jan's mother and stepfather, it was clear to the psychologist that their daughter was reacting to the stress of the new marriage. He explained to them that Jan had continued to do well at school and with friends because she had numerous developmental strengths. He emphasized the good upbringing Jan had received and pointed out that Jan's mother had been able to avoid burdening her daughter with many of the common stresses divorce can bring to children. The psychologist explained that mothers and daughters often develop close relationships that are rewarding to each. However, when daughters feel they have an exclusive emotional tie to their mother and there are no other loving adults centrally in their lives, they can become notably possessive of their mother. He elaborated on this idea by adding that it is upsetting to girls when they have to begin to share mother's time and loving attention for the first time. They become unsure of their place in their mother's heart and can become sad and worried about losing her. He went on to say that Jan was probably warding off these unpleasant feelings by becoming angry and critical towards her mother. Anger can often be used to sweep away helpless feelings of sadness, loss, and anxiety. The normal difficulty many girls have in making the transition from having lived in a single-parent household with their mother for a long time to being part of a remarried family was also described.

This developmental context permitted Jan's mother and stepfather to see her problems as an understandable reaction to the stress of the remarriage rather than as an indication that she was an emotionally disturbed girl. The psychologist outlined a three-pronged plan to help Jan adjust to her new family circumstances. First, he suggested that Jan's mother arrange to do some of the same things with her daughter that they had done prior to the marriage. This included going shopping together and then to lunch on an occasional Saturday, walking in the woods near their home looking for different types of butterflies, and attending a children's movie from time to time. Jan's mother had for the most part stopped these mother–daughter activities and had tried to include her new husband, Jim, in all of them. Her reasoning (which is so common in this kind of situation) was that if they did all these things as a threesome it would help build a sense of family more quickly. She had not been aware of the fact that many youngsters perceive this approach as a loss of special, exclusive time with their mother, rather than as a newfound feeling of family togetherness. The psychologist brought this to her attention and noted that including Jim in these activities could be done, but only in a gradual way. The second part of the plan was to do just that: include Jim in these mother–daughter interactions from time to time. The final ingredient was to have Jan's mother talk with her about their new family using displacement communication. This overall plan, and the specific content of the displacement messages, was very similar to the strategy used by Meredith's recently remarried mother (see chapter 7).

Jan's mother and stepfather moved quickly to implement the first two parts of this intervention. Then Jan's mother, with the help of the psychologist, developed a displacement communication approach. Using Jan's large collection of stuffed animals, she showed her daughter a "stepfamily play." She had a mother bear and her daughter bear living together after a divorce, "They did lots of neat things together like walking in the woods and looking for honey. The daughter bear loved her mother and they had a lot of good times together." Then Jan's mother showed the mother bear getting married to a big "Stepdaddy Bear." He moved in with the mother and daughter. After setting the stage in this way, Jan's mother proceeded to use the first four steps of displacement communication. She had the girl bear acting angrily toward her mother: "I don't feel like helping set the table, Mom. Why don't you and Stepdaddy Bear do it. And how come we have to have cereal for breakfast. Why can't you fix my toast and honey like you used to? You make cereal just because Stepdaddy Bear likes it." This represented Jan's observable signs of distress. The second step, showing the youngster's unhappiness with her own distress, was carried out by, "The daughter bear doesn't like feeling mad at her mom. She loves her mom a lot and she wants things to be real nice like they used to be." At this, Jan angrily said, "Well, maybe the mom could get divorced!'' Jan's mother was tempted to respond directly to her daughter's comment. But she heeded the psychologist's advice and simply went on to step three of the displacement process by representing her daughter's underlying emotional pain: ''The daughter bear is mad at her mom for paying attention to the Stepdaddy Bear. Deep down it makes the daughter bear feel sad because she thinks her mom doesn't love her as much as she used to. The daughter bear saw how much her mom loved the stepdaddy, and the daughter bear felt sad and left out.'' Jan muttered, ''The mom is a jerk, and the stepdad is a dodo.''

Jan's mother moved along to the fourth step by correcting Jan's belief that she was no longer loved as she had been, ''The girl bear feels mad at her mom but she's also sad because it feels like her mom doesn't love her as much as she used to before she married the stepdaddy bear. The girl bear doesn't know that mom bears love their daughters just as much as before they got married. It's like there are two big honey love pies. The mom bakes one pie for her daughter and gives it all to her. It's only for her daughter. Then when she gets married, the mom bakes a whole new honey love pie for her new husband. It's a different kind of pie, and girl bears don't like how it tastes. It only tastes good to grown-up stepdaddy bears. Girls have one pie and stepdaddies have another. That's because mother bears love their girls in a very special way, and they love their new husband in a different kind of way.''

The third time Jan heard this story, she asked, ''What if the mother bear baked two or three honey pies for the girl bear and didn't make any for the stepdad? Then the girl could have more because she's real hungry.'' Jan's mother reiterated the difference between the honey love pies, ''The mom bear uses all of her love for her daughter to bake the honey love pie that is only for her. She puts every bit of her big loving feelings into it. The honey love pie for the stepdaddy bear is different. It has loving feelings that a mom has for a grown-up man bear.'' She then added, ''You know that you hate spicy spaghetti sauce and Jim likes it. You wouldn't want me to put spicy sauce all over your spaghetti, would you?'' Jan said: ''Yuck! That stuff stinks!''

As all three parts of the plan were being put into effect, Jan began to return to her old self. She enjoyed resuming the times alone with her mother but also began asking if Jim could come along sometimes. She genuinely liked him and resonated to his warmth and good humor. Within two months the displacement communication seemed no longer necessary. Jan's mother continued to spend occasional special, exclusive times with her daughter, which both liked, but more time was spent with all three family members together.

Overview

In helping early elementary school children cope with divorce, parents need to attend both to external and internal sources of distress for their children. Directly acting to reduce the former and using displacement communication to alleviate the latter increases the likelihood of children adapting successfully to divorce. However, these efforts may require a great deal of time, energy, and patience from parents. Structuring the youngster's environment so as to minimize stress may be difficult especially when parents are immersed in their own anger or emotional anguish. And attending to a child's inner concerns can be hard for parents who feel too uneasy, overwhelmed, or fatigued to confront their child's distress.

When parents seek to help their children they must also be prepared to examine carefully their own feelings, needs, and behaviors as well as those of their youngsters. It takes both courage and love for parents to avoid giving in to urges to make themselves feel better about the divorce without considering the possible impact on their children. Such impulses can lead parents to continue being at war with their former spouse, enmeshing their youngsters in inappropriate parent–child relationships, or fleeing their parental responsibilities in work or social activities. Parents also often have an understandable wish to blind themselves to the emotional pain of their children. Resisting each of these tendencies can be emotionally draining for parents. But the outcome for children depends upon it.

10

►◄

The Divorce Experience for Later Elementary School Children

The next phase of childhood extends from the middle of third grade through the end of sixth grade. Youngsters in later elementary school are usually between nine and twelve years old. During this period cognitive development proceeds to the point that children can achieve a realistic understanding of divorce events. They are aware of divorce as a legal process involving attorneys and the courts, and they know that it means the end of their parents' marital relationship. There is also significant social and emotional growth in later elementary school that contributes to an increasingly firm sense of independence from home and family. This permits youngsters to gain a more objective, at times even cynical, perspective on their parents' marital troubles. At the same time, the considerable developmental strides of older elementary school children provide the impetus for greater involvement in the wider world of school, friendships, and extracurricular activities. This is a time of transition from early childhood to adolescence.

The enhanced psychological maturity of older elementary school children brings greater complexity to their experience of divorce. This is manifested in two ways. First, children of this age are prone to develop internal conflicts over their perceptions of and reactions to divorce. For younger children the main sources of internal stress are frightening fantasies and self-blaming beliefs. Later elementary school children are also burdened by these stresses at times. But their more sophisticated sense of interpersonal relationships results in competing wishes and concerns, which form the basis for internal conflicts. An example is the child's impulse to side with one parent against the other, which is at odds with the youngster's need to be even-handedly loving toward each parent. This gives rise to feelings of divided loyalties that can become especially painful as one or both parents attempt to enlist the child on "their side" of the adversarial divorce process. The second way later elementary school children exhibit complexity in their reactions to divorce is in their use of more elaborate psychological defenses against experiencing emotional distress. These defenses are invoked automatically by the child's mind and protect him from becoming aware of potentially upsetting feelings. Internal conflicts and complicated sequences of defenses take on lives of their own which can be far removed from the external sources of stress. This makes it more difficult to discern links between the realistic environmental stresses of divorce and the youngster's observable reactions to them and often makes it harder for adults to understand and empathize with the child's underlying anguish.

Older elementary school children frequently convert painful feelings of helplessness and sadness into anger. This bit of psychological alchemy prevents them from feeling unhappy and emotionally vulnerable; anger is much more tolerable to most older elementary school children. While feelings of loss, sadness, and vulnerability characterize the divorce experience for many early elementary school children, anger and active attempts to master both external and internal stresses are the hallmarks of how these older children respond to their parents' divorce. It is as if they are saying, emotionally and behaviorally, that they refuse to take the divorce lying down.

The Immediate Crisis Stage

The initial parental separation jars most later elementary school children. Though they are frequently aware of marital discord between their parents, the majority of youngsters tend to accept it as part of normal, day-to-day family life. Other kids' parents may get divorced, but not theirs!

Two common sources of external stress in the immediate crisis stage of divorce are parental warfare and the loss (partial or complete) of the relationship between the youngster and the noncustodial parent (usually father). However, unlike their younger counterparts, later elementary school children do not simply resonate to parental anger or feel overwhelmed by sadness over losing their sense of family togetherness, which parental hostilities signal. Nor are most older elementary school children openly and visibly depressed over their father becoming more peripheral to or disappearing entirely from their lives. They often do not appear to long for or miss him. All of these reactions would indicate feelings of emotional vulnerability and/or helplessness. Children in the upper elementary school grades are far more likely to seem emotionally detached from the divorce process, almost as if it had nothing to do with them. Boys may display academic and aggressive behavioral problems in school. Girls can become overly solicitous of one or both parents and sometimes appear to bend over backwards to be helpful and congenial both at home and in school.

These observable reactions are the end products of complex interactions between the child's internal stresses (that is, internal conflicts, fantasies, beliefs) and the youngster's defenses, which are automatically and unwittingly mobilized to cope with these internal sources of distress. The feelings and behaviors of the child which adults can see directly often seem to have little if anything to do with the actual nature of the divorce events. Parents and other adults may think that the youngster is not being affected by the divorce at all. Either she seems cheerfully cooperative, or he is just acting up and getting into trouble for no apparent reason. Neither is true. Children actively strive to master the psychological pain of the internal conflicts, fantasies, and beliefs stimulated by divorce events. Their defenses are often so effective at protecting them from this pain that neither they nor adults who observe them are aware of what lies beneath the surface of their conscious thoughts and feelings. The forces that drive them have become invisible both to the children themselves and the adults in their lives.

TODD's parents angrily separated when he was ten-and-a-half years old. They had been arguing bitterly and openly for nearly six months. After one such blow-up, Todd's mother insisted that her husband pack his belongings and leave the family home immediately. Swearing loudly, he threw some clothing into a suitcase and stormed out of the home near midnight.

Todd's mother had become increasingly unhappy and enraged over her husband's insensitivity to her view of what their marriage should be like. She wanted him to participate in household chores and respect the fact that she, too, worked full-time outside the home and contributed financially to the family. She resented his expectation that she cater to his needs while also having nearly complete responsibility for raising Todd and his seven-year-old sister, Jackie. Todd's father experienced his wife's complaints as nagging and "bitching." He worked long hours as a house painter and believed that it was his wife's job to keep house, take care of the children, and see to it that he could relax and unwind when he came home from work. He angrily derogated his wife's wishes that he share household chores and child-rearing responsibilities referring to them as "women's lib crap."

After leaving the household, Todd's father rented a small apartment about five miles away. His wife filed for divorce and gained temporary custody of the two children. Todd and his sister saw their father every other weekend from Saturday morning to Sunday afternoon.

Todd could not believe it when his father left. For weeks he was certain that his parents would reconcile and that his father would return home. As the reality of the separation and impending divorce became clear to him, Todd began having difficulties at school. He had been an average student who had never been overly invested in doing well academically. Now he seemed to lose all interest in his schoolwork. His teacher reported that he seemed preoccupied. He would become occasionally sullen when given work to do and rarely completed assignments. Within a month, he had fallen behind the rest of the class in reading and in math.

But Todd's behavior with other children was of even greater concern to his teacher. Todd had always been a good athlete; now he began using his abilities to hurt and belittle other boys. In one soccer game he deliberately kicked the ball into a boy's stomach and laughed derisively when the youngster cried. On another occasion Todd became furious at a boy who insisted that Todd's kick had not scored a goal. He wrestled this boy to the ground, punched him repeatedly, and swore loudly. During a softball game a few days later, Todd went out of his way to charge into the catcher from the opposing team while crossing home plate to score a run. He knocked the boy down and then began calling him a "wimp" and a "loser" until the child cried.

At home things were not any better. He angrily kicked his sister as they argued over which television to watch. He teased her unmercifully about her schoolwork calling it "stupid," "easy," and "for dopes." Todd had also begun verbally demeaning his mother. From time to time he referred to her as an "air head" and a "dork" while muttering about her request to help set the dinner table or to clean up his bedroom. Todd's mother became increasingly angry at him and had begun to see him as acting just like his father, insulting her while refusing to help with household chores.

She told her husband about Todd's difficulties at home and at school. However, his father dismissed her concerns and attributed them to her not knowing how to handle their son. He noted, truthfully, that Todd was respectful and cooperative when the children were with him. Todd did what he was asked to do and did not pick on his sister during weekend visits at the apartment. Todd's father claimed that "Women don't understand how to deal with boys." All Todd needed was a firm hand. He just shook his head and smiled when his wife told him about Todd's behavior at home and in school.

After several months, Todd's problem behaviors had become a regular part of his daily life. When his mother tried talking with him about his behavior, Todd usually responded with sullen silence. Occasionally, he blamed other boys at school or his sister for provoking him and insisted that the trouble he got into was their fault, not his. Todd's mother believed that he was becoming unmanageable. She felt frustrated and angry about her son's demeaning attitude toward her and his hurtful behavior toward other boys and his sister.

At first Todd tried to deny the reality of his parents' separation and the fact that they were going to get a divorce. However, as he accepted that irreversible reality, Todd became an angry, hostile youngster. He seemed unconflicted about attacking and belittling other children, including his sister, and was all too comfortable derogating his mother.

The environmental stress of overt parental warfare provoked rage in Todd. He was furious at both parents for their attacks on one another and for upsetting the predictability and security of his world by separating. However, his anger at his father was not at all in evidence. Nor did he express his feeling toward his mother for her role in the marital discord and separation. Todd's fury at his parents created an internal conflict for him; he loved his parents but at the same time had a powerful urge to vent his anger at them for their behavior and for the divorce. To act on this rage toward them would stimulate intolerable feelings of guilt and fears of retaliation from them. So Todd found safer, more acceptable targets for his anger. He picked on other boys at school and tormented his sister. He displaced his rage from his parents to these whipping boys. This defense permitted Todd to discharge his pent-up anger while avoiding the internal conflict between his loving and furious feelings toward his parents. And this defense had an added psychological payoff for Todd; instead of feeling helpless and frightened by his parents' anger toward each other, he could feel powerful and in control both at home and in school. Todd, his parents and his teachers were entirely unaware that these dynamics, the presence of a particular internal conflict and the defense it evoked, were the forces propelling him to behave as he did.

Todd dealt with the stress of partially losing his relationship with his father in a different way. Initially he used the defense of denial as he ignored the reality of his parents' separation and waited expectantly for his father to come home. However, this defense is one that older elementary school children rarely permit themselves to continue for too long; it contradicts their mature and accurate perception of reality. As this way of coping with the absence of his father from the household gave way, Todd was faced with impending feelings of sadness and longing. He became like his father in order to feel close to him. Thus, Todd quite unwittingly adopted his father's attitudes toward household chores and his negative views of women. He refused to help his mother at home and demeaned her by calling her names under his breath. The developmental bonus of this defense for Todd was to further consolidate his emerging sense of masculinity, in that he was not taking any of his mother's "women's lib crap." And his father approved. Todd's mother responded in the way many women do in this situation; she became furious at her son and was also worried because he seemed to be turning out to be just like his father.

Todd's ways of coping with the painful feelings and internal conflicts precipitated by the divorce generally, and parental warfare and the partial loss of his father specifically, did not endear him to his mother, teachers or other youngsters. He was seen as acting in unacceptable ways at home and school. But neither he nor the adults in his life were aware of the connections between his behavior and the impact of the divorce on him. Rather than eliciting understanding, compassion, and support, Todd provoked frustration and anger in everyone around him, with the exception of his father.

Todd's reactions to parental hostilities and the partial loss of his relationship with his father are fairly common among older elementary school boys. Though the majority of these boys do not usually have as many behavioral problems as Todd did, their emotional reactions, internal conflicts and defenses are quite similar. Thus, while most boys will not be this physically hurtful toward peers or siblings, many will start teasing or belittling other youngsters. Instead of openly refusing to listen to their mother as Todd did, boys of this age may become more subtly uncooperative. They might repetitively "forget" to do chores they have been asked to perform or insist that they will do them later. Even after finally complying with such requests, boys will often complain bitterly about having had to do them. Many boys also have a tendency to identify with a father who has moved out of the family home. Sometimes this leads to a child adopting characteristics of his father that are antagonistic to his mother. But more positive identifications are possible, too. Boys may develop an interest in something their father cares about, such as sports or classical music. Or a boy may begin using phrases or displaying mannerisms of his father. These can inadvertently irritate mothers as they are then faced with frequent reminders of their ex-spouse and the difficulties of their previous marital relationship. When parents become aware of the private feelings and internal conflicts these defenses are meant to cope with, they can be more empathic with and feel less angry at their sons.

Girls in later elementary school often react quite differently. They are less likely to exhibit problematic aggressive behavior or difficulties in academic performance, or to identify with their noncustodial father. In the earliest stage of parental divorce, older elementary school girls seem to fare much better than their male peers.[1] Though clearly the same external stresses confront girls as boys and they give rise to similar internal conflicts, girls cope very differently from boys.

When a girl in later elementary school becomes frightened by parental warfare, angry at her parents for attacking one another (verbally or physically), or sad about missing her noncustodial father, she is likely to direct her coping efforts toward maintaining good relationships with both parents. She automatically banishes these painful feelings to distant and largely inaccessible corners of her mind and substitutes her intellectual understanding of the divorce and a desire to be solicitous of and helpful to both parents. These defenses of intellectualization (to understand without experiencing any accompanying unpleasant feelings) and reaction formation (to convert anger into pronounced loving and helpful feelings) serve girls well. They thus free themselves of emotional pain while achieving a greater realistic understanding of the divorce and gaining praise and affection from parents and teachers alike for being so helpful and caring. When these defenses work well, and they often do, girls are able to adjust to the initial phase of their parents' divorce.

However, there are hidden costs that some girls pay for these very real benefits. Perhaps the most common is to delay until adolescence coming to terms with their anger toward parents and their yearning for a close relationship with the absent father. It is as if there were a significant psychological agenda that is temporarily on hold. Even during the later elementary school years, there are prices girls sometimes pay for their good adjustment. In being so solicitous, so "other-directed," they in part sacrifice their own assertiveness. And conflicts over expressing anger or feeling sadness may not be fully contained by the defenses of intellectualization and reaction formation. At times more costly defenses must also be invoked. Among the most typical of these is somatization in which conflicts become expressed as physical problems such as headaches or stomachaches. This is not simply malingering nor is it evidence of a youngster becoming melodramatic. Real physical pain is substituted for emotional pain. Though the majority of older elementary school girls cope adaptively with the initial distress over divorce, it is wise for parents to be aware of the possibility that some of these more silent difficulties may be present.

The Short-Term Aftermath Stage

When a parent is having difficulty adjusting to the stresses of divorce, she may turn to one of her children for help. Though either parent may feel sufficiently beleaguered to do this, it is more likely for mothers who have custody of their youngsters to do so. Custodial mothers frequently feel understandably burdened by the social, emotional, and economic consequences of divorce.[2] They are often in the position of raising children largely on their own, holding down a job, having fewer financial resources than when they were married, and trying to fashion a new social life. This juggling act usually does not begin in earnest until the initial upheaval of the separation passes and the divorce process moves into the short-term aftermath stage.

Mothers of early elementary school children, and those even younger, usually must be in considerable distress before they enlist the aid of youngsters in their single-parent struggles. However, children in the upper elementary school grades are capable of being genuinely helpful to a distressed parent. The cognitive, emotional, and social strides older elementary school children have made are obvious to parents. They can effectively prepare dinners, do laundry, and look after younger siblings. These youngsters can also empathize with and understand the feelings of an adult far more readily than younger children and are able to engage in adult-like discussions around complex, divorce-related issues. These characteristics are especially true of girls in later elementary school who, on the average, are more interpersonally attuned and verbally skilled than their male counterparts.

Because parents recognize the abilities of older elementary school children, especially girls, they are more likely to turn to them for help with single-parent stresses. It is no longer necessary for a parent to be emotionally distraught before reaching out to a child. Instead, parents appear to be mobilizing a potentially effective resource that is readily available to lend a much-needed hand. Children of this age are usually willing to try to please parents and are concerned about their parents' well-being. Yet despite the realistic support youngsters are able to willingly provide their parents, especially girls helping their custodial mother, children feel burdened when they play this kind of role. They become distracted from the normal developmental tasks of gaining greater independence from their family and investing emotionally in relationships with friends and important adults outside the family. As they are pressed into this service, they are drawn back into the maternal orbit, partially sacrificing their efforts to establish a life of their own outside their family.

DANA was ten years old and her brother Blake was six when her parents separated. Her mother had been a full-time homemaker and her father was a branch manager for an outlet of a large chain of shoe stores. After ten years of marriage, Dana's father announced his plan to seek a divorce. He was unhappy with what he experienced as a progressive lack of intimacy and excitement in his marital relationship. Their lovemaking had diminished to about twice a month and it felt perfunctory to him. It seemed that his wife devoted all of her energy to raising their two children and socializing with other housewives in the neighborhood. At age thirty-three, he was not willing to continue in a marriage which he described as being "an old folks relationship."

His wife was stunned by his decision. She felt they had a good marriage and was comfortably content in her role as a homemaker. She had a good relationship with her youngsters and believed that her marriage was solid and satisfying. She and her husband had few disagreements and rarely argued. Initially, she tearfully tried to get her husband to reconsider his intention to leave the home. She suggested that they go off on a "second honeymoon," discuss his dissatisfactions, or see a marriage counselor. She claimed she was prepared to do anything, make any changes, to preserve their marriage. But her husband was adamant. He had made up his mind over several years and was not about to change course now. He left the house and rented an apartment about twenty miles away in the community where he worked.

The first several months of their separation was characterized by Dana's mother trying to persuade her husband to return to the family home. She called him frequently at work and at his apartment with ideas about how they might breathe new life into their marital relationship. When he came to pick up Dana and Blake for their biweekly visits, his wife cried and pleaded with him to give her another chance. She asked him to come to dinner, and suggested that they might "date." Her husband gently, but firmly, refused and reiterated the fact that he had thought over his decision for a long time and was convinced that it was right for him.

Gradually, Dana's mother became resigned to the reality of the divorce. She felt terribly wounded by her husband's having left her and began to try to understand what it was that caused him to be so unhappy. But as the initial shock of the separation began to pass and the divorce process moved into the short-term aftermath stage, she grew increasingly aware of the fact that she was now on her own as a single parent with two young children to raise. Although her husband made child support payments on time, she would have to sell the family home and move with her children to a smaller, more affordable house unless she found a job. These pressures began to frighten Dana's mother. At this point she started turning to her daughter for emotional support.

It began with her tearfully muttering to herself about not understanding what had gone wrong in her marriage. Dana frequently saw her mother in this distress and heard her lament. She began to try to console her mother awkwardly saying, "It'll be okay mom, you'll see." Instead of musing aloud to herself, Dana's mother began to talk directly to her daughter. She tearfully asked, "What did I do wrong?" and "Was I such a bad wife?" Dana was uncomfortable hearing these questions but did her best to reassure her mother. In the evenings, when her husband would have been home from work, she became especially upset and began asking Dana to help her brother get ready to go to bed. Dana willingly cooperated and saw to it that Blake had a snack, washed up, brushed his teeth, and got into his pajamas. She read him bedtime stories and tucked him in. Soon it became part of the household routine for Dana to get Blake to sleep.

Within a few months, Dana took on other parental tasks as well. She offered to cook dinner every other night, and when it was her mother's turn to prepare dinner, she looked after Blake from when they came home from school until mealtime. Dana spent less time playing with friends after school as she began to share the parenting role with her mother.

Dana also became her mother's confidant as well as Blake's part-time substitute parent. After her brother was in bed for the night, Dana and her mother talked about the divorce, the family's financial situation, the possibility of having to move to another house, and mother's anxieties over looking for a job. At times Dana's mother asked her point-blank, "What should I have done differently to make your father happy?" "Would it be better to get a full-time job or just work part-time?" and "What kind of job should I look for?" Having just turned eleven, Dana was at a loss about what to say in response to these adult concerns. But she was empathically in tune to her mother's anxieties and sadness. She comforted her mother primarily by hugging her and reassuring her that she had been a good wife and she would be able to get a job. However, after several months in her role as mother's confidant, she began to tell her mother that the divorce was not her fault. She had no reason to feel bad. It was her father who had left the family; he did not care enough about his wife or children to stay.

Emotionally propping up her mother in these ways began to take its toll on Dana. Her teacher reported that although Dana continued to do well in school academically, she seemed to have become socially isolated. The other girls rarely included her in games at recess anymore, and she did not have any close friends in the class. The teacher thought this might be because Dana had taken on a somewhat prissy, pseudo-adult air. She "shushed" her classmates when they were talking instead of paying attention to the teacher, always volunteered to help her teacher, and frowned disapprovingly at children when they did not know an answer to a question. The girls began referring to her as the "teacher's pet" and the boys occasionally called her "Miss Hot Snot." Though these insults did not appear to bother Dana, it was clear to her teacher that things were not going well for this youngster.

According to her mother, Dana seemed to be doing well at home. Although she rarely played with friends after school anymore, instead spending her time at home taking care of Blake, cooking dinner, and talking with her mother, she appeared to be responsible, thoughtful, and generally on even keel emotionally. Her mother did report that Dana had begun having three or four headaches a week, usually in the evenings. But perhaps most troubling was the fact that Dana had started refusing to go to her father's apartment for their every other weekend visits. She claimed it was boring at her father's place and that there was nothing to do. She told her mother that Blake could go, but she would rather be at home with her mother.

Her father had become upset about his daughter's resistance to seeing him and discussed it with his ex-wife. Dana's mother did not see her daughter's behavior as problematic. She claimed that Dana was a big girl and had the right to decide whether or not to spend time with her father. Besides, he had "abandoned" his family, so it was understandable that Dana might not want to see him. When Dana's father called to try to talk with her about her reluctance to see him, she was distantly polite but insisted that it was just too boring at his apartment. Her father thought that his ex-wife was inappropriately supporting Dana's puzzling need to avoid him. He filed a complaint with the court noting that the visiting arrangements specified in the divorce decree were not being adhered to. This triggered a referral by the court to a mental health professional for an evaluation of Dana and her home situation.

Actively helping her mother as a coparent and confidant fit well with Dana's need to cope with an internal conflict she began to experience when her parents separated. She was furious at her parents for not working out their marital difficulties and held each responsible for the divorce. However, she also loved both her parents. Her mind automatically protected her from the guilt this conflict threatened to produce by becoming especially loving and helpful to her mother. She convinced herself that she was a good, affectionate daughter who could not possibly harbor any angry feelings toward anyone, least of all her parents.

Dana was also wrestling with another internal conflict. She had an urge to side with one of her parents against the other by fixing blame for the divorce on one of them. Yet this offended her sense of fairness and interfered with her loving feelings toward each parent. This kind of loyalty conflict often produces intolerable tension within a youngster and therefore a strong psychological pressure to resolve it by coming down in favor of one parent. Dana eventually sided with her mother for two reasons. First, she felt that her mother needed her more than her father did. He seemed to be pleased with the divorce and was adjusting well to it. He could afford not having her support whereas her mother could not. Secondly, Dana experienced her father's leaving the home as an indication that he did not really love her. This belief, common to younger children as well as later elementary school youngsters, created distress in Dana because it made her feel unlovable and unworthy. If she were only prettier or nicer, then her father would have stayed. This belief often leads to depressive reactions in younger children as we observed earlier (see chapter 8). In older elementary school youngsters, it is more likely to see anger and/or retaliatory rejection as defenses against feeling the pain of sadness and battered self-esteem. So Dana resolved her conflict over which parent to be loyal to by taking her mother's side. In doing so, she also simultaneously supported her needy mother and protected herself from feeling awful about her father having left her as well as her mother.

Dana's defenses, while strong and in many ways adaptive, were not able to fully contain her emotional distress. She developed headaches, primarily a somatic expression of the anger she experienced toward her mother. This second line of defense served to keep her unaware of her underlying rage but at the cost of feeling physical pain. Her need to reject her father brought her into conflict with the legal establishment as well as interfering in her maintaining a loving and developmentally valuable relationship with him. A close, caring relationship with her father enhances a girl's self-esteem, paves the way for her feeling comfortable with and acceptable to males when she reaches adolescence and adulthood, and protects her from becoming emotionally enmeshed with her mother.[3] These benefits were in danger of being lost.

Most girls who take on adult roles during the extended divorce process do not typically reject their father so openly or forsake peer relationships to the extent Dana did. Their enmeshment with a needy mother and emotional distance from father usually has a lower profile. These youngsters infrequently come to the attention of either the courts or mental health professionals. But these psychological forces are at work in the lives of many older elementary school girls. As we shall see later, the results of these factors are more likely to become visible in adolescence than in preteen years.

While a distressed custodial parent may draw a youngster into adult matters of divorce as a coparent or confidant, warring parents will also inappropriately involve their children in the divorce process by encouraging them to take sides in the conflict. This may be done openly and blatantly by trying to convince a youngster that the other parent is bad or defective, attempting to use a child as a spy to bring back information about the other parent, or by having the child act as a messenger between parents who are hostile to each other. Rather than asking the youngster to be supportive of a distressed parent, the child is put in the middle of two angry parents. More subtle expressions of this dynamic are for parents to rail loudly or mutter about the faults of the other parent in the youngster's presence. Although the parent is not directly addressing the child at these times, the message is clear: I am right, reasonable, and decent while your father [mother] is wrong, irrational, and bad. If the youngster tries to defend the parent being maligned, he risks the wrath of the parent he is with at the time. If he stays silent, it feels as though he is tacitly agreeing.

The emotional cost to children when their parents draft them into their adult conflicts can be considerable. First, the older elementary school child's naturally occurring tendency to feel a loyalty conflict over which parent to side with is inflamed. The result is strong feelings of guilt and shame over participating repetitively, with one parent and then the other, in being disloyal to each. Second, it adds substantially to the child's anger over the disappointment and upset of the divorce. What begins as a typical angry reaction escalates to palpable rage that is at odds with the youngster's love for his parents. This internal conflict triggers defenses which may result in anger being acted out directly against peers and/or siblings or in more subtle expressions of resentment toward parents. Third, it places the child in a position of considerable and developmentally inappropriate power. While parents may try to involve the child in their dispute, in part because they realize that his enhanced reasoning and verbal skills make him capable of being an effective ally, no late elementary school child is ready to handle this power or the stress it creates. Whether or not he sides with a parent can provoke strong reactions in that adult. What he chooses to tell one parent about the other can lead to greater or less parental warfare. This is a daunting and burdensome responsibility that can also fuel the child's belief that he is the cause of his parents' disagreements. Collectively, these internal conflicts add a substantial amount of stress to the child's divorce experience.

Unfortunately, the use of children as allies or pawns in the hostilities between parents fits all too well with the propensity of older elementary school children to strive actively to master the stresses associated with divorce. They seek to avoid feeling like innocent bystanders caught in the turbulence of divorce. Becoming participants in the conflict is preferable despite internal conflicts this creates.

THE INITIAL STAGE of Ryan's parents' divorce was marked by intense acrimony. Charges of marital infidelity, drug use, and poor parenting were hurled back and forth for nearly a year before they finally separated. These accusations continued during the immediate crisis phase of their divorce and led to a bitter fight over the property settlement, the legal custody arrangement of the children, and the extent to which Ryan would spend time with his father. Ryan had just turned nine when his father moved out of the house into an apartment less than a mile away.

Ryan's mother taught in the foreign language department of a two-year community college. During her eleven-year marriage to Ryan's father, she and her husband had smoked marijuana together nearly weekly and had experimented with other illegal psychotropic substances as well. As Ryan got older she became uncomfortable about this behavior. She worried that Ryan would learn about it, and take his parents' use of drugs as license to do the same. She was resentful of her husband's unwillingness to give up smoking marijuana regularly. She felt he was being too self-absorbed and irresponsible in his parenting role. Their arguments over this issue became increasingly heated and rancorous. The intimacy they had shared, in part facilitated by their mutual recreational drug use, was replaced by a distant and resentful relationship. Ryan's mother immersed herself in her teaching and began a friendship with a colleague who was twenty years older than she. They frequently met for coffee after classes and faculty meetings and started having dinner together occasionally.

Ryan's father was also dissatisfied with the direction the marriage was taking. He was a dentist in private practice and had disliked his work from the beginning of his career. He had reduced the amount of time he spent at his office and got high on marijuana several times a week. At the same time, he resented his wife's new resolve to avoid drugs and was jealous of her friendship, which he believed was probably an affair, with her colleague. In part out of loneliness and to some degree because of his jealousy, he began an affair with a dental hygienist who worked in his office. They smoked marijuana together at her apartment, where he was spending a great deal of his after-work time.

As both parents fled their marital relationship in their own ways, Ryan was increasingly left on his own. He had heard his parents argue and use the word "divorce," but he never really believed it would come to that. When they separated, his hopes that they would get back together died quickly in the face of their intense hostilities. Throughout the first year of their separation they fought any time they talked. Fourteen months after Ryan's mother filed for divorce, it became legally final. However, this did not put an end to their antagonistic relationship.

Ryan lived with his mother and stayed with his father every other weekend from Friday night to Sunday afternoon. They also had dinner together every Wednesday, usually at a restaurant. This schedule had been established at the time of the initial separation and had continued undisturbed. Every time Ryan's parents saw each other, when Ryan was being picked up from one parent's home or dropped off at the other's, they argued. His father complained about the child support payments being too high and made snide references to his ex-wife's "sugardaddy" friend. Ryan's mother returned fire (and frequently initiated it) by sarcastically asking whether his "feet were touching the ground today" (a reference to his getting high on marijuana), berating him for being late even by a few minutes, and wondering how his "very un-hygienic assistant" was doing.

Each parent bad-mouthed the other in Ryan's presence. His mother frequently made comments about her ex-husband's affair and his lateness picking Ryan up for their biweekly visits. She portrayed him as an irresponsible man and an uncaring father, at times using these terms directly. Similarly, Ryan's father was critical of his ex-wife. He commented on her being away at work a great deal instead of looking after her son and made sexual innuendoes about her relationship with her colleague. He also claimed she was acting like a little girl in search of a "daddy" to take care of her.

In addition to exposing Ryan to their mutual derogation of one another, his mother and father also used Ryan to carry messages between them and act as a spy for each. His mother would remind Ryan to ask his father when the next child support check was coming when he visited his father next. His father often had Ryan let his mother know of changes he needed to make in the visiting schedule. Each parent quizzed Ryan about what the other was doing. When he returned from a visit with his father, his mother frequently asked Ryan whether his father's girlfriend had been with them and if his father was smoking and "acting strangely." Ryan's father pumped Ryan for information about how often his ex-wife was seeing her "friend," whether the man had been at the house recently, and if he had slept over.

Ryan dutifully did what his parents asked him to do. He carried their messages and answered their questions. But in doing so, he became sarcastic and argumentative with his mother and sullenly withdrawn with his father. When he was at his mother's house, he was resistant to helping her with chores, arguing in a legalistic way about whether it was really his turn to clear the dinner dishes, if he should have to take turns with her doing the laundry, and why he had to mow the lawn on Saturday instead of Sunday. He also mounted impressive arguments about why he should be permitted to stay up until 10 o'clock or 10:30 on school nights rather than having to be in bed by 9:30. He frequently became sarcastic during these altercations, making comments such as, "Sure, I'll clear the dishes and make dinner and do the laundry so you can go be with Jerry (her friend) and have a good time"; and "I don't have to be your slave and do everything you say." With increasing frequency, these debates ended with Ryan screaming that his mother was being unfair, running to his bedroom, and slamming the door. When he was at his father's home, Ryan seemed impossible to please. His father would plan an activity he thought

Ryan would like and have his suggestion greeted with a sullen, uncaring shrug of the shoulders. He said, ''I don't know'' when his father wondered why the plan did not seem like fun or invited Ryan to think of something he would really like to do. The times they went to a movie or sports event, Ryan did not appear to enjoy himself at all. His father's attempts to generate enthusiasm and ''talk up'' these outings were met with monosyllabic replies and exaggerated expressions of being bored. Both parents became increasingly resentful over Ryan's attitude.

In school Ryan began to do poorly. His academic work had consistently been above average, and he had liked school. Now toward the end of the fourth grade, he seemed uninterested in learning. His teacher was concerned about his underachieving. Though he was in no danger of having to repeat fourth grade, he was performing well below his previous level and far short of what his achievement tests indicated he could do. Ryan was also withdrawing from participating in athletics. He had been on the team of a local swim club but had recently quit, claiming he ''didn't feel like swimming anymore.'' His parents and coach tried valiantly to convince him to continue, but he was immovable. Ryan was not a behavior problem, but he had retreated from being appropriately engaged in schoolwork and peer relationships.

The environmental stresses of parental warfare and of being drawn into these hostilities as an active participant provoked several internal conflicts in Ryan. Most prominent were his divided loyalties and affections for each parent. As he alternately took one parent's side and then the other, he felt increasingly guilty and ashamed for being disloyal to both. He kept himself from being consciously aware of this inner tension by becoming uncooperative with each, not in their requests to carry messages and spy, but in other areas of his relationship with them. It was as if he were saying to himself, ''I can't refuse to do what seems so crucial to my parents, but I can be independent and not go along with their wishes in other ways.'' At the same time, his feelings of guilt forced him to unwittingly sacrifice numerous pleasures as a way of paying for his misdeeds. He gave up the gratifications of having a good time with his father, feeling close and loving to his mother, and enjoying the successes of good schoolwork and swimming. These were the prices his conscience exacted from him for being disloyal to each parent.

Ryan was also wrestling with intense anger at his parents for demeaning one another to him and for insisting that he become a party to their mutual hostilities. This precipitated another internal conflict; his rage was pitted against his love for both. His mind quickly defended him against becoming aware of this painful conflict. Instead of feeling furious toward each and then becoming frightened over their possible retaliation against him as well as guilty about being angry at them, Ryan began legalistically debating with his mother and was impossible to please with his father. These behaviors are frequently maddening to parents and quickly make them feel that they are at their wit's end about what to do. In these subtle ways, Ryan got even with his parents for placing him in the emotionally wrenching position of being in the middle of their warfare. Although he was not fully aware of this, it satisfied his urge to retaliate against them. However, at times his anger was so great that it required an outburst to fully express it. Then he would scream at his mother and slam his bedroom door.

Ryan's observable behavior could not easily be linked to his reactions to the divorce. He and his parents were unaware of the hidden, internal conflicts created by his parents' hostilities and the roles they assigned to him in them. These conflicts in turn automatically evoked age-appropriate psychological defenses that spare children the pain of having to confront their distress over the conflict directly. The end results of this private sequence of conflict and defense, invisible to the eye of most observers, were troubled relationships with each parent and a withdrawal from previously pleasurable activities.

Because older elementary school children are realistically capable of participating actively in adult conflicts and assuming adult roles vis-à-vis their needy or warring parents, the short-term aftermath stage of the divorce process can be prolonged for years. The involvement of youngsters in these ways serves to facilitate and sustain the difficulties one or both parents are having in coming to terms with the end of their marriage. At the same time, the developmental progress of the children is interfered with and delayed as energies are devoted to these conflicts instead of to the usual activities of peer relationships and learning in school. Continued parental warfare, the ongoing absence or near-absence of the noncustodial parent, and a constantly needy parent have their effects on children in the long-run. These environmental stresses will stimulate difficult-to-manage feelings, internal conflicts, and the defenses evoked by both in much the same ways as described earlier in this chapter. The more sustained these external sources of stress, the more consolidated and difficult it is to ameliorate the child's conflicts and defenses.

The Long-Range Period

Important environmental sources of stress for older elementary school children during this stage of the divorce process are parental dating and remarriage. Though dating can begin in the immediate crisis phase following the marital separation, and often occurs in the short-term aftermath stage, it is likely to be quite common and more serious in the long-range period. As parents successfully resolve their distress over the end of their marriage and learn to cope with the demands of being a single parent, they are freed up emotionally to become involved in significant dating relationships. And the majority remarry. Regardless of the child's gender, dating and remarriage by the custodial parent seems more upsetting to youngsters than the non-custodial parent engaging in these activities. The emotional connection to the custodial parent is often stronger than to the noncustodial parent (especially when that parent has had less than weekly contact with the child), and their day-to-day lives are more directly affected by actions of the parent with whom they live.

When a custodial parent (usually mother) begins to date in earnest, children must confront the fact that she will often have less time and energy for them. Her emotional investment shifts from a near-exclusive focus on the youngsters and their needs to her own desires for adult companionship and intimacy. This gives rise to several internal sources of distress in children. First, even older elementary school children tend to confuse having less of their mother's time and attention with the belief that she loves them less. This belief assaults the young-ster's sense of being lovable and important. They may develop fantasies that their mother would care more deeply about them if they were smarter, prettier, or nicer, but they automatically defend themselves against this depressive reaction, frequently becoming angry instead. The anger may be expressed directly at mother or, more often, is disguised in subtle ways, such as being sullen and uncooperative at home or picking on peers or siblings.

A second conflict generated by parental dating is the need to prematurely recognize their parents' sexuality. Many older elementary school youngsters are aware of the connection between reproduction and sex. But most keep this understanding out of consciousness. They realize that their parents must have "done it" at least once. However, they have great difficulty imagining their parents engaging in sex (they do not usually conceptualize it as "lovemaking") for pleasure! The connotation of sexual intercourse for older elementary school children is usually that it is exciting, forbidden, and dirty. Even in these enlightened times and in families that have educated their youngsters in liberal and thoughtful ways about sexuality, this seems to be the case. As parents develop serious dating relationships, the sexuality of the parent and the sexualized ambience of the relationship is much harder for children to avoid and keep out of mind. They are faced with the strong suspicion, if not knowledge, that their mother is doing something they consider very wrong. This conflict, between their image of their mother as good and nice and the idea of her having sex, must be reconciled. Some children try to blind themselves to the sexual nature of the dating relationship. But most older elementary school children will not permit themselves to carry on this distortion of reality for too long. It is often replaced by angry, derogatory feelings directed at their mother or her partner.

A third conflict aroused by parental dating is the feeling youngsters often have about whether it is all right for them to like and enjoy being with their mother's partner. Many men will try to be engaging with their partner's children. They may genuinely care about the youngsters or only recognize that it is important to their partner that they treat her children well. Youngsters find themselves feeling affectionate toward this new man, which creates a loyalty conflict for them. If they really like him does that mean that they are being disloyal to their father? If they have fun when they are with him, give him a hug, or accept a small gift when he comes over for dinner, are they in effect saying that they like him more than their father? Will their father be mad? This is a different sort of loyalty conflict from the issue of which parent to side with in their marital or postdivorce disagreements. But it is a surprisingly powerful source of distress for many youngsters. The most typical way for them to resolve it can be very upsetting to their mother: they act aloof, cold, or openly hostile to her dating partner. This creates an emotional distance between the child and this new man and constitutes an unwitting affirmation of the youngster's undying loyalty to his father.

HEATHER was six years old and her sister Jamie was ten when her parents separated. The anger and tension between spouses, which so commonly attends this first stage of the divorce process, subsided relatively quickly for Heather's parents. Both believed that the divorce made sense and had been discussing it privately between themselves for nearly a year before deciding to separate. Heather's mother worked as a hostess at an up-scale restaurant four afternoons and three evenings a week. Her yearly income was approximately $14,000. Heather's father was a police officer and earned $31,000 a year. They were able to arrive at a property settlement that seemed fair to each: Heather's mother got full possession of the house and Heather's father paid $550 per month in child support plus half of the monthly house mortgage payments. This allowed mother and children to continue their previous life-style, with only some belt tightening. Heather and her sister lived with their mother and saw their father every weekend, alternating between a Friday to Saturday and Saturday to Sunday schedule. He also took the children to his apartment, three miles away, for dinner once during the week.

During the short-term aftermath stage, Heather's mother coped increasingly well in her role as a single parent. She had a good relationship with each of her daughters, and with the exception of the two girls getting into heated disagreements and mutually provoking each other from time to time, things went smoothly. Although Heather's mother rarely dated, she felt confident about reentering the social scene at some time in the future. She was an attractive thirty-two-year-old woman who got along well with people and generally felt good about herself. Heather's father enjoyed being a bachelor. He had married when he was twenty and had always sensed that he had missed out on being an independent, single man. He enjoyed his work and delighted in purchasing his own small home two years after the separation. He dated casually and reveled in the sexual freedom of his single life. Since he had not developed a serious relationship, he avoided having Heather and Jamie meet the women he went out with. He saw no purpose in having his children get to know each of his partners in these short-lived relationships.

Four years after her marital separation, Heather's mother met and seriously began to date a man who played in the symphony orchestra of a large, nearby city. She had always appreciated music deeply and had played the flute throughout grade school and high school. George was forty-one, six years older than Heather's mother when they met. He, too, had married when very young and his

262

one child from that marriage, a son, attended a college several hundred miles away. George had been divorced for five years.

Although George was a hard-working perfectionist when it came to his career, he was a tender and caring man in his close, personal relationships. He became enamored of Heather's mother after meeting her at a private party at the restaurant where she worked. They began to date and he was delighted to learn that she had two daughters. Heather was ten and Jamie fourteen at that time. Though he loved his son, he had always wanted a daughter, too. Heather's mother and George quickly began seeing a great deal of one another. She attended the symphony's concerts when she did not have to work, and they met many late afternoons after his rehearsals and before either had to work later in the evenings, for a drink and light dinner. Within three months, it was clear to both of them that this was more than a casual relationship and could even result in marriage.

Heather's mother began inviting George for dinner at her home so he and the children could get to know one another. Though he had picked her up at her house several times in the early stage of their dating, he had not spent any time there. The first time he came to dinner, he brought each girl a different copy of an album recorded by the symphony orchestra. He wanted very much for them to like and accept him. Initially, everything seemed to go well. The girls found him funny and easy to be with, and his love for their mother grew stronger with each passing week. Heather's mother found herself falling in love with George and was pleased and relieved to see that he and her daughters got along so well.

Five months into their relationship, Heather's mother was spending nearly all of her free time with George. The two girls, their mother, and George began engaging in family-like activities during the parts of the weekends that the children were not with their father. They went to the zoo, canoed on a nearby river, attended movies, and went out for dinner. At fourteen, Jamie often elected to be with her friends during some of these times and occasionally had to stay home to do homework. Heather began to complain from time to time about having to go on these outings; she claimed she would like to be with friends like her sister was.

Heather also started acting cool toward George, a departure from her previous attitude. She quickly excused herself and went to her bedroom when George came to the house and preferred to play video games and read rather than watch television or listen to music after dinner with her mother and George. She became contrary with her mother, bickering about when familiar chores were to be done, when she was supposed to do her homework, whether or not she could sleep over at a friend's house on the weekend, or have a friend sleep over at her home. These rarely escalated to the point of angry exchanges between Heather and her mother. But both George and Heather's mother were aware of Heather's tendency to withdraw from them and of an undercurrent of hostility coming from her.

This behavior became more pronounced over the next several months. Heather seemed to be avoiding George when he was at her house. She resisted with increasing intensity accompanying her mother and George on their family-like outings. Her mother was confused about this behavior, somewhat embarrassed by Heather's obvious wishes to stay away from George, and felt bad for George that Heather did not seem to like him anymore. She tried to discuss this with her daughter, noting that it seemed that Heather had stopped being fond of George and appeared to be avoiding him. Heather responded matter-of-factly. She said George was "okay" but she just liked doing things besides sitting around with grown-ups. She would rather play video games, read, or talk to her friends on the telephone. When her mother pressed her further by pointing out that Heather's behaviors might hurt George's feelings, her daughter said, with some annoyance, that she "didn't mean to do that."

Heather's requests to have a friend sleep over or to go to a friend's house for the night became more strident. While other bickering did not lead to full-blown arguments, this issue did. Heather whined and wheedled to try to get her way on this score and if she could not, she angrily went to her bedroom while yelling that her mother was "unfair" and "mean." Heather had also begun to walk to the corner at the end of their street to wait for her father to pick her up for their weekly time together at his home. Her mother was puzzled about this, but when she asked Heather why she did it, her daughter just said, "I feel like it." It seemed to Heather's mother that this was yet another instance of her daughter avoiding her and George as well as not wanting her father to know that George was at the house.

At school, Heather continued to do splendidly. She had many friends, got along well with her teachers, and was progressing nicely in her academic work. Her teachers described her as a delight: smart, personable, and cooperative. Heather's mother was pleased to learn this, but was struck by the discrepancy between her daughter's excellent adjustment in school and her resentful, avoiding attitude at home towards her and George.

The closeness between Heather's mother and George stirred up painful feelings of not being as special to her mother as she, Heather, used to be. She loved her mother and enjoyed a close relationship with her. But now she felt unimportant compared to George. To protect herself from the belief that she was no longer as lovable and as worthy as she had been, she started to feel resentful towards her mother. Her usual cheerful, cooperative attitude gave way to her bickering when her mother asked her to do something. However, her resentment was at odds with her love for her mother. This created an internal conflict between these opposite feelings. She attempted to resolve this inner tension by distancing herself from her mother and thus from seeing her mother be so affectionate with George. This essentially was an attempt to use the defense of denial. If she did not have to observe her mother with George then she did not have to feel envious, left out, and therefore angry. Her desperate attempts to have a sleep-over with a friend, at her own house or at the friend's, was an example of Heather trying to use denial; if she were occupied with a friend she could have a good time and not have to think about her mother and George having a loving, close relationship.

The romantic relationship between her mother and George also made Heather uneasy. She sensed, and intellectually expected, there to be a sexual aspect to their relationship. For the first time in her life, Heather had become aware of her mother's sexuality. Her efforts to avoid George and her mother thus also served to ward off her having to face the sexuality of their closeness.

Heather was also wrestling with another internal conflict. Her love for her father felt threatened by her initial interest in George and the good feelings she had when she was with him. At first she really liked George and enjoyed his caring, humorous attention. But this seemed vaguely disloyal to her father. How could she like a man other than her father? Why did she feel so good when George paid attention to her? Would her father feel hurt because she liked George? This is a different sort of loyalty conflict from children trying to decide which parent to side with in their disagreements. Here, a child must reconcile her affectionate feelings toward a parent's dating partner and for the parent of the same sex as that dating partner. For Heather, the loyalty conflict was not whether to side with her mother or father. Instead she was burdened by the decision of whether or not it was really all right for her to care a great deal about George without that being evidence of her betraying her father's love. Heather coped with this conflict by giving up her interest in George. She avoided him whenever possible and became unresponsive to his efforts to engage her. In doing so, she was "demonstrating" her love for her father.

Heather was not consciously aware of her painful fantasy that she was less special to and less loved by her mother. Similarly, she was not in touch with the content of her two internal conflicts. Her mother felt that she loved Heather as much as she ever had, and was unaware of her daughter's internal conflicts. Thus Heather's behaviors were unexpected and seemed inexplicable.

A custodial parent's dating does not necessarily lead to the sorts of impending emotional pain and internal conflicts Heather was confronting. While these issues are common for girls in later elementary school, they arise less frequently for boys. The developmental agendas for the two sexes are quite different. Older elementary school girls often still feel comfortably close to their mother and naturally seek to solidify their identifications with her. When daughters of this age and their mother do chores, shop, talk, and go on pleasurable outings together, they are seen by others as having a good, especially close relationship. There is no term for girls that connotatively corresponds to "momma's boy." If a boy between the ages of nine and twelve and his mother spend a great deal of time together in different activities, this epithet is often thought, if not actually voiced, by other adults as well as the boy's peers. Older elementary school boys are expected to have greater emotional and physical distance from their mother than their female counterparts.

When a later elementary school boy's custodial mother develops a serious dating relationship, there are several developmental payoffs for him. First, the mother's dating relationship may help create a comfortable degree of distance between mother and son. Boys at this age sometimes find it difficult to achieve an optimum emotional distance when their single-parent mother is overly close to them out of their own needs. A boy is more able to escape the burdensome closeness with his mother of being the "man of the house" when mother, in fact, has a man in her life. Second, boys in the upper elementary school grades are psychologically looking for a man with whom to identify and after whom they can model themselves. Having a caring, interested man in their lives affords boys whose parents have divorced an opportunity to further develop and consolidate their masculine identity. Though older elementary school boys must confront feeling less special to their mother than they used to be as well as the loyalty conflict in their affections for their father and toward mother's new partner, these developmental bonuses tend to make it easier for them to accept and profit from their mother's dating relationship.

JEFF's mother began a serious dating relationship with Evan, a man she met at a dinner party given by a friend, when her son was nearly twelve years old. Jeff had been eight years old when his parents separated. His two younger sisters were six and three at that time.

During the first two stages of the divorce process, Jeff's mother had put her energy into her work and spending all her free time with her children. She coped successfully with the rigors of single-parenting. She was economically self-sufficient and was respected at her place of work. She was also a caring and effective parent. Her youngsters thrived under these conditions. They knew their mother was competent at work, organized at home, and loving with them. She was fortunate in not having to burden them with feelings of depression or neediness, nor was she preoccupied with her life apart from her children to the extent that she was unaware of their needs or uninvolved in their upbringing.

Though all three children were generally faring well across the board developmentally (that is, in family relationships, peer friendships, schoolwork, and how they felt about themselves), Jeff's sisters were doing better than he. At age ten, two years beyond the marital separation and well over a year after the legal divorce had been granted, Jeff developed several inhibitions. He avoided participating in sports except at school during gym where he was required to. At the same time, he began spending long hours involved in a variety of computer games, especially football and baseball. When neighborhood boys came to ask him to play with them, he begged off, making up the excuse that he had too many chores to do at home. He frequently asked his mother to go out in the backyard with him to play catch with a football or baseball (depending on the season of the year) and to play board games with him indoors when the weather was bad. When she had other things to do around the house or was involved with one or the other of her daughters, Jeff became angry and exclaimed, "You never have time to do any stuff with me!" It seemed that his entire social-emotional life revolved around his mother.

Jeff also began to sulk and complain whenever his mother asked him to do the few household chores he had. He frequently said he was too tired or that he just had to finish the computer game he was involved in. Then he "forgot" the task his mother had asked him to do. When she reminded him, Jeff told her to "quit nagging" him. His mother became increasingly irritated by his general passivity; he did not spend much time with friends, was not involved in sports or extracurricular activities at school, and played computer programs or watched television for hours each day. She angrily told him on several occasions that pushing computer buttons and changing the channels on the television set was not enough exercise for a boy his age. She also resented his constant demands for her to play with him coupled with his unwillingness to be actively helpful around the house. Gradually, she found herself devoting more of her family time to her daughters, playing with Barbie dolls, putting on puppet shows, and playing "dress up" with them. Jeff had no place in these activities, and withdrew further into imaginary play with the computer and watching television.

When his mother began dating Evan, Jeff's demeanor began to change for the better. Evan frequently invited Jeff to throw a football or baseball together, took him to sporting events that only the two of them attended, and also occasionally played computer games with him. With Evan's gentle encouragement, Jeff reluctantly agreed to try to play Little League baseball that summer. Evan helped Jeff practice his throwing, fielding, and batting, praising him freely for his efforts. Over the course of the summer Jeff became more confident in his athletic abilities and in fact did reasonably well.

At the end of the summer, Evan and Jeff's mother married. They bought a new home in the same neighborhood and Evan involved Jeff in moving the furniture, painting some of the bedrooms, and putting up wood paneling in the basement. He told Jeff that this was "men's work" and they spent long hours together in these tasks. Jeff also noticed that his new stepfather helped set the dinner table, cleared the dishes after meals, and put them in the dishwasher. Jeff responded well to Evan's request that he help with those chores so that they could get them done and have more time to play catch or practice batting afterward.

As the relationship between Evan and his stepfather flourished, Jeff's attitude toward his mother improved. He was more cooperative and even volunteered from time to time to be helpful to her. However, Jeff continued to be reluctant about investing himself in peer activities after school and on the weekends. He easily and happily played with Evan and was helpful around the house, giving up much of his previous passive retreat to television and solitary computer play. But he resisted joining neighborhood youngsters in playing ball, riding bicycles together, or spending time at each other's homes. He had come a long way, but had not yet transferred his emotional investment from home to peer relationships.

After his parents' divorce, Jeff had to cope with the environmental stress of not having his father available to help him grow up. He found himself the only male in a household with three females. His mother was neither distressed nor needy, so even the developmentally interfering role of "man of the house" was not available to him. Further, he had no adult male role model around which he could begin to consolidate his masculine identity. Thus, he did not have the confidence that he would be accepted in the world of male peers. Nor did he have the experience of relating to a man and thereby becoming comfortable in interacting with boys. He retreated from peer interactions which, in later elementary school, are nearly exclusively same-sex relationships. Instead he stayed with his mother or involved himself in the more predictable and less anxiety-arousing activity of computer games. He did not have to worry about how to act, what to say, or whether he would be accepted in a group of boys.

Jeff also faced a difficult internal conflict which all older elementary school and adolescent boys must wrestle with when they are being raised in a single-mother household. On the one hand, they tend to feel that they have to rely on their mother for the parenting support and love they realistically still need. Yet they are notably uneasy about giving in to the usual demands parents make of children because doing so feels tantamount to being a "momma's boy," a "wimp," or worse, effeminate. While younger boys are far less vulnerable to this fear, it is a central issue for those in later elementary school and adolescence. Without a firm sense of their emerging masculine identity, these boys experience closeness with their mother or being cooperative with her as evidence of their lack of assertiveness or masculinity. Coercive struggles between single-parent mothers and their sons can ensue over household chores, bedtime, and completing homework assignments from school. Nearly any area of normal parental authority or guidance can become a source of conflict between mother and son precisely because many boys experience such requests as a threat to their shaky masculine identity. Thus, a boy's need for parental affection and direction is at odds with the pressure he feels to resist and fight his mother's influence because to give in means that he is sacrificing his sense of masculinity. Jeff wished to be close to his mother and felt the need to rely on her, as well. But he also found it necessary to fend off her authority. He was buffeted by this internal conflict, alternating between imploring her to play with him and resisting her requests to listen to him and do his chores.

When Evan came into his life, Jeff was developmentally ready to accept a relationship with a man. He needed an adult model of masculinity close at hand to facilitate the growth of his own sex role identity. How do men act in different situations? How do they speak? What is it like to feel manly? Without a father, or some other involved man (a grandfather or an uncle) present, boys are left with the unrealistic, and therefore unattainable, images of manhood that are frequently found in the popular media. Most older elementary school boys whose only models for masculinity are of the Clint Eastwood variety retreat from the impossible task of measuring up to them. They console themselves by vicariously experiencing the masculinity of sports or television idols while eschewing attempts to develop their own masculine competence.

When Jeff threw a baseball or football with Evan, he could see Evan's competence as well as his realistic shortcomings. Sometimes Evan dropped a pass or threw inaccurately. But he accepted his lack of perfection with good humor and equanimity. Thus, Jeff began to learn that being manly did not mean having to be a top-notch professional athlete or, even more unrealistically, a perfect character in a movie. Jeff could identify with this very real and engaging man.

He also had a new and gratifying alternative to the mother–son relationship. When Jeff did things with Evan, he was doing even more than enhancing his own masculine identity and developing realistic athletic skills. He was also shifting some of his emotional investment in his mother to Evan. This began to create a developmentally appropriate emotional distance between Jeff and his mother. It was not that he loved his mother less, but rather he did not have to feel that she was the only adult in his psychological universe.

Jeff's growing sense of and confidence in his own masculinity along with his feeling less emotionally dependent on his mother permitted him to be more cooperative and pleasant with her. It was also enormously helpful for Jeff to observe that Evan could set the dinner table, wash the dishes, and participate generally in household chores without feeling that his manhood was threatened. It became clear to Jeff that helping his mother and being reasonably responsive to her authority did not mean that he was being a "wimp" or was in some other way sacrificing his masculinity.

Although Jeff was prospering psychologically with the entrance of Evan into his life, he still avoided (with the exception of playing in Little League) opportunities to interact and form friendships with peers. It was as if he did not yet feel sufficiently confident about his newly acquired sense of masculinity to risk rejection, or perhaps even ridicule, at the hands of the neighborhood "guys."

The long-range period commonly involves children coping with life in a single-mother household, the custodial mother's serious dating, and/or her remarriage. For many youngsters, all of these life experiences characterize the long-range period of divorce. Each has its own potential for creating distress and for offering developmental support to older elementary school children. Boys and girls often react differently to these life events just as they do to the environmental stresses associated with the immediate crisis and short-term aftermath phases of divorce.

Recognizing Distress in Later Elementary School Children

Unlike younger children, later elementary school youngsters display distress in ways that do not make them appear vulnerable or in need of help. The visible signs of their emotional upset often do not suggest that they are feeling distressed. Later elementary school children are more likely to exhibit behaviors and feelings which make it seem that they are either upset with another person (for example, a peer, sibling, parent, or teacher) or are not experiencing distress at all. Their complex psychological reactions to divorce frequently disguise the fact that they are struggling with painful feelings about their parents' divorce.

Anger is the most common expression of distress in children in later elementary school, especially boys. It can be expressed in direct, physical fighting with peers or siblings or in bitter, verbal aggression directed at one or both parents. But anger also can be displayed in quieter, more subtle ways. A child may argue with a parent or complain about having to do household chores, how late he can stay up at night, how much television he can watch, when to take a bath or shower, whether he can have a friend over to play, the food that is served in the home, and even the type of clothing he should wear on a particular day. Nearly any facet of day-to-day living can be a vehicle for this more indirect expression of anger.

Parents rarely connect either these overt or disguised manifestations of anger to reactions the child is having to the divorce. Instead, the youngster seems, to parents and other adult observers as well, to be generally hostile, explosive, or out of control when he is being openly angry, or as uncooperative, argumentative, willful or "passive aggressive" (a favorite term of mental health professionals and educators) when more subtle forms of anger are being expressed. In short, these expressions of anger lead adults to characterize the child in general ways. Unfortunately, such global descriptions fail to recognize the reasons for the anger and the specific links between it and the divorce. This may result in self-fulfilling prophesies: The youngster begins to "live up to" the expectation that he is a generally angry, unpleasant, or uncooperative child, as if that were the main feature of his personality.

Somatic complaints are also frequently observed expressions of distress in later elementary school children. Headaches and stomachaches are among the most common of these. Parents may regard these physical ailments as evidence of a medical problem such as a virus or "flu." Trips to the pediatrician or family physician, while appropriate and prudent, especially when the physical symptom has persisted for days, often reveal that there is no underlying medical condition. Parents sometime dismiss these sorts of somatic complaints, believing that the child is making them up or exaggerating them. However, many youngsters can have headaches or stomachaches that are very real and painful. This comes about through the unconscious defense of somatization. This defense is automatically triggered at times in order to protect the child against feeling anger (associated with the production of "tension headaches") or longing for the attention and love of a noncustodial father or an emotionally unavailable custodial mother (often linked to stomachaches). Parents rarely make the connection between these somatic complaints and the child's experience of the divorce.

Social withdrawal is another common sign of emotional distress among later elementary school children. Though some youngsters display this reaction in easily recognized ways, such as moping about the house claiming they have nothing to do, it is far more typical for children to appear to be overly involved in activities that just happen to be solitary in nature. The child who spends a great deal of time in imaginative play with action figures or Barbie dolls, playing computer games, reading, organizing and reorganizing a large collection of baseball cards, and the like is actually withdrawing from developmentally appropriate peer and family interactions rather than simply being caught up in a special interest. They avoid hidden anxieties over being rejected, humiliated, or even being hurt in peer relationships by clinging to the safety of home. They often engage in very active fantasies that serve to bolster their low self-esteem and lack of confidence. Children imagine they are powerful beings, well-known sports figures, famous entertainers, or simply that they are popular with their peers while playing in these ways. Parents often begin to be concerned about the youngster's lack of friends after a while but do not usually link this social withdrawal to distress over divorce related issues.

A variation of social withdrawal is when the child wants to spend her after-school and weekend time talking to the custodial parent, helping out around the house, and accompanying the parent on errands. Here the child's withdrawal does not involve solitary play. She avoids peers, but not her family, and is especially close to her custodial mother. The fact that the youngster is not appropriately involved with peers may be overlooked by a distraught or needy custodial parent who values the realistic support she is getting from her youngster. However, peer relationships are crucial to the social-emotional development of children in later elementary school. Any pronounced lack of involvement in peer activities outside school should be a signal to parents that the child is in distress.

Although these are among the most common signs of distress in older elementary school children, they are by no means the only forms it can take. Expressions of distress described for early elementary school children occur for later elementary school youngsters, too. General anxiety expressed in nervous habits such as nail biting, hair twirling, and the like is not unusual. Similarly, sadness and depressive reactions, especially among children at the younger end of the later elementary school age range, can be displayed. Children mature at widely varying rates, and thus there is some understandable overlap in how later and early elementary school children respond to their parents' divorce.

Overview

Later elementary school children struggle to cope actively with divorce. In doing so, they bring surprisingly mature cognitive abilities and greater social-emotional independence to bear on the problems parental divorce creates for them. They organize their experience of divorce rather than simply responding to it. But new internal sources of distress are created in the form of internal conflicts. These arise from perceptions of and concerns about divorce that could not even occur to younger children. The greater complexity of defenses, which older elementary school children have at their disposal for protecting themselves against emotional pain, are automatically used to cope with both external and internal sources of stress. Frequently, both the child and the adults in his world are unaware of the nature of the distress and the connection between the child's observable reactions and the ways in which he is experiencing the divorce.

11

►◄

Helping Later Elementary School Children Cope

Parents can begin helping their later elementary school children cope with divorce by directly confronting with them the fact that a marital separation is about to occur. It is not unusual for parents to avoid discussing the separation and the changes it will bring into the child's life. Some parents feel that talking about the divorce will cause their child undue emotional pain. They try to protect the youngster by not mentioning anything about divorce. Others are uneasy about the possibility that their child will be angry at them and do not talk with the youngster in order to protect themselves from the child's fury. And, while many parents of early elementary school children believe that discussing divorce with their child will be unhelpful because he will not be able to understand it, parents of older elementary school children frequently think that it is unnecessary to explain divorce to them because they are mature enough to see for themselves what is happening.

When parents choose not to discuss the divorce with their children, they are inadvertently giving youngsters unhelpful messages. The child may experience this lack of communication as a statement that her parents do not think she is capable of dealing with the stresses of divorce. This vote of "no confidence" may undermine the child's efforts to cope with the divorce. Or a child may sense that a parent is frightened by the prospect of the youngster getting angry. This can give children the impression that their anger is too strong and dangerous for parents to manage and therefore must be kept under wraps. Not discussing divorce may also make children think that there is nothing of importance to talk about. This suggests to many children that there is no reason to be upset or concerned when their parents separate. Children are then burdened by the discrepancy between this message and the fact that they are indeed feeling distressed by their parents' divorce. It is natural for children to turn to their parents for understanding, reassurance, and emotional support in times of stress. When parents do not take the initiative in discussing the divorce, it cuts children off from the primary way they have of coping with questions, worries, and troublesome feelings, irrespective of their source. The child is left on his own to deal with his reactions to the divorce. The result for many children is an increased sense of distress.

Parents can explain the divorce to their older elementary school children in much the same ways as described earlier for younger elementary school children (see chapter 9). The main points in these discussions are telling the child about the fact of the marital separation; explaining what it will mean to the youngster regarding where he will live, with which parent he will be staying, where the other parent will be living, and how frequently (if at all) he will see the noncustodial parent; giving reasons for the divorce in terms appropriate to the child's level of development; and, reassuring the child that the parents love him and that he was in no way responsible for the divorce. These parent–child discussions should be brief (usually under five minutes) and should be repeated several times throughout the immediate crisis stage of the divorce.

In addition to discussing the divorce openly with their children, beginning early in the initial crisis stage and even a week or two before the separation has taken place, parents can strive to minimize the environmental sources of stress. These include parental warfare, the loss of the child's relationship with the noncustodial parent, and emotional distress of the custodial parent. Parents can be mindful of the deleterious impact on youngsters of hostilities between divorcing spouses. Physical confrontations, verbal assaults, and insults can be avoided through mutual agreement, by restricting communication to written messages, and if necessary, via legal steps to reduce contact between the parents. The loss of the child's relationship with the noncustodial parent can be mitigated to a great extent by parents working together to establish a schedule of regular and frequent times for the youngster to be with the noncustodial parent. This should be done early in the immediate crisis stage because patterns of visitation set down then tend to continue.[1] A custodial parent who is distraught about the divorce can seek support and relief from friends, relatives, and mental health professionals to contain the negative effects of this stress for youngsters.

Two more subtle sources of external stress that parents of later elementary school children must guard against are placing the child in adult roles such as coparent or confidant and involving the youngster in parental conflicts as a messenger or spy. The older elementary school child's cognitive, social, and emotional maturity can easily result in parents putting them in these untenable and stressful positions. It is helpful for parents to reflect on whether they are asking their child to perform functions *on a regular basis* that are really meant for adults. How often does the child prepare meals or look after younger siblings? Have these become tasks that the child is asked to do nearly every day? If so, the youngster has become a coparent. Does the parent share concerns about finances, the relationship with the (ex-)spouse, or dating? When the parent discusses these adult issues with the child, the youngster becomes a confidant. Similarly, how frequently do the parents use the child to convey messages back and forth between them or report on each other's activities? Is the child told to ask the other parent about support payments or changes in the visiting schedule? Does either parent pump the child for information about the other's drinking, dating, or money spending? Parents are often unaware that they are putting the child squarely in the middle of their conflict by making these requests.

Frequently, a parent calls out to a youngster who is on his way to the other parent's home to ''Remind your dad about the support check'' or ''Don't forget to tell your mom that I'll be picking you up at 6:30 next Saturday instead of 5:00.'' Parents may also greet a child coming from the other parent's home with questions such as ''Did you see Mary [father's girlfriend] this time?'' or ''Did your mom buy you any new clothes last week?'' Often these comments and questions seem casual and innocuous to parents. But older elementary school children usually experience them as pressures to participate in the parents' divorce battles.

In addition to avoiding or minimizing these external sources of stress, it is crucial for parents and other adults with whom the child has contact to be aware of the internal sources of stress that divorce often stimulates in older elementary school children. These private sources of stress are pivotal forces in shaping the later elementary school child's experience of divorce. It is generally the case that the older the child, the more important it is for adults to be sensitive to the youngster's internal sources of distress.

Earlier we saw that fantasies of what might occur in the course of the divorce and egocentric beliefs about the reasons for current and past divorce events can frighten children and damage their self-esteem. Later elementary school children are also vulnerable to these two sources of internal distress, though usually to a lesser degree than preschoolers and early elementary school youngsters. In the upper elementary school grades, the primary sources of internal stress are conflicts within the child. Competing wishes, needs, and feelings pull children in opposite emotional directions and thus create inner tensions that can become painful and upsetting. Children and parents are usually unaware of the presence of these conflicts, let alone the nature of them. A brief list of centrally important, common internal conflicts for older elementary school children is given below.

- Anger at one or both parents
  versus
  Love for both parents
- Loyalty to each parent
  versus
  Impulses to take sides in parental conflicts
- Affection for one parent's partner
  versus
  Loyalty to the other parent
- Wishes to be involved with peers
  versus
  Urges to help a distressed parent

These conflicts are rarely visible to children or their parents. But just as it is the submerged part of an iceberg that can scuttle ships passing by, these unseen conflicts can destroy a child's healthy developmental progress.

Older elementary school children have available to them a wide array of complex psychological defenses against the emotional pain and tensions that threaten to be evoked by both external and internal sources of distress. These defenses are elicited automatically and protect the youngster from even being aware of the presence of the conflict. Moreover, the behavioral and emotional results of these defenses are often so far removed from the initial sources of distress, external or internal, that it is difficult for adults to recognize that the child is struggling with divorce-related issues. Once adults can see the defensive aspect of a youngster's observable actions and feelings, they are more able to empathize with and help him. It also becomes possible to infer the nature of the specific divorce stresses that the child is trying to cope with. Common psychological defenses and some examples of their visible expressions are outlined below.

Defenses	**Observable Behavior/Feelings**
Intellectualizing feelings	Unemotionally discussing events which would seem upsetting; explaining why it was reasonable not to be upset in the face of distressing events.
Denying feelings	Appearing aloof and untouched by realistically upsetting events; creating emotional distance from a parent or parent's partner to avoid painful feelings.
Displacing feelings	Teasing or fighting with siblings or peers (instead of being angry at a parent); being uncooperative or argumentative with one parent and on especially good behavior with the other.
Somatizing feelings	Having headaches or stomachaches; frequently complaining about feeling tired.
Converting one feeling to another	Becoming overly devoted to a parent (instead of feeling angry); acting angrily invulnerable or bossy (instead of feeling helpless, frightened, or sad).
Identifying with an absent parent	Becoming strikingly like that parent in mannerisms, attitudes, and/or interests (instead of longing for and missing the parent).

By their very nature, these defenses are automatic psychological reflexes that are below the level of the child's conscious awareness.

It is not helpful for parents to mount frontal assaults against these defenses. To begin with, they serve an important, self-protective purpose, sparing the child distress he would experience in their absence. Further, the youngster is not cognizant of the fact that he is defending himself against emotional pain. If a parent were to say to her child, "You're not really mad at your brother, you're just taking out your anger toward me on him," or "You're having headaches because you're really very angry at me," the child would most likely respond by insisting that he was indeed mad at his brother or that he did not feel angry at anyone, he just had a bad headache. In addition, children often feel confused, put on the spot, misunderstood, and even criticized when parents (or other adults for that matter) make direct statements of these sorts.

It is likely to be far more useful for parents to approach these defenses and the potentially upsetting internal conflicts and feelings they are often protecting through the indirect means of displacement communication. When a boy has been getting into trouble at school for teasing or fighting, a parent can say: "Sometimes guys have some pretty big mad feelings when their parents are getting a divorce. Guys can feel real angry at their parents even though they love them. A lot of boys take those mad feelings to school with them. Then they start feeling angry at other kids and get into trouble for teasing (or fighting with) them." If a girl has been having headaches, it can be helpful for a parent to tell her: "You know, it's kind of interesting that lots of times when a girl is having some mad feelings toward her parents for fighting with each other and getting a divorce, she can start getting headaches. Girls don't like having headaches, but they love their mom and dad and don't want to be mad at them. Feeling mad makes most girls pretty tense, so they get headaches instead."

These one-step-removed communications are valuable because they permit the child to hear what the parent is saying instead of pushing it away. They usually do not feel that the parent is shining an uncomfortable spotlight on them nor are they likely to feel misunderstood or criticized. To the contrary, by verbalizing the link between the child's defense and the underlying conflict giving rise to it in the context of talking about "a lot of boys" or "most girls," the parent is reassuring the youngster in several ways. When parents make these sorts of comments they are letting their child know he is not alone in his trouble; there is an explanation for the difficulties he is having, and therefore relief can be achieved; he is not solely responsible for what he is experiencing because it is a reaction to the divorce; and, he is not bad, after all "lots" of children have similar problems when their parents separate.

This is not to say that children will usually respond to displacement communication by directly acknowledging the correctness of the parent's statement, feeling immediate emotional relief, quickly altering their behavior, or beginning to openly discuss their internal conflicts. Nor are they likely to look their parent in the eye and say, "Thanks, I needed that." Initially, most older elementary school children react by either saying nothing at all or somewhat weakly denying the parent's assertion. Although some may express interest by asking questions such as, "You mean that the reason I have a headache is because I'm mad at you and dad [mom]?" Fortunately, however, the usefulness of displacement communication does not hinge on whether the child directly accepts the parent's statements. It can work even though the youngster denies them or seems oblivious to what the parent is saying. It therefore takes a great deal of patience on the part of parents to proceed with this type of communication while getting so little feedback from their children about its possible beneficial effects. But as long as the parent continues this indirect form of communication (often for a month or more) and resists the temptation of moving away from the displacement method by making direct statements or asking direct questions, this way of talking to a child can be surprisingly helpful.

The reactions children initially have to their parents' marital separation are filtered through their elaborate system of internal conflicts and defenses. Unlike infants, toddlers, and many preschoolers, children in later elementary school are not reacting directly to specific environmental stresses, which if reduced alleviate the child's distress. Nor is the source of their difficulties a single frightening fantasy and/or burdensome belief. Older elementary school children are often reacting to multiple internal conflicts and using several unconscious defenses simultaneously. Each conflict-defense constellation must be addressed.

TODD's (see chapter 10) mother talked with her son's teacher, the school social worker, and friends for months about her concerns. The advice she got from nearly all sources was that Todd needed to be in psychotherapy. His mother was not enthusiastic about this idea. She felt that parents should solve any problems their children were having and, besides, the cost of therapy would be burdensome to bear. However, she was deeply worried about her son and realized that she had to do something to help him.

Todd's mother made an appointment with a mental health professional at a low-fee university clinic specializing in work with children and families. She told the psychology intern assigned to see her about Todd's angry, explosive behavior at school, his being hurtful towards his sister, and his uncooperative, derogating attitude with her. She tearfully claimed that she had tried talking to Todd as well as disciplining him but that nothing seemed to work. She angrily explained that she had attempted to discuss these issues with Todd's father and that he had made it clear he believed the problems their son was having were due in large measure to her ineffective parenting.

The intern, under the supervision of an experienced social worker, told Todd's mother that the difficulties her son was having were not at all uncommon among boys his age whose parents were in the process of getting divorced. He explained that her son's behavior was the result of his trying to cope with conflicts he was having about the divorce. By their third session, the intern felt he had enough information about this boy's problems to begin to outline for Todd's mother the specific nature of the internal conflict and defenses causing her son to act in the ways she had been describing. He explained that when parents separate, boys of Todd's age feel angry at both parents for disrupting their sense of being in a secure, predictable family environment. But they also love their parents and are uneasy about letting their parents know that they are angry at them. Boys fear retaliation from their parents and also feel guilty for feeling angry at them. So they solve this dilemma by taking their rage out on safer targets, such as peers and siblings.

Todd's mother was greatly relieved by the intern's comments. The fact that her son's difficulties were not an indication of mental illness and were not even uncommon reassured her that she was not a bad parent. However, she was still hurt and confused by her son's demeaning, unpleasant attitude toward her. The intern put this behavior into an understandable context as well. He told Todd's mother that no matter how well cared for and loved by his mother a boy Todd's age may be, it is in the nature of how boys develop emotionally for them to want to model themselves after their father. Boys need to figure out what being male and growing up to be a man really means. They look to their father and identify with him in order to further the sense of their own emerging masculinity. The intern explained that a man does not even need to be a caring, warm, involved father for a boy to feel drawn to identify with him. A problem arises, however, when a father disparages his wife. Even when there is no divorce, a boy begins to take on his father's characteristics. When these traits include looking down on women, or at least demeaning his wife, many boys will often automatically follow suit. When parents separate and a boy's father moves away from the family home, it is sometimes the case that a youngster will identify even more strongly with his father as a way to avoid missing him.

The intern reviewed these two conflicts and Todd's defenses against them. He underscored the fact that this was not Todd's mother's fault by stating, "I know it sounds strange, but it really doesn't make any sense to take your son's behavior personally. It sounds odd that a mother should not take it personally when her son is getting into trouble at school and demeaning her at home. But these behaviors really have nothing to do with your mothering. They are the end result of your son trying to deal with his anger over the divorce and his need to identify with his father in order to further his own sense of masculinity." Todd's mother gradually accepted the logic of this formulation. She and the intern agreed to meet once a week for a month or two so that they could develop a plan for Todd's mother to implement with her son to help him cope more adaptively with the divorce. The intern had called Todd's father, after discussing it with Todd's mother, and invited him to participate in these sessions with his wife or to meet separately with the intern to discuss Todd's difficulties. However, Todd's father insisted that his son was "doing just fine." He added that he was glad his wife was going to be seeing a therapist "because all the problems are in her head anyway."

The intern outlined a displacement strategy for Todd's mother. They agreed to focus on Todd's conflict around his angry feelings toward his parents about the divorce and his finding safe targets for that anger. When Todd's mother received a call from the school about Todd's belittling other children or fighting, she could begin talking about it with him by saying, "I heard from the school that there was some trouble today. It reminded me of something I heard the other day. Most boys have angry feelings when their parents are getting a divorce. A lot of guys even start getting mad at kids at school and then they get into trouble. Guys usually don't like getting into fights or having to go down to the principal's office. They wish they didn't have to get into trouble at school because school can be a fun place.''

She then went on to verbalize the underlying conflict: ''When guys get mad at their mom and dad it feels real crummy. Most boys love their parents and don't want to be angry at them. So guys have a problem: what should they do with their mad feelings about the divorce. Well, lots of kids take their angry feelings to school with them. Instead of showing their mom or dad how angry they are at them, they take their mad feelings to school and sort of dump them on kids there.'' His mother then corrected the belief Todd seemed to have, that his anger would be unacceptable to her: ''Boys sometimes think that their mom will get upset or mad if they get angry at her. That really isn't true. Most mothers know that guys hate divorce and wish it never happened in their family.'' Todd seemed bored during these brief (under two minutes) comments from his mother, but he did not leave the room or turn on the television set. It was as if he were listening, but almost against his will.

The next day, Todd became furious at his sister because she used his hair brush. He angrily shoved her against the wall of the bathroom, loudly calling her names. Todd's mother again went through the steps of displacement communication, restating what she had told him earlier. Todd, again, seemed uninterested in what his mother was saying. But he sullenly asked: ''So what should I do? You want me to push you and kick you?'' Though he sounded angry, there were tears welling up in his eyes. His mother took this opportunity to suggest alternative ways of expressing difficult feelings and managing painful conflicts. She gently said: ''No. I think any guy would feel terrible about hurting his mom. But there are other ways to let a mom know you're mad. Some guys tell their mom how much they hate the divorce and how mad they are at her for letting it happen. Other guys write down those things and give it to their mom to read. Some guys even pretend that their pillow is their mom and they punch it real hard. There are lots of ways a guy can feel mad at his mom without hurting her at all.'' At that point, Todd angrily told his mother to ''bug off,'' went to his bedroom and played his radio loudly.

In her weekly sessions with the psychology intern, Todd's mother expressed her frustration. After two weeks of trying these displacement communications, Todd had not changed at all. Further, he always seemed bored whenever she talked to him. The intern noted how much patience it takes to stick with this kind of plan. He told her that he knew how much more gratifying it would be to yell at a boy who is acting the way Todd was, discipline him, and insist that he change. The only problem is that she had already tried that for nearly five months, and it just did not work. He also suggested saying to Todd from time to time that, "It takes a real grown-up guy to handle big, angry feelings so that he doesn't get into trouble with them. Even thirteen- and fourteen-year-olds have to work at it." In this way Todd's mother was holding out the expectation that he would be able to manage his anger adaptively, like the teenagers he looked up to, while at the same time acknowledging how difficult it was to do so.

The intern and Todd's mother also talked about alternative vehicles for displacement communication. Repeating the sequence she had been using began to feel awkward to her, as if she were playing a well-worn record over and over. They discussed Todd's interest in G.I. Joe action figures. Though Todd did not seem amenable to having his mother participate with him when he played with them, she wondered if she could mention the G.I. Joe figures in her comments. After completing the usual statements she had been making, she added references to the G.I. Joe characters from time to time: "It's sort of like if Recondo (a "good guy" character) got real mad at his lieutenant about something. He might get worried about what the lieutenant would do if he got mad at him and told him to 'drop dead.' So instead he takes his angry feelings out on the other guys in his army like Roadblock and Gung Ho. But then pretty soon it isn't going to be any fun for him because all the guys in the army won't want to do anything with him and he'd be lonely. It'd be a lot easier if Recondo told the lieutenant what was bugging him and maybe even wrote him a note about it."

At first Todd seemed startled by his mother knowing some of the G.I. Joe characters. But he quickly got into the spirit of things. He said, "Yeah, he could blow up the lieutenant's tent or wait for him to be walking alone and machine gun him!" Todd's mother just nodded. She did not know what to say. After consulting with the psychology intern at her next appointment, she was able to talk with Todd about how Recondo could do something besides hurting the lieutenant. She said: "Well, he could do things like blowing up the lieutenant's tent or machine gunning him, I guess. But he doesn't really want the lieutenant to be killed or hurt, he's just very mad at him. He'd feel bad if he really hurt the lieutenant. Besides, he and the rest of the army need the lieutenant to help them against the Cobra army. But it sure sounds like he's got some pretty big, mad feelings."

Within six weeks from the time the displacement communication was begun, Todd's behavior started to change for the better. He rarely got into fights at school anymore, and his teacher reported that he was getting along well with the other boys. He began to catch up in his schoolwork and generally seemed happier. At times he occasionally called his sister names and argued with her, but his mother claimed that it seemed like "normal brother–sister stuff now." It was interesting that Todd at no point took his mother's suggestions about expressing anger toward her in constructive ways. Instead, all of the psychological work he had to do in coming to terms with his anger was done via discussing G.I. Joe scenarios with his mother. He gleefully told her many times what Recondo "might do" to the lieutenant. In addition to machine gunning him or blowing up his tent, Recondo could humiliate him by defeating him in a fight in front of all the other soldiers, urinate in the lieutenant's food without him knowing it, sneak into his tent and pour catsup on his uniform, and so on. In listening to these stories, Todd's mother was accepting her son's anger. She also verbalized the fact that Recondo was angry and empathized with how hard it is, even for a "tough soldier," to be mad at someone he really cared about and liked. She even finally got Todd to play out a scene in which Recondo (manipulated by Todd) and the lieutenant (spoken for by Todd's mother) talked about Recondo's anger.

Todd's mother was pleased with his progress and her active hand in being so helpful to her son. But he still bridled when asked to do household chores and called her names under his breath at those times. It was time to address the second conflict: Todd's identifying with his father's attitudes towards housework and towards his estranged wife as a way of trying to consolidate his own masculine identity.

When Todd refused to do a task such as clearing the dinner dishes, his mother noted this visible sign of his underlying distress and underscored how unpleasant this is for most boys: "Lots of guys feel like it's just not right for them to have to help their mom with chores. It feels like they shouldn't have to do any of that stuff. But most guys don't like arguing with their mom and calling her names either." She then elucidated the conflict Todd was having, corrected the implicit misperception that it was unmanly to help at home, and accepted Todd's feelings. She told her son: "Most guys want to be like their dad. Dads are very special to boys. If a dad likes football, then most guys try to like football, too. If a dad hates meatloaf, then lots of guys decide that they hate meatloaf, too. And when a guy's dad and mom get divorced, and his dad says bad things about his mom, then the guy figures that it's also okay for him to say bad things about his mom. Sometimes guys, even teenagers, think it's sort of wimpy to help their mom at home because it sure isn't what their dad used to do before the divorce. But it really doesn't have to be like that. Most guys can love their dad and even act like him in a lot of ways, but they don't have to be exactly like him. It's fine for guys to keep loving their dad after a divorce, and to want to do the things he does. But every guy is his own person. It'd be sort of silly for him to be exactly like anybody." Todd's mother went through this brief sequence three or four times a week, but not every single time that he balked at doing a chore.

The psychology intern encouraged Todd's mother to be alert to finding examples of athletes or movie actors identified with particularly manly roles who were involved in household tasks. A televised interview with a well-known football player and his wife provided an opportunity to show Todd that helping out at home was not "wimpy." The telecast was during half-time of a professional football game, and the player was shown drying dishes after his wife washed them as well as shopping with her at a food store. His mother casually asked Todd, "Do you think that football player is a wimp?" Todd was shocked, he said, "A what?" His mother repeated the question. Todd replied, "Are you kidding? That guy is six foot seven inches and weighs 270 pounds. He's the best player on the team. Nobody messes with him. He'd kill them." His mother said: "Well, I was just wondering. I saw him helping his wife shop for food, and it looked like he was also helping her do the dishes. I guess it doesn't bother him to help a woman do stuff around the house. Heck, he even let them put it on TV!'' Todd said, "Well, it's his wife, not his mother." His mother agreed, but added: "If he's helping his wife, he probably helped his mother, too. Some men don't help their wives at all and even think that doing chores around the house are something a man shouldn't do. They probably didn't help their mother either." Though Todd's mother wisely never mentioned Todd's father directly, the comparison was inescapable. Todd's father had not helped around the house, and he did not think a man should.

Todd's mother also creatively enlisted the aid of a friend who lived nearby. She asked if her friend would be willing to help her show Todd that it was all right for men to do chores around the house. Her friend's husband was an airline pilot and Todd admired and liked him. Todd's mother's friend invited Todd, his sister, and his mother for Sunday brunch. The man volunteered to set the table. After the meal, his wife asked him to clear the dishes, rinse them off, and put them in the dishwasher while she talked with Todd's mother in the family room. This man asked Todd to help him, which he readily agreed to do. The airline pilot told Todd about a close call he had on an emergency landing the previous week as they worked together in the kitchen. He made no mention of their shared task, treating it matter-of-factly. It was just another job that had to be done. And he did all jobs well whether it was piloting an aircraft or washing the dishes.

In subsequent comments about Todd's conflicts over doing household chores, his mother occasionally mentioned the football player and the airline pilot. The psychology intern suggested she also ask Todd from time to time, when they were quietly watching television in the evening or running an errand on the weekend, what he would like to be when he was all grown up. Todd sometimes said he wanted to be a policeman. Other times he stated that he would like to be a pilot in the Air Force. His mother occasionally (not always, for that would feel heavy-handed and critical) said, casually: "I guess it isn't necessary for guys to grow up to be *exactly* like their dad and do just what he does." Todd never responded directly to these comments, but he seemed thoughtful.

Within four months of her first meeting with the psychology intern, Todd's mother reported that she did not feel it was necessary for her to have any more sessions. Todd was doing well at school, his altercations with his sister, while occasionally quite heated, seemed to be well within normal limits, and he had become reasonably cooperative and pleasant with her. Though he sometimes complained about being asked to do a chore, he usually just went ahead and did it without much grousing. He also rarely called his mother names anymore. Todd's mother thought things were very much on the right track for her son, and she felt confident of her ability to continue helping him adjust to the divorce.

When older elementary school children will permit parents to engage them in play activities (for example, with dolls, puppets, and various action figures), then these toys may be used in displacement communication in much the same way as with preschoolers and early elementary school children. However, some later elementary school children balk at playing with parents. The parent then must rely nearly exclusively on verbal displacements (for example, "some guys," "lots of girls," and so on). This can become stilted and awkward through repetition because the opportunities for variations and the pleasure provided by directly engaging in play activities are unavailable. Todd's mother was able to avoid this by weaving her son's interest in G.I. Joe characters into her displacement statements. It is helpful for parents to reflect on their child's interests and incorporate them into verbal displacements when the youngster will not allow them into their play.

Todd's mother was also able to draw on other indirect methods to communicate to her son that he need not follow exactly in his father's footsteps. She made use of her son's respect and admiration for other men (for example, athletes and the airline pilot neighbor) to show Todd that there were alternative ways of being a man. Boys who have little or no contact with their father, or whose identifications with their father put them at odds with their mother, peers, or school authorities, often need more than displacement communication with their mother. Her statements, alone, will usually not be sufficiently compelling to a son in these circumstances. Other models of masculinity must be offered in order for a boy to modify his identification with his father. However, it is wise for mothers to encourage some partial identifications with his father. The message should not be, "Don't grow up to be like your dad." This is equivalent to a total condemnation of a boy's father and will often be intolerable to a son. Instead a boy can be helped to see that he can be like his father in some respects, just not in every way.

Todd had to adjust to the external stresses of parental warfare and the partial loss of his relationship with his father. But the impact of these stresses were experienced through the development of internal conflicts and the automatic psychological defenses they stimulated. After the marital separation, the hostilities between his parents were substantially reduced. Todd did get to see his father every other weekend, though they had not been particularly close before the separation. The extent of Todd's difficulties could not be explained in terms of intense environmental stresses. Rather, it was the internal conflicts and defenses that accounted for his reactions to the divorce. This is frequently the case for older elementary school children.

At times, however, children are faced with a significant, ongoing environmental source of distress. These not only provoke powerful feelings in youngsters but also create and sustain internal conflicts as well. A child must then defend himself against emotional pain on two fronts: from distress over the external stressor and the internal conflicts, too. This sorely taxes a child's defenses and is burdensome in ways that threaten to interfere with the normal course of child development. It is not that parents are simply being insensitive to their youngster's needs, but rather that they are so caught up in their own reactions to the divorce that they are temporarily blinded to the impact they are having on the child. Developing an enmeshed relationship with the child and placing her in adult roles is one such common environmental stress. It is more likely to be seen in later elementary school children who are old enough to be capable of entering into this sort of enmeshed relationship and not yet enough of a rebellious adolescent to avoid it.

DANA (see chapter 10) was referred by the court to undergo a psychological evaluation when she refused to go to her father's home for regularly scheduled visits. The divorce decree was being violated, and Dana's father had filed a complaint with the court.

This evaluation began with the psychologist interviewing Dana's mother alone. (Most psychological assessments with preadolescent youngsters, court-ordered or not, begin in this way in order to obtain a parent's perception of the current life situation and the child's developmental history.) Dana's mother was furious. She saw this involuntary evaluation as harassment by her ex-husband and had no wish to cooperate. She answered questions in as brief and unrevealing ways as possible. She insisted that her daughter was doing well academically and was not causing any trouble at school or at home. When the psychologist confronted her with the teacher's report about Dana being socially isolated, her mother scoffed and claimed that Dana was a personable, bright youngster who got along well with everyone. Dana's headaches were dismissed with the explanation that, "Kids are always picking up some bug or another; it's normal for kids to feel under the weather sometimes." Questions about how Dana spent her free time after school elicited glowing statements from her mother about how helpful Dana was at home. She put her brother, Blake, to bed each night, cooked dinners every other evening, and enjoyed long chats with her mother. The psychologist agreed that Dana was a real asset to her mother, but wondered about her spending so much time at home instead of being with friends. Dana's mother minimized this claiming that, "All kids go through phases where they just don't feel like playing with friends."

Toward the end of their second session, the psychologist explained that most girls Dana's age have angry feelings about divorce. Her mother readily agreed and noted that Dana was indeed angry; that was why she did not want to see her father. Attempts to get her to see that girls have angry as well as loving feelings toward their mother, too, were met with disbelief and examples of how cooperative and helpful Dana was with her. When the psychologist outlined the loyalty conflict children often have over which parent to side with, Dana's mother pointed out that her daughter had no such problem; she was only angry at her father for "abandoning" the family. The psychologist expressed concern about Dana taking on the adult role of coparent (her role as confidant was not addressed directly), but Dana's mother countered by claiming that Dana was only developing a precocious maturity by becoming so responsible at an early age.

When the psychologist suggested that Dana's mother might explore how her daughter felt about her current situation by using displacement communication, she stared in disbelief. She told the psychologist that she knew exactly how her daughter was feeling because they had a splendid, close relationship. There was no need to "play word games" with Dana.

Dana's father was furious at his ex-wife for "turning Dana against me." In his sessions with the psychologist, it became clear that he was also frightened of losing his daughter because of her mother's influence. He believed that he had a good relationship with his daughter prior to the divorce and wanted very much to continue to be in his daughter's life.

The psychologist had three sessions with Dana alone and saw

her once with each parent. In their individual meetings, Dana insisted that it was "boring" at her father's home; there was nothing to do there. She painted the kind of forced, overly rosy picture of her current situation that is so common to older elementary school children, especially girls. She liked school, had friends, loved her mother, and loved her father, too. It was just that it was not fun being at his place. Her headaches did not really bother her, they only lasted a short time and did not hurt much. Everything was "fine."

In their second session, the psychologist invited Dana to play with the dollhouse or puppets. She refused, saying they were "for little kids." But she did like to draw. She drew a picture of a house, some flowers around it, and a smiling-faced sun. The psychologist said, "That's how girls would like to feel after a divorce." He drew a picture, also. He had two houses, mother's and father's, in it and a sun with half its face smiling and the other half angry. He told Dana: "Girls usually have mad feelings after their parents split up and get a divorce. But they try to keep smiling. They help their mom in lots of ways and that helps them feel good. Sometimes they don't feel like being such a goody-goody girl, and they hate getting headaches and stomachaches." The psychologist was implementing the first two steps of displacement communication; representing the child's overt signs of distress and noting how unpleasant they were.

He went on to verbalize one of Dana's underlying conflicts, correct a misperception, and accept her anger. He said, "Most girls feel that it's wrong to have angry feelings toward their mom. They love their mom and they can see she's having a hard time with the divorce. But pretty much all girls have angry feelings, because they hate divorce and wish it never happened. Sometimes girls worry that their mom will be very hurt by these mad feelings so they try to be a big help to her instead. But moms are grown-ups and they can usually handle a girl's mad feelings. It really is okay, actually it's pretty normal, for girls to have mad feelings and loving feelings, both, toward their mom." Dana listened carefully and then claimed: "Well, I'm not mad at my mom. I just like to help her out. Besides, it was my dad that wanted the divorce." The psychologist said, "I think most girls have some angry feelings toward their mom even if their dad was the one who left. When a divorce happens, most girls figure that both parents sort of made a mess of things.'' Dana replied, ''My mom didn't want the divorce at all. She's still sad about it.'' She added bitterly, ''She'd like for her and my dad to get back together, but he doesn't feel like it.'' The psychologist casually noted that, ''A lot of girls might feel mad at their dad for that. Then a girl might want to get back at him by not going to visit him. Most girls would think that then their dad would be just as hurt as their mom so he'd know how it feels.''

With the psychologist's help, Dana was able to elaborate this idea. The psychologist suggested that they draw an imaginary family with mother and children living in one house and the father in another. They made up names for the family and for the children. The psychologist said, ''Okay, let's see what happens when the girl says she doesn't want to go to her dad's.'' Dana drew the father crying. She said he did not even feel like watching television or driving his new car. She angrily put a big ''X'' across his house and said, ''He's history.'' The psychologist verbalized this observable manifestation of Dana's distress by saying, ''Girls can get real angry at their dad for the divorce and want to get back at him for it for making their mom feel so bad.''

He then went on to the second step of displacement communication, underscoring how unpleasant it was to feel that way. He told Dana, ''Girls get real mad at their dad after a divorce, but it doesn't feel good. They really don't like hurting their dad's feelings and not seeing him.'' Next he verbalized the underlying conflict: ''Most girls love their dad even though they're mad at him. They want to see him and feel good with him. But they also hate him for a while.'' The misperception, that her father left because he did not care enough about his daughter to stay, was put into words and corrected. The psychologist said, ''A lot of girls feel that if their father loved them enough then he wouldn't have gotten the divorce and moved out. That hurts a girl's feelings and makes her mad. But dads don't get divorced because they don't care enough about their kids. They get a divorce because their marriage just isn't working.'' Dana became teary but did not cry.

When the evaluation was completed, the psychologist recommended that the court enforce the visitation schedule stated in the divorce decree. Failure to comply would result in Dana's mother being cited for contempt of court. He also recommended that Dana see a therapist regularly, once weekly, to help her adjust to the divorce. Because Dana's mother was angrily resistant to the whole evaluation and was furious over the recommendations, she would not cooperate in beginning to change the nature of her interactions with her daughter in order to reduce the environmental stress created by their enmeshed relationship. Dana's father could not address the conflict his daughter had with her mother. To do so would make it seem that he was subtly criticizing Dana's mother. The only alternative was a neutral therapist.

Dana was not able to deal with her love-anger conflict towards her mother. Thus, she could not see that she had defended herself against the pain this conflict could cause her by converting her angry feelings into inappropriate devotion and also, at times, into the somatic symptom of headaches. The displacement communication directed at this conflict foundered on correcting the "misperception" that Dana's mother could not tolerate anger from her daughter. In fact this was no misperception. Dana knew, if not consciously then at a level below direct awareness, that her mother was incapable of coping with Dana's rage, at least at this stage of the divorce process.

Dana was, however, able to make use of the three sessions she had with the evaluator to become aware of a major reason for her not visiting her father. She had not been in touch with her anger toward him for hurting not only her mother but also wounding Dana's pride and sense of self-esteem by "rejecting" her when he left. Through displacement communication, the psychologist helped Dana to significantly reduce this conflict and the defensive behavior it had led to. Thus, Dana, with the help of the court, could resume her relationship with her father. Without a resolution to this conflict, Dana might have experienced the court order that she visit her father as an arbitrary, prison-like sentence.

Unfortunately, Dana's subsequent therapy was undermined by her mother's spoken, as well as implicit, needs. Dana continued living out her enmeshed relationship with her mother, sacrificing opportunities for the friendships and emotional independence that most later elementary school children enjoy. She was, however, able to maintain a loving relationship with her father that would serve her well in adolescence and beyond. As we shall see in the next chapter, girls who are overly enmeshed with their mother can encounter serious problems when the demands of adolescence add a powerful push for emotional independence from both parents. An ongoing relationship with father can reduce the severity of difficulties caused by an enmeshed mother–child relationship.

Another common type of ongoing environmental stress is parental warfare. This has a corrosive impact on children who must contend with their rage at both beloved parents for hurting one another and also with their feelings of divided loyalty. These internal conflicts give rise to psychological defenses that exact developmental costs, to a greater or less degree, from the child. When continuing hostilities between parents include involving the youngster as a participant in them (for example, as a messenger or spy), these internal conflicts are exacerbated. Sometimes reducing these sources of external stress can result in dramatic improvement in the child with only minimal use of displacement communication to address the internal conflicts.

RYAN'S (see chapter 10) parents had become increasingly concerned about his withdrawal from peer activities and his deteriorating academic work. They had agreed to consult a mental health professional about these issues. Though they disliked each other intensely, they were both caring parents who were unaware of the effects their warfare was having on Ryan. Nor did they realize that they had been enlisting their son as an active combatant in their continuing discord.

The social worker to whom they had been referred by the school offered them a choice of meeting separately with her or coming to an appointment together. Ryan's parents did not get along, but both felt they could work together on behalf of their son. They elected to meet jointly with the social worker. In their first session, Ryan's parents told the social worker about their son's social isolation from peers and his declining schoolwork. Though these were the concerns uppermost in their minds, Ryan's mother also described her son's argumentative posture with her. Ryan's father then noted that he had not observed that when Ryan was with him, but shared his increasing frustration over the fact that his son seemed impossible to please. As the parents elaborated what each had seen, it became clear that Ryan was having difficulties with both parents. The social worker asked Ryan's parents to closely observe their interactions with their son over the next week and scheduled another appointment for that time. She urged the parents to pay specific attention to their own comments to Ryan as well as his reactions to them.

During their second meeting, it became clear that the parents were bad-mouthing each other in Ryan's presence. Further, when the social worker asked them to recall their conversations with Ryan just before he left each parent's home to see the other parent and on returning, what emerged was how frequently both parents put Ryan in the roles of messenger and spy. The social worker gently pointed out: "Parents are often curious about what is going on in each other's lives after a divorce. If they aren't on particularly good terms, they naturally ask their children about what's happening in the 'other house'." She also noted how convenient it feels to parents who do not get along well to use their children as go-betweens about things like the visiting schedule and child support payments.

At the beginning of their third session, the social worker explained to Ryan's parents how painful it is for youngsters to see the two people they love the most, their mother and father, verbally attacking and belittling each other. She underscored the fact that when children become participants in these conflicts it feels even worse because they are being asked to betray each parent by reporting what is going on in the other parent's life. The social worker explained that putting children in the middle of two parents who dislike each other is extremely stressful for youngsters. Even though the parents were civil to one another, were not harassing each other, and were not involved in protracted litigation around their divorce, all of which was to their credit, they did dislike one another and looked down upon each other's life-styles. The social worker told Ryan's parents that she was not asking them to love and honor each other, but that it would be a great relief to their son if they could contain their feelings of animosity in his presence. She also noted how relieving it would be for Ryan to hear from them what they seemed to believe: they did not care for one another, but each thought that it was important for Ryan to have a good relationship with the other.

Ryan's parents had not recognized that they were insulting each other and asking Ryan to be a spy and messenger. These insights prompted them to move quickly to change their styles of interacting with their son. They were able to bite their tongue when they felt they were about to make derogatory comments about the other parent. The social worker suggested that if a statement slipped out, they could easily recover by telling Ryan, "I know I just said something about your dad [mom] that was not very nice. When grown-ups get divorced, it takes them a while to get over their hurt and mad feelings. But I know that your dad [mom] is a good parent and that you love him [her]. That's the way it should be. I think it's important for you to be with your dad [mom], love him [her] and have fun when you're together.'' In this way the social worker was helping Ryan's parents give their son permission to love and feel close to the other parent. The parents' reactions to one another were explained and it was made clear to Ryan that the parents did not expect him to share those feelings. To the contrary, they told Ryan that they hoped and thought it was important for him to love and think well of both parents.

The social worker also helped Ryan's parents find alternative ways of communicating with each other that did not involve Ryan. She suggested regular weekly or biweekly telephone conversations to take care of the business of coparenting. This might include discussing issues of Ryan's schedule, how he was doing when he was with each of them, and child support payments. The social worker also said: ''It's really all right for you to ask each other how you are doing. After all, you were married for eleven years. It isn't surprising that you may want to know, from time to time, what is happening in each other's life.'' The social worker suggested that if these telephone calls began to stir up too many difficult feelings and thus threaten to be unproductive, they could write each other brief notes about these issues as long as they did not use Ryan as the ''mailman.''

Toward the end of their third meeting, the social worker explained that since they were making significant changes in their styles of relating to Ryan, it might be helpful for them to acknowledge this to their son. She provided them with some examples of how they might talk to Ryan about the changes: ''I know that your mom [dad] and I haven't been very nice to each other. We've both said things because we're still mad about all of the divorce stuff. And sometimes I ask you to talk to your mom [dad] about grown-up divorce business like changing the time for a visit or stuff about money. We've talked to someone who knows a lot about how guys feel when their parents act like that. She told us that most guys feel mad and sad about it. Your mom [dad] and I are going to change all that. We'll still be divorced and have our separate lives, of course. But I want you to love your mom [dad]. I'm not going to ask you to talk to your mom [dad] about grown-up divorce stuff, and I'm not going to ask you about what's happening in her [his] house, anymore.'' Ryan's parents and the social worker agreed to meet again in a month to discuss how Ryan was doing.

In that session, the parents reported that Ryan seemed much happier and less tense. His difficulties with each of them had substantially subsided, and he was seeing more of his friends again. They both told the social worker that Ryan seemed grumpy and a bit sad when returning to each of their homes after being with the other parent. The social worker explained the need children have to emotionally ''decompress'' during these times of transition between being with each parent. She suggested that they might say, ''It's kind of hard for guys to go back and forth between his parents when there's been a divorce. It's like guys have to say 'goodbye' to one parent so that they can be with the other one. Most guys would like to be with both parents at the same time. I know that's hard. But it gets better after a while.'' In this way Ryan's parents were acknowledging his observable distress and how uncomfortable it was. They were also verbalizing the underlying conflict (that is, the wish to be with both parents versus the need to separate from each in order to be with the other), accepting his being upset, and reassuring him that transitions would become easier over time. Both parents called about six weeks later to express their gratitude for the help they had gotten from the social worker. Each felt Ryan was doing very well.

Some environmental sources of stress for children are naturally occurring, happy events. Parental dating and remarriage are two such events. Here the aim is not to minimize or eliminate the stressor, but to understand its impact on children. It makes no sense for a parent to avoid dating or decide not to remarry because their youngsters are not thrilled about those circumstances. To do so breeds resentment in the parents toward the children and gives youngsters a sense of inappropriate power over what should be adult decisions. Some parents quite consciously plan to put off dating (at least serious dating) and/ or remarriage until the children are older because they think it would be another big, stressful change for them. Often this is actually a defense the parent uses to avoid the anxiety they might experience about a new, intimate relationship. Regardless of the reason for such a decision, it is not helpful for adults or children for parents to eschew intimate, postdivorce relationships ''for the sake of the children.''

This makes as much sense as staying in a troubled, unfulfilling, or conflict-ridden bad marriage because the parent believes that the stress of divorce would be too much for the youngsters to handle.

When parents do begin dating, it is important for them to discuss this change with their youngsters. There are several purposes in doing so. First, the parent can explain that it is appropriate for them to date. Older elementary school children sometimes harbor the unspoken belief that even though their parents are divorced, it is somehow wrong for them to be attracted to an adult who is not the other parent. Second, later elementary school children will often fear that parents will stop loving them if they start a romantic relationship. They seem to believe that there is a finite, limited amount of love that the parent is capable of giving. Thus, if they fall in love with a dating partner, there will be less (or no) love for the children. Third, children often worry about their parents suddenly marrying someone they are dating. The child would gain a stepparent "overnight." Perhaps they would have to move to a new house and go to a different school. Children whose parents have divorced are frequently frightened by the prospect of important family changes. They do not want another surprise that could affect their lives dramatically. They have already had one surprise, the divorce, and they are understandably wary about others.

Parents can use a mixture of displacement and direct communication when they talk to their children about dating. It is useful to do this as a parent is actually beginning to date so that the three issues described above will feel relevant to youngsters. Preparing a child for the possibility that a parent might date at some unstated time in the future will seem too abstract for most youngsters. Here is one possible way to present parental dating to children. (Either parent can say this to children. For simplicity of exposition, wording is given from the mother's perspective.) "You know that your dad and I are getting [have gotten] a divorce. That means that we live in different places. But when a mom gets divorced, it doesn't mean that she stops liking all men. It's nice to care about a man and feel close to him. Divorce doesn't mean that a mom shouldn't like another man. Actually, the court says it's okay to have dates and like another man. So I'll be having dates. This Saturday night I'll be going out to dinner and then to a movie with a new man. You can meet him and say 'hi.' I've heard that sometimes kids have some worries when their mom starts to go out on dates. Some guys and girls worry that their mom will give most of their love to the person that they're dating and stop loving them as much. Sometimes kids even worry about whether their mom will get married all of a sudden and there will be a lot of big changes. But moms always keep loving their kids when they're having dates. No matter how much a mom or dad cares about someone they are dating, they always love their children. And I'll always love you very much. If I ever decide to get married again, I'll tell you way before it happens so that you can have a lot of time to get used to that idea. But right now I'm only going out on a date this Saturday.'' It is a good idea to say these sorts of things somewhat casually and to pause from time to time during the course of this explanation to allow children to ask questions or make comments. Most older elementary school children will be silent, though sometimes they might ask the name of the person with whom the parent has a date, which movie they are going to see, who will ''baby-sit'' with them, or what time the parent will be home.

While it can be a great help to children to have the reality of a parent's dating acknowledged and to be reassured about some worries dating tends to evoke in youngsters, such an explanation cannot cover all possible tensions that dating might create for children. Nor is it the case that saying these things once will lay to rest all current and future concerns children may have about a parent dating.

HEATHER'S (see chapter 10) mother decided to consult a psychologist in private practice about her daughter's behavior toward George and her. She had enjoyed a close, loving relationship with Heather and was disturbed by the recent welling up of resentment in her daughter. She was also upset by her daughter's cool attitude toward George and her obvious wishes to avoid him. Heather's mother believed that she and George would very likely get married soon and did not want her new family to be burdened by her daughter's negative feelings toward George. She wondered what she had done wrong. Had she been spending too much time with George? Was she inadvertently neglecting Heather's needs? Did she put too much pressure on Heather to join her and George in family-like outings?

The psychologist listened to these self-doubts. He also gathered a history of Heather's development and of the divorce events. Heather's age at the time of the marital separation, her initial reactions to it, how she had adjusted during the immediate crisis and short-term aftermath stages, her reactions when Heather's mother began dating George, and Heather's first impressions of George were all explored in the first session.

In their second session, the psychologist asked Heather's mother to describe the changes she had observed in her daughter. When had they first appeared? How did they begin to manifest themselves? Heather's mother tearfully reported how Heather had seemed genuinely fond of George at first. She had looked forward to his coming to the house and going on outings with him and her mother. The psychologist asked how Heather was doing at her father's home. Heather's mother said that her ex-husband had not noticed anything different about their daughter. He saw her and her sister every weekend at his house and had them to dinner there one day during the week. He was a caring, affectionate father who was committed to continuing to parent his daughters after the divorce. The psychologist asked Heather's mother if she would object to his contacting and perhaps meeting with her ex-husband. She thought that would be fine.

Heather's father agreed to come to an appointment with his ex-wife and her partner, George. Now four-and-a-half years after the marital separation, he was on good terms with his former wife and wished her well in her relationship with George. During this meeting, the adults in Heather's life expressed their puzzlement over her avoidance of George and her increasing resentment toward her mother. They all noted how well Heather had continued to do in her peer relationships, in her schoolwork, and with her teachers. Her father also noted that Heather was still cheerful, cooperative, and affectionate with him. He insightfully wondered whether Heather was worried about losing her mother's affections to George.

The psychologist explained that it seemed two very different conflicts were causing Heather's difficulties. First, she was frightened and saddened by the fantasy that her mother did not love her as much as she had because she seemed to care so much for George. Instead of feeling sad as many early elementary school children do when they imagine this, Heather reacted by trying to cut her losses emotionally; she became angry at her mother. It was as if she were subscribing to the idea that the best defense was a good offense. She was rejecting her mother instead of waiting to be rejected by her. However, this was inconsistent with her loving feelings toward her mother. She tried to resolve this internal conflict by attempting to ignore the fact that her mother had fallen in love with George. Spending less time with him at home, no longer going on outings with them, and having a sleep-over with a friend to distract her from seeing how much her mother cared for George were ways Heather had of putting the relationship between her mother and George out of mind. After all, if she did not have to think about her mother's love for George, she did not have to feel displaced by him in her mother's affections, and therefore did not have to feel defensively angry at her mother.

The psychologist carefully explained that this was a fairly common conflict for girls Heather's age who had not had to share their custodial mother's affections with an adult for several years. Living in a single-parent home with a concerned, loving mother builds a very close mother–daughter relationship. When a mother develops a romantic interest, girls feel threatened with the possible loss of their mother's love. Rather than being a sign that Heather's mother had done something wrong, it was testimony to the loving closeness between them. Needless to say, Heather's mother found this explanation enormously reassuring.

The psychologist added that Heather was old enough to be aware of the sexuality implict in a romantic relationship between adults. He described the uneasy feelings and forbidden curiosity a youngster Heather's age experiences amid the naturally occurring sexual ambience of a courtship involving a parent. Heather's avoidance of George and her mother was a way for her to minimize her awareness of this issue and is common among older elementary school children.

The psychologist went on to explain the second conflict Heather was struggling with. Heather had a fantasy, most likely one that she was not even aware of, that her father would be hurt and angry about her liking George. It felt vaguely disloyal to her. Thus, she had still another motive for avoiding George: it allowed her to preserve a feeling of loyalty to her father.

The psychologist suggested that Heather's father be the one to talk with her about this loyalty conflict. Reassurance on this score would carry far more weight coming from the person she imagined she was being unfaithful to and possibly wounding. Using displacement communication, her father could begin by describing Heather's overt signs of distress and acknowledging the discomfort she was experiencing: "I hear that you haven't been spending much time with George anymore. I read that a lot of times girls do that. They sort of avoid the person their mom is dating and act like they don't care about him. It's too bad when that happens, because girls can have fun with their mom's friend. It's like part of a girl wants to like him but another part of her won't let herself like him, and then she misses out on having a nice time.'' Heather's father could then verbalize the hidden conflict his daughter was trying to deal with, correct the misperception implicit in it, and give her permission to like George, ''A lot of girls like the guy their mom is dating and want him to like her. But sometimes girls feel that if they really like that new man then it would mean that they were sort of not being nice to their dad. Lots of girls figure that they're only supposed to care about their dad, and if they like another man, it might hurt their dad's feelings. Then girls feel that they're being a bad daughter. But, you know, it's really okay for girls to care about their mom's dating partner. I know it would be fine with me. I like George and I think he's a good guy.''

When Heather heard this from her father, she listened thoughtfully and then said, ''But George is yucky. He likes crummy music. Besides, he and mom are always looking at each other funny, like they don't even know anyone else is around.'' Here Heather was unwittingly testing her father's resolve. If she criticized George, would her father seize that opportunity to agree? Would he take pleasure in Heather's comment? Heather's father passed this test. He responded, saying, ''George isn't yucky at all. He's a terrific musician. I've talked with him and I like him. And I know he cares about you and wants you to be happy. He looks funny at your mom because he loves her a lot. That makes her happy, and I'm glad about that.''

Although Heather's father did an excellent job with his daughter's loyalty conflict, he was not able to help Heather come to terms with her sense of being displaced by George in her mother's life. She continued to refuse to spend time around George and her mother. In subsequent sessions with Heather's parents and George, the psychologist pointed this out and suggested that Heather's mother talk with her about this issue. She could use the displacement method to articulate Heather's visible signs of distress, how uncomfortable Heather felt, and the internal conflict she was trying to cope with.

Heather's mother told her, ''It's not easy for girls when their mom really cares about someone she is dating. Most girls don't like that. Lots of times they try to stay away from the person their mom is dating and even get mad at their mom for liking that man so much. That makes girls feel crummy because they don't want to feel left out and mad. I've heard that the reason that happens is because a lot of girls feel that they are not as special to their mom when she starts loving a new man. Girls figure that if their mom loves that new guy, then she doesn't love their daughter as much as she used to.'' Heather's mother could then correct this misperception, accept her daughter's competitive and angry feelings and reassure her, "But, you know, moms still love their daughters just as much as they used to before they started dating. A mom's love for her daughter is very strong and it's different from how she loves a man. It's like when a girl spends a lot of time with her friends and really likes them. That doesn't mean she stops liking her parents. I know that a lot of girls are mad when their moms date, and they think that things would be better if she didn't go out on dates. But after a while things get better because a girl can see that her mom still loves her.'' Heather's mother made these statements several times over a two-week period. Her daughter sullenly listened, but nothing changed.

The psychologist noted that perhaps Heather's difficulties were continuing because she was responding to her mother's actions. The words in the displacement communications could not outweigh the fact that her mother was spending nearly all of her free time with George. He advised Heather's mother to begin setting aside regular times each week for her and Heather to be together without George. They could do the things they used to do before Heather's mother began dating George: shopping trips at a nearby mall, occasional lunches at a restaurant, and eating dinner at home together instead of always having dinner with George and just preparing meals for her daughters without joining them.

At first Heather was resistant to her mother's invitations to do these things together as they used to. But after two months, she began to enjoy them again. In these ways she could see, concretely, the proof of her mother's continuing love for her; her mother sometimes gave up being with George in order to do things with her. Also being with her mother, apart from George, permitted Heather to enjoy her mother's company without always having to face the romantic and sexual nature of the relationship between her mother and George. Her behavior toward her mother began to change. She seemed more like the way she used to be; cooperative and loving. Though she often still avoided spending time with her mother and George together, she occasionally accompanied George on errands he had to run and seemed to enjoy those times with him.

The psychologist suggested that Heather's mother and George each continue to build and strengthen their individual relationships with Heather and not try to involve her with the two of them together. Apparently, it was going to take some time for Heather to accept them as a couple. Trying to force that process and speed it up was not going to be helpful.

Although the displacement communication that both of Heather's parents had implemented with their daughter was useful, it was not sufficient to help Heather change all of her troublesome attitudes and behaviors. For some children, especially older elementary school youngsters and adolescents, actions speak much louder than words. In her courtship with George, Heather's mother had in fact been spending substantially less time with her daughter than she had earlier. It is not unusual for a parent who is involved in a romantic relationship and is falling in love with a new partner to unwittingly withdraw from individual relationships with her children. It often does not feel to the parent that she is ignoring her youngster because of her attempts to include the child in family-like activities with her and her partner. But the underlying message is clear: I have no time to spend with you apart from my partner; if you want to be with me, you must also be with him. When the parent devotes special time and energy to being alone with the child, she is demonstrating her continued love and commitment to that youngster. It can be a difficult juggling act, dating and also having separate time with children, but it is well worth it.

Dating and remarriage can also have salutary effects on older elementary school children, especially boys who have little or no contact with their father in the long-range period of divorce. Boys in this situation can gain experience relating to a man, identify with the man's masculinity in order to further his own, and achieve a developmentally optimal emotional distance from their custodial mother as they transfer some of their affections to the new man. In these ways, a boy's stepfather can serve as a progressive developmental force in the youngster's life.

However, being mother's long-term serious dating partner or her new husband is not an easy role for most men. They must walk a fine line between being important to the youngster and yet not taking a parental role too quickly. When a man prematurely begins to assign chores or become involved in discipline, most boys react negatively. They become angry at the man for presuming to act with the authority of a parent and are angry at their mother for allowing this to happen. The resulting difficulties will depend on how the child handles his anger. Some sullenly withdraw from and resist their parents' demands, others act out their anger with peers or siblings, and still others develop somatic symptoms such as headaches. These are not mutually exclusive; a boy may display more than one of these ways of coping with his distress.

It is helpful if men in these positions initially adopt an avuncular posture toward the children. They can play with them, take them to the movies or sports events, offer to help them with homework, joke with them, and talk with them about their interests. They can even gently suggest that it is getting late and it is probably a good idea for the child to go to bed soon so that he will be well rested the next day. Dating partners and stepparents can also ask for the youngster's help in some task. However, giving orders ("It's time for you to go to bed," "Pick up your jacket and hang it up, please") or disciplining a child ("You're grounded tomorrow because you yelled at your mother," "I told you to clear the dinner dishes and you didn't, so there won't be any TV tonight") are sure ways to alienate a child and even create tension between the adults. Dating and live-in partners should avoid entirely trying to take on these parental roles. Even stepparents should keep a low parental profile for at least several months after the marriage. Children need time to adjust to a parent's remarriage, and it takes a while for most youngsters to feel that a stepparent is a legitimate parental authority.

JEFF (see chapter 10) began to blossom developmentally after his mother married Evan. His new stepfather played a role of a caring, involved uncle with him during the initial stage of the marriage. Evan played ball with Jeff, encouraged his athletic interests, and involved him in tasks as a helpmate and companion rather than as a demanding authority figure. He became a readily available and much-needed model of masculinity for Jeff. The difficulties Jeff had been having while living in a single-parent household with his mother and sisters were not uncommon for older elementary school boys. The absence of his father, not only from the home but entirely from his life, made it hard for Jeff to give direction to his emerging sense of masculinity. He also found it difficult to accept his mother's authority because it threatened his masculinity. Evan's entry into the family permitted Jeff to regain his developmental stride.

Jeff, his mother, and his stepfather were not seen for clinical reasons. They were participants in an in-depth study of postdivorce families. Jeff's stepfather seemed to know intuitively that he first had to build a loving and trusting relationship with his stepson before attempting to move into a parental role. Most parental authority derives not from being legally or biologically entitled to it, but from the emotional bonds that exist between parents and children. Though youngsters can be coerced by adults (parents, stepparents, teachers, or coaches), it is usually at great cost to the adult-child relationship and to the child's individual psychological development. This is not to say that assigning chores, setting behavioral limits, conveying expectations for appropriate speech and actions, and disciplining children are unimportant. They are essential to healthy development. But it is crucial for them to occur within the context of a caring, ongoing relationship in order for them to be helpful to the child.

Though Jeff prospered developmentally when he acquired a caring, sensitive stepfather, it is unwise for custodial mothers to remarry in order to provide their children with a man in their lives. Just as it makes no sense for parents to stay together in a bad marriage ''for the sake of the children,'' or to avoid dating or remarrying for that same reason, it is foolish to remarry to do something helpful for the children. These are adult decisions that should be made on the basis of the nature of the adult relationships involved.

Overview

Parents can be helpful to their children by reducing external stresses and being aware of the internal sources of stress and psychological defenses common to older elementary school youngsters. Using displacement communication to verbalize the child's distress and underlying conflicts, correct private misperceptions, and reassure the child can be enormously valuable for many children of this age. However, later elementary school children often need more than words. Parents must demonstrate their commitment to and love for the child through specific actions (for example, sharing activities). It is also helpful to provide the child with experiences that are developmentally important, such as having contact with a man who can appreciate a girl's femininity and thus boost her self-esteem or who can serve as a role model for a boy. Relatives (such as, grandfathers and uncles), neighbors, and teachers can serve the child well in these ways.

12

►◄

The Divorce Experience for Adolescents

Adolescence is the last phase of child development. Although this period is usually thought to span all the teenage years, the focus here will be on youngsters between thirteen and seventeen. There seems to be a notable shift in maturity after seventeen. The years between seventeen and approximately twenty appear to serve as a bridge between adolescence and young adulthood. Thus, this later stage is set apart from the core of the adolescent experience. Further, surprisingly little is known about how offspring over seventeen respond to their parents' divorce.

Developmentally, adolescence is a time of remarkable change. The biological move into puberty ushers in a host of dramatic physiological changes. Youngsters become acutely aware of their bodies and of their sexuality, which contributes to a quality of being self-absorbed. At the same time, there are significant social changes attending adolescence. Exclusively same-sexed peer groups and activities give way to parties, friendships, and dating relationships with members of the opposite sex. Adolescents become sensitive to the complexities of more mature friendships and romantic relationships. They also face new social environments as they make the transitions from the relatively calm haven that elementary school has become to the more exciting and as yet unmastered worlds of junior high and high school. Emotionally, adolescents struggle to adapt to these internal biological and external social changes while at the same time trying to carve out their own niche apart from their parents. Teenagers are conscious of their physical growth, sexuality, greater understanding of their world, and emerging sense of independence. These must be integrated into a new self-image.

Collectively, these factors make adolescence a period of normally occurring and substantial flux on all developmental fronts. More than ever, adolescents need emotional support, love, and firm guidance from their parents as they confront the considerable developmental challenges. Despite their strides toward (and often loud claims for) independence, at some level of consciousness they are aware that they still very much need their parents. Yet adults amid the dramatic emotional, social, and financial dislocations that characterize so many divorces frequently have less time and energy as well as fewer emotional resources for parenting.

When parents divorce, adolescents face the formidable task of adjusting to two sets of significant changes in their lives: those that normally arise in this period of development, and those accompanying the divorce process. And the stakes are higher than ever, because youngsters are capable of expressing their feelings of distress and internal conflicts in alarming new ways. Teenagers can, and unfortunately too many do, use illicit drugs, abuse alcohol, precociously (and at times promiscuously) engage in sexual activities, physically hurt others or themselves, get into trouble with the law, and/or run away from home. These behavioral expressions of internal conflict and distress are virtually absent at every other stage of child development. They can put the adolescent in positions of serious risk that potentially have far-reaching consequences. It is precisely this capacity to up the ante, so to speak, that characterizes the divorce experience for adolescents.

The Immediate Crisis Stage

The majority of adolescents are genuinely shocked when they learn that their parents are separating. Though they usually have been aware of ongoing dissension between their parents, they experience it as a predictable part of their everyday life. It seems unthinkable to most teenagers that the parents they have lived with all their lives, for so many years, will get divorced. Surprise is quickly followed by anger, dismay, and sadness. They also feel a more subtle but nonetheless keen disappointment in their parents for not being able to keep the family together.

Many youngsters are aware of these reactions. However, their feelings are so strong, fueled by the surging impulses of adolescence, that they experience the emotions in diffuse yet overwhelming ways.

310

They often know how they feel, but rarely understand exactly why they are so angry, so sad, or so intensely critical of their parents. Without the knowledge of the forces that are giving rise to their feelings, many adolescents cannot contain them. They spill over into actions that upset and concern parents and threaten the developmental progress of youngsters.

When parents initially separate, adolescents must confront several stressors at once. First, they have to deal with the frightening prospect of losing the stability, support, and protection provided by their sense of family cohesiveness. Most teenagers are unaware of this fear, though occasionally some will articulate it, to themselves and possibly to others, as feeling that they "have to grow up fast" or that they "are on their own now." The multitude of changes that adolescence imposes on youngsters leads to uncertainty and anxiety when parental support appears less likely.

A second stress for adolescents is the rapid shift in their perceptions of and feelings about their parents. During the teenage years, most youngsters gradually modify their views of parents. Parents come to be seen as complex human beings with realistically admirable qualities as well as true limitations and faults. The process often includes periods of idealizing parents and having great expectations for what they can do that alternate with derogating parents as mean ogres who act arbitrarily and are nearly always wrong. Often a more integrated and true-to-life picture eventually emerges and is accepted in early adulthood. When parents separate, this process can be derailed as adolescents begin to perceive their parents in extremely negative terms. Parents are selfish, stupid, weak, or cruel, and their divorce-related behaviors "confirm" these impressions. This is no mere temporary derogation based on commonplace frustrations and anger over not being able to stay out past a curfew, having to do household chores, or being grounded for a weekend. Divorce can bring a more lasting, bitter, and demeaning view of parents. When this occurs, it creates internal conflicts for adolescents. Their disappointment in their parents and derogation of them is at odds with their love for their parents, their need to have appropriate guidance and limits, and their need for loving, involved role models to help them in consolidating their identity.

A third source of stress stems from the adolescent's tendency to revert to the egocentric thinking so typical of preschoolers and early elementary school children. They frequently develop unconscious beliefs that place responsibility for the marital discord and separation squarely on their own shoulders. These self-blaming beliefs stimulate burdensome feelings of guilt. A variation on the theme, especially common in adolescence, is for teenagers to personalize the divorce. The separation is "proof" that their parents do not really love them or want to be with them. Some youngsters will directly verbalize these beliefs, "If he really cared about me, he wouldn't have left," "If my mom really loved me, she would have tried harder to make the marriage work," or more subtly, "I remember how bad I felt when my dad left *us*," and "I guess *we* weren't worth my mom staying." When the youngster experiences divorce in such personal ways, it causes great emotional pain and may seriously damage feelings of self-esteem. The very fact of the divorce, apart from specific external stressors (like parental warfare) evokes fear, anger, and emotional pain. These reactions, which may be recognized consciously or remain below the level of awareness, occur because of the meanings and implications of divorce to adolescents.

PHIL was fifteen when his mother told him that his father would be moving out the following week. She tearfully and angrily related the fact that her husband was having an affair with a co-worker of his and had decided to seek a divorce in order to pursue the relationship. She truthfully said that she did not want a divorce, but that she certainly was not going to put up with her husband staying in the home while he saw another woman. Phil's father did not talk to his son about the separation or his extramarital relationship.

Phil's parents had been married for nearly eighteen years. His father was twenty-six and his mother twenty-four when they married. When Phil was four and his brother Kenny two, their mother returned to work on a full-time basis. She was initially employed in a medical research laboratory as a skilled technician and at the time of the marital separation had risen to the position of associate director of the laboratory, earning $24,000 a year. Her husband, a research chemist, worked for a manufacturing company and earned $35,000 a year. Their marriage had been stable but was characterized by increasing emotional distance. Neither parent was particularly warm or affectionate, but their marital relationship had not been stormy. However, Phil's father had grown dissatisfied with the humdrum quality of his marriage. He became enamored of a colleague fifteen years his junior and had begun an affair with her. Phil's father enjoyed the excitement of the relationship, felt young and attractive when he was with her, but had no plans to marry again.

Phil took the news of his parents' impending separation stoically. He asked no questions and appeared to have little reaction to it. This posture did not change after his father moved out into an apartment a few miles from the family residence. Phil and his brother saw their father every other weekend from Saturday afternoon to Sunday at noon. They went out to dinner together on these Saturdays, and Phil's father prepared a Sunday brunch just before the boys were to return to their mother's home. Phil's father never offered to discuss the marital separation with his sons, and they asked no questions. When the three of them were together, they talked about sports, politics, the boys' schoolwork, and little else. Occasionally, they played board or video games together. Phil's relationship with his father had never been especially close, but he had always looked up to his father and admired his intellect.

After the marital separation, Phil gradually became more resistant to his mother's authority. He yelled at her to "leave me alone" when she inquired about whether he had finished his homework. When she asked him to hang up his jacket or straighten up his room, he sometimes screamed, "Quite bugging me." Requests that he do some chores around the house were met with: "You're always on my back! Why don't you ask Kenny to do it." Phil seemed sullen around the house even when he did not feel intruded upon by his mother.

Two months after his father had moved out, Phil was caught shoplifting in a large department store. He had taken a small, portable cassette/radio. The store called the police and his parents and formally pressed charges. Phil had to appear in court and was given a sentence of performing fifty hours of community service. His mother was tearfully upset and tried to talk to her son about why he had tried to steal the cassette/radio. Phil sullenly replied that he had, "just felt like it" and refused to discuss it further. Phil's father was furious. He angrily told Phil, "I'm not interested in having a thief for a son! I don't care why you took that thing, but you better not do anything like that ever again. You're grounded for a month, and it'll be a lot worse if it ever happens again." Phil said nothing.

A few weeks later Phil was caught drinking beer in the high school parking lot when he should have been in class. The school did not call the police but suspended him for a week. Though he had been a solid B student, his grades had fallen to C's and D's for the first half of his first semester of tenth grade. He had been cutting classes, and this drinking episode underscored the problems he was having in school. Phil's father was so enraged that he slapped his son across the face, calling him a "worthless piece of shit" who was going to turn out to be a "real loser." Phil began to cry tears of fury as well as pain. He screamed back at his father, "Yeah, well at least I wasn't screwing around behind my wife's back with some broad young enough to be my daughter!" Phil's father grabbed him by the hair and slapped hard several times across the face. He hissed at Phil, "Don't you ever speak to me like that again." Phil grabbed his jacket and ran from the house crying.

Phil's mother was distraught. Her son had been a cheerful, agreeable youngster whom she had always felt close to. During his elementary school and even early teenage years, Phil had been open with his mother, sharing his experiences at school and with his friends. He had not only been easy to get along with but also a genuine delight to her. He was always well-groomed in a somewhat preppy style, had done well academically, was liked by his peers, and was loving and cooperative at home. Now in the space of three months, he had been in trouble for shoplifting, drinking, and cutting classes. His grades had fallen dramatically, and he seemed uninterested in doing well in school. His relationship with his father had deteriorated, and his mother felt she could not reach him and get him to talk with her about what had been happening in his life. She was greatly worried that her son was headed for even more trouble and did not know how to help him.

Phil is a good example of how quickly a teenager's life can change after a marital separation. As is so often the case with adolescents, Phil kept most of his thoughts and feelings to himself. Thus, his behavior seemed inexplicable to his parents. But Phil also kept himself as well as his parents in the dark about how he was reacting to his parents' divorce. It was not that he knew consciously that he was having strong feelings and conflicts over their separation, but simply refused to share them with his parents. He was aware of his actions, but only dimly recognized the thoughts and feelings that accompanied them. And he did not understand at all the forces that were driving his behavior.

Phil's parents were not at war with each other. Though his mother was understandably sad and angry about her husband leaving her for another woman, she only occasionally criticized him in front of Phil. They had quickly agreed on a settlement and were not embroiled in hostile litigation, nor was either parent so distressed that their pain was burdensome to Phil or his brother. Phil's father did not seem overcome by guilt. To the contrary, he was enjoying his romantic relationship. Phil's mother was a psychologically sturdy woman who had a rewarding career of her own. She was not overly worried about finances, and though her husband's leaving was a blow to her pride, she believed his actions were a product of some sort of "mid-life crisis" he was caught up in. While she expected this "fling" to pass, she was committed to ending the marriage. She was confident of doing well on her own, and in fact had begun to enjoy the freedom of being single.

Rather than being upset by the sorts of environmental stresses that can so often accompany divorce, Phil was reacting to several internal conflicts aroused by his parents' separation. The most prominent of these was the dramatic negative change in his view of his father that was at odds with his wish to continue to admire and identify with him. Phil's outburst at his father revealed his moral condemnation of him. Adolescents develop a rigid sense of right and wrong, in part to contain their own emerging impulses. When Phil learned of his father's extramarital affair, he no longer saw him as an intelligent research scientist committed to painstakingly pursuing truth and discovery in his laboratory. Instead he was an adulterer and a sneak, a man who lied to his wife and broke the rules of the marital contract. Yet at the same time, he had the developmental need to continue to identify with his father in order to consolidate his own masculine identity.

A second and equally powerful internal conflict for Phil was the clash between his love for his father and his rage at him for disappointing him so terribly and for being unfaithful to Phil's mother. Phil unwittingly tried to resolve these conflicts, neither of which he was sufficiently aware of to be able to articulate, even to himself, by getting into trouble. He identified with his father in a special way: he enacted the negative image he had of him by breaking the rules. By stealing, drinking, and cutting classes, he was becoming like the father who did not play it straight. At the same time, these behaviors served to punish his father. Phil knew how important grades and good conduct were to his father. By acting like a delinquent, Phil could deprive his father of the pleasure he took in his son's accomplishments without having to express his anger directly.

Consciously, all Phil was aware of was that he did not give a damn about being a "good boy" anymore. He realized that he thought his father's affair was wrong and that he did not like it. But he was unaware of how angry and condemning he felt toward his father. Nor could he verbalize to himself that he wanted still to admire and love his father. Both internal conflicts were below the level of consciousness and were expressed in actions rather than ideas, fantasies, or words.

However, these two internal conflicts do not explain Phil's behavior toward his mother. There were two additional internal conflicts Phil was wrestling with that were focused on his relationship with his mother. First, the wish to comply with her authority was pitted against the belief of many adolescent boys that to do so was unmasculine and "wimpy." Second, his urge to step into the vacated role of "man of the house" and be lovingly helpful was at odds with a vague but powerful sense of uneasiness over deeply unconscious feelings of sexuality that this position implies. Phil did what many adolescent boys tend to do in this situation: he put as much emotional distance between himself and his mother as possible. To be compliant and loving meant being a wimp, or even more frightening, would elicit a loving but forbidden closeness between him and his mother. Teenage boys are often awkwardly uneasy about hugs and kisses they used to seek from their mother before they were so acutely aware of their own sexuality. They fend off this physical closeness in part because it feels as though they are being treated as a "little kid" and partly because of the forbidden, sexualized meanings that it takes on in adolescence. Phil did not have to derogate his mother as Todd (see chapter 10) did. But he needed to put emotional distance between them. Like a porcupine, who when frightened throws his quills, Phil threw verbal barbs at his mother so that she would keep her distance.

Phil was not consciously aware of the internal conflicts he was experiencing toward his mother and father. But they were powerful currents in his mind that found expression in behaviors. Despite the trouble he got into, and the prices he was paying for it, his action defenses protected him from having to confront the emotional disruption that recognition of his internal conflicts threatened to cause.

316

Not all adolescents are spared having to cope with external sources of stress. Parental hostilities can be extremely upsetting to teenagers, especially when the youngsters find themselves caught in the middle. Like older elementary school children, adolescents, who are even more mature and capable, are especially vulnerable to being used as spies and messengers in conflicts between divorced parents. However, adolescents who are caught in the crossfire of their angry, divorcing parents, in a heated and protracted custody dispute often undergo more stress than younger children. Vigorously contested custody disagreements are painful and potentially developmentally disruptive for all youngsters. They often involve psychological evaluations, and youngsters are frequently asked, indirectly and skillfully or directly and heavy-handedly, which parent they wanted to live with. They may be interviewed by a host of adults in this process, including court-appointed case workers, a judge, mental health professionals, and each parent's attorney. In addition to the stresses of this legal battle, it usually fuels a powerful internal loyalty conflict in children as well as anger at parents that is at odds with the youngsters' loving feelings.

As painful as custody disputes are for children, preadolescent youngsters are often protected to some degree from direct attempts by a parent to convince the child that he should live with him [her]. It is difficult to discuss these issues with very young children who cannot cognitively grasp the relevant concepts. And if parents try to persuade preadolescent children to choose them, it is likely to be seen by the court as inappropriate coercion or bribery. Further, the wishes of children under twelve years old do not carry pivotal weight in custody determinations in most states. Collectively, these facts tend to spare many preadolescents from having to face the full extent of their parents' warfare over custody.

As hard as these custody disputes are for younger children, they can be exquisitely painful for adolescents. Because the courts in most states seriously consider a teenager's preference for which parent to live with, it is expected that parents will discuss custody issues with their adolescent children. This opens the door to subtle and not-so-subtle attempts to coerce or persuade youngsters to make a particular decision. It also tends to result in court case workers, judges, attorneys, and mental health professionals asking adolescents very blunt, direct questions about the nature of their relationship with each parent, their views of each parent, and their preference for whom to live with.

Since most teenagers love their parents, despite whatever conflicts they may have with them, it places them in the troubling position of having to choose one parent over the other.

Divorcing parents who are enraged at one another usually do not lovingly and supportively try to ascertain which household their youngster prefers, given the fact that she cannot continue living with both parents. It is more common for parents who are at war with one another to try to persuade the child that she will be happier in their home and to derogate the other parent in this process. Teenagers are acutely aware of the battle their parents are waging over them. As one youngster put it, "It's like my parents are having a big tug of war, and I'm the rope." This phrasing captures well the adolescent's sense that it is not simply that she is a prize being fought for, but that she is also a vehicle for her parents' rage, hurtful feelings, and enmeshed hostilities. The "rope" is the instrument of their struggles and at the same time is the tie that keeps them connected emotionally.

MANDY was two months shy of her fourteenth birthday when her mother decided she could no longer tolerate her marriage and moved out of the family home to an apartment with her daughter. Mandy's parents had been married for seventeen years and had been seniors in college when they married. Mandy had an older brother, Justin, sixteen, who elected to stay in the family home with his father after his mother left with Mandy. Mandy's mother had begun her career as a free-lance commercial artist while still attending college. Now as she approached forty, she was quite successful, earning nearly $45,000 a year doing art work for newspaper and magazine advertisements. Her husband, too, was doing well in his career as director of personnel for a large department store.

Mandy's mother had felt that her marital relationship had begun deteriorating four years before her decision to leave. She had found herself becoming depressed and did not, at first, understand why. She sought professional help, and after two years of therapy had come to the conclusion that she had been ignoring strong negative feelings about her marriage. She was an outgoing woman who enjoyed parties, concerts, and the theater. She loved a fast-paced social life. Her husband, on the other hand, took great pleasure in puttering around the house, gardening, and coaching soccer and basketball teams in his city's youth recreation leagues. During the fall, spring, and summer, he dashed home from work, ate a hurried meal, and was off to coach. On weekends nearly all of his time was spent coaching or organizing athletic schedules. His wife felt lonely and at the same time angry over being neglected. Eventually, she became depressed, because she would not let herself recognize these feelings. However, her therapy permitted her to see how lonely and enraged she was. She tried discussing this with her husband, but he was not particularly psychologically minded or emotionally sensitive. Mandy's mother decided to try doing what she preferred socially even if it meant going out without her husband. She began attending concerts and plays with friends she met through her work. She became aware of how much she had been missing in her marriage and decided to separate from her husband to pursue a more sociable life style and the possibility of a more gratifying, intimate relationship.

When Mandy's mother told her husband of her plan to leave him, he was stunned and then furious. He had believed that his marriage was stable. His rage was an automatic defensive reaction, which served to protect him from feeling hurt and abandoned. He was completely unaware of these painful feelings and only knew that his wife was acting "selfishly and irrationally." He told her that if she began dating it would be "proof" that she was a "slut" and that he would never take her back. He shoved her against a wall and slapped her several times across the face. Mandy was in the house during this episode and had overheard her parents' loud exchange and the slaps that followed.

Mandy's mother told her about her decision to separate from her husband and get a divorce. She honestly said that she felt she no longer loved her husband but that he did not want a divorce. She went on to explain to her daughter that she had been very unhappy for several years and realized that she had "fallen out of love" with her husband. Instead of being depressed and sad, she was going to end her marriage and would probably be dating other men. She told Mandy that she wanted her to come live in her new apartment, about a mile from the family home. Mandy could continue attending the same school if she lived with her mother.

Mandy readily agreed to go with her mother. They had always had a close, loving relationship. She saw her father as distant and uninvolved with her. He spent a great deal of time coaching boys' sports teams, including ones her brother played on. It seemed to her that she naturally belonged with her mother and her brother should be with her father. In fact, Justin elected to stay in the family home with his father and shared his father's angry, critical feelings toward his mother. When she talked with her son about her plans to leave and invited him to live with her, Justin angrily refused.

Mandy's father talked with her about staying with him. He told her that her mother was "acting really stupid." Besides, if she continued living at home she would still have her own bedroom and be in a big house instead of a "dinky" apartment. He told her, "There's nothing to do in an apartment building. There probably won't be any kids your age there and your bedroom will be real small." He added that if she stayed at home, she could have a color television set for her bedroom. Mandy silently nodded but went with her mother when she moved out. She saw her father every weekend from Friday after school until Saturday afternoon. During these visits, he continued to try to persuade his daughter to come back home to live with him and her brother. Her father also questioned her closely about whether her mother was going out in the evenings, how late she stayed out, and if her mother was having dates with men. Mandy just shrugged and uncomfortably looked down at her hands.

Two months after the separation, it became clear that there was going to be a custody fight over Mandy. Her mother had asked the court for joint legal custody and for Mandy to live with her. Mandy's father petitioned for sole legal custody and physical possession of his daughter. Mandy told her mother that she wanted to live with her. She said her father never had time for her and that when she visited him, her brother picked on her and called her names. Justin would not let her sit in the family room, claiming that, "You're not part of this family anymore. You went with mom. This isn't your house. I'll tell you where you can sit and you sure can't come into the family room. That's only for the family." Mandy also told the court case worker and the judge of her preference to live with her mother. But she never said that to her father. Whenever he asked whether she wanted to live with him, Mandy remained silent and just looked uncomfortable. At other times when she was with him, she seemed reasonably happy and acted friendly with her father.

Three months after the separation, Mandy began angrily exploding at her mother several times a week. These outbursts seemed to come out of the blue. When her mother casually asked her how things went at school or if she had much homework, Mandy screamed, "Leave me alone! I don't have to tell you every little thing that happens in my life." She would run to her bedroom, slam the door, and throw herself on her bed crying. However, at other times, the same questions would lead to Mandy openly sharing her school experiences of the day or matter-of-factly telling her mother about her homework assignments. Occasionally, she even asked her mother for some help with them. Her mother was bewildered by Mandy's unpredictable responses and tried talking with her about what was bothering her. Mandy never responded, but after a half an hour or so in her room, she would be back to her usual, pleasant way of interacting with her mother. She acted as if nothing had happened. She always apologized, but was unable to explain her behavior to her mother.

Over the following two months, Mandy's angry outbursts toward her mother escalated. Instead of only yelling, she began throwing things such as plastic dishes and shoes at her mother. She also cut up two of her own sweaters with scissors after running to her bedroom after one such explosion. Mandy had also begun angrily threatening to kill herself. She screamed obscenities at her mother (an extremely uncharacteristic behavior) and said, "Everything sucks! It'd be better if I was just dead. Then everyone would be happy. There wouldn't be any fighting or problems anymore." Mandy's mother was worried and frightened. She contacted Mandy's school to find out how she was doing there. The school reported that Mandy was doing well and that they had not noticed any changes in her. She was maintaining her usual B average, was attentive in class, and had several good friends. Academically and socially, she was doing fine and was certainly not a behavior problem.

Mandy's mother told her that she had talked to people at school and that they were very pleased with how Mandy was doing. Mandy's mother complimented her daughter on this score and went on to try and discuss with her what had been happening at home. She wondered about Mandy's anger and her ideas of hurting herself. Mandy said: "Nothing's happened. I'm fine. I just get upset sometimes.

The custody litigation continued with Mandy being reinterviewed by the court case worker and the judge. She again told them that she wanted to live with her mother and added that she no longer wished to visit her father. The court conveyed this to Mandy's father who insisted it was not true. He told them that Mandy never said anything like that to him and that she was loving when she was with him. He said that he was prepared to "go to the mat" to have his daughter live in a proper, morally upright home. He claimed that it might hurt Mandy in the short-run to have a bitter custody fight, but that she would be better off with him in the future than she would be living with her morally unfit mother. He directly asked his daughter why she would even think of living with a "whore," which, after all, was all her mother was. Mandy just shrugged and looked away.

Mandy was caught in the maelstrom of her father's rage at his wife. He appeared to have unwittingly identified his daughter with his wife because of their both being female and the fact that Mandy had chosen to leave with her mother. He was entirely unaware of his wounded masculine pride and his sadness over the ending of his marriage. His rage protected him from these painful feelings. He was equally unaware that this fury spilled over into his feelings toward his daughter. Despite his knowledge of how cruel Justin was being to Mandy, he never made any attempt to intervene, rationalizing that brothers and sisters had to work out their own conflicts. Similarly, he dismissed the fact that the custody dispute was hurting Mandy by claiming he was pursuing this legal battle for Mandy's ultimate, greater welfare. Men who wrap themselves in such self-righteous rage are rarely amenable to efforts aimed at sensitizing them to the effects of their behavior on their youngsters. They are convinced they are acting on behalf of their children by protecting them from the bad influence of the mother.

Mandy's mother was far more able to see what her daughter needed. She was careful not to criticize her husband, and supported Mandy having an ongoing relationship with her father. She encouraged her daughter to continue visiting her father regularly and tried to explain her husband's actions to Mandy as products of his being upset about the divorce. However, she appropriately was not prepared to sacrifice her daughter's best interests and stated custody preference to her husband's rage. And so the custody battle continued.

Mandy was furious. She was angry at her mother for leaving the marriage and thus creating the current strife. But she was both hurt by and enraged at her father for calling her mother awful names, permitting her brother to treat her badly, and not being sensitive to her needs. She was very much aware of her anger over her mother's decision to seek a divorce. But she had blinded herself to her fury at her father. She never expressed it when she was with him, nor did she even tell him directly of her preference to be with her mother (though he could see that she was living with her). In fact, she often seemed affectionate when she was with him.

Developmentally, Mandy was at an age when girls very much need their father. Fathers help confirm for their daughters that they are femininely lovable, competent, and attractive. A father can also help his daughter separate from her mother emotionally by providing an alternative, caring relationship to the mother–daughter one and by acting as a buffer to the friction that so often arises between mothers and their daughters in the separation process.[1] Thus, she could not easily afford becoming aware of her rage at her father. She tried to cope with this internal conflict by unwittingly shifting her anger fully onto her mother and by eventually turning the force of her rage against herself. This permitted her to feel close and loving when she was with her father. However, the cost of these defenses was increasing in alarming ways. She found herself inexplicably enraged at her mother several times a week. And since these outbursts had become insufficient to keep her anger at her father out of awareness, she turned to a more dangerous defense: she directed her fury at herself, destroying her own clothing, and threatening to kill herself. In fact, it is well known that suicidal feelings and actions are frequently the result of rage toward a loved one that is warded off and converted into impulses to maim and kill oneself.

Mandy was at risk for acting out her defenses against the pain of her internal conflict over her love and need for her father and her intense anger towards him. As is so often the case with adolescents, her defenses against the anguish over a hidden conflict were being expressed in worrisome and potentially dangerous behaviors.

The Short-Term Aftermath Stage

One of the most difficult tasks for adolescents during the short-term aftermath stage is to accept the irrevocable fact that their parents are going to be divorced. After the shock and emotional turmoil they experience in the immediate crisis stage, teenagers must come to terms with the finality of their parents' divorce. Many adolescents secretly harbor fantasies of their parents reconciling their differences and getting back together. Often these wishes are consciously recognized by youngsters. They talk with one or both parents about how they might work on their relationship, how the marriage really was not so bad, and how much better it would be for them to be reunited. Some teenagers engage their parents in intellectual discussions or debates aimed at convincing them of the wisdom of reconciling. They may recall good times the family used to have and point to realistic financial and emotional difficulties the parents are experiencing in the wake of the separation. Other adolescents appear to accept the divorce but are unaware of powerful wishes to have their parents get back together. They may seem sad, angry, or especially critical of one or both parents but are unable to see that these feelings are the result of a frustrated longing for the divorce to be negated and for things to go back to being the way they were before the marital separation.

As noted earlier in this chapter, adolescents have many developmental reasons for wanting their parents to stay married. Their needs for a stable and secure home base and for their parents' love and guidance during this time of normally occurring major changes makes it especially difficult for them to accept divorce. Though most teenagers are unaware of these developmental needs, and their worries that divorce will undermine the support and love they require, these issues contribute to their experiencing divorce as intolerable.

When strong wishes for parental reconciliation are at play, youngsters perceive certain events as roadblocks in the path of their parents getting back together. These become external sources of stress because of the meaning adolescents attach to them; they will make it harder (or even impossible) for parents to reunite. External events that thus become stressful include the noncustodial parent buying a house (instead of renting a less permanent apartment), selling what had been the family residence (a symbol of the predivorce family togetherness), and parent dating (a clear demonstration of a lack of commitment to the former spouse).

CHRISTOPHER was thirteen and his brother Sean was ten when his parents separated and his father moved to a nearby apartment complex. After fourteen years of marriage, his mother increasingly felt stuck in an unfulfilling marriage. She experienced her husband

324

The Divorce Experience for Adolescents

as self-centered and believed that he looked down his nose at her because she was "only a housewife." She was an intense woman who thought of herself as a frustrated artist. She believed she never had the time or the support of her husband to pursue her talents. She painted in oils and had begun numerous canvases only to leave them uncompleted because they "were not turning out quite right." She felt her creative energies were sapped by day-to-day child rearing and household tasks and were intruded upon by her husband's wishes for sexual intimacy. At thirty-seven, she thought that unless she made a commitment to her art, she would never bring her talents to fruition.

Christopher's father was an easygoing man who sold insurance for a living. He enjoyed his work, which fit well with his extroverted personality style. But he was not overly invested in his career. He had many interests that he pursued with friends and with his two sons. He took them fishing frequently, spontaneously threw a baseball or football with them after work and on the weekends, and involved both of them in his hobby of building elaborate model trains with complete scenes. At first he was angry with his wife's wish for a divorce but soon after became depressed. He tearfully talked out his feelings with his brother and a close friend. Within a few months he had not only accepted his wife's decision but began to enjoy being single. For years he had been upset over his wife's lack of interest in sex and her constant accusations that he was somehow at fault for her not achieving success and recognition as an artist. He found it a delightful relief to be living apart from her and was flattered by the interest some of his women co-workers began to show in him. By the time the divorce was legally finalized, a year after the marital separation, he had adjusted well.

At first Christopher cried when his parents told him of their plans to divorce. He sobbed openly and asked them directly if they were separating because of his having done something wrong. They were taken aback by this concern and quickly reassured him that the divorce had nothing to do with their feelings about him. They both told Chris that they loved him and would continue to love him. Together they explained that Chris's mother was not happy being married and wanted to devote her energies to being an artist. They truthfully acknowledged that Chris's father did not want the divorce, but that he would get used to it. In fact, several months later, his father told him that he was feeling fine about

325

the divorce and that it was a good thing for him. Appropriately, neither parent discussed their sexual incompatibility with Chris or his brother.

Chris's parents told him of their agreement that the boys would live with their mother and be with their father in his apartment for part of every week, alternating between Thursday night through Saturday noon and Saturday noon to Sunday evening. They quite reasonably offered him the opportunity to modify this schedule at any time. However, Chris accepted it readily, and it continued into the short-term aftermath stage.

After Chris's initial display of distress over his parents' separation, he seemed to adjust to it. He continued to do well at school, both academically and socially. He received mostly B's, played in the school band, and enjoyed getting together with friends to listen to music and play sports and video games. He got along reasonably well with both parents, though each had noticed that he was clearly more moody since their separation. As the divorce moved into the short-term aftermath stage, six months after the marital separation, Chris seemed to have come to terms with it.

At that point Chris's father began to date. He became especially fond of a woman, a secretary who worked in the same office he did. After seeing Louise for a month, he decided to introduce his sons to her with the hope that they would hit it off and become friends. In their first times together, Chris seemed interested in Louise and invited her to listen to some tapes of rock groups he enjoyed. She also liked this music and it appeared that a bond between them was beginning to develop. However, after a month, Chris's demeanor toward Louise changed. He became cool and was unresponsive to her continued overtures for friendship. When they were at the dinner table he monosyllabically answered her attempts at conversation. He also began to correct her incessantly—about the name of the rock group whose music he was listening to, the score of a football game, and the results of recent election polls. He snickered when she made a slip of the tongue or used a word incorrectly. After meals at his father's apartment, he "forgot" to help clear the dishes despite her reminding him several times. And he began to leave articles of clothing, tapes and books strewn about the living room in clear opposition to Louise's wishes to have the apartment tidy. Though she was not living with Chris's father, she had taken on housekeeping responsibilities when she was there.

Chris's father was upset about this change in his son's attitude toward Louise. He talked privately about it with Chris and asked him directly why he was acting so unfriendly. Chris openly told his father that he did not really like Louise. She was picky about neatness in the apartment, seemed "out of it," and chewed her food with her mouth open. "Besides," he claimed, "she's always over at the apartment." Chris's father patiently explained that Louise only wanted things to be nice at the apartment and for Chris to like her. He said that it hurt Louise's feelings when Chris put her down. Chris argued that he was not doing anything wrong; it was not his fault that she did not know much of anything and talked like a "hillbilly." At that point, Chris's father became angry. He told his son that Louise was his girlfriend and that he really liked her. He added that Chris had no right to say nasty things about her and hurt her feelings. Chris angrily replied, "Fine! If you think she's so great, then you talk to her. I don't need to be around her." After this exchange, Chris began to have reasons not to visit his father for the full amount of time they usually spent together. He had a school party, a band practice, or plans to go to a movie with some friends. Chris's father felt frustrated; his budding relationship with Louise seemed pitted against the close bond he had enjoyed with his son.

Though Chris rarely spoke about it, things were not going well at his mother's home. In the fourteen months since the marital separation, she had still not completed a painting. Money was becoming increasingly tight, but she had not sought a job. She had neglected caring for the house and cooking for her sons in order to spend time painting. When he picked the boys up, Chris's father noticed that her household had fallen into disarray and was concerned about their lack of decent meals and clean clothes. He and his ex-wife were on fairly cordial terms. She apologized for the way her house looked, but cheerfully noted that "sometimes artists just can't be bothered with making sure everything is picked up off the floor." Chris's father did not press this issue. He felt that his former wife was "living in a fantasy world" and that she would never become a productive artist. But he saw no reason to confront her and possibly precipitate a fight between them.

However, he continued to be distressed about the widening emotional gulf between him and his son. His efforts to discuss Chris's feelings about his relationship with Louise seemed to have no impact on Chris except to make him angry. Two months later, he announced his plans to buy a house and have Louise move in with him. Chris muttered, "Jesus H Christ! That's just great. Wonderful. Soon I'll have a dip for a stepmother." Chris's father confronted his son about this reaction saying, "See. That's what I mean. You won't give her a chance. What did she ever do to you, except try to be nice?" Chris sarcastically replied, "Sure, she's just great." Within two weeks, Chris became despondent. His mother and father both noticed that he was spending a great deal of time lying in bed listening to tapes. Though he continued to do well at school and did perk up when he was with his friends, he appeared remote and depressed in each parent's home. Chris's father was increasingly concerned about his son. He knew that Chris resented Louise and was acutely aware of the rift between him and Chris. Now Chris also seemed depressed. He was at a loss about how to reach and help his son.

Chris's difficulties illustrate a major alternative to adolescent conflicts being expressed in explosive, potentially dangerous actions. His underlying emotional pain over the divorce became evident in more quiet ways. His gradually increasing resentment of Louise, his feelings of alienation from his father, and his depression indicated that he had never really come to terms with the end of his parents' marriage and of his family as he had always known it. When his father's relationship with Louise threatened to endure, and this possibility was underscored by his father's plans to buy a house and live with Louise, Chris began to have trouble.

Chris's attempts to derogate his father's partner was motivated by a wish to drive a wedge between Louise and his father. To do so would serve two purposes: it would prevent his father from emotionally leaving him for Louise, and at the same time leave open the possibility that his mother and father would resolve their differences and reunite. As is so often the case, Chris was unaware of these aims and did not even realize that his behavior and attitude represented attempts to put an end to his father's relationship with Louise. All he knew was that he did not like Louise and wanted his father to stop seeing her.

The fact that Chris felt that he needed his father more than ever added to his desperation. He was at a point in his development which required a strengthened identification with his father in order to further his own emerging sense of himself as a young man. Moreover, the lack of structure and stability in his mother's house made him uneasy. Her withdrawal from parenting in order to pursue her artistic endeavors left him feeling that he no longer had a secure home base. His father's solid adjustment to the divorce and his more organized life-style made him a potential anchor for Chris in the face of the strong currents of change characterizing adolescence. Thus, any perceived threat to his relationship with his father had serious and far-reaching implicit meanings for Chris. Chris was not consciously aware of these issues either. It is sadly ironic that Chris's attempts to ensure a continued, prominent place in his father's life and to keep the door open for his parents reconciling had the effect of creating the emotional distance between him and his father that he feared.

Chris was able to adjust well to his parents' separation and the immediate crisis stage for several reasons. Both parents loved him and were able to tell him so. They reassured him about the fact that the divorce was due to their marital problems, and that he had no role in bringing it about. It was also enormously helpful to Chris that there were no significant environmental stresses. His parents were on reasonably good terms, he continued to see his father frequently and regularly, and neither parent was distraught over the divorce. The divorce settlement also permitted Chris to continue living in his house and thus attend the same school and keep his network of friends. The importance of school and peers is central for adolescents, and the divorce did not require the changes in residence, school, and therefore the peer relationships that so often accompany divorce.

Rather than a reaction to internal conflicts stimulated by turbulent environmental stresses, Chris's problems were the result of developmentally understandable responses to the very fact of his parents' divorce and his father's subsequently having a serious dating relationship. The marital separation threatened Chris's need for security and stability amid the changes of adolescence, and his father's romantic involvement raised the spectre of Chris losing the closeness of the father-son tie at a time that it was especially important to maintain it. Chris defended against the anxieties aroused by each of these issues by clinging to an unspoken fantasy that his parents would reconcile and undo their divorce. This would restore a feeling of having a secure home base and at the same time ensure a continued close relationship with his father. When the reconciliation wish was in danger of being thwarted by Chris's father's relationship with Louise, Chris unwittingly tried to interfere. And when his efforts appeared fruitless, he became despondent as he had to face the prospect of both giving up his fantasy of his parents' reunion and also possibly losing his father to Louise.

Many youngsters in Chris's position give the appearance of generally coping well with their parents' divorce. They continue doing well academically and stay involved in appropriate and pleasurable peer relationships. They get along well with adults (other than their parents), including other relatives, teachers, and coaches. Most do not act out their conflicts in ways which get them into trouble or draw the concern of adults. In fact, parents, themselves, are usually not sensitive to these more quiet kinds of difficulties and dismiss their teenager's behavior as irritating or as a reflection of normal adolescent moodiness. However, children like Chris are in emotional pain, and their developmental progress can be hampered.

Although the focus here has been on boys' reactions to divorce and their noncustodial father dating, girls frequently display similar attitudes and behaviors when their parents divorce and their custodial mother begins to date. They, too, have a wish for their parents to reconcile, and girls need to identify with their mother for the same developmental reasons boys require their father as a role model. And when a girl's mother is involved romantically, it causes an additional strain for her; at just the time that an adolescent girl is wrestling with concerns over her own emerging sexuality and the internal as well as external pressures about how to conduct herself in dating relationships, her mother becomes clearly active both socially and sexually. This can threaten a girl's emotional equilibrium by fueling her feelings about dating. Some girls then begin to act in a precocious manner sexually, taking an inadvertent cue from their mother. They may seem mature beyond their years and are vulnerable to the dangers of growing up too fast in these ways. Others retreat from the anxiety that this arouses and seem stuck in early adolescence. They defensively shun dating, often turning their energies (at times quite productively) to academic work and extracurricular activities. These girls rarely provoke adult concern, but their developmental progress has nonetheless been compromised. Often they successfully avoid feeling any conflict until the expectation (internal and external) for having intimate relationships becomes more pressing in young adulthood.

Adolescents' conflicts over divorce can be inflamed in both the immediate crisis and short-term aftermath stages of divorce by the presence of significant environmental stresses. However, a "friendly" divorce of the sort Chris's parents had can create another kind of stress. It often results in teenagers feeling more surprised by their parents' divorce and less able to understand the reasons or need for it. These youngsters cannot even console themselves with the perception that at least things are better in some ways after the divorce because strife in the household has been reduced or an emotionally upset parent feels happier. More silent and less visible (to the adolescent) marital tensions or dissatisfactions make the divorce more of a shock. The teenager is likely to feel more keenly the loss of a comfortable, pleasurable, and reassuring sense of family cohesiveness. These youngsters are prone to acute sadness. It is somewhat paradoxical that intense feelings of loss and despair may be more pronounced, at least in the short-run, when there is a notable lack of environmental stresses.

The Long-Range Period

Many adolescents whose parents' divorce took place years in the past appear to do very well.[2] This seems to be the case when the marital separation occurred during the teenager's infancy, toddlerhood, or preschool years, the custodial mother remarried within a few years, and the stepfather established a caring, involved relationship with the youngster. For these children, the stresses of the immediate crisis and short-term aftermath stages are usually beyond recall, lost in the dim memories of early childhood. They are not burdened by vivid and painful recollections of parental hostilities or the emotional distress of one or both parents. Nor do they have to come to terms with the loss of remembered family closeness and yearnings for the reestablishment of a treasured sense of family togetherness.

The remarried family *is* their family, and the stepfather is very much the child's psychological parent. Key stresses of the extended divorce process in single-mother households (for example, economic insecurity, use of children for the parent's emotional support) do not come into play. And the conflicts stimulated by a custodial mother's remarriage at a later point (competitive feelings toward the stepfather for mother's love and attention, resentment over the new stepfather becoming too parental, and curiosity about the intimacy between mother and stepfather) often do not arise, and if they do, rarely are carried forward into adolescence when the remarriage takes place prior to the child's elementary school years. For many of these adolescents, their remarried family is their only psychological family and divorce may not even be a concept they apply to their own situation.

This is not to say that an adolescent whose parents divorced when she was very young will be necessarily free of all divorce-related stresses. Continued parental warfare and the absence of a relationship with the noncustodial father are two common problems for adolescents in the long-range period of divorce. However, when the marital separation has taken place long in the past, many parents (and mental health professionals, as well) often fail to recognize that a teenager's difficulties may be related to divorce. Adolescents, themselves, do not usually make this connection. When it is suggested that a teenager's troubles may have something to do with the divorce, adults and youngsters frequently will say, "But that was a long time ago." They point to the fact that it is unlikely that the child will remember "the divorce." The implicit assumption is that divorce is a circumscribed event consisting of the parental separation and/or the legal finalization of the divorce. Ongoing stresses stemming from the divorce are not recognized.

But there are more subtle processes at work, too. Growing up in a single-mother household and having little or no contact with a man, affects the developmental trajectory of both boys and girls.[3] And long-standing ill-will between parents, even if it is short of open warfare, can have a cumulative corrosive effect on youngsters. Internal conflicts that these conditions often create in children can lie dormant, and may not spring to life until the developmental issues in adolescence provide the necessary impetus for them.

KIM was four years old when her parents separated. They had been married when each was nineteen years old. Kim's mother had worked full-time as a secretary since Kim was two years old in order to support her husband's efforts to finish college. When he failed several courses and had to leave college, he vented his frustration and anger on his wife. He accused her of being unsupportive and uncaring. After being fired from a succession of part-time jobs, his scapegoating of his wife increased and their marital relationship deteriorated. He moved out and went to a distant state. Since he had no wish to pay child support, he kept his whereabouts unknown for nearly five years. His parents told Kim's mother that they knew that he was in a state over a thousand miles away.

Kim's mother was anguished by her husband's abandonment.

She was twenty-four, alone with her young daughter, and completely on her own financially. At first she partly accepted her husband's beliefs that she had been a failure as a wife. She was depressed and frightened, but she was also an emotionally resilient woman. She continued working as a secretary, found an excellent child-care facility for Kim, and began to date casually. When Kim was seven, her mother opened a gift shop with another woman. She managed the business while her partner provided nearly all of the initial capital. Kim's mother was a hard worker with good organizational skills. Within a year the shop was providing her with a solid income that permitted her to live a comfortable middle-class life. Because of the nature of her work, and the fact that she was a co-owner of the business, she had a great deal of flexibility in the time she could spend with her daughter. After school, Kim took a bus to her mother's shop and helped out there by straightening out shelves and putting customers' purchases into bags. As she got older, Kim worked in her mother's shop as a salesperson and also helped her mother keep track of the inventory. On weekends they spent time together at the gift shop, went to lunch frequently, and took in movies together in the evenings.

Kim's mother was a loving parent and a competent business person. She was grateful that she could arrange for her and Kim to spend a lot of time together, and took pride in providing a stable, middle-class upbringing for her daughter. They worked and played together, took week-long summer and winter vacations, and very much enjoyed each other's company. Over the years, a powerful and mutually pleasurable emotional bond was forged between them.

When Kim was thirteen her mother developed a serious dating relationship. Though she had dated frequently since her divorce, she had not found anyone she wanted to marry until Chuck. She had rarely brought these men to her home, preferring to keep her romantic life separate. At times she had slept at a dating partner's home and had gone on weekend trips with a man after arranging for Kim to stay at a friend's house. Although Kim complained about these activities, the relationships ended before she had to fully confront her feelings about her mother dating and spending time with someone other than her. However, when Chuck moved in with her mother and her six months after they had begun seeing one another, Kim had to face two important issues: her mother's affection for and emotional commitment to someone else, and the obvious (to an adolescent) sexual nature of her mother's relationship with Chuck.

Shortly after Chuck moved in, Kim began voicing her displeasure to her mother. She pointed to Chuck's less-than-perfect table manners and his tendency to laugh loudly. She told her mother that Chuck was "gross"; he watched television in his undershirt, smoked smelly cigars, and belched after drinking soda pop or beer. She seemed to resent his very presence. At one point she said to her mother: "I can't stand him! He's always watching some stupid football game so I have to miss my programs. And if I want a snack at night, I have to put on a damned bathrobe to go down to the kitchen. Just to get an apple! In my own house!" Though she was not directly hostile toward Chuck, she kept her distance from him and privately barraged her mother with her dissatisfactions.

Kim's mother was concerned about her daughter's reactions to Chuck. However, she thought that Kim would gradually accept her romantic relationship and was confident that the close bond between her and her daughter would sustain and help them through this difficult time. She also believed that if she married Chuck, Kim's objections to him would be reduced because their relationship would then be more permanent and "legitimate." Besides, Kim had always been a thoughtful, bright youngster who got along well with adults and peers. She would recognize the importance of the relationship to her mother and would be able to accept Chuck.

Kim's mother married Chuck shortly after her daughter turned fourteen. But her mother's expectation that this would alleviate Kim's tension over Chuck's presence was not met. Kim continued to feel that Chuck was an intruder. Outwardly, she only acted cool and distant toward him, but inside she was fuming over his being a part of her household and his relationship with her mother.

Kim began to express her anger toward her mother. Rather than confidentially telling her mother about her unhappiness with Chuck, which underscored her special closeness with her mother, Kim became resistant to her mother's authority and critical of her as well. She complained about having to help prepare dinners and argued with her mother about just how neat her bedroom had to be kept. She began to resent having to go to bed at a regular time (10:30 P.M.) on school nights. Her mother dreaded the evenings because she knew that as half past ten approached, she and Kim would get into a battle over bedtime. Kim pleaded with her mother to be able to stay up "just a little longer." When her mother told her reasonably that she had to get enough sleep in order to feel good the next day and be alert in school, Kim told her she was being "stupid."

After Chuck married Kim's mother, he believed that he had the right and obligation to take a parental role with his stepdaughter and a supportive position with his new wife. He tried to come to his wife's aid in her battles with Kim by telling Kim to listen to her mother. When Kim ignored him, Chuck became angry and told her to go to her room. In addition to siding with his wife in her efforts to get Kim to take appropriate responsibilities at home and observe rules about bedtime, he started threatening Kim with disciplinary actions for not complying. Kim was increasingly enraged over Chuck acting parental toward her. She privately told her mother: "Who the hell does he think he is? He's not my father! He's got no right to order me around." In Kim's eyes, Chuck was not a legitimate parental authority.

As much as they fought over household tasks, the greatest conflicts between Kim and her mother were over weekend curfews and Kim's manner of dress. At fourteen and a half, Kim had begun wearing mini skirts with black net panty hose. She also started using a great deal of make-up. On Fridays and Saturdays she wanted to stay out until one o'clock in the morning, frequently going to parties that her mother was not sure were supervised by adults. Her mother told Kim that she did not approve of what she was wearing and that she had to be home no later than midnight on weekend evenings. Kim was furious. She berated her mother for being "out of touch with what was happening." She told her mother that all of her friends dressed as she did and that coming home by midnight on weekends would make her look like a baby to the other kids. She accused her mother of being unsympathetic and trying to ruin her social life. Kim also bitterly asked her mother, "Why can't you be like Jennie's mom or Courtney's mom? How come their mothers understand them? Why do you have to be so weird?" Kim's mother was deeply hurt by her daughter feeling that their relationship was not as good as those that her friends had with their mothers. She had always felt very close to Kim and thought that they had a special, treasured bond between them. To placate her daughter, Kim's mother agreed to a 1:00 A.M. curfew on Fridays and Saturdays.

One night Kim came home at 2:00 A.M. clearly drunk. She

awakened her mother as she threw up in the bathroom. Her mother was furious and told Kim how "dumb" it was to drink, that it would get her into big trouble, and was also illegal. Kim was contrite, but a similar episode occurred a month later. This time Kim's mother went into a tearful and angry tirade about her daughter's lack of responsibility and poor judgment. She grounded Kim for two weeks and insisted that when she resumed going out on weekends that her daughter call her at eleven and at twelve o'clock to "check in" before coming home absolutely no later than 1:00 A.M. Kim argued about having to call home and told her mother that everyone would laugh at her. But her mother was adamant and made this a condition of Kim being permitted to stay out until one in the morning.

Kim's mother was becoming increasingly concerned about her daughter's behavior. She asked Kim's high school counselor to talk with Kim's teachers about her academic progress and general adjustment in school. She learned that Kim was doing well. Though her grades had dropped from A's and B's to B's and C's, her teachers felt that Kim was applying herself to her work and participated in class discussions. They saw no evidence of Kim being in any trouble; she got along well with teachers and classmates and was responsible about getting homework assignments in. They thought that the slip in her grades was the result of taking harder courses now that she was in high school.

Still, Kim's mother was worried about her. Their once close relationship had deteriorated, her daughter was dressing "like a sex pot," and she had been drinking at parties to the point of being intoxicated on at least two occasions that she knew about. Kim's mother felt that she had to keep more of an eye on her daughter. She believed Kim was at risk for getting into serious trouble and decided to have her daughter see a therapist.

Kim's difficulties illustrate well a problematic confluence of developmental issues and long-range divorce events. She was struggling with two important developmental tasks of adolescence: emotionally separating from parents, and adaptively integrating sexual feelings into a new self-image. These normal developmental challenges had become more difficult for Kim for several reasons. First, the emotional closeness between her and her mother was much greater than it is for many girls. She and her mother had only each other for many years. Without an alternative caring relationship that a father (or stepfather, uncle, grandfather) can provide, all of Kim's emotional eggs went into one basket; her relationship with her mother. During elementary school this usually does not pose problems for girls. Mothers and daughters can be very close without developmental or social pressures against this sharing of their lives. And although Kim's mother was actively engaged in her career and also dated, her needs for intimacy were primarily met through her relationship with her daughter. The result was keenly gratifying for each. However, in adolescence, there are internal, developmental demands to be emotionally separate from parents and to carve out one's own identity apart from them. There are also new social expectations from peers to be independent of parents. Girls who have enjoyed an overly close mother–daughter relationship earlier must struggle that much harder to escape the maternal orbit during adolescence.

A second factor was Kim's mother's relationship with Chuck. Rather than Kim gradually (and, it must be noted, with probably some conflict) pulling away from her mother, she had to face the precipitous loss of her special place in her mother's life. Her mother's love for Chuck and her increasing emotional commitment to him, disrupted Kim's relationship with her mother. Rather than beginning to actively disengage from the tie with her mother, Kim felt abruptly pushed away. She was hurt and automatically defended herself against this pain by becoming angry. But her anger was at odds with her loving feelings and continued wishes to be close to her mother. In the face of this internal conflict, she displaced her rage onto Chuck while at the same time trying to reinforce her special position with her mother; they had long, confidential talks about Kim's dissatisfactions with Chuck.

This equilibrium shifted after Kim's mother and Chuck married. From Kim's point of view, they seemed to be ganging up on her which underscored her mother's allegiance to Chuck rather than to her. Chuck compounded this by acting as so many new stepparents do. He supported his wife against her child and also assumed a parental role too quickly. Teenagers mightily resent both. The former drives home the special marital bond which necessarily excludes children, and the latter seems entirely illegitimate to most adolescents. As these events unfolded, Kim's anger toward her mother could no longer be contained by her unwittingly shifting it to Chuck. She became furious at her mother directly and was constantly at odds with her. But her rage also served to continue a highly charged emotional tie between mother and daughter. For many adolescent girls, this dance of anger replaces the earlier bond of affection; mother and daughter may no longer be lovingly close, but they are still partners, each attentive and responsive to the other's moves.

Kim's awareness of the sexual aspect of her mother's relationship with Chuck also contributed to her difficulties. At the time that most adolescents have to manage their own emerging sexuality, Kim had to confront the sexual intimacy between her mother and Chuck. Even before they were married, Kim showed that she was uncomfortably cognizant of this issue when she told her mother that she had to put on a bathrobe "just to get an apple." Teenagers are usually curious about their parents' sexuality, but when there has not been a divorce, most push these thoughts out of mind. One sixteen-year-old expressed this particularly well. He told his therapist one day that he was furious because his mother's dating partner had slept over the previous night. He said, "I knew what they were doing! He didn't stay over just so they could play cards in bed. Steve (a friend whose parents were not divorced) doesn't have to deal with that crap." His therapist gently asked him if he meant that Steve's parents never had sex. The boy became uneasy and then blurted: "Well, at least Steve doesn't have to know exactly when they're doing it! They sleep together every night." Adolescents are both curious about their parent's sexuality and repelled by that very idea.

Kim's sexually provocative style of dress and her getting drunk at parties were, in part, responses to her mother's intimate relationship with Chuck. Her normally occurring adolescent sexual feelings and curiosities had been further stimulated by her awareness of the sexuality between Chuck and her mother. Kim's actions represented an attempt to cope with her own sexuality as well as an unwitting identification with the image she had developed of her mother. She seemed to be flirting with the idea of becoming sexually active; she would unconsciously feel close to her mother by being like her. The tendency for adolescent daughters of divorce to seem more sexually aware and to act more sexually provocative than girls whose parents have not divorced has been noted by several observers.[4]

However, the behaviors of concern to Kim's mother also served another, more subtle purpose. They were in effect invitations for Kim's mother to be close to her in particular ways. Though Kim was completely unaware of this hidden motive, the fact was that her actions resulted in her mother paying a great deal of attention to her, involving herself in her daughter's life beyond what adolescents usually need or consciously want, and keeping Kim home with her (that is, grounding her). At the same time that Kim was vociferously insisting on her right to be independent, she was identifying with her mother and acting in precisely the ways that were guaranteed to give her less freedom and have greater controls imposed by her mother.

The lack of an ongoing, loving relationship with her noncustodial father tends to intensify a girl's closeness with her mother. Most teenage girls who have not seen their father in years do not consciously experience his absence as stressful. When asked about their feelings about their father, they frequently say, "I really don't think about him much. He left a long time ago," or "I don't miss my dad anymore. I used to, but I got over it when I was in fourth or fifth grade." Despite this calm acceptance of not having a father in their lives, many adolescent girls are burdened by his prolonged absence. The bond with their mother can become overly strong and thus interfere with the normal task of emotionally separating from her and beginning to travel their own path in life. When a mother does not remarry, her daughter may continue to feel especially close to her and fail to emotionally separate from her. Such girls may not develop close friendships, avoid dating, or choose to live with or near their mother after high school, forsaking good job or college opportunities. They dedicate themselves to the mother–daughter relationship, at times paying enormous prices for it.

Adolescent girls whose fathers have stayed centrally involved in their lives after the divorce, seem less vulnerable to these sorts of problems. Similarly, girls who were very young when their mother remarried also appear to do well in adolescence. In each of these situations, a loving relationship with someone (perhaps, father or stepfather) other than mother reduces the likelihood of an enmeshed mother–daughter relationship developing. By the time a girl reaches adolescence, after having lived for years with a stepfather, she does not usually see him as a competitive threat for her mother's affections. Nor is the sexual ambience of dating and courtship present. The adolescent girl is unencumbered by these potential stresses.

As we have pointed out before, the absence of a father figure can have long-range effects on teenage boys, too. It is well-known that fathers play a crucial role in the development of their sons' masculine identity. An adolescent boy's capacity to feel comfortable with his masculinity, to experience himself as competent, to be appropriately assertive, and to develop internal controls over his behavior are in large measure derived from modeling himself after and identifying with his father.[5] When boys are raised without a loving, available man in their lives, they are vulnerable to a host of problems including performing below their abilities in school, being inhibited in social and competitive situations with other boys, and/or having difficulties controlling aggressive impulses.[6]

As discussed earlier, boys whose parents divorce and live with their custodial mother face other stresses as well. They are in a position of having to accept their mother as the primary parent, responsible for assigning chores, setting appropriate behavioral limits, and disciplining. Boys often have problems accepting these controls from their mother, especially in adolescence. Many older elementary school and teenage boys experience yielding to their mother's authority and direction as being unmasculine. Usually boys are not consciously aware of this issue. Instead they feel generally resistant without knowing why. Some youngster may voice a vague recognition of these feelings by saying: "She's always on my back about something," "She won't give me any freedom," "She worries about me too much," or, "She's always treating me like a little kid." The overall impression is that the boy feels that his mother is holding the reins on him too tightly and not giving him credit for being responsible. There is an undercurrent of feeling vaguely humiliated by having to give in to his mother's authority, and therefore this goes beyond typical adolescent chafing at restrictions.

The combination of having a less solid sense of his masculinity due to the absence of his father, and being in a position of having to submit to his mother's authority, can lead the adolescent boy to have to prove (to himself and to his peers) that he is not a "wimp" or "sissy." This internal conflict, between strivings for masculine identity and an underlying lack of conviction about it, may result in hypermasculine behavior. Fighting, vandalism, conflicts with school authorities, refusal to do homework assignments, driving in a daredevil manner, and constant challenges to mother's parental role are fairly common outcomes. These behaviors are not consciously planned attempts to demonstrate one's masculinity. The teenage boy often feels compelled to engage in these activities without having a clue about the forces which are driving him to do so.

ANDY was seven and his sister Leslie was five when his parents separated. His mother was a supervisor for the telephone company and his father an electronics repairman who worked in the service department of a national chain of home appliance and electronics stores. After nine years of marriage, Andy's mother decided to divorce her husband. She regarded him as childish and insensitive. When she turned thirty, she made up her mind to leave him in the hope of finding a more compatible partner. Her income was sufficient to maintain a middle-class life style, and her job was secure. Andy's father was angry when his wife left him, not because he was especially hurt, but because she had made the decision to leave rather than he. He had felt trapped in an ungratifying marriage for years and was on the brink of filing for divorce, himself. He resented his wife beating him to the punch because he did not like the way it looked, that she found him unacceptable rather than the other way around.

During the immediate crisis stage of their divorce, Andy's parents argued bitterly about the property settlement and the level of child support Andy's father would pay. There was never any question between them about custody and visitation; they agreed that the children would live with their mother, she would have sole legal custody, and he would have "liberal visiting privileges."

At first, Andy was shocked and saddened by his parents' divorce. He cried frequently, withdrew from peer activities, and pleaded with his parents to get back together. His mother sensitively explained that the divorce was not in any way his fault and empathized with his sadness over losing his sense of family. She joined a support group for recently separated mothers, and made excellent use of the parenting suggestions of the group leader and other group members. Within a few months, Andy's depressive reaction had lifted.

Andy's father became "superdad" after the hostilities of the immediate crisis stage had passed. He saw his children every weekend from Saturday afternoon to Sunday night, took them to dinner every Wednesday evening, and had them sleep over on Wednesdays, as well. He showered them with presents and took them to movies, the zoo, and sporting events, regularly. Andy's mother noted that her ex-husband did far more with the children after the divorce than before.

Andy continued to do well in the short-term aftermath stage of his parents' divorce. Environmental stresses were at a minimum; his parents were not embroiled in conflict, both had adjusted well to the divorce, and he saw a great deal of his father. Internal stresses (such as, self-blaming beliefs and frightening fantasies about what the future might hold) were successfully addressed by his mother.

Three years after the separation, when Andy was ten, his father remarried and moved to a city over 500 miles away. Their time together was reduced to a week at Christmas and three weeks over the summer. Andy did not show any signs of distress at that time, but his schoolwork began to decline about a year after that. He also occasionally got into trouble at school for fighting with other boys. However, these difficulties were not causing significant problems in his life. His mother might have paid more attention to them except that she had begun dating a man seriously and married him a year and a half later, when Andy was twelve. Between the demands of her job and her emotional involvement in this relationship, her usual keen sensitivity to the lives of her children had been reduced. Though she continued to be an effective, loving parent, she was not as attuned to the day-to-day experiences of her youngsters as she had been in the past. As long as they were not displaying clear emotional upset or getting into serious difficulties, she assumed that they were doing well. And, generally speaking, Andy was progressing reasonably well developmentally.

Andy accepted his new stepfather, but never felt especially close to him. Howard was a thoughtful, caring man who taught English in junior high school. He was particularly fond of nineteenth-century poetry and tried to interest Andy in it. However, Andy preferred professional and college sports of all kinds, as his father did, and also played soccer and baseball in his city's recreational leagues. Howard frequently attended his stepson's games, encouraged him, and supported his athletic efforts. But he was neither knowledgeable about nor proficient in sports. Over the next few years, Andy came to see his stepfather as a loving man who treated him well, even though he was a bit of a "nerd."

After Andy entered high school, his grades began to fall further. He regularly got C's and D's even though his achievement test scores indicated that he could do solid B work in most courses. His mother talked with him about this discrepancy between his abilities and his academic performance. She underscored the need for him to do well now that he was in high school because his grades would count in terms of applications to college. Both she and her current husband had earned college degrees and her former husband had a two-year community college certificate. She very much hoped that Andy would attend college and have a successful career. Andy agreed that he wanted to go to college but complained about his dull, boring classes and the "jerks" he had for teachers. Efforts on his mother's part to set up study schedules were unsuccessful.

At sixteen, in his junior year of high school, Andy got into several fights, something he had not done for two years. These had occurred at weekend parties. But twice they happened at school, and Andy's mother was called in to discuss her son's behavior. She learned that Andy was well liked by his teachers who felt he could be doing a lot better than he was academically. His high school counselor also told her that Andy had several good friends. The fact that he played on the high school baseball team added to his popularity. However, the counselor shared her concern that Andy was like a "bantam rooster," always seeming to have to prove himself by being tough. She felt that Andy's fights could have been easily avoided if he felt more comfortable walking away from a confrontation.

Andy's mother discussed this fully with her son. He replied: "What should I have done? This guy bumped into me at school and said, 'Watch where you're going.' So what should I do? Just say, 'Oh, excuse me, I'm sorry'? He bumped into me. I couldn't let him get away with that. Everyone was standing around watching. So I just said, 'Fuck off, man.' Then he says something back. So I shoved him. He called me a name, so I hit him. What else was I supposed to do? If I let him get away with that, it would have looked like I was a weenie!''. Andy's mother was exasperated by her son's attitude but took a deep breath and tried to explore the options in this situation. She suggested that after they each swore at one another, Andy could have just gone to his next class and forgotten about it. It was not a big deal. Andy said, "No way. He bumped into me. If he walked away after I said something to him, well, okay. But he had to go and call me a name. I couldn't let it go at that." Andy and his mother went round and round with no resolution. Each felt the other just did not understand the issues.

Later in his junior year of high school, Andy got into a car accident. According to the police report, he was traveling ten miles over the speed limit, failed to yield at an intersection, and hit another car broadside. No one was seriously hurt, but Andy was shaken. Still he insisted that it was the other car that should have stopped. He was furious at his mother for grounding him for a month.

Before the month was up, Andy sneaked out late one night, met two of his friends, and went to a party. He drank some beer and got into a fight. His mother found out about this when she received a call at 1:00 A.M. from the hospital. Andy had broken his hand in the fight, and her permission was needed in order for the physician to set the bones.

His mother was furious and worried. Andy had gone out despite his grounding restriction and, once again, had gotten into trouble. Andy apologized for going out but claimed that the fight was not his fault. Another guy had taken his house key and was playing "keep away" with another boy. He had refused to give it back. Andy warned him that he better give him his key. Finally, the other youngster gave Andy the key. But that was not enough. Andy told the first boy: "You better apologize, dick face." The reply was another profanity, so Andy "had to" hit him.

Andy's mother and stepfather had a long talk with him the next day. They told him that they were concerned about him. They pointed to his poor grades, his car accident, and his fighting. Andy sullenly listened but refused to acknowledge that he was having problems. There was a "reason" for each of the things they mentioned: his classes were boring and the teachers were "losers"; the other car should have stopped; and the fights he had gotten into were really not his fault. Andy's mother and stepfather were frustrated. They could not get Andy to see his role in these difficulties.

Andy's mother called her ex-husband and shared her concerns about her son. Andy's father drove to see him the following weekend. He loudly berated his son about how he was "screwing up" and told him: "You'd better get your act together." Andy was enraged. He screamed, "Who're you to tell me what to do? You're not even around to see what's happening! You don't know a damn thing about me. You've got no right to tell me what to do." Then he stormed out of the house.

His mother was at her wit's end. She decided to talk to the mental health professional who had led the parenting group she had participated in after her separation. He suggested that it would be a good idea to consult a particular psychologist who specialized in helping adolescents. He indicated that Andy might need to be in therapy to resolve his difficulties.

Andy was wrestling with a worry that he was not really masculine. This concern was far below his level of awareness, but it drove him to have to prove his masculinity to himself and to his friends. In his mind, anything that was even remotely associated with weakness or femininity was a threat to his feeling like a respected "guy." Doing well in school and driving carefully were things girls did. Giving the slightest appearance of being less than tough was being a "weenie" (that is, being a "wimp"). His counselor's sense that Andy was like a "bantam rooster" fell short of capturing the intensity of Andy's need to demonstrate his masculinity and his great sensitivity to possible challenges to his manhood. So many things were perceived as a threat to his sense of masculinity, indicating how fragile and vulnerable his masculine identity was. Consciously, Andy felt that he was "cool" and was acting appropriately. But in fact he was unwittingly engaged in a chronic internal battle to ward off feeling weak and ineffective. He kept these unacceptable feelings out of awareness, drowning them out by becoming behaviorally hypermasculine. These internal issues may account for some of the aggressive problems and difficulty with schoolwork that characterize many (but by no means the majority) of adolescent boys from divorced families.[7]

The relative absence of a father after divorce is quite common, affecting over a third of children whose parents have separated.[8] For boys, the lack of a continuous relationship with an emotionally available adult male role model interferes with developing a solid, internal conviction about their masculinity. Having to submit to their mother's parental authority can exacerbate these concerns; she is a woman, and there is little to be gained developmentally by acceding to her power. When boys follow their father's direction, they can identify with his strength, wisdom, and consistency. This becomes a developmental "payoff" that enhances a boy's sense of masculinity. There is no equivalent advantage to giving in to one's mother. Single mothers do better to parent their adolescent sons through reasonable compromise rather than force. (Actually, most adolescents respond better to this approach.) In this way, the boy's sense of efficacy, independence, and masculinity can be acknowledged and respected.

Andy was also attempting to cope with an internal conflict created by his father having so little contact with him after he remarried and moved away. Andy felt hurt and abandoned by his father having left him. But it was "unmasculine" to reveal, even to himself, these tender feelings. Further, Andy had a developmental need to preserve an ideal image of his father with whom he could continue to identify. The result was that Andy could not let himself feel how much he missed his father or how angry he was about his removing himself from his son's life. He had to be "tough." But Andy vented some of his anger toward his father in a disguised way; he fought with peers. The intensity of Andy's feelings about not having his father available erupted into view when his father confronted him about the problems he was having.

Unfortunately, the fit between Andy's personality and his stepfather's was not particularly good. Though he liked his stepfather, Andy could not look up to him; he was just too bookish, too nice, and too unaware of sports. Had the personality match between them been better, Andy could have shifted the developmentally appropriate need for a male role model to his stepfather. This probably would have created some loyalty conflicts in his affections for both his father and stepfather, but most likely they would have been outweighed by the contributions to Andy's enhanced sense of certainty about his masculinity.

Andy's mother could not step into this breach and impart to her son a confidence about masculinity and a model for it. Neither she nor her husband were doing anything wrong. In fact, both were thoughtful, loving people who treated Andy well. But Andy's developmental needs were not being met, and his internal conflicts over masculine identity and feelings about his father were not being addressed. Neither Andy, nor the adults in his life, were aware of the psychological forces at work and how they contributed to the problems Andy was having.

The long-range period of divorce is fertile ground for the development of difficulties in adolescence by boys and girls. The most common environmental stresses in this phase of divorce are the loss of the father–child relationship, parental dating, and remarriage. These can stimulate powerful internal conflicts that lie below the level of teenagers' conscious awareness and are unrecognized by parents. Defenses are unwittingly and automatically mobilized against having to experience the emotional pain and distress that awareness of these conflicts would elicit. The result can be behaviors that get adolescents into trouble and worry their parents.

Recognizing Distress in Adolescents

It is frequently difficult to recognize undue distress in adolescence because of the rebelliousness and mood swings common to this period of development. Though the picture of the adolescent as being in constant turmoil has been overdrawn in the popular and professional literature,[9] it is nonetheless true that teenagers must cope with the array of internal and environmental pressures described at the beginning of this chapter. These normally occurring stresses often result in unpredictable behaviors and emotional states. Rapid shifts between cooperation and obstinacy, affection and antagonism, mature reasonableness and childlike outbursts, responsible behavior and flightiness, and calmness and irritability are typical of many adolescents, at least for periods of time during this developmental stage. Parents, teachers, and mental health professionals have the formidable task of distinguishing between the expectable ups and downs of adolescence (which are manifestations of normal stresses) and unusual levels of distress.

Important guidelines for determining whether or not signs of distress indicate problems beyond the range of normal is the extent to which the youngster's developmental progress and adjustment is being significantly interfered with. Is academic performance reasonably consistent with abilities? Does the teenager have a pleasurable relationship with one or more friends his age? Are family relationships at least tolerable? Does the adolescent exercise good enough judgment to avoid physically dangerous actions? Does the youngster stay out of trouble with school and legal authorities? If the answers to any of these questions is no, the adolescent is probably distressed beyond normal limits.

Anger is one of the most frequently observed expressions of distress for teenagers. It may be directed towards parents and/or siblings at home, teachers and/or peers at school, physical objects, or more than one of these. Physical fighting, destruction of property, and verbal hostility are the clearest examples of anger in action. But there are many other behaviors which can serve as vehicles for anger. Substance abuse (alcohol and/or illicit drugs), getting poor grades, skipping school, stealing, and other delinquent-like activities are frequently the result of anger being expressed in disguised ways. Often the teenager is not even aware that anger is driving these behaviors. The youngster who is furious at a parent may unwittingly turn his rage inward against himself by hurting himself with drugs or even consciously being suicidal. The teenager who knows how important grades or social appearances are to a parent may unconsciously seek to fail in school or engage in antisocial behavior that will reflect poorly on the parent.

The central issue here is the extent to which the ways the youngster displays anger are self-defeating. Many adolescents get poor grades in certain subjects or have a bad semester academically. Similarly, experimenting with alcohol and/or marijuana, or in some communities even using these substances occasionally in social situations, is not atypical. And a large percentage of teenagers have tried shoplifting small items. Many well-adjusted adolescents engage in some of these behaviors, and most are never caught. Nor is their developmental progress in the realms of school, peer relations, and family life interrupted. However, when their behavior results in seriously impaired academic work, loss of friends, trouble with the law, physical danger, and/or chronic family friction, it is an indication that their anger is so great that it not only spills over into action but also sufficiently impairs their judgment that they find themselves in difficult predicaments.

Depression is another common sign of distress during adolescence. It may manifest itself in irritability (or depressed mood), feelings of worthlessness, difficulty concentrating in school, poor appetite (or overeating), insomnia (or sleeping too much), and/or constant fatigue. If two or more of these indicators are present nearly every day for over two months, it is likely that the youngster is suffering from a depression. At times thoughts of suicide or actual self-harming behavior can be part of the depressive picture. These should promptly be brought to the attention of a mental health professional. The notion that those who talk about suicide will not try to hurt themselves is a myth. Professional help is needed when teenagers voice suicidal ideas.

Normal adolescent moodiness, fluctuations in appetite, preoccupation with social events (making concentration in school difficult), and erratic sleep patterns make noticing depression difficult. At times parents dismiss a real depression as being simply the result of these commonly observed characteristics. Other times parents too quickly become concerned, mistaking the expectable ups and downs of adolescence for depression. One important distinguishing factor is duration; at least two of these signs must be present nearly every day for two months or more. Another key factor is the extent to which the youngster's developmental progress is being interfered with in the domains noted above in the discussion of anger. Finally, some of these behaviors and emotions can be the result of physical problems. Adolescents are notorious for avoiding physical examinations. Apart from a cursory work-up to complete the medical forms often required for entrance into junior high or high school, many teenagers have not seen a physician. It is wise to have a complete medical evaluation when these signs of depression persist.

Somatic complaints are also fairly common in adolescence. Headaches, stomachaches, a preoccupation with one's body, and fatigue can be examples of distress. Teenagers can convert internal conflicts into physical expressions in much the same way that younger children do. The reader can review the specifics of somatization in chapters 8 and 10 for a fuller discussion of this issue.

There are also general alarm bells in adolescence. Some of these have already been discussed because they may be used as means to express anger or depression. Nonetheless, they are of sufficient importance to warrant a separate list.

- Substance abuse (alcohol and/or other drugs)
- Large discrepancy between ability and academic performance
- Suspension from school
- Precocious/promiscuous sexual behavior
- Physical fighting
- Self-injuring behavior
- Accident proneness
- Trouble with the law
- Running away from home

This list of alarm bells still requires that parents and other adults distinguish between behavior that is within the limits of normal adolescent development and that which is an indicator of undue distress. What is the difference between substance abuse versus occasional social use of illegal substances? What is a "large discrepancy" between abilities and grades, and how do you measure abilities? What is "precocious" sexual behavior? Is it sexual intercourse before sixteen? Is having two "fender benders" in the space of six months "accident proneness"? For all of these signs, the line between what is understandable and no cause for worry and what constitutes evidence of significant distress can be disconcertingly fuzzy. If a parent is wondering about just how distressed or off the normal developmental track a youngster

349

is, consultation with school authorities (who often have a good sense of the boundaries between what is expectable at different ages in particular communities and what is beyond the pale) and/or mental health professionals can be helpful.

Overview

Adolescents must cope with the normal vicissitudes of this developmental period as well as the external and internal stresses created by divorce. Their capacities to manage stress are frequently taxed by the combination of developmental and divorce challenges. Many teenagers automatically and unwittingly try to avoid directly confronting the things that bother them. Their primary posture seems to be that of an ostrich with its head deeply planted in the sand. At times, this defense serves them well, as they are able to weather the forces threatening to derail their developmental progress. However, teenagers are prone to having their internal conflicts translated into actions. These behavioral products of stress can interfere substantially with a youngster's social, emotional, academic, and even physical well-being.

Though many parents and other adults are mindful of the stresses on adolescents in the immediate crisis and short-term aftermath stages of divorce, most are not attuned to divorce-related stresses in the long-range period. It is helpful to remember that divorce is an extended process creating events and situations that can exert their effects on children years after ''the divorce.''

13

►◄

Helping Adolescents Cope

By this stage of development, youngsters are well aware of the fact that many families experience divorce. They will have known other children whose parents have separated and who live in single-parent or remarried households. Furthermore, the near-adult cognitive abilities of adolescents permit them to understand many of the realities of divorce. They can grasp concepts such as child support, property settlements, custody, and visitation. They also understand that there are many possible reasons for divorce. Teenagers know about alcoholism, infidelity, financial problems, falling out of love, and marital strife. Intellectually, they comprehend a great deal about divorce, including that it cannot possibly happen to their parents.

It is crucial for both parents to discuss the divorce directly with their adolescent children in order to help them deal with the shock they typically experience over it. If the parental relationship is such that they can talk to their youngster together, it is helpful. It conveys a shared caring for the teenager and a commitment to continue to coparent on his behalf. However, if tensions between the spouses are running too high for them to do this together, it is important for each to tell their adolescent about the divorce separately. At times this task automatically falls to the primary parent alone, typically mother. When this occurs, teenagers rightly believe that they are getting only part of the story. It also leaves open the question of whether the other parent is committed to continuing his relationship with the youngster.

It is useful for parents to discuss the divorce with their teenager about two to four weeks before the marital separation occurs. The youngster is then more likely to feel that he is being informed before any actions are taken and will tend to be more trusting of his parents in the future. If there is one teenager in the family, it is best for the parents to talk with him apart from the younger children. This allows the adolescent to feel that his greater maturity is being recognized. Parents can begin by telling him of their plans to separate and seek a divorce. They can truthfully point to the general nature of their marital problems by noting the arguments they have had, that they have grown apart over the years and no longer love each other, and/ or the unhappiness of one or both parents in the marriage. It is important for both adults to underscore that it is their marital relationship which is causing the divorce and that their love for the children will continue. Here, the aim is to head off the youngster's potential fantasies that he was part of the marital difficulties and therefore, to some degree, responsible for the divorce, and to reassure the teenager of the fact that the divorce will not change his parents' love for him.

It is also a good idea to let the adolescent know, as much as possible, how the marital separation will immediately affect her life. Who will be moving out of the family home and when, where the youngster will be living and with whom, where the other parent will be living and how frequently the adolescent will see him are all questions that are best answered during this first talk. If any of these issues are unclear at the time of this discussion, it is helpful for parents to acknowledge that and tell the youngster that they will let her know about whatever matters are in doubt as soon as they are resolved.

Both parents, separately or together, should address the divorce openly and directly with their teenager. The following example assumes both parents are present, though each parent could have a similar conversation separately with their youngster:

Mother: Your dad and I have something important to talk to you about.

Father: It'll only take a little while but it is important.

Mother: I guess you know that things haven't been going too well between your dad and me. We argue way too much.

Father: And we don't have the good times together that we used to. I've been more and more unhappy, and so has your mom.

Mother: We think you're old enough to know what happens when a marriage isn't working well; parents start to feel that everyone would be better off in the long-run if they didn't live together anymore. It looks like that's what's going to happen with your dad and me.

Father: That's right. We're going to get a divorce.

Mother: You [your sister, brother] and I are going to keep living here in the house and your dad's going to be moving out to an apartment soon.

Father: It's on the other side of town. I'll give you the address and my phone number as soon as I know them for sure, probably by next week. I'll be seeing you pretty much every week [every other week, once a month]. We'll have that all figured out real soon.

Mother: I know this is hard on a girl [guy]. Sometimes she [he] even starts to wonder if there's anything she [he] could have done to stop a divorce from happening. But that's not how divorce works. It's grown-up business.

Father: That's right. It just has to do with the parents not getting along. Your mom and I love you and we always will.

Mother: Right. We'll always love you. That's not going to change.

It is helpful if this first talk is kept brief. Many times a teenager, unlike younger children, will ask questions during this explanation. The parent should not ignore these questions by rigidly sticking too closely to the above illustration.

A first discussion of this sort assumes that the parents have talked together carefully about the details of their separation before telling the children. This level of organization implies a capacity on the part of both parents to stay sufficiently in control of their feelings so as to have worked out the way that they will separate. Such planning serves adolescents well. It provides structure for the enormous changes that divorce will mean in the family life and helps youngsters anticipate the impact of the divorce on them. However, feelings frequently are too intense for parents to be able to take this reasonable approach. Their initial parting is undoubtedly accompanied by emotional fireworks, deep sadness, and/or anxieties. But adolescents still need some structure and explanation. Even if there is great uncertainty about the immediate future, and if the parent remaining in the house is distraught, it is helpful for that parent to tell the teenager that a marital separation is occurring and divorce is imminent. This talk should be kept quite brief (under five minutes). The parent can simply acknowledge the fact of the separation as well as her lack of clarity regarding whatever issues are up in the air (for example, the reasons for the marital rift, where the other parent will be living, with whom the child will ultimately reside). Just verbalizing the reality of the situation helps the adolescent recognize what is occurring and that divorce-related issues can be voiced.

As in divorces involving younger children, the adolescent will fare best when environmental stresses are kept at a minimum. Parental warfare, loss of the child's relationship with the noncustodial parent, the emotional distress of a parent, and imposing adult-like responsibilities on the youngster (that is, taking care of younger siblings, comforting a parent) burden teenagers and make adjustment to the divorce more difficult. Furthermore, because of the substantial physical, emotional, and social changes that normally occur in adolescence, teenagers tend to do best when their parents can reassure them that the divorce will not create dramatic upheavals in their lives. For example, parents can strive to arrange for the adolescent to continue to live in the family residence. When this is not possible, a move not requiring a change in the school the youngster attends, and therefore a disruption in the peer network he has developed, is helpful.

Even when environmental sources of stress are minimal, many adolescents must cope with internal stresses that arise in response to the very fact of divorce, stemming from the meanings teenagers unwittingly attach to the divorce. For the most part, these perceptions of divorce remain below the level of conscious awareness and at best are only dimly recognized, if at all. They are not even necessarily true, but nonetheless create inner tensions for a large number of adolescents. These sources of internal stress are rooted in the concerns common to youngsters in this period of development. A few frequently experienced, troublesome meanings teenagers attribute to their parents' divorce are given below. The wording of these concerns reflects what the youngster might say *if* she were aware of them.

- I will no longer have the safety of my parents' support to help me manage my impulses; I can do whatever I want now.
- I can no longer trust my parents' love; if they can stop loving each other, they can stop loving me.
- I can no longer maintain the fiction that my parents are basically asexual; they are clearly sexual people who indulge these impulses when they date.

- I am no longer sure I want to be like my father [mother]; his [her] actions are wrong (that is, hurtful, deceitful, ineffective, self-indulgent).

What these usually unspoken ideas have in common is that they dramatically change the teenager's sense of his parents and of himself. Views that he had held with unquestioned conviction are precipitously disrupted and altered. Cut loose from these psychological moorings, the teenager is faced with being buffeted by the biological, social, and emotional currents of adolescence. This heightens the anxiety of many youngsters.

In addition to the internal stresses caused by these perceptions, adolescents are also frequently burdened by internal, divorce-engendered conflicts. Their competing wishes and feelings pull them in opposite emotional directions, and this creates additional sources of inner tension. Some of the internal conflicts discussed for older elementary school children are present for adolescents, though issues of sex-role identity and sexuality come into prominence during adolescence. A list of common internal conflicts for teenagers is given below.

- Anger at one or both parents
   versus
   Love for both parents
- Loyalty to each parent
   versus
   Impulses to take sides or choose one parent over the other
- Affection for a parent's partner
   versus
   Anxiety over the sexuality in the parent's dating relationship
- Wishes to be helpful to a custodial mother
   versus
   Needs to be emotionally independent of mother

These internal conflicts typically lie below the level of the adolescent's conscious awareness.

Internal stresses, arising from the meanings adolescents give to divorce and from inner conflicts are kept out of consciousness for the most part through the automatic and unwitting use of psychological defenses. These defenses, and their resulting observable behaviors and feelings, are identical to those listed for late elementary school children in chapter 11. Adolescents are especially prone to intellectualizing, denying, displacing, and somatizing painful feelings stemming from internal stresses. But for many teenagers, these defenses are not sufficient to contain distress all the time. They then resort to acting out their inner tensions. It is precisely this tendency to engage in "action defenses" that can make adolescence so difficult for young-sters, parents, and other adult authorities. For example, a teenage boy may perceive his father as untrustworthy and unloving after he leaves the marriage and moves away from his children. The boy may also be furious at his father for acting in this way, yet love him deeply at the same time, thus creating a powerful internal conflict. As a first line of defense, this teenager may automatically deny his painful feelings and intellectualize them. He may consciously think to himself: "It's no big deal [use of denial]. I know lots of kids whose parents split up. They just can't get along. They have problems, so they split up. My parents fell out of love and now they don't want to live together anymore. That makes sense [use of intellectualiza-tion]. It doesn't affect me one way or the other [use of denial]." Though this combination of intellectualization and denial can serve youngsters well, in some cases it may not be sufficient to keep the inner tensions under wraps. A more costly defense may then have to be automatically rushed in to keep the emotional distress at bay; the youngster may begin to somatize his anger through "tension head-aches" in order to continue to be unaware of his internal distress. Now he is not only cut off from his true feelings, he is in physical pain. At times, even this is not enough to contain the distress. The adolescent may engage in actions that partly express some aspects of his inner tensions. His behavior is like a safety valve in that some of the pressure of the internal distress is temporarily relieved. The youngster avoids having to experience emotional pain (for example, keen disappointment in and rage at a loved parent), but now must pay the cost of the trouble his actions may bring.

Action defenses such as fighting, vandalism, stealing, substance abuse, and sexual acting out carry high price tags. Consciously, the youngster experiences himself as being in conflict with peers, specific authorities (for example, teachers, police) or rules of society (for example, disapproval of sexual behavior at an early age). Thus the inner distress is transformed into a struggle between the teenager and something or someone outside himself. This serves to distract the adolescent from internal tensions and, instead, become immersed in conflicts outside himself. This defensive style has been termed "externalization" and stands in contrast to "internalization," which includes intellectualizing and somatizing as well as directly experiencing the underlying emotional distress (that is, becoming depressed or anxious).[1]

The multiple internal sources of distress and the complex psychological and action defenses against becoming aware of inner tensions make it difficult for parents and other adults to help teenagers cope with their reactions to divorce. So much of what is going on for adolescents lies below the level of their conscious awareness. And their defenses against recognizing what is bothering them are strong, at times intimidating or infuriating adults. It is useful for parents, teachers, family physicians, and mental health professionals to keep firmly in mind the likely nature of the adolescent's internal distress and the defenses teenagers automatically mobilize against it. In doing so, adults are then more able to understand, empathize with, and, therefore, help the adolescent adjust to divorce.

A combination of reducing environmental sources of stress, using both displacement and direct communication, and adopting a reasonable position of compromise are the best ways of approaching a teenager who is having difficulty adjusting to her parents' divorce. Unlike very young children, adolescents need more than relief from environmental stress to adapt well to divorce. They generate a great deal of internal distress apart from what is going on around them. Extensive use of displacement communication, which works so well for both young and older elementary school children, is not enough for teenagers. Exclusive use of the displacement method makes many teenagers feel that they are being treated like younger children, they are being lectured, or both. Direct communication and compromise have to be added in order to facilitate the adolescent's successful adaptation to divorce and permit developmental processes to continue on track.

Ways of reducing environmental sources of stress have been discussed extensively in previous chapters focused on helping children cope with divorce. And how to implement the indirect style of displacement communication has been presented in considerable detail earlier. However, achieving the often delicate balance between displacement and direct communication, in the context of acknowledging the adolescent's capacity and need for autonomous thought and action, is considerably more difficult than strategies already discussed. This approach requires great patience as well as sufficient self-control to avoid the teenager's tendency to invite and provoke power struggles. Adolescent youngsters are in a somewhat paradoxical position when their divorced (or divorcing) parents try to help them. Much of the adolescent's inner distress is related to perceptions of and conflicts in their feelings toward the same parents who are trying to be helpful, and the developmentally normal thrust toward independence can make teenagers less receptive to help and direction from their parents.

PHIL's (see chapter 12) mother set up an appointment with a psychologist in private practice to discuss the concerns she had about her son. She sadly said that she felt she had lost the son she loved so much. He had gone from being a loving, good-natured youngster to an angry boy who had gotten into increasingly serious trouble. She noted that her efforts to talk with Phil about his difficulties and what was causing these dramatic changes in his behavior had been fruitless.

In their first two meetings, the psychologist took a detailed history of Phil's developmental progress and of the events surrounding the divorce. This information led him to conclude that Phil appeared to be a psychologically healthy youngster who had been doing well prior to the stress of his parents' divorce. He told Phil's mother this but added that whenever there are sudden, startling changes in an adolescent's behavior patterns, it is wise to have a test to see if the youngster is using drugs. He explained that the screening procedure for drug abuse is simple and inexpensive; it involves obtaining a urine sample and sending it to a laboratory. He said that since family physicians, pediatricians and many mental health clinics can perform this test, she should choose where to have it done.

Phil's mother set up an appointment for him with their family physician for a physical examination. She told Phil that it had been some time since he had had one and that it was important to have a check-up periodically. She truthfully added that part of the examination would include a test for drugs. As is the case with many teenagers, Phil was furious about the drug screen. He screamed: "You don't trust me! I told you I wasn't doing any drugs. Why don't you believe me?" Phil's mother wisely asked her son to discuss this matter with the doctor. Fortunately, their family practitioner matter-of-factly told Phil that he automatically included a test for drug use whenever there has been a big change in a teenager's behavior or school performance. He explained that when an adolescent was having other kinds of problems, he ordered different tests such as special blood tests or X rays. Phil was mollified by this talk, and the screening indicated that he was free of the six substances (including marijuana and amphetamines, two common street drugs) that he was tested for. The rest of the physical examination showed Phil to be in excellent health.

The psychologist was then more certain of his initial conclusion: Phil's difficulties were a response to the stresses of divorce in adolescence rather than a result of long-standing psychological problems, drug involvement, or some underlying medical condition. This, in itself, was reassuring to Phil's mother.

After discussing it with Phil's mother, the psychologist called Phil's father and told him that his wife had consulted the psychologist about Phil's difficulties. He invited Phil's father to participate in trying to figure out what was troubling his son and how to help him. Phil's father agreed and in his first meeting with the psychologist gave substantially the same picture of Phil's development and of the divorce that his wife had. He was also able to describe more fully the angry interactions that he had with his son. At the end of their session, Phil's father agreed to further meetings in which he and his wife would meet together with the psychologist to find ways of helping Phil get back on track in his life.

Over the course of three meetings with Phil's parents, the psychologist outlined the nature of their son's internal conflicts and how they were causing him to get into trouble. He described Phil's rage at his father and the dramatic shift in his view of him. These feelings were at odds with Phil's love for his father and his developmental need to continue to identify with him. The psychologist suggested that Phil's father talk to his son about these issues using a mixture of displacement and direct communication. As a way to begin this discussion, it was suggested that Phil's father acknowledge his own distress over his son's behavior. The psychologist illustrated how this might proceed: ''I've been thinking about how things have been going, and I'm not happy with the ways I've been acting. I've lost my cool each time I heard about some trouble you were having, and I've come down on you too hard. I know you're a good kid, and something must really be bugging you for you to get into trouble.'' Starting this sort of conversation with a focus on the parent's actions and feelings accomplishes several things. It focuses the topic of discussion without placing an uncomfortable spotlight on the youngster; it avoids sounding as though the parent is lecturing the adolescent; and it provides a model for sharing ideas and feelings.

Phil's father could then shift from this sort of direct communication to using displacement in order to comment about Phil's conflicts. "I've been talking to a psychologist who knows a lot about teenagers and I've learned something interesting. When teenagers start getting into trouble after their parents split up, it can be because they're having some real strong feelings about the divorce. Most guys don't like getting into trouble with the law or getting lower grades than they used to." After representing Phil's observable signs of distress and his discomfort about them, Phil's father could then go on to describe the underlying conflict his son was experiencing, accept the difficult feelings in the conflict, and offer alternative ways of handling this inner tension. Usually a combination of direct and displaced communication works best. The former makes the adolescent feel the personal relevance of what is being said while the latter permits painful subjects to be introduced more comfortably. "I know you're really mad at me for the divorce and my dating. You told me how you felt about my 'screwing around.' Sometimes guys can find some pretty good ways to get back at their dad when they're really pissed at him. Like if a guy knows his dad wants him to do well at school, keep out of trouble, and go to college, one way to really make the dad feel awful is to start messing up. I sort of wonder if that's what's been happening with you. You know I love you and I want you to do well. I think you've sort of been sending me a message, and the message is: 'Go to hell, Dad. You screwed up and I'm going to show you what it feels like when someone screws up.' "

Phil's father thus addressed Phil's anger, his wish to retaliate against his father, and his identification with his father. He then accepted his son's anger and disappointment and also offered alternative ways of handling his distress about the divorce: "I know you're mad at me. And I know I've acted in a way that makes you feel you can't sort of look up to me anymore like you used to when you were a kid. I'm sorry I've hurt you. I didn't mean to. Adults sometimes do things their sons don't like. But it doesn't make any sense for a guy to mess up his own life just to stick it to his dad. When you're feeling angry at me, tell me. And if you can't tell me, write me a note or make a tape of what you're feeling and give it to me. I'd rather have you dump on me than on yourself.''

Phil's father implemented a close version of this discussion. His son at first was withdrawn and sullenly silent. But by the end of the talk, Phil was crying. He poignantly asked his father, ''Why did you have to do it? Couldn't you and mom just stay married? Why did you have to go wreck everyone's life?'' Phil's father sadly and quietly told his son, ''I wish it could have worked out the way you wanted it. But you're old enough to know that sometimes marriages just can't stay together. People fall out of love sometimes. But, you know, your mom's doing fine and I'm okay, too. I think we're both happier now. And I know we both love you and don't want our divorce to mess things up for you. If there's anything I can do to make sure you can start to feel good again, let me know.''

Two weeks after their talk, Phil reminded his father of his offer. He said, ''You know how you said you'd like to help me about the divorce? Well, how's this. You quit dating.'' Phil's father initiated a compromise with his son. He gently told him, ''It doesn't make any sense for me to have you tell me whether I can date or whom I should go out with. But I'll make a deal with you. I won't have anyone I'm dating over when you and I are together. When you and your brother are at my place, it'll just be the three of us. Phil seemed satisfied with this and was especially pleased when his father suggested a weekend camping trip with ''just guys allowed.''

Phil's mother still had to contend with his irritability and lack of willingness to be helpful around the house. The psychologist outlined a way she could talk with him about the conflict between them. He suggested that she use direct statements to set the stage for discussions with Phil and a combination of displacement and direct communication to address his internal conflicts over being cooperative. Phil's mother said to him, ''I think it would be a good idea for us to talk about what's been happening between us. I've been sad about it. I've always loved you a lot, and we used to get along real well. It's upsetting to me to see you so bugged whenever I ask you to do something.'' Here, Phil's mother initiated the discussion in much the same way Phil's father did, by focusing on *her* feelings and perceptions. In this way she could draw Phil's attention to his irritability and uncooperative behavior without putting him on the spot or making him feel criticized. She went on to articulate, using displacement and direct statements, the tensions in her son that were contributing to these overt signs of distress; "You know your dad and I have been talking with a psychologist about what's been happening. It's helped me see that a lot of guys feel angry and don't want to help out at home after a divorce because it sometimes feels to them that they're being a little kid or a wimp if they're nice to their mom. I don't think that, but you seem to." Phil muttered: "I have to do everything around here. You're always telling me 'do this, do that.' "

His mother then suggested a reasonable compromise, which acknowledged her son's autonomy and avoided his feeling controlled by her and forced to submit to her wishes: "I think it makes sense for you to help around the house. Teenagers are big enough and capable enough to have some jobs to do. But you're also grown up enough to help decide how you can help out. Why don't you make a list of some things you think you could do that would help this house run better. Then we can figure out together which ones you do each week. Phil dragged his feet in making a list, in part to test whether his mother would go back to arbitrarily assigning him chores and in part because many teenagers would just rather not have to do work around their house. His mother gently reminded him, from time to time, "Have you decided on your jobs yet?" The psychologist had counseled her to proceed slowly and not give in to the urge to angrily confront Phil with his failure to make the list, his lack of responsibility, and other derogatory responses a parent's anger tends to generate. Two weeks later, Phil sullenly gave his mother a small, tattered slip of paper. On it he had written: "Take out garbage, clear dinner dishes into dishwasher, clean up room." Phil's mother said, "These make a lot of sense, and they'll be a big help. But I don't think you need to do these every day. How about doing them on Monday, Wednesday and Friday and taking the other days off?" Phil was taken aback by this response. He had anticipated criticism for the list being so short and for his mother to insist that he do the chores he had noted every day. He was prepared to angrily storm out of the room, accusing her of always being on his back. He silently nodded his agreement to his mother's suggestion.

Within two months, Phil was acting more like his old self at home with his mother. He had not gotten into further trouble, and had begun gradually improving his grades. This did not mean, however, that he had suddenly become an adult's view of a model child. He still became irritable at times when his mother reminded him of a chore he had left undone, and occasionally made snide references to his father's girlfriend when he was at his father's apartment. His room at his mother's house sometimes looked like a cyclone had hit it, and he argued from time to time about his mother's requests that it be straightened up. Phil seemed back on track developmentally, but he was, after all, still very much a teenager.

The capacity of Phil's parents to work on understanding the nature of their son's conflicts enabled them to empathize with the trouble he had been getting into. But they went further than this. They were able to take their son's perspective about their own behaviors in order to understand his reactions. His father could admit that his role in the divorce and his dating angered his son. Phil's mother acknowledged that what seemed to be reasonable requests for her son to help out at home in fact were experienced by many teenage boys as arbitrary demands for the youngsters to submit to parental authority. Both parents had the courage to face these issues, discuss them with Phil, and make reasonable compromises which indicated their respect for their adolescent son. And they were able to avoid the temptation of expressing their frustration with Phil by becoming angry, demeaning him, and flexing their parental muscles by insisting he do exactly as he was told.

When parents cannot find it in themselves to do what Phil's parents did, it is usually necessary for the youngster to see a therapist. A mental health professional would deal with the conflicts described for Phil in much the same ways that a parent would. The combination of direct and displacement communication would unfold in very similar ways. However, it is usually more powerful and can work more quickly if parents can implement this strategy directly. And to the extent that one or both parents are exploding angrily at their adolescent, demeaning him, and refusing to compromise or negotiate with him, the therapist's efforts are usually not as successful as they could otherwise be. The result, even with therapy, will then be considerably less happy than the outcome was for Phil.

Parental warfare is a source of potent psychological stress for adolescents. Teenagers must normally come to terms with and manage their own anger and the impulse to act on it. Open hostilities between parents can fuel a youngster's anger to the point that she feels flooded by rage, which then becomes too powerful to keep under control. She is compelled to seek special outlets for this excess fury. The safety valve she chooses depends on her own personality and the models she observes for how to handle anger. Some teenagers pick fights with friends, siblings, teachers, or parents. Others engage in antisocial behaviors such as stealing, vandalism, substance abuse, or even precocious sexual behavior. These are externalizing ways of trying to cope with a surfeit of anger and often bring the youngster into conflict with authorities. But many teenagers, especially girls, gravitate toward internalizing ways of managing anger. These include developing somatic symptoms (for example, headaches, stomachaches, unusual fatigue), withdrawing from social activities and isolating oneself, becoming depressed, or turning the anger inward and having impulses to hurt oneself. Often adolescents use a mixture of externalizing and internalizing modes of handling their rage.

The most effective way to help teenagers who are being overwhelmed by their own anger is to remove the stresses giving rise to their fury. Intense conflict between parents is among the most common sources of stress that results in the adolescent feeling enraged. She is furious that the two people she loves most are being hurtful to each other, and she is subtly learning by observing them that the unfettered expression of anger is acceptable. She will also strongly resent it if her parents use her as a vehicle for attacking each other (that is, asking the child to take sides, arguing over child support, custody, or visitation) and, at the same time, will feel miserably guilty over being at the center of their hostilities. Reducing parental warfare alleviates a major cause of a youngster becoming flooded with angry feelings.

THE COURT CASE WORKER had become increasingly concerned about Mandy's (see chapter 12) self-destructive impulses. Mandy's mother was also worried about her daughter and discussed Mandy's behavior with the case worker. It seemed to both of them that Mandy's angry outbursts at her mother and her tendency to channel her anger toward herself were being exacerbated by the prolonged, bitter custody battle over her. The case worker suggested that Mandy's mother consult a particular social worker at a child guidance clinic who specialized in helping teenagers cope with family stresses such as divorce.

Mandy's mother met with the social worker, and during the course of their first three sessions described her daughter's current behavior, her developmental history, and the ongoing custody fight. The social worker asked her if she could contact Mandy's father to invite him to participate in trying to understand their daughter's difficulties and help her with them. After Mandy's mother agreed to this, noting that it was unlikely that he would come to an appointment, the social worker called him. Mandy's father tightly and grimly told the social worker that neither he nor his daughter needed anyone else meddling in their lives. It was bad enough to have attorneys, a judge, and a court case worker involved. The social worker explained that Mandy was voicing thoughts of hurting herself and had destroyed some of her own clothing. She went on to share her concern about any girl who was distressed enough to act in those ways. Mandy's father angrily replied, "Well, she never does any of that stuff when she's with me. If you really want to help, tell the judge to give Mandy to me. Then everything will be just fine." The social worker stated that her role was to help Mandy not to become involved in the custody battle or take sides in it. Mandy's father said, "It doesn't sound to me like you're going to be any use to anyone," and hung up. A follow-up letter to Mandy's father encouraging him to participate in the social worker's efforts to help Mandy drew no response.

The social worker told Mandy's mother about her husband's unwillingness to be involved in sessions with the social worker. She counseled Mandy's mother to discuss with her attorney the possibility of obtaining a court-ordered custody evaluation with an expert in the community. Mandy's mother followed through on this, and she, her husband, and both children were seen over a period of a month by the court-appointed expert, a forensic psychiatrist. Though Mandy's father wanted no part of this evaluation, he had to participate or be cited for contempt of court. The psychiatrist concluded that Mandy's mother should be awarded sole legal custody and that Mandy should live with her mother and see her father every weekend, but only for a day and without sleeping over. This strongly worded recommendation to the court, coupled with Mandy's repeatedly stated preference to live with her mother, resulted in the judge finally deciding the case by taking all of the expert's recommendations.

Mandy's father was enraged at his ex-wife, the forensic psychiatrist, the court case worker, and especially the judge. He withheld child support payments for a month. The judge jailed him for fifteen days. She angrily told him that she would send him to the county jail again if he were even so much as a week late with subsequent payments.

Much of Mandy's explosive behavior toward her mother was reduced after the custody fight was over. Her comments about everyone being better off if she were dead also diminished. The social worker pointed out that these positive changes were largely due to Mandy's mother moving assertively to get a court-ordered, expert evaluation, thus ending the protracted custody struggle. She explained that in doing so, Mandy's mother had been able to help take her daughter out of the middle of this parental battlefield. The divorce decree also protected Mandy to some extent from the cruelty she had been suffering at her older brother's hands by limiting her visits with her father to an eight-hour period on a weekend day.

However, the social worker added that it would be helpful to Mandy if her mother could talk with her daughter about what had been happening and articulate the inner tensions that had been created in her. The social worker explained that the primary internal conflict for Mandy had been between her rage at her father and her love for him. She was furious over his open and vicious derogation of her mother, for not protecting her from her brother, and for spending so little time with her. But she had to keep herself unaware of how angry she was at him because she also loved him and hoped he would love her in return. The social worker also noted that a second source of internal stress for Mandy was her belief that she was responsible for her parents' fighting; if she did not exist, then they could go their separate ways without trying to annihilate one another. Mandy's defenses against these two internal sources of stress were then outlined. Mandy kept her anger toward her father out of her awareness by displacing it onto her mother and, subsequently, by also turning the force of this rage against herself by destroying her own clothing and voicing the idea of destroying herself, as well. Further, her cutting up her sweaters and having feelings of doing away with herself also served as self-inflicted punishments for the guilt she experienced (but did not recognize consciously) over her belief that she was the cause of her parents' warfare.

The social worker helped Mandy's mother find the words to

address her daughter's internal stresses and the worrisome defenses against them. She suggested a mix of direct and displacement communication, beginning with a focus on Mandy's mother. She could say to her daughter, "I'm glad the divorce fight is over. It was a hard thing to go through. And I was real upset and worried when I saw you getting so mad at me and even at yourself." These comments set the stage for Mandy's mother to begin focusing on her daughter's observable signs of distress as well as the underlying conflicts and defenses they led to: "It's hard for any girl to be mad at her mom. It feels awful when girls have such big mad feelings that they take them out on their own clothes. And even think of hurting themselves. When mad feelings get that strong, they have to be coming from a special place. I've heard that lots of times girls get mad at their dad, but they also love him. They have to do something with their mad feelings. They want to throw them at their dad, but they don't really want to hurt him. So those mad feelings come back at them, like a boomerang. You know, you throw a boomerang, but it comes right back at you."

Mandy said, "But I'm not real mad at dad, just a little bit." Her mother replied, "I know you love your dad. And you want him to love you back. But I think it felt awful to you when he let Justin treat you so bad, and when he said some things about me." Mandy angrily exclaimed: "Justin's a real jerk! That's not dad's fault. Dad's never done anything bad to me." Mandy's mother gently acknowledged her daughter's love for her father, but added, "It's really okay for a girl to have some angry feelings toward her parents when there's been a divorce. Most girls have some mad feelings toward their mom and some toward their dad. It seems like you put a lot of those mad feelings onto me. That's okay. But it makes me sad when you take your mad feelings toward someone else out on yourself."

Mandy's mother then went on to reduce some of the guilt Mandy was feeling about "rejecting" her father by living with her mother: "You're a good kid and you haven't done anything bad. It's normal for girls to want to live with their mom after a divorce, just like it's normal for guys to sometimes want to live with their dad. Justin is living with his dad, and you're living with me. I miss Justin, but it's okay if he wants to live with his dad. I hope your dad can get over being so mad about the divorce, so he can see that it's okay for you to live with me.'' Mandy listened to this and quietly nodded in agreement. Mandy's mother raised these issues with her daughter from time to time. She used hearing about another couple's divorce and wondering how their children might react to it or having read about divorce issues in a magazine as ways of reintroducing these points.

Occasionally, Mandy's mother also noted briefly that, ''Sometimes kids can get the idea that because their parents are fighting over them, it means that it's the kids' fault. But when parents get divorced, sometimes one of them, or even both of them, gets so mad about the divorce that they'll fight over anything. If it isn't kids, it's money, or who gets the house, or the other parent's drinking, or the other parent dating, or whatever. It's sort of like when two little kids get mad at each other. One of them might pick up a ball, a toy, or even a stone to throw at the other one. It doesn't matter what they throw; they're just trying to hurt each other.'' The aim of these comments was to correct Mandy's belief that she was partly responsible for the ugly warfare between her parents.

Within a few months, Mandy's behavior had returned to its normal, predivorce style. She got along well with her mother, and dutifully but unenthusiastically kept to the visiting schedule with her father. However, after three months, she began to make excuses for why she could not see her father on particular weekends. She was still being mistreated by Justin and wanted to avoid him. At the same time, her father did very little with her when she did visit. The rift between them was growing greater. It was painful for Mandy to have to experience this emotional distance and her frustrated longings for closeness with her father on a weekly basis. By not visiting her father frequently, she could avoid having to confront this pain as well as the misery her brother put her through.

At times a parent is so entirely unamenable to changing behaviors that have a negative impact on his child that restricting contact between them is the only solution. The most obvious examples of this are when a parent is sexually or physically abusing a youngster. But open, unremitting emotional abuse in the form of verbally attacking the child or, more subtly, acting in ways that create intense emotional pain in the youngster can also be psychologically destructive. Reducing the amount of time the child spends with the parent can alleviate major sources of environmental stress for her. This and the resolution of the custody battle resulted in rapid improvement in Mandy's case.

Divorcing parents are frequently angry at each other, and therefore tend to perceive one another in extremely negative ways. Therefore, it is wise to seek the advice of a mental health professional who is an expert in assessing divorce conflicts and their potential impact on the children involved before unilaterally deciding to limit or interfere with the child's relationship with the other parent. Having a parent's dating partner, relatives, or even his therapist agree with him about how bad the child's relationship with the other parent is for the youngster are insufficient grounds to interfere in that relationship. A proper assessment of the possible effects the divorce-related conflicts may be having on a child requires an expert in this area who meets with each parent separately, with the child alone, and sometimes with each parent and the child. If the expert has not directly met and spoken with both parents (usually separately) and the child, it is unlikely that any resulting recommendations will be valid. Parents can be very persuasive when they are painting an estranged spouse as unloving, uncaring, irresponsible, or abusive. In part they are convincing because they often truly believe what they are saying. And at times they may have observed their ex-spouse acting in these ways toward them or the child. But the nature of a parent–child relationship after a marital separation may not be what it was like before the separation. At times it is better than the other parent can imagine. And occasionally it is worse.

Environmental sources of stress for adolescents need not be dramatic. Most adults realize that the heat of parental warfare, the anguish of a parent, and the sudden loss of the child's relationship with one of his parents are likely to cause distress in youngsters. But when parents date after divorce, they often expect, quite unrealistically, that their adolescent children will understand and accept their trying to create a new life for themselves. Parents count on their teenagers' well-developed intellect and knowledge of social relationships to lead them to take parental dating in stride. Often this is in fact the case. Conflicts in the adolescent engendered by a parent dating are contained or resolved because the teenager can acknowledge the reasonable wishes of his parent to have adult intimacy. But adolescents sometimes do not readily accept the reality of parental dating.

The kinds of conflicts and concerns that adolescents tend to experience when a parent dates depend to a large extent on the stage the divorce process is in. Which parent is dating and the youngster's gender also shape teenagers' responses to parental dating. During the immediate crisis and short-term aftermath phases, adolescents may be upset about a parent beginning to date, because it often represents to the youngster the finality of the divorce. The adolescent must then give up treasured wishes and fantasies that her parents will reconcile their differences and get back together. Youngsters may also see a parent's dating partner as a rival for the parent's time and affection. Teenagers can also be upset by the clear, if only implicit, sexual nature of dating relationships. Their own emerging sexuality makes adolescents especially uneasy about their parents clearly acting in sexualized ways; it fuels these new and difficult to manage feelings.

It is useful for parents to directly address the issue of their dating with teenage children. It is most helpful to do this when a parent is about to begin to date. This makes the discussion more immediately relevant and also signals to the adolescent so that there will be no surprises. The following is an illustration of what a parent can say. For simplicity of exposition, it is assumed that a father is speaking: "There's something I think is important for me to tell you about. You know, it's been about six months [or whatever the time interval has been] since your mom and I split up. I know that when that happens it isn't easy for guys [girls]. There are a lot of changes to get used to. I want to talk to you about another kind of change. That has to do with parents starting to date other people. Just because your mom and I have split up, it doesn't mean that I don't like women. And a divorce [legal separation] means that the adults are free to start going out on dates. The law says it's okay to start having a new social life. So I'm going to start dating. I wanted to tell you that ahead of time because it's another change, and I didn't want you to feel surprised by it. And in case I ever get serious about someone I'm going with, I'll talk to you about it. I've heard that sometimes guys [girls] can start wondering if their dad is going to get married again, especially when he's been dating someone for a while. But if that ever looks as though it might happen, I'll tell you about it way in advance. No surprises, right?" This kind of discussion acknowledges the reality of the parent beginning to date, articulates the reasons for it, and underscores the fact that the parent will not surprise the teenager with another big change in his life.

Despite sensitively preparing adolescents for parental dating, they may still have to cope with their teenager's distress over this common element in the extended divorce process. Even when adults are adjusting well to their divorce and there are no obvious environmental stresses in evidence, adolescents can experience their parents' dating as painfully upsetting. Being aware of the nature of a teenager's distress over parental dating is a major step toward helping the youngster cope with it. This permits parents to empathize with the teenager's concerns and address them openly. At times this is difficult for parents to confront, especially since some are, themselves, uneasy about reentering the world of dating. Parents can thus become defensively angry at their adolescent youngsters when they do not readily accept parental dating or react negatively to it. It is enormously helpful to teenagers when parents can accept their youngsters' distress over parental dating as a normal response, recognize the sources of it, and have the courage to face it constructively with them.

CHRIS (see chapter 12) appeared to be coping well with his parents' separation until his father became seriously involved with a woman he was dating. Chris's rejection of Louise and his deepening depressive reaction led his father to contact a child and family clinic. He met with a social work graduate student who was doing her internship under the supervision of a senior staff psychologist at the clinic. Chris's father related his son's difficulties with Louise and his increased moodiness. The social work intern gathered information about Chris's developmental history, the divorce, and the current situation in each parent's household. Based on Chris's continued good adjustment at school and with friends as well as the clear links between Chris's problems and his father's dating, the social work intern and her supervisor concluded that this youngster was reacting to the meanings he had attached to his father's involvement with Louise.

In their fourth meeting, the social work intern explained the nature of Chris's difficulty to his father. She said that Chris was upset by his father's emotional involvement with Louise because of the private ways he was experiencing that relationship. She went on to emphasize that it was not that Chris's father was doing anything wrong. To the contrary, he seemed to care deeply about his son and was attuned to his feelings. But his father's relationship with Louise posed two threats to Chris: first, it reduced the likelihood that Chris's parents would reconcile and get back together, and thus undermined Chris's wish for that to happen; and second, it made Chris feel comparatively less important to his father and therefore not as close to him. The social work intern explained that these two issues were only dimly recognized by Chris. She went on to say that Chris's moodiness occurred because his sadness and underlying anger over the loss of his predivorce family could no longer be contained by harboring the hope that his parents would reunite. His father's deepening commitment to Louise meant, in Chris's mind, that he was also losing the special place in his father's heart.

Chris's father had been aware that his son felt he was in competition with Louise for his father's love, but he had not realized that Chris resented Louise because she represented an obstacle to his father and mother getting back together. The social work intern suggested that she and Chris's father meet every other week to discuss how he could help his son with these two issues. She also noted that the absence of other environmental sources of stress (such as, parental warfare), the history of a warm, caring father–son relationship, and Chris's good academic performance and positive peer relationships made her optimistic about their helping Chris cope with his parents' divorce.

In their next two sessions, the social work intern explained how displacement communication works and the importance of combining it with direct statements. She also explained the need for parents to begin to talk with an adolescent by at first focusing on their own feelings and thoughts about what was occurring. The social work intern suggested that Chris's father initiate the following discussion: "I think there's something we need to talk about. I've been feeling sort of caught in the middle. You know that I love you and want you to feel good. And since your mom and I split up, I've been trying to get my own life together. I like Louise, and I think she and I have something special going. But it makes me sad when it sort of feels like I've got to pick between you and her."

By revealing his own feelings and perceptions in this way, Chris's father set the stage for the mixture of displaced and direct communication he would use to talk about Chris's reactions. He could go on to discuss Chris's observable signs of distress and his discomfort with them by saying, "It's pretty clear that you're not real happy about my relationship with Louise. She seems to bug you just by being around. It can't feel good to a guy when it seems that he just can't be with his dad and have everything be okay.'' Then Chris's father was able to put his son's underlying emotional pain into words, ''I've heard that when a guy's parents get divorced and then one of them starts dating, it's hard. And one reason it's especially hard on guys is that they start to see that their parents really aren't going to make up and get back together. Most teenagers want their parents to quit being divorced and get back together. But when one parent starts dating, it gets pretty clear that they're going to stay divorced.'' Chris's father then assured his son that, ''It's tough to take at first, but after a while it gets better.''

Chris listened to his father, and then said, with some irritation, ''I know you and mom are going to stay divorced. I'm not dumb. It's just that Louise is, you know, she's not with it. I mean, she's not too cool. Besides, it's just easier when she's not around.'' Rather than defending Louise and pointing out that she cared about Chris, as he had done in the past, Chris's father accepted his son's feelings. He said, ''I know it bugs you to have her around. But one big reason that a lot of guys feel that way about their dad's girlfriend is that she sort of stands for the fact that the marriage is really over. If a dad is dating someone, and maybe starts living with her, it's a pretty sure thing that he's not going to get back together with the guy's mom.'' Chris responded by insisting, ''Uh-uh. If you were going with someone else, I'd probably like her. Louise is just, well, I guess she just bugs me. Like telling me to do the dishes and not leave my stuff around the living room. She gets on me like she was really my mom or something.'' Here Chris's father could accept his son's resentment instead of explaining the reasonableness of Louise's wishes for tidiness and then negotiate about the reality of Louise acting too parental. He told Chris, ''I can see where that would bug most teenagers. How about you and I and Louise agreeing that she doesn't tell you what to do. She isn't your mom, or even your stepmom. If I want you to do something, I'll be the one to tell you. I guess I just got into the habit of not asking you to do things, just like before the divorce it was always your mom, not me, who said what you needed to do around the house.''

Chris was surprised by how his father handled his criticisms of Louise. In the past, he always rose to Louise's defense and seemed to take her side. Now he accepted his son's unhappiness and even agreed with him about limiting Louise's parent-like stance toward him. When Chris seemed especially moody or resentful, his father reintroduced this way of talking about having to give up the understandable reconciliation wishes that so many youngsters have. He said, "Looks like you're down in the dumps today. Sometimes it's hard to feel good. Maybe it's some of those divorce feelings we've talked about. You know, when it really sinks in for a guy that his parents are going to stay divorced. It makes guys feel kind of down when they see their dad having a good time with his girlfriend 'cause they know for sure that their mom and dad just aren't going to get back together. But it really does start to feel better after a while." Chris often reacted to comments like this by saying, "Oh, dad, not that again!" or "I'm fine," or "I'm just thinking about all the homework I've got to finish by Monday." His father just accepted these defensive responses saying, "Well, sometimes feelings about divorce can be pretty strong," and left it at that.

In addition to addressing Chris's pain over having to give up his reconciliation wishes, his father also began to articulate his son's feelings of rivalry toward Louise. He said: "Sometimes it feels to me like you and I aren't having the same good times together as we used to. Between my work and dating Louise and getting ready to buy a house and move in with her, we just haven't been doing as much together as we used to." These statements about his own feelings and ideas focused the discussion on his son's competitive feelings toward Louise without making Chris feel on the spot or criticized. Chris's sense that he was not as important to his father as he used to be could then be discussed using both displacement and direct communication. Chris's father began by describing his son's observable signs of distress and noting how unpleasant it was for Chris, "Sometimes guys feel real irritated about their dad's girlfriend being around. It bugs them and then they start bad-mouthing her and sort of putting her down. It sure doesn't make a guy happy to feel bugged like that."

Next he went on to voice Chris's underlying fantasy, a source of internal stress, that he was less loved by and less important to his father than Louise was, "Guys sometimes get the idea that just because their dad is dating and really cares a lot about a special, new woman in his life, it means that their dad doesn't love them as much as they used to. A guy figures that his dad would rather be with his girlfriend than with him." Then Chris's father could directly correct this fantasy, "Maybe that's how you feel sometimes. But it's just not true. I love you as much as I did before Louise. One nice thing about loving feelings is that there's plenty to go around. It's not like having only one big hamburger (a favorite food of Chris's). So if I give her part of it, you get less. It's like I've got a whole supermarket full of hamburger meat, and you can have as much as you want. When your mom and I were married and we used to love each other, you know I still had plenty of love for you. And you have friends whose moms and dads aren't divorced and still love each other a lot. Do you think Dan's (Chris's best friend) dad doesn't love him just because he loves Dan's mom?" This startled Chris. His father's likening his affection for Louise to the love a never-divorced father has for his wife drove home the point that loving feelings were not finite and limited. From time to time, his father added, "I think you're just not sure yet that I'll keep loving you even though I care a lot about Louise. When a guy's parents aren't divorced, it means he's grown up with the fact that his dad loves his mom and he's sure that his dad loves him, too. After a divorce, it takes a guy a while to get convinced it'll be that way when his dad loves the woman he's dating, or living with, or even has gotten married to. But you'll see that I'll keep loving you. It doesn't matter whether I love your mom, like I used to, or Louise. Either way, I still love you."

After three months, Chris's father reported that his son was doing much better. He and the social work intern agreed to discontinue their sessions with the idea that he could contact her when and if it seemed like a good idea. Four months later he called in to set up an appointment to discuss his plans to marry Louise, and how he could talk with Chris about this. They met twice. In their sessions, the social work intern emphasized the need to reassure Chris of his continued love and that Louise would not suddenly turn into a controlling stepmother. Chris was invited to participate in the wedding along with his brother Sean. Both boys agreed to this, Sean with overt enthusiasm and Chris with a sense of doing his father a favor. A year later Chris's father contacted the clinic to let the social work intern know how well things were going for Chris and for him and Louise.

Chris's generally good psychological adjustment before the divorce and his father's capacity to understand, empathize with, and help his son were critically important to this positive outcome. However,

Louise's ability to understand the issues and her willingness to follow Chris's father's plan was also a significant factor. Some dating partners of divorced parents are unwilling or unable to assume this kind of low profile. They feel they must get the youngster to like them, and their efforts become overbearing and intrusive. This only inflames the adolescent's conflicts. And Chris's mother played a key role, too. She did not criticize Louise or her ex-husband to Chris. Some divorced parents feel hurt and then reflexively angry when their ex-spouse finds a new and gratifying intimate relationship. Their self-esteem can be threatened by the possibility that their ex-spouse can find happiness and fulfillment with someone else. It is as if they believe that such a relationship is "proof" that the marital failure was due to some shortcoming in them. Fortunately, Chris's mother was not burdened by these ideas and feelings. She did not need to poison her son against Louise or his father. Though she took no dramatically visible actions on her son's behalf, the absence of rancor on her part was important in Chris adjusting to his father's relationship with Louise.

When a parent becomes serious about a dating partner or remarries during the long-range period of divorce, the potential distress for adolescents is different from their reaction when a parent has a significant intimate relationship shortly after the marital separation (that is, within the first two stages of the divorce process). When a noncustodial parent who has been relatively peripheral to a youngster's life for years dates or remarries, the impact on most teenagers seems relatively minimal. However, when the parent has been centrally involved in the child's life, as is the case for a custodial parent, dating and remarriage stir conflicts that may be very difficult to resolve. Boys must face the likely feelings of experiencing the custodial parent's (typically mother) partner as a rival for her affections and as a new and initially unwelcome source of potential adult authority. For these reasons, boys may resent their custodial mother's partner and act in an aloof or provocative manner toward him. Girls must also confront these issues, but at times it is harder for them because of the especially close relationship that can evolve over the years between single mothers and their daughters. Both boys and girls have to cope with the sexualized nature of their custodial mother's new relationship, a task made more difficult by the fact that youngsters are more keenly aware of this when it is the parent with whom they live who is involved in an intimate relationship. Girls can be particularly troubled by the sexual aspects of their mother's relationship. They are uneasy about the sexuality of their mother's partner and may feel self-conscious. And their mother is unwittingly being a role model for sexual behavior at precisely the time in her daughter's development when a girl is struggling with how to conduct herself sexually.

Parents are often reluctant to deal with these issues. They may feel conflicted about a serious dating relationship, wondering whether it is really all right to be sexually active, especially with teenagers around. Or they may experience the uneasiness shared by many parents, divorced or not, about discussing sexual issues with their adolescent youngsters, even though they may be comfortable about their own sexual behavior. Nonetheless, it is crucial for parents to be able to overcome these inhibitions and talk with teenagers about the difference between an intimate relationship in adulthood and what is developmentally appropriate behavior regarding sexuality for a youngster. Further, it is important for parents to distinguish the pleasure they experience from being involved in a caring, intimate relationship from the very different ways their adolescent children will tend to feel about that relationship.

KIM'S (see chapter 12) mother consulted a psychologist in private practice about her worries regarding her daughter. She described her daughter's excellent adjustment up until the time she began to get serious about Chuck. Kim's mother tearfully recalled the good times she and her daughter had enjoyed for years, emphasizing their especially close and mutually pleasurable emotional bond. She expressed her bewilderment at Kim's intense, negative reactions to Chuck and her escalating anger at her. She also said she was "worried sick" about her daughter's drinking and wanting to appear sexy.

The psychologist spent two sessions with Kim's mother collecting information about Kim's developmental history, the end of the marriage, the lack of contact between Kim and her father, and Kim's reactions to Chuck at various stages of her mother's involvement with him. He concluded that Kim was struggling with conflicts and feelings stimulated by her mother's intimate relationship with Chuck, her emotional commitment to him, and the adolescent context for these issues. However, he added that since Kim had been drinking, it would be best to have a drug screen to see if other substances were a problem. Kim reacted angrily but did agree to this urine test, conducted at the family physician's office, and it was negative.

The psychologist set up an appointment to see Kim. She reluctantly agreed. In the session, Kim was at first sullenly unwilling to talk. But for the last twenty minutes of the meeting, she launched into a vitriolic attack on her mother. Her mother was "unreasonable" in her efforts to monitor Kim's social behavior and was a "worry-wart." And she could not fathom why her mother loved Chuck, "She never should have married him. He's gross and stupid." Kim also firmly stated that she was not going to come for another session, "I don't need a shrink. My mother's the one who should come. She's all bent out of shape and crying and weirding out all the time. I'm fine." The psychologist empathized with Kim's anger at her mother and her unhappiness about Chuck. He also pointed out that sometimes it is helpful for girls to be able to talk out their feelings about big changes in their lives, such as when their mother remarries. Kim stubbornly reiterated her views.

The psychologist met with Kim's mother and discussed her daughter's insistence about not coming to appointments. He outlined the issues Kim was wrestling with: her rage at Chuck and her mother for disrupting their very close mother–daughter relationship; her anger over Chuck's becoming parental by disciplining her; and her anxieties over the sexual ambience of her mother's relationship with Chuck, which intensified her own concerns about sexuality. He also explained that Kim's wish to dress in a sexually provocative manner was, in effect, a subtle invitation to her mother to impose restrictions and keep a careful eye on her, both of which had the effect of reducing Kim's independence and driving mother and daughter closer together. The psychologist underscored the fact that Kim was not consciously aware of these issues, except for her indignant rage over Chuck acting in a parental way.

The psychologist suggested that Kim's mother begin to help her daughter by having Chuck give up his efforts to openly support his wife in her altercations with Kim and refrain from disciplining Kim or assigning her chores. He invited Chuck to come in with Kim's mother to the next session, and explained how resentful teenagers usually feel about a new stepparent taking on a parental role or inserting himself into conflicts between the children and their parent. The psychologist told them: "It's okay for you (Chuck) to be supportive with your wife in private and to discuss ways she might respond to Kim's difficulties. But when Kim's around, it would be best for you to keep a low profile. You can offer to drive her to a friend's house when she's planning to go there, drive her and her friends to the mall or to a movie, and ask her if she would like help with her homework or a chore. But that's about it. Your role is to be useful to her, although she may even reject that for quite a while. She's got an important emotional agenda to work out with her mother, and those are the ways you can help her and your wife.''

Chuck understood these issues, and the psychologist's advice made sense to him. However, he did not like having to "back off.'' He claimed it was his home, too, and that he should have an active role. The psychologist acknowledged that feeling, and added that the ways he had suggested of being helpful called for patience and the ability to tolerate the frustration of not leaping immediately to his wife's aid in her conflicts with Kim. His consistent willingness to be helpful to Kim (for example, driving her to a friend's house), avoiding becoming entangled in mother–daughter battles, and not disciplining or giving Kim chores collectively formed a strategy that often pays off for stepparents. However, the psychologist cautioned Kim's mother and Chuck about having the somewhat unrealistic expectation that Kim, at her age, would eventually come to love her new stepfather as if he were her father.

Kim's mother and stepfather implemented this first step in the plan to help Kim. At the same time, the psychologist continued to meet weekly with Kim's mother, joined for some sessions by Chuck, to discuss how she could talk with her daughter. With the psychologist's help, Kim's mother began to confront her daughter's feelings about the marriage. She began by sharing her own perceptions and emotions, "We used to be so close. Remember how you used to help out in the store and how we went to movies together? I really miss those times. Sometimes I get sad about how things have changed so much.'' Kim responded sarcastically: "*I* didn't change anything. You're the one who got married to Mr. Grossness.'' Kim's mother refrained from responding to this provocative statement and went on instead to articulate her daughter's visible signs of distress as well as how unpleasant it must be for her, "I know you're not happy about Chuck. There are lots of things you've told me that you don't like about him, like his smelly cigars and his watching sports on TV. I think most girls sort of feel like they'd be happier if their stepdad disappeared and it sure doesn't feel good for anyone to have to feel so mad and upset about what's happening in their own house." Kim angrily said: "I sure don't need him around! He's on my back about stuff and he even grounds me. Who gave him the right?"

Kim's mother took this opportunity to accept her daughter's feelings as well as her view that Chuck had been overstepping his bounds as a stepfather, "I know Chuck's tried to act like a dad. He and I have talked about that, and we both think you're right. He's not going to tell you what to do or ground you anymore. That's between me and you; I'm your parent, not him." Kim was surprised by these comments and wary about the truth of them. She asked, "You mean even if I yell at you and tell you I'm not going to do something, he won't ground me or start telling me what to do?" Her mother answered, "That's right. I raised you by myself for ten years. You're my responsibility. I know Chuck wants to help, but it will be better if you and I take care of our own disagreements by ourselves." While Kim was relieved, she was also incredulous, and set out to test these new ground rules. She tried to resist her mother's authority, verbally attacked her at times, and argued constantly about bedtime, weekend curfews, and the clothing she wanted to wear. However, her mother and Chuck stuck to their plan.

Kim's mother had used her daughter's willingness to talk with her to accept the validity of Kim's feelings and wishes regarding Chuck trying to be parental. She also told Kim that there would be real changes made to correct that problem, and then she and Chuck followed through on them. In doing so, she had interrupted the usual way that this kind of talk proceeds: she stopped after the first two steps (that is, articulating the visible signs of the youngster's distress and noting how uncomfortable the child is about them) that follow a teenager's parent focusing the discussion by sharing her own thoughts and feelings about what has been happening. In subsequent talks with Kim, her mother went on to address the internal sources of her daughter's distress and help her cope with it.

Kim's mother began by acknowledging how difficult it was for a girl when her mother remarries. After repeating the earlier elements of the discussion (that is, setting the stage by focusing on her own ideas and feelings and then articulating Kim's distress as well as her discomfort with being so upset), she went on to say, "It's not easy for a girl when her mother gets remarried. Teenagers start getting independent of their mom, but they like to be the one who sort of decides to not be as close to her as they used to. Sometimes girls feel pushed away when their mom gets married, almost like they're not as important to their mom as they used to be." Kim said: "Are you kidding me, or what? *I'm* the one who wants to be independent. *I'm* the one who wants to stay out later on the weekends and have you off my back!" Kim's mother nodded her agreement but went on to the fourth step, correcting the fantasy Kim had that her mother did not love her as much as she had before meeting Chuck, "Maybe you have the same idea a lot of girls do, that you're not as important to me now that Chuck is here. But that's not true. I love you every bit as much as I ever did." Kim responded by jokingly pleading with her mother to love her "a little less" so she could have more freedom.

Kim's response is not unusual for adolescents in her position when they are being reassured of their parents' love. Developmentally, they are so focused on their struggles for autonomy that they try to blind themselves to their wishes to be loved. For some teenagers those yearnings can feel too childlike to be accepted. When this is the case, a parent must do what a therapist usually does: interpret the hidden wishes for closeness embedded in the adolescent's demands for freedom. A few days later, Kim's mother reminded her daughter of their earlier discussion and of Kim's joke about wanting to be loved a little less: "I was thinking about what you said about how now that you're a teenager you'd sort of like it if I loved you less, so you could have more freedom. I think you're right about needing more freedom. But there's something I can't quite figure out. If you want more space, why do you keep doing things that you know are going to make me ground you and check up on you? I'm not saying I expect you to be an angel. I know that girls can go to a party and have something to drink there without their parents knowing about it. And I know that lots of girls do put on more make-up after they leave the house because they figure that if they did it before they left, they'd just get into a fight with their mom or dad. I'm not saying you should be having something to drink at a party or that it's right to wear a lot of make-up and dress real sexy. And I don't want you to feel you can't be honest with me. But a little bit of that kind

381

of sneakiness, together with being responsible when you're out with friends, is how teenagers get their independence. So why are you rubbing my nose in stuff that you know is going to worry me and get me to not trust you?''

Kim was startled by her mother's comments, and after fumbling around for what to say, she replied, ''So I'm supposed to be a sneak? You want me to keep secrets from you?'' Kim's mother gently said: ''I'd like you to be responsible, and I think you are. But one big difference between a teenager like you and a younger girl is that teenagers usually don't tell their parents everything. That doesn't mean that they go and do dumb things that can get them into trouble. But it does mean that teenagers want to feel independent enough to not have to share with a parent everything they're thinking, feeling, or doing. I hope that you and I can have a good relationship so that when you have questions or worries, you can feel okay about coming to me about them.'' Kim appeared thoughtful, but did not say anything more at the time.

Kim's mother then dealt with the subject of sexuality. With the psychologist's help, she began to distinguish between her adult sexuality and sex during adolescence. She again began with a focus on herself. She said to her daughter: ''You know that I haven't been exactly delighted with how you've been dressing. But I've been thinking more about it. It seems like I've been upset because how you dress and the make-up you wear is making me think about sexy stuff. Parents start getting concerned about how their teenage daughter is going to handle the whole sex thing. I guess I've been worried about that and that's why I've been bugging you about it.'' Kim listened and gave the standard adolescent response, ''But all my friends are dressing that way and using make-up! It's normal. You want me to dress like a geek?'' Her mother went on to describe common, though often not immediately visible, signs of distress that adolescent girls experience about sexuality: ''I just know that girls have their own questions and even some uncomfortable feelings about sexy stuff. Like wanting to be attractive, not looking like a geek, but also not wanting their girlfriends or guys at school to think they're really ready to do a lot of sexy things. And girls don't want to get a bad reputation, like other people thinking they're a slut. It's a hard line to walk— trying to look good and be popular but also wanting to stay out of trouble and keep a good reputation.''

As is often the case, Kim began to look embarrassed. She blushed and said, "Oh, mom!" Her mother said, "I know this isn't easy to talk about, but it's important." She then went on to the underlying issues: "This sexy business isn't easy for teenagers. But it can be especially hard when your mom is dating or has just gotten remarried. Teenagers are old enough to know that there's a sexy side to their mom's relationship with a man. It's not easy to realize that. It can make girls more aware of sex, and some girls even figure that if their mom has that kind of relationship, then it's okay for them to have one, too." Kim's mother was then able to differentiate between an intimate relationship in adulthood and one in adolescence: "Being a teenager is different from being an adult. I hope that you'll have a good romantic relationship, lovemaking and all, when you're older. Not only will you be able to handle it responsibly when you're older, but the guy you choose will be able to treat you right. Guys take a long time before they can deal with a love relationship. So it's not only how you would handle it that's on my mind, but how the guy will treat you."

As this plan took its course, Kim became less angry and provocative with her mother. She also tolerated Chuck and even acted friendly at times. There were no further episodes of coming home drunk. And although Kim continued to dress in a more sexualized way than her mother liked, it was (according to her mother's perception and that of the high school counselor she talked with about it) within reasonable and normal bounds for girls her age in her school. After meeting weekly for two months, the psychologist and Kim's mother agreed to have only one session a month, and within another three months, neither felt that further work together was necessary.

Kim's mother and stepfather were able to eliminate a pivotal source of environmental stress for Kim: the tendency of stepparents to become too parental soon after a remarriage. This tends to produce enormous feelings of resentment among many adolescents. The removal of this key external stressor also led Kim to feel heard and understood. In addition, Kim's mother constructively talked with her daughter about two crucial internal stresses: the loss of her special closeness with her mother that the marriage meant to Kim, and the sexual concerns stimulated by her mother's intimate relationship with Chuck. Interpreting Kim's provocative stance with her mother as a disguised invitation for closeness was also helpful. However, at times adolescents will begin to act out more seriously than Kim did. Their rage may spill over toward authorities at school or be expressed in provocative use of drugs. And conflicts over their parent's sexuality may propel them toward precocious involvement in sexual activities. At those times, direct professional help is often necessary. Even when an adolescent refuses individual treatment, family or joint mother–teenager therapy can be successful.[2]

The long-range period can create significant stresses for adolescent boys who have had minimal contact with their father over the years. Many seem to lack a solid self-confidence about their masculine identity. Some of these youngsters develop notable inhibitions over moving fully into adolescence and may appear more like an older elementary school boy than a teenager. They avoid peer relationships with adolescents their own age, preferring to be with younger boys, or at home alone engaged in fantasy play with video games, remote-controlled cars, or action figures. These youngsters may continue to do well academically, be liked by teachers and other adults, and give their custodial mother no trouble. They often evoke no concern in either their parents or teachers. And custodial mothers are frequently pleased about having raised such a good boy. Thus, they rarely are referred for counseling. But they are stuck developmentally, eschewing the pleasures of gratifying friendships and emotional independence in favor of the safety of remaining a little boy.

Other teenage boys respond differently to their deep-seated uncertainty about their masculine competence and effectiveness. Rather than retreating from the challenges of adolescence, they mobilize for action and meet their unconscious uneasiness head-on. These youngsters are burdened by the fantasy that they must always prove, to themselves as well as others that there is absolutely no question about their strength, daring, or courage. This fantasy lies entirely below the level of most boys' awareness. When they get into trouble, as they often do, they nearly always experience it as someone else's fault or simply bad luck.

Whether a teenage boy copes with his unconsciously felt lack of confidence in his masculine effectiveness through inhibitions or trying to actively prove himself, it is helpful for parents to be alert to their adolescent's developmental progress. Is he spending his free time with younger children or in excessive fantasy play? Is he frequently at home rather than with friends his own age? Is he uneasy about

384

participating in extracurricular peer activities such as athletics, band, the school newspaper, or school math club? If the answers to any of these is yes, a parent might consider the possibility that their youngster is avoiding adolescence. Such boys can then be encouraged to become more involved in age-appropriate activities. On the other hand, if a boy is getting into trouble with peers or authorities at school, getting into fights, having car accidents, or getting into trouble with the law (for shoplifting, vandalism, use of illegal substances), it may be that he is struggling to prove his masculinity. But in neither case is it the boy's sexual preference that is at issue. Divorce does not influence a youngster in the direction of homosexuality or heterosexuality. This sort of fear lurks in the minds of some parents and prevents them from recognizing that their son may be having to cope with an uncertain sense of his masculine prowess.

When parents can permit themselves to think about the possibility that their boy may lack confidence in his masculinity, they can try to help him achieve a more solid sense of what it means to be a teenager and a boy. Parents can encourage their sons to become more involved in peer activities and help arrange for such opportunities. They can try to increase their boy's involvement with his father, stepfather, or other adult male who might serve as an appropriate role model for him. And if these efforts do not seem to be enough, parents can consult a mental health professional and help their youngster get into counseling, preferably with a man.

ANDY'S (see chapter 12) mother and stepfather consulted a psychologist who had extensive experience working with teenagers. They related their concerns about Andy, noting the trouble he had been getting into. They shared their view that Andy seemed to have a need to act tough with peers. They also told the psychologist about Andy's strengths: his athletic abilities, his popularity with youngsters his own age, and the fact that they saw him as basically a "good kid" who was a pleasure to be with most of the time.

In their second session, the psychologist outlined the conflicts Andy seemed to be wrestling with. He told Andy's mother and stepfather that Andy seemed to have to prove constantly that he was not weak or frightened, no matter what the situation was. The psychologist emphasized that boys who are so worried about appearing, as Andy put it, like a "weenie" are struggling with their own lack of confidence in being solidly masculine. He explained that the minimal contact with his father over the past six years and the fact that Andy and his stepfather seemed to have very different interests (and therefore had not formed a close relationship), meant that there had been no consistent and psychologically available male role model in Andy's life for a long time. The psychologist also reassured them that Andy's difficulties were not due to how they were treating him. Rather, these problems can arise when a boy has to carve out his changing masculine identity essentially on his own during adolescence. He told Andy's mother and stepfather that it was also probably the case that Andy was furious at his father for "abandoning" him by moving so far away. His getting into trouble may also be a way to express this anger as well as punish his father by not living up to his father's hopes and expectations for him. The psychologist underscored the fact that Andy was unaware of these issues and that simply talking to him about them directly would only elicit incredulous denials or defensive anger.

As this session drew to a close, the psychologist also suggested that they have a urine drug screen performed by their family physician. He explained that marked shifts in behavior during adolescence could signal a substance abuse problem. Though this did not seem to be the case for Andy, drug screens are inexpensive and, at the very least, would lay to rest the possibility of substance abuse should the test be negative. Andy's mother arranged for a general physical check-up and a urine test for several common drugs. Andy did not object strenuously to this and, according to his mother, seemed almost proud that she wondered about his "doing drugs." Here, Andy's "macho" posture served to facilitate the evaluation of his physical health and potential drug involvement. His examination revealed that he was in excellent health and was not abusing any of the six common substances that the urine screen tested.

The psychologist also contacted Andy's father by telephone, after discussing it with Andy's mother and stepfather. Andy's father was chagrined by his son's behavior but insisted that Andy would "grow out of it." He claimed that he, too, had been a "hell-raiser" during adolescence, and he had turned out just fine. Nonetheless, he agreed to pay for his share of any costs should Andy appear in need of counseling and indicated a willingness to talk with the psychologist from time to time.

The psychologist then met with Andy's mother and stepfather, and outlined a plan to help Andy. He suggested that both parents, separately, begin to raise with their son the hypermasculine nature of his behavior. He explained displacement communication and the need to mix it with direct statements when talking to teenagers about their inner conflicts. The psychologist also noted that it is usually best to begin with the parent focusing on him/herself so as not to make the adolescent feel that he is on the spot or being criticized. Andy's mother or stepfather could say: "It's been upsetting to me to see you in trouble. I worry about your fighting, even if someone else starts it. I know you can handle yourself, but when people get into fights, they can get hurt no matter how tough they are. And the car accident got me worried, too. I know that no one got hurt, but now I get tense when you're out at night on the weekends. I want you to be safe and not get hurt." Andy's mother and stepfather did not blame him for the fights or the accident. Instead they expressed their own concerns and feelings.

Andy cared about his mother and stepfather and responded to each by trying to reassure them. He claimed that he really did not get into too many fights, that he certainly would not fight if someone had a knife or a gun, and that he considered himself to be a safe driver who just had one "freak accident." Needless to say, these comments did not have a calming effect on Andy's mother and stepfather.

Andy's stepfather decided to implement the combination of displacement and direct communication that follows this sort of parent-focused introduction. He said: "Most guys really don't like getting into fights. It's a tense situation when that happens. And no matter how brave or tough you are, it's kind of scary. You seemed a lot happier when you weren't getting into the kind of fights that can happen between guys your age." In this way, Andy's stepfather was addressing Andy's aggressive behavior and noting how unpleasant it was for him. He then went on to articulate the underlying conflict that was driving this posture: "I've heard that sometimes guys just feel like they have to prove that they're no wimp. They really don't want to fight, but they don't want anyone to even get the idea that they're a weenie. But why do you have to prove anything? You're a real good athlete, you're real popular with the guys, and girls keep calling you all the time. So what's happening?" Andy earnestly replied that he did not start fights and that there were plenty of arguments he walked away from. He gave several examples of his willingness to avoid these physical confrontations and appeared unable to see that he was trying to prove his masculinity.

Andy's mother took a slightly different tack. After focusing the discussion by sharing her feelings and concerns about Andy's difficulties, much as her husband had done, she talked with her son about how the absence of a good relationship with a man can lead a teenager to feel unsure of how to act in certain situations. She said: "I've been talking to a psychologist about why guys sometimes get into fights or have a hard time studying in school. He said that most guys don't like to feel like they have to fight in order to show everyone how tough they are. And most teenagers like getting good grades and showing off their smarts in school. But he told me something very interesting. He said that sometimes when a guy's parents get divorced, it's hard to grow up really knowing that it's okay to avoid fights. It doesn't mean you're a wimp. And it's okay to study; not only girls study. Guys usually want to feel good about themselves, and one way to do that is to get good grades in school and then go to college. When a guy's dad is there to tell him all that, and even show him that he doesn't get into fights just because someone is being rude or nasty to him, then a guy can really learn what it's like to be a man." Andy seemed somewhat bored by these comments. He insisted that his dad not being around had absolutely nothing to do with anything that had been going on in his life.

After a month of Andy's mother and stepfather trying to talk with him in these ways, they reported that it did not seem to be working. The psychologist then initiated a telephone conversation with Andy's father, explaining to him how he might discuss these issues with his son. But Andy's father was not particularly psychologically minded. Instead of approaching Andy with a mix of displacement and direct communication aimed at alleviating underlying conflicts, he confronted his son about his difficulties and insisted that he "better shape up" if he wanted to get anywhere in life. Andy was furious and got into a shouting match with his father. Eventually this led to his father angrily stomping out of the house.

The psychologist recommended Andy begin once weekly psychotherapy. He explained to Andy's mother and stepfather that Andy was not able to make use of their efforts to help him. He underscored the fact that they had carried out the plan faithfully, but that Andy's conflicts were too solidly entrenched to be corrected quite so easily. He further noted that many teenage boys with Andy's sort of long-standing problems could not make use of direct help from their mother. Mothers often cannot effectively convey the idea that a teenage boy's attitude and style of dealing with interpersonal conflicts was defensive rather than reasonable and appropriate. Adolescent boys too easily dismiss their mother's comments as just that: a mother's (female's) ideas. The psychologist added that Andy also could not make use of his stepfather's help: Andy saw his stepfather as too kind and mild-mannered to be an arbiter of what was appropriate behavior in a situation that could conceivably call for battle. Further, Andy's distant and strained relationship with his critical father closed that avenue for intervening effectively with Andy.

Andy's therapy lasted for eighteen months. In the course of their work together, the psychologist raised and addressed many of the same issues that his mother and stepfather had. But he could do it within the context of Andy's need to see him as particularly manly. Despite having no direct knowledge of the psychologist's personal life, his style of managing interpersonal conflicts with other males, or what his therapist had been like as a teenager, Andy seemed convinced that the psychologist was solidly masculine. In their sessions the psychologist could, after several months, even jokingly confront Andy about his readiness to defend his masculine honor: "So yesterday a guy cut in front of you in the lunch line and you're ready to duke it out with him. So you start mouthing off to him, and pretty soon you feel you can't back down. Are you Clint Eastwood or something? Did you also tell him 'Make my day' when you were getting ready to fight. Do you think Clint Eastwood really acts that way in real life? If he did, he'd be up in the state prison instead of making a million bucks a picture." In these ways, the psychologist could help Andy separate his fantasy of what it took to be masculine from the reality. He was able to offer specific suggestions about how to deal with these kinds of situations. And, when the timing was right, he interpreted Andy's underlying lack of confidence in his courage and physical abilities, linked it to his not having had a man consistently in his life to model himself after, and showed him how this led to the sorts of problems he had been having.

Therapy was discontinued when Andy eventually was accepted

to a college and moved away. He had been able to find a measure of certainty about his masculine identity and could then give up the defenses he had unwittingly mobilized against his private fear that, at bedrock, he was nothing more than a weak, scared little "weenie."

The strategy that Andy's mother and stepfather each had implemented frequently works well for boys with conflicts of this sort that have not been in formation for a long time. Adolescents who have lived in a single-mother household for years, have had minimal or no contact with their father (or a poor relationship with him), and have not been able to accept their stepfather as a masculine role model (though they may have accepted him as a member of the household and as their mother's husband) are likely to require counseling. Though this example is of a boy who was acting out his problems in ways that provoked concern in his parents and teachers, youngsters who avoid this struggle by developing inhibitions can also profit from counseling, especially with a male therapist. For it is not simply the interpretation of conflicts that makes therapy work for these teenage boys. It is also the opportunity to be in regular contact with an adult male who can serve as a new source of masculine identifications. These identifications are not with the actual behaviors of the therapist (since therapists are rarely viewed in interaction with others by their patients) but with his perspective on masculinity, his approach to problems, and his style of relating to the youngster.

Overview

Parents can be of great help to adolescents who are struggling with environmental and internal stresses created by divorce. It is crucial for parents, and other adults in the youngster's life, to be especially aware of the inner tensions of teenagers when their parents separate. However, it is equally important for parents to recognize that divorce is a process consisting of many life changes that unfold over time and collectively challenge the youngster's abilities to cope effectively and get on with the business of growing up. Because "the divorce" occurred years in the past, many parents are unaware of the impact of the extended divorce process. When parents recognize that divorce-initiated life changes (for example, residential moves, dating, remarriage) continue to affect children, they are in a better position to help ameliorate the stresses on adolescents. But whatever the divorce-related vicissitudes are for an adolescent, he is still a teenager. Parenting styles that are most effective with youngsters in this period of development involve a sensitive balance among direct statements, indirect communications, negotiations, and respect for the emerging autonomy of the youngster.

▶◀

Afterword

Parents who divorce did not grow up imagining a future that included the end of their marriage, being a single parent, or marrying more than once. In our society we are socialized to the notion of marriage beginning as a romantic adventure and enduring forever. The marital relationship itself has come to be seen as potentially providing all the needs of adulthood: love, economic security, sexual fulfillment, companionship, understanding, emotional support, and an unending source of self-esteem. Yet this view is relatively new. For centuries past, marriage was perceived as an economically advantageous union, a way to continue one's bloodline, an acceptable outlet for sexual needs, or as an escape from loneliness. Many adults hoped to achieve no more than one or two of these goals. Now we freight marriage with so many expectations that keen disappointments are commonplace, discontent is nearly sure to arise, and the likelihood of divorce is greater than ever.

But divorce is not something people plan for. It is a wrenching experience for most adults, and one of the most painful that young and middle-aged adults encounter. Yet divorce as a widely shared experience is too new for society to have developed generally accepting and constructive responses. And there has not been enough time as yet to have an agreed-upon set of expectations for the course of psychological recovery after divorce. Often, divorced parents are not quite sure about what to expect from themselves or others. Nor is it clear what they can do to help themselves and their children.

By mapping the nature of stresses that divorce creates for children, this book attempts to fill the gap left by the absence of societal expectations in this area. The division of stresses into those stemming from environmental versus internal sources not only makes the divorce experience for children more understandable, but also provides specific strategies for alleviating the pain divorce brings for so many youngsters.

The great majority of parents are able to meet the needs of their children when they have sufficient knowledge to understand what is affecting a child, why the child is responding in a particular way, and what to do about it. When parents do have problems helping a child cope with stress, it is frequently because they cannot communicate effectively with their youngster about them.

To be most helpful to children across the whole divorce process, it is essential that parents be aware of the nature of the stresses youngsters are likely to encounter and specifically how to reduce these stresses. For children of all ages, environmental stresses such as parental warfare, the loss of the relationship with the noncustodial parent, and the emotional distress of a parent (especially the custodial parent) are key sources of emotional pain for children. Less obvious environmental stresses include parental dating and remarriage. However, as a child grows and matures, new sources of stress come into play in the form of the child's own beliefs, fantasies, and inner conflicts. These internal sources of stress can exact a great toll on children. It is crucial for parents to keep these sources of stress in mind and to recognize the different ways children experience them at different ages.

Perhaps the most difficult task of all for parents is to recognize when a child is reacting to the stresses of divorce. In part this is due to the disguised forms that expressions of distress can take at different stages of child development. But another major factor is the parent's own inability to see a son or daughter as being in distress. Such blinders are of several different types: for example, a parent's emotional distress over the divorce; a father's preoccupation with his ex-spouse; a mother's guilt over the divorce causing pain for her child. It takes courage and perseverance for parents to remove these blinders and look squarely at their children.

However, it is not enough for parents to realize that a child is having trouble adjusting to divorce. Merely being aware of the child's distress, without knowing how to help, places a parent in the impossible position of knowing the youngster is in pain and feeling helpless to do anything about it. This book attempts to provide parents with the understandings and strategies necessary to help their child cope well with and adjust successfully to divorce. In feeling better prepared to help, parents can then more readily afford to see the difficulties their child may be struggling with.

Ultimately, aiding children in their efforts to grow up with divorce is best done by parents. Who else knows their child so well? Who does the child depend upon more? And who else cares so deeply?

Notes

Chapter 1
Introduction

1. P. C. Glick, "Children of Divorced Parents in Demographic Perspective," *Journal of Social Issues*, 35 (1979): 170–182. F. Furstenberg, C. Nord, J. Peterson, and N. Zill, "The Life Course of Children of Divorce," *American Sociological Review*, 48 (1983): 656–668.

2. B. L. Bloom, S. J. Asher, and S. W. White, "Marital Disruption As a Stressor: A Review and Analysis," *Psychological Bulletin*, 85 (1978): 867–894.

3. L. J. Weitzman, *The Divorce Revolution: The Unexpected Social and Economic Consequences for Women and Children in America.* (New York: Free Press, 1985).

4. J. Guidubaldi and J. D. Perry, "Divorce, Socioeconomic Status, and Children's Cognitive-Social Competence at School Entry," *American Journal of Orthopsychiatry*, 54 (1984): 459–468. J. Guidubaldi and J. D. Perry, "Divorce and Mental Health Sequelae for Children: A Two-Year Follow-up of a Nationwide Sample," *Journal of the American Academy of Child Psychiatry*, 24 (1985): 531–537. J. S. Wallerstein and J. B. Kelly, *Surviving the Break-up: How Children and Parents Cope with Divorce* (New York: Basic Books, 1980).

Chapter 2
The Stages of Divorce

1. N. Kalter and J. W. Plunkett, "Children's Perceptions of the Causes and Consequences of Divorce," *Journal of the American Academy of Child Psychiatry*, 23 (1984): 326–334. J. W. Plunkett and N. Kalter,

"Children's Beliefs About Reactions to Parental Divorce," *Journal of the American Academy of Child Psychiatry,* 23 (1984): 616–621. J. S. Wallerstein and J. B. Kelly, *Surviving the Break-up: How Children and Parents Cope with Divorce* (New York: Basic Books, 1980).

2. R. Emery, "Interparental Conflict and the Children of Discord and Divorce," *Psychological Bulletin,* 92 (1982): 310–330. R. E. Emery, E. M. Hetherington, and L. F. DiLalla, "Divorce, Children and Social Policy," *Child Development Research and Social Policy,* vol 1, ed. H. W. Stevenson and A. E. Siegel (Chicago: University of Chicago Press, 1984). Wallerstein and Kelly, *Surviving the Break-up,* 1980.

3. L. J. Weitzman, *The Divorce Revolution: The Unexpected Social and Economic Consequences for Women and Children in America* (New York: Free Press, 1985).

4. D. L. Chambers, *Making Fathers Pay: The Enforcement of Child Support* (Chicago: University of Chicago Press, 1979). Weitzman, *The Divorce Revolution,* 1985.

5. Wallerstein and Kelly, *Surviving the Break-up,* 1980.

6. F. Furstenberg, C. Nord, J. Peterson, and N. Zill, "The Life Course of Children of Divorce, *American Sociological Review,* 48 (1983): 656–668.

7. A. Arbarbanel, "Shared Parenting After Separation and Divorce: A Study of Joint Custody," *American Journal of Orthopsychiatry,* 49 (1979): 320–329. J. Grief, "Fathers, Children and Joint Custody." *American Journal of Orthopsychiatry,* 49 (1979): 311–319. S. B. Steinman, S. E. Zemmelman, and T. M. Knoblauch, "A Study of Parents Who Sought Joint Custody Following Divorce: Who Reaches Agreement and Sustains Joint Custody and Who Returns to Court," *Journal of the American Academy of Child Psychiatry,* 24 (1985): 554–562.

8. M. B. Isaacs, B. Montalvo, and D. Abelsohn, *The Difficult Divorce* (New York: Basic Books, 1986).

9. Furstenberg, et al., "The Life Course of Children of Divorce," 1983.

10. H. B. Biller, "The Father and Sex Role Development," in *The Role of the Father in Child Development,* 2nd ed., M. E. Lamb, (New York: John Wiley, 1981).

11. R. S. Weiss, "Growing Up a Little Faster: The Experience of Growing Up in a Single-Parent Household," *Journal of Social Issues,* 35 (1979): 97–111.

12. National Center for Health Statistics 1985, *Monthly Vital Statistics Report* (D.H.H.S. Publications, 33–11) (Washington, D.C.: U.S. Government Printing Office, 1985).

Chapter 4
The Divorce Experience for Infants and Toddlers

1. A. Thomas and S. Chess, *The Dynamics of Psychological Development.* (New York: Brunner/Mazel, 1980).

2. D. Finkelhor and A. Browne, "The Traumatic Impact of Child Sexual Abuse: A Conceptualization," *American Journal of Orthopsychiatry,* 55 (1985): 530–541.

3. N. Kalter, "Long-Term Effects of Divorce on Children: A Developmental Vulnerability Model," *American Journal of Orthopsychiatry,* 57 (1987): 587–600. V. J. Machtlinger, "The Father in Psychoanalytic Theory," in *The Role of the Father in Child Development,* 2nd ed., ed. M. E. Lamb (New York: John Wiley, 1981).

4. R. Spitz, "Anaclitic Depression," *Psychoanalytic Study of the Child,* 2 (1946): 113–117.

Chapter 6
The Divorce Experience for Preschool Children

1. E. L. Abelin, "The Role of the Father in the Separation-Individuation Process," in *Separation-Individuation,* ed. J. B. McDevitt and C. F. Settlage (New York: International Universities Press, 1971). J. Herzog, "Sleep Disturbance and Father Hunger in 18–28-Month-Old Boys: The Erlkönig Syndrome," *The Psychoanalytic Study of the Child,* 35 (1980): 219–233.

2. M. E. Lamb, "Father and Child Development: An Integrative Overview," in *The Role of the Father in Child Development,* 2nd ed., ed. M. E. Lamb (New York: John Wiley, 1981). M. E. Lamb, "The Development of Father-Infant Relationships," in *The Role of the Father in Child Development,* 2nd ed., ed. M. E. Lamb (New York: John Wiley, 1981).

3. H. B. Biller, "Father Absence, Divorce, and Personality Development," in *The Role of the Father in Child Development,* 2nd ed., ed. M. E. Lamb (New York: John Wiley, 1981).

4. V. J. Machtlinger, "The Father in Psychoanalytic Theory," in *The Role of the Father in Child Development,* 2nd ed., ed. M. E. Lamb (New York: John Wiley, 1981).

Chapter 8
The Divorce Experience for Early Elementary School Children

1. H. B. Biller, "Father Absence, Divorce, and Personality Development," in *The Role of the Father in Child Development,* 2nd ed., ed. M. E. Lamb (New York: John Wiley, 1981). N. Kalter, "Long-Term Effects of Divorce on Children: A Developmental Vulnerability Model," *American*

Journal of Orthopsychiatry, 57 (1987): 587–600. V. J. Machtlinger, "The Father in Psychoanalytic Theory," in *The Role of the Father in Child Development*, 2nd ed., ed. M. E. Lamb (New York: John Wiley, 1981).

2. F. Furstenberg, C. Nord, J. Peterson, and N. Zill. "The Life Course of Children of Divorce," *American Sociological Review*, 48 (1983): 656–668.

3. N. Kalter and J. W. Plunkett, "Children's Perceptions of the Causes and Consequences of Divorce," *Journal of the American Academy of Child Psychiatry*, 23 (1984): 326–334. J. W. Plunkett and N. Kalter, "Children's Beliefs About Reactions to Parental Divorce," *Journal of the American Academy of Child Psychiatry*, 23 (1984): 616–621. J. S. Wallerstein and J. B. Kelly, *Surviving the Break-up: How Children and Parents Cope with Divorce* (New York: Basic Books, 1980).

4. K. Tooley, "Antisocial Behavior and Social Alienation Post Divorce: The 'Man of the House' and His Mother," *American Journal of Orthopsychiatry*, 46 (1976): 33–42.

5. J. S. Wallerstein, "Children of Divorce: Report of a Ten Year Follow-up of Early Latency-Age Children," *American Journal of Orthopsychiatry*, 57 (1987): 199–211.

Chapter 9
Helping Early Elementary School Children Cope

1. L. K. Brown and M. Brown, *The Dinosaur's Divorce: A Guide for Changing Families* (Boston: Jay Street Books, 1988). J. Sinberg, *Divorce Is a Grown-up Problem* (New York: Avon Books, 1978).

2. National Center for Health Statistics 1985, *Monthly Vital Statistics Report* (D.H.H.S. Publications 33–11) (Washington, D.C.: U.S. Government Printing Office, 1985).

Chapter 10
The Divorce Experience for Later Elementary School Children

1. R. E. Emery, M. E. Hetherington, and L. F. DiLalla, "Divorce, Children and Social Policy," in *Child Development Research and Social Policy*, vol 1, ed. H. W. Stevenson and A. E. Siegel (Chicago: University of Chicago Press, 1984). E. M. Hetherington, "Divorce: A Child's Perspective," *American Psychologist*, 34 (1979): 851–858.

2. Emery et al., "Divorce, Children, and Social Policy," 1984. L. J. Weitzman, *The Divorce Revolution: the Unexpected Social and Economic Consequences for Women and Children in America* (New York: Free Press, 1985).

3. H. B. Biller, "Father Absence, Divorce, and Personality Development,"

in *The Role of the Father in Child Development*, 2nd ed., ed. M. E. Lamb (New York: John Wiley, 1981). N. Kalter, "Long-Term Effects of Divorce on Children: A Developmental Vulnerability Model," *American Journal of Orthopsychiatry*, 57 (1987): 587–600. V. J. Machtlinger, "The Father in Psychoanalytic Theory," in *The Role of the Father in Child Development*, 2nd ed., ed. M. E. Lamb (New York: John Wiley, 1981).

Chapter 11
Helping Later Elementary School Children Cope

1. M. B. Isaacs, B. Montalvo, and D. Abelsohn, *The Difficult Divorce* (New York: Basic Books, 1986).

Chapter 12
The Divorce Experience for Adolescents

1. N. Kalter, "Long-Term Effects of Divorce on Children: A Developmental Vulnerability Model," *American Journal of Orthopsychiatry*, 57 (1987): 587–600.

2. J. S. Wallerstein and S. Blakeslee, *Second Chances: Men, Women, and Children a Decade After Divorce* (New York: Ticknor and Fields, 1989).

3. H. B. Biller, "Father Absence, Divorce and Personality Development," in *The Role of the Father in Child Development*, 2nd ed., ed. M. E. Lamb (New York: John Wiley, 1981). Kalter, "Long-Term Effects of Divorce on Children," 1987.

4. E. M. Hetherington, "Effects of Father-Absence on Personality Development in Adolescent Daughters," *Developmental Psychology*, 7 (1972): 313–326. N. Kalter, "Conjoint Mother–Daughter Treatment: A Beginning Phase of Psychotherapy with Adolescent Daughters of Divorce," *American Journal of Orthopsychiatry*, 54 (1984): 490–497. N. Kalter, B. Reimer, A. Brickman, and J. W. Chen, "Implications of Parental Divorce for Female Development," *Journal of the American Academy of Child Psychiatry*, 24 (1985): 538–544. J. S. Wallerstein, "Children of Divorce: Preliminary Report of a Ten-Year Follow-up of Older Children and Adolescents," *Journal of the American Academy of Child Psychiatry*, 24 (1985): 545–553.

5. Biller, "Father Absence, Divorce and Personality Development," 1981.

6. Biller, "Father Absence, Divorce and Personality Development," 1981.

7. Kalter, "Long-Term Effects of Divorce on Children," 1987.

8. M. Gold and E. Douvan, *Adolescent Development: Readings in Research and Theory* (Boston: Allyn and Bacon, 1969).

Chapter 13
Helping Adolescents Cope

1. T. M. Achenbach and C. S. Edelbrock, "The Classification of Child Psychopathology: A Review and Analysis of Empirical Efforts," *Psychological Bulletin*, 85 (1978): 1275–1301.

2. N. Kalter, "Conjoint Mother–Daughter Treatment: A Beginning Phase of Psychotherapy with Adolescent Daughters of Divorce," *American Journal of Orthopsychiatry*, 54 (1984): 490–497.

Index

Abandonment, fantasies of, 98–100, 174, 225, 228–231
Abstract thinking, 94–95, 100, 161, 162
Abuse, physical/sexual, 62–63, 188
Academic performance, impaired, 2, 349
Accident proneness, 349
Action defenses (acting out), 356–357; *see also* Aggressive behavior in children
Adjustment: *see* Coping by children
Adolescence
  avoidance of, 385
  delay of coming to terms with anger at parents into, 248
Adolescents, 309–391
  chores assigned to
    mother–son conflict and, 313, 340, 362–363
    by stepparent, 378, 379
  coping (by), 351–391
    with anger-vs.-love conflict, 359–363
    compromise and, 357–363
    direct and displacement communication to assist in, 36–39, 357–363, 367–368
    discussing divorce and, 351–354
    earliness of divorce and, 331–332
    internal conflicts and, 355
    internal stresses and, 354–355, 357
    with masculine identity problems, 384–390
    minimizing environmental stresses and, 354, 357
    with parental dating, 369–375
    with parental warfare, 363–369
    with parent's sexuality, 377, 382

    psychological defenses and, 355–357
    with remarriage, 377–384
    restricting abusive parent's contact and, 368–369
  developmental capacities of, 309–310, 351
  drug screening of, 358–359, 377–378, 386
  emotional separation (independence) from parents, 335, 336–337, 381–382
  in enmeshed relationships, 294
  evolving view of parents, 311
  fantasies about mother's economic distress, 324
  immediate crisis stage of divorce and, 310–323
    bottled up reactions during, 313, 314
    custody disputes during, 317–323
    initial reactions to separation, 310–311
    moral rigidity during, 315–316
    stressors in, 311–312, 315–317
  importance of school and peers to, 329
  long-range period of divorce and, 331–346
    lack of contact with father during, 322, 339–346
    masculine identity problems during, 339–346
    parental dating during, 333–334
    parental warfare during, 332
    remarriage during, 334–335, 337
  need for structure and stability, 328–329
  parental dating and, parent's unrealistic expectations about acceptance of, 369
  parent's sexuality and, 376–377
  recognizing distress in, 347–350
    "alarm bells," 349–350

Adolescents (*cont.*)
  anger, 347–348
  depression, 348–349
  difficulties in, 347
  somatic complaints, 349
  short-term aftermath stage of divorce and, 323–331
  difficulties in accepting divorce during, 323–324, 330–331
  external stressors in, 324
  fantasies of parental reconciliation during, 324–330
  noncustodial parent's purchase of house during, 324, 328
  parental dating during, 324, 326–327, 328
  suicidal feelings in, 321, 323
  trouble with intimate relationships in, 2
  verbal displacement techniques for communicating with, 36–39
Adulthood, trouble with intimate relationships in, 2
Adult-like behavior in children, 277; *see also* Enmeshed relationships
  enmeshed mother–son relationship and, 179–180
  girls as coparent and mother's confidant, 248–254
  in late elementary school, 290–295
  "parenting child" phenomenon, 14–15, 22
"Affective flooding," 45
Affect storms, 42
Aggressive behavior in children, 2, 173–174, 232; *see also* Anger in children; Father(s); Masculine identity problems
  bullying, 121
  controlling behaviors, 125–126
  as displaced anger at parents, 246
  displacement and direct communication to address, 387–388
  fighting, 34–35, 102–103, 130, 342, 343–344, 349
  in later elementary school, 244–245
  parental warfare and, 191, 193–195, 225
  toward peers, 140–141, 143
Alcohol abuse, parental, 101–104, 141–145
Anger in children, 2, 173–174, 253; *see also* Aggressive behavior in children; Conflict(s), internal; Conflict(s), parental; Warfare, parental
  adolescents, 347–348
  chronic, 9–10, 69

conversion of feelings of helplessness and sadness to, 242
defenses against, 364
defensive, 7, 56–57, 233
in early elementary school, 200–201
infants and toddlers, 71
in late elementary school, 272
manifestations of, 347
parental conflict and, 46, 79, 103–104, 119, 245–246, 363–364
in preschool, 130–131
over remarriage, 123–127, 198–199, 236, 337–338, 378, 379–380
somatic expressions of, 253
Anger in parent(s), 43, 50, 55, 140
Anxiety
  from continued parental warfare, 119
  general, 132, 201, 273–274
  stranger, 69
Arguments between parents: *see* Conflict(s), parental; Warfare, parental
Attorney(s), 52, 172, 191–192, 317
  animosity toward, 102
  assistance in preventing harassment from ex-spouse, 82–83, 188
  communication with children, lack of training in, 28
  court-ordered custody evaluation and, 365
  divorce negotiations exclusively through, 227
  financial settlement negotiations, 170
  impact of advice, 96
  use of displacement technique, 31
  vigilance in child abuse accusations, 63
  as weapons in divorce conflicts, 106

Baby-sitting arrangements, 43, 76–77
Bed wetting, 102, 140, 142, 143, 194
Behavioral problems, 25, 29–30, 179, 232; *see also* Aggressive behavior in children; Defense(s), psychological
Beliefs, self-blaming: *see* Egocentric logic/beliefs
"Blended families," 234–235; *see also* Remarriage
Boys: *see also* Father(s); Gender differences; Masculine identity problems; Mother(s)
  avoidance of closeness to mother, 152
  difficulty in accepting maternal authority, 340, 345
  living with mother, internal conflicts in, 269–270

mother's new romantic interest and, 376–
377
reactions to parental dating, 266–268

Causal relationships, preschooler's understanding of, 93; *see also* Egocentric
logic/beliefs
Child abuse, 62–63, 368
Child care arrangements, 51, 74–76
Child-rearing practices, 47
Child support payments, irregular or absent,
10
Chores assigned to children
age-appropriate, 221, 223
coparenting phenomenon and, 14–15,
277
early elementary child's changed perception
of, 198
enmeshed relationship and, 251
by mother's boyfriend or new husband, 20,
21, 235, 378, 379
mother–son conflict over, 270–271, 340,
362–363
resistance to performing
as expression of anger, 272, 313
as mirror of absent parent's attitude toward, 246–247, 286–289
parental dating and, 264, 267, 269, 306,
307
parental warfare and, 257
Cognitive maturity, 29; *see also specific child
developmental stages;* Development,
child
Communication, adult–child, 25–40; *see also*
Direct communication; Displacement
communication
day-to-day, 27–28
difficulties of, 27, 28
about divorce, 134–135, 206–208, 275–276,
299–300, 351–354
false assumptions hindering, 28–30
psychosocial stressors and, 23
purposes of, 26
relief provided by, 25–26, 27
Community services, 154
Competition with stepparent. *See* Rivalry with
stepfather
Compromise, adolescent coping and, 357–363
Confidentiality, rule of, 234
Conflict(s), internal, 290
of adolescents, 310, 355

affection for parent's partner vs. loyalty to
other parent, 261, 263–266, 278, 300–
303
affection for parent's partner vs. sexuality
in parent's dating relationship, 355
anger at vs. love for parent(s), 278, 291,
355, 359–363, 366–367
acting as coparent and confidant to cope
with, 252–253
delay in resolving, 248
displacement communication to address,
292–293
disruption of family environment and, 282
father–daughter relationship and, 322–
323, 366–367
father's infidelity and, 315–316, 359–361
parental warfare and, 245–246, 295–298
partial suppression of, 186
psychological defense against, 259
arising from more sophisticated sense of interpersonal relationships, 241–242
bed wetting as expression of, 194
over being cooperative with mother, 361–
363
in boys raised in single-mother household,
269–270
over feeling of responsibility for parental
conflict, 366, 368
identification with vs. wish to punish absent
father, 315–316, 359–361, 386
independence vs. love, 381–382
loyalty vs. side-taking, 242, 253, 258, 278,
291, 293–298, 322–323, 355
about masculinity, 316, 340, 345–346, 385–
386
maternal intimacy vs. male adolescent sexuality, 316
mental professionals to assess, 369
from parental dating/remarriage, 301–302
peer involvement and independence vs. urge
to help distressed parent, 278, 355
from sleeping with parent, 14
Conflict(s), parental, 6–7, 12–14, 17–18; *see
also* Warfare, parental
anger and fear in children and, 46, 79, 103–
104, 119, 245–246, 363–364
child development and, 53
chronic or persistent, 17–18, 83
over divorce settlements, 104–108
emotional resonance to, 45–47, 100, 101,
103
escalation of, 104–108

Conflict(s) (*cont.*)
  infant/toddler's reactions to, 50, 51–54
  internal conflicts about feeling responsible
    for, 366, 368
  joint physical custody and, 12
  overwhelming effect on child, 51
  preschooler's reactions to, 100–104, 107–
    108
  recruitment of children in, 13–15, 366, 368
  reducing
    displacement communication to assist in,
      34–36
    infant/toddler's coping and, 79–81
    preschooler's coping and, 123, 140–145
    for successful joint physical custody, 88
    during short-term aftermath stage, 12–13
Conflict-defense constellation, 281
Confusion/disorientation in infants and tod-
    dlers, 43–45, 50, 51
Consistency: *see also* Schedule, daily
  environmental, 45, 90, 95–96
  interpersonal, 90
  need for, 96
Controlling behaviors, 126
Coping by children, 5, 51, 247–248; *see also*
    specific child developmental stages;
    Communication, adult–child; De-
    fense(s), psychological; Direct commu-
    nication; Displacement communication
Crying, differentiation among types of, 68
Custody: *see* Joint legal custody; Joint physical
    custody
Custody disputes, 317–323, 364–366

Dating, parental, 9, 324; *see also* Remarriage;
    Sexuality, parental
  adolescent sexuality and, 330, 383
  avoidance of, as defense, 298–299
  children's reactions to
    avuncular approach of new partner and,
      305–306
    competitive feeling toward parent's part-
      ner, 371–372
    developmental level and, 73–74
    fear of losing central role in parent's life,
      265, 301–304
    fear of losing parent's affections, 301–
      304
    infants and toddlers, 44
    internal conflicts, 16, 301–302
    later elementary school children, 260–271
    stage of divorce and, 376

  compromising on, 361
  coping with
    by adolescents, 369–375
    discussing with children and, 299–300
    displacement communication to assist in,
      32–34, 156–158, 303–304
    by infants and toddlers, 63–65
    by late elementary school children, 298–
      307
    partner's low profile and, 376
    by preschoolers, 155–158
  ex-spouse's reactions to, 52, 192–193, 376
  live-in arrangements from, 19
  loyalty conflict arising from, 302–303
  mother–child relationship and, 197, 333–
    334
  as obstacle to reconciliation wishes of child,
    326–327, 328, 330, 370, 372
  salutary effects on children, 305
  sexuality and, child's awareness of, 302
  time spent with children and, 304–305
  unrealistic expectations of teenager's accep-
    tance of, 369
Day-care arrangements, 43, 44, 76–78, 95–
    97
Death, preoccupation with, 141
Defense(s), psychological, 355–356; *see also*
    specific child developmental stages;
    Aggressive behavior in children; Anger
    in children; Conflict(s), internal
  adolescent coping and, 355–357
  against anger, 364
  anger-based, 7, 56–57, 104, 233
  avoidance of parental dating as, 298–299
  conversion of one feeling to another, 279
  denial, 200, 210, 265, 279, 356
    by early elementary school children, 173–
      174
    in fantasy, 113
    of parents' separation, 245, 246
    of sadness or upset feelings, 209
  displacement, 279
  displacement communication and, 280–281
  against external and internal stressors, 290
  externalization, 357, 364
  hostility as, 194–195
  identification with absent parent, 279
  intellectualization, 247–248, 279, 356
  against internal conflicts, 259
  internalization, 357, 364
  maladaptive behaviors as, 25, 29–30
  parent's restructuring of family life as, 181

reaction formation, 247–248
retaliatory rejection, 253
somatization
  in adolescents, 349, 356
  in late elementary school children, 248, 253, 272–273, 279
  reasons for, 186
Depression, 2, 9–10
  in adolescents, 348–349
  low self-esteem and, 167
  in parent, 84–85
    anger and guilt arising from, 55
    infant/toddler's reactions to, 55–58
    who initialized divorce, 43
  recognizing, 348–349
  sense of loss and, 167
Depressive reaction(s) in children, 195, 253, 274; see also Sadness in children
  to custodial parent's restructured life, 186–187, 215
  in early elementary school, 166–167, 200, 210
  to loss of father–child relationship, 111–113
  to parental warfare, 166–167, 225, 226–227
  symptoms of, 166, 186
Development, child: see also Adolescents; Elementary school children, early; Elementary school children, later; Infants and toddlers; Preschool children; Regression
  abdication of parental role and, 179–181
  coping success and, 5
  displacement techniques and, 31
  disruption of continuity and, 45
  effect of distress on, 70
  emotional separation from parents and, 336–337
  enmeshed mother–child relationship and, 116–117
  failure to achieve appropriate levels of, 129–130, 202
  father–child relationship and, 60, 162
  joint physical custody and, 89–90
  parental conflict and, 53, 232–234
  parent's attention to, 384–385
  parent's new romantic involvement and, 65
  parents' obliviousness to, 90
  part-time parenting and, 86, 87
  sex-role development, 162
  trajectory of, 70–71
Dinosaurs' Divorce, The, 229

Direct communication, 32, 34; see also under Displacement communication
Discipline, mother's boyfriend's administration of, 19–21
Displacement communication, 30–40, 81
  to address anger at remarriage, 237–238
  to address anger-vs.-love conflict, 283–286, 292–293
  to address child's sadness and sense of loss, 208–209, 210
  to address egocentric beliefs about cause of divorce, 213–214
  to address fantasies and self-blaming (egocentric) beliefs, 138–140
  to address fantasies of parental rejection, 150–151
  to address fears of displacement by parent's partner, 32–34, 156–158, 303–304
  to address feelings of loss and abandonment, 215, 217–219, 228–231
  to address identification with father, 286–288
  to address loyalty conflict, 293–294
  to address mother–son enmeshment, 220, 222–225
  to address private worries (fantasies), 142–144
  to address reconciliation fantasies, 373–375
  to address sense of family loss and loss of father–child relationship, 146–147, 148, 211–215
  aims of, 31
  approaching psychological defenses through, 280–281
  basic strategy of, 31–32
  children's initial responses to, 281
  child's developmental level and, 31
  common pitfalls of, 212
  difficulties with, 39–40
  direct communication balanced with, 357–358
    to address aggressive behavior, 387–388
    to address masculine identity problems, 387
    to address parental dating, 299–300, 372–375
    adolescent coping and, 357–363, 367–368
  including child's interests in, 289
  lack of contact with father and, 289
  parental conflicts and, 34–36
  parents' doubts about, 229, 231
  play materials used in, 36

Displacement communication (*cont.*)
  story-telling method of, 214–215
  termination of, 34
  through drawings, 217
  using children's books on divorce, 229, 231–232
  verbal, 26–29, 36–39, 289
Displacement of feelings, 279; *see also* Aggressive behavior in children
Divorce Is a Grown-Up Problem, 229
Divorce rate, rise in, 1
Dolls, use of anatomically correct, 62–63
Drugs: *see* Substance abuse
Drug screening, 358–359, 377–378, 386

Eating, regression in, 67, 128
Economic difficulties, 2, 10, 17, 22
  changes in residence due to, 118
  of mother, 188, 331, 333
    anger elicited by, 55
    avoiding discussion of, with child, 220, 222, 223, 224
    depression from, 55
    empathizing with, 219
    fantasies about, 205, 324
    return to work force and, 15
    turning to children for help and, 14, 248
Egocentric logic/beliefs, 159; *see also* Fantasy(ies)
  adolescent's reversion to, 311–312
  about changes in mother–child relationship, 215
  damaging effects of, 278
  in early elementary school children, 162, 167, 205–206
  about father's reasons for leaving home, 173
  in preschoolers, 93, 100, 113, 122, 133–140
  self-esteem and, 206
Elementary school children, early, 161–239
  coping by, 205–239
    discussing divorce with children and, 206–208
    displacement techniques to assist, 36
    empathizing with children and, 208–209
    with loss of father–child relationship, 209–215
    with mother's emotional distress, 219–225
    with mother's new life, 215–219
    with parental warfare, 225–234

    with remarriage, 234–239
    through denial, 173–174
  developmental capabilities of, 161–163
  egocentric logic/beliefs in, 162, 167, 205–206
  environmental and internal stressors on, 205–206
  fantasies of abandonment, 174
  immediate crisis stage of divorce and, 164–174
    father–child relationship during, 162, 167–174
    parental warfare during, 164–167, 190
  joint physical custody of, 161
  long-range period of divorce and, 187–199
    mother–daughter relationship after remarriage, 195–199
    parental warfare during, 190–195
    separation during infancy and, 187–190
    variability in child development trajectory during, 187, 199
  loss and sadness in, 163, 171–173, 175, 185
  mother's economic distress and avoidance of involving child in, 220, 222, 223, 224
    fantasies about, 205
  recognizing distress in, 200–203
    abnormal and normal signs, 202–203
    anger, 200–201
    depressive reactions, 200, 210
    fear, 201–202
    general anxiety, 201
    regression or failure to achieve developmentally appropriate levels, 200, 202
    sadness, 200
  sense of family, 206
  short-term aftermath stage of divorce and, 174–187
    custodial parent's creation of new life during, 181–187
    custodial parent's emotional distress during, 175–181
    father–child relationship during, 174–175
    parental warfare during, 174
Elementary school children, later, 241–308
  aggressive behavior in, 244–245
  chores assigned to, resistance to performing coparenting phenomenon and, 277
  enmeshed mother–daughter relationship and, 251
  as expression of anger, 272

mother–son conflict and, 270–271
parental dating and, 264, 267–269, 306–307
as reflection of absent parent's attitude, 246–247, 286–289
connotation of sexual intercourse for, 261
coping by, 275–308
awareness of internal sources of stress and, 277–278
discussing divorce with children and, 275–276
displacement communication and, 36, 280–281
with enmeshed relationships and adult role playing, 290–295
gender differences in, 247–248
minimizing environmental sources of stress and, 276–277
with parental dating and remarriage, 298–307
with parental warfare, 289–290, 295–298
with partial loss of father relationship, 289–290
psychological defenses and, 278–280
developmental capacities of, 241–242
immediate crisis stage of divorce and, 242–248
defenses-vs.-internal conflicts dynamic during, 243, 245–246
father–child relationship during, 242–243, 246
parental warfare during, 242–247
long-range period of divorce and, 260–271
environmental stresses during, 260
parental dating during, 260–271
remarriage during, 260, 268–269
main environmental (external) stressors on, 242
mother's economic distress and, 248
recognizing distress in, 271–274
anger, 272
other signs, 273–274
social withdrawal, 273
somatic complaints, 272–273
short-term aftermath stage of divorce and, 248–260
custodial mother's emotional distress during, 248–254
parental warfare during, 254–260
Emotional disturbance in children, persistence of parental warfare and, 144–145

Emotional lability, 67–68, 71, 129–130
Emotional resonance: see Resonance, emotional
Enmeshed relationships
adolescence and, 294
correcting, 220, 222–225, 290–295
factors working against, 235
mother–child, 22, 115–117
mother–daughter, 151–155, 339
relationship with father and, 294–295
social relationships and, 251–252
mother–son, 178–181, 186–188, 220, 222–225
Environment: see also Stress(es) and stressor(s), psychosocial
alteration to reduce stress, 133
fear of, 131
Externalization defenses, 357, 364

Family(ies)
"blended," 234–235
early elementary school children's sense of, 163, 206
loss of sense of, 164, 167, 210, 211–215
Fantasy(ies), 159; see also Defense(s), psychological; Egocentric logic/beliefs; Reconciliation wishes of children
of abandonment, 98–100, 174, 225
of consequences of child's rage, 201
damaging effects of, 278
denial in, 113
in early elementary school children, 161, 174, 205
fear arising from, 202
of masculinity, 384
about parental warfare, 100–104, 140–145
in preschoolers, 95, 133–136
about being abandoned, 98–100
blurred distinction between reality and, 93
disruption of daily routines from, 98–100
about outcome of parental conflict, 100–104
from visitation anxieties, 149, 150–151
Father(s): see also Parent(s); Visit(s) to noncustodial parent
alcoholic, 141–145
child abuse, 62–63
daughter's relationship with
anger-vs.-love conflict in, 322–323, 366–367

Father(s) (*cont.*)
   daughter's rejection of, 252, 253–254
   self-esteem and, 253–254
  elementary school children's relationship
   with
    early, 162, 167–175, 209–215
    late, 242–243, 246–247
  infant/toddler's relationship with, 58–62
   coping and, 85–87
   experiential definition of "father" and,
    60, 89, 121–122
  joint physical custody and, 87–90
  loss/disruption of relationship with, 11–12,
   15, 58–59, 210
   adolescents and, 322, 339–346
   children's peer relations and, 120, 122–
    123
   child's developmental level and stress
    from, 74
   coping with, 209–215
   depressive reaction to, 111–113
   displacement communication to address,
    211–215, 289
   distancing effect of, 119–123
   father's grief over, 111
   father's previous level of involvement
    and, 74
   later elementary school children's re-
    sponses to, 246–247
   maintenance of emotional bond with fa-
    ther, 169
   preschoolers and, 133, 145–148
   sense of loss over, 167–174
  mother–daughter relationship and, 123, 162,
   336–337, 339
  role as progressive force, 108, 113
  preschoolers' relationship with, 108–113,
   133, 145–148
   attachment, 94
   gender differences in, 109–113
   independence and, 108–109
  as primary caretakers, 47–49
  self-righteous rage of, 322
  sex-role development of children and, 162
  son's relationship with: *see also* Masculine
   identity problems
   disruption of father's dating and, 328–329
   identification, 194–195, 247, 282–283,
    286–288
   identification-vs.-wish-to-punish conflict
    in, 315–316, 359–361, 386
Father-presence, atmosphere of, 11

Fear(s)/fearfulness
  arising from fantasies, 202
  of being unloved by mother, remarriage and,
   123–127
  from continued parental warfare, 119
  in early elementary school children, 201–
   202
  of environment, 131
  in infants and toddlers, 69, 71
  normal, 202
  from parental warfare, 46, 52–53, 79, 103–
   104, 191, 193
  from parent's anxieties, 84
  in preschoolers, 131
Fighting, children, 34–35, 102–103, 130, 342,
  343–344, 349
Fighting, parental: *see* Conflict(s), parental;
  Warfare, parental
Financial difficulties. *See* Economic difficulties
Frustration, 68, 69

Gender differences
  in coping, 5, 247–248
  in father–child relationship, 109–113
  in reactions to parental dating, 266–267
General anxiety, 132, 201, 273–274
Girls: *see also* Enmeshed relationships; Gender
  differences; Mother(s)
  as coparent and mother's confidant, 248–
   254
  mother's new romantic interest and, 330,
   376–377
  reactions to divorce, 247–248
  reactions to parental warfare, 195
Guilt-remorse, feelings of, 9, 43, 55

Half-siblings, 21
Headaches, 272
Helpless feelings, conversion into anger, 242
Home(s)/house(s)
  changing, 118
  chores in, compromising on, 362
  joint custody and proximity of, 89
  noncustodial parent's purchase as obstacle
   to reconciliation fantasy, 324, 328
  running away from, 349
  selling of, 324
Homosexuality, 385
Hostility in children, 194–195; *see also* Aggressive behavior in children
Hostility in parents: *see* Conflict(s), parental;
  Warfare, parental

Index

Hyperactivity, misidentification of nervous
    habits for, 53

Identification with absent father: *see* Father(s)
Immediate crisis stage of divorce: *see specific
    child developmental stages;* Stages of
    divorce
Independence
  of adolescence, 310, 335, 336–337, 381–
    382
  of early elementary school children, 162,
    182
  father–child relationships and, 108–109,
    336–337, 339
  internal conflict involving, 278, 355, 381–
    382
  preschoolers' struggle for, 93–94
  regression in, 67, 129
Infants and toddlers, 41–91, 187–190
  attachment to mother, 108
  confusion/disorientation in, 43–45, 50, 51
  coping by, 73–91
    child-care arrangements and, 74–77
    consistency in daily routine and, 74–79
    father–child relationship and, 85–87
    joint physical custody and, 87–90
    with parental dating, 63–65
    parents' emotional equilibrium and, 83–
      85
    reduction of parental hostilities and, 79–
      83
    with remarriage, 189
  developmental capacities of, 41–43, 49, 58,
    65
  ego immaturity of, 58
  experiential definition of parenthood, 60, 89,
    121–122
  immediate crisis stage of divorce and, 42–
    49
    confusion during, 43–45
    father as primary caregiver during, 47–
      49
    parents' emotional state during, 45–47
  long-range period of divorce and, 58–65
    loss of father–child relationship during,
      58–62, 73–74, 86
    mistreatment or abuse by father during,
      62–63
    parent's romantic involvement during,
      63–65, 74
  main stressors on, 73–74
  mother's economic distress and, 55

  parental dating and, 44
  recognizing distress in, 66–71
    anger, 68–69, 71
    common sources, 73–74
    emotional lability, 67–68, 71
    fearfulness, 69–70, 71
    normal and abnormal signs, 70–71
    from physical problems, 73, 760
    regression, 66–67, 71
    withdrawal and listlessness, 70, 71
  resonance to parental warfare, 100, 101
  short-term aftermath stage of divorce and,
    49–58
    disruption of daily routine during, 50, 51
    parental conflicts during, 50, 51–54
    parental depression during, 55–58
    working custodial parent during, 55–58
  supportive measures for, 30
  temperament of, 42, 52, 90
Infidelity, divorce due to, 50, 315–316, 359–
    361
Intellectualization, 247–248, 279, 356
Internal conflicts: *see* Conflict(s), internal
Internalization defenses, 357, 364
Interpersonal conflicts of son, mothers and,
    389
Intimacy, problems with, 2
Irritability, chronic: *see* Anger in children

Jealousy, 17–18
Joint legal custody, 11–12, 192
Joint physical custody, 11–12, 48, 87–90, 183,
    184, 210, 211, 217
  awareness of child developmental needs and,
    89–90
  of early elementary school children, 161
  incidence of, 168
  parental cooperation and, 88–89
  parent's fitness for, 87–88
  physical proximity of homes and, 89

Language, regression in, 67, 128
Law, trouble with, 349
Lawyer(s). *See* Attorney(s)
Listlessness, 70, 71, 132
Loneliness of single parent, 14–15, 113–117
Long-range period of divorce: *see specific child
    developmental stages;* Stages of di-
    vorce
Loss: *see also under* Father(s)
  depression and, 167

411

Loss (*cont.*)
  displacement communication to address, 208–209, 210, 228–231
  disrupted father–child relationship and, 167–174
  in early elementary school children, 163
  parental warfare and, 225
  of sense of family, 164, 167, 210, 211–215
Loyalty conflicts: *see under* Conflict(s), internal

Male role model, absence of, 386; *see also* Father(s)
Marriage: *see also* Remarriage
  divorce vs. persevering in troubled, 1–2
  modern vs. historic views of, 393
Masculine identity problems
  adult male model and, 267, 269–270, 282–283
  coping with, 384–390
  fighting and, 342, 343–344
  incompatibility with stepfather's personality and, 346
  internal conflicts related to, 340, 345–346, 385–386
  loss of father–son relationship and, 339–346
  maternal authority and, 345
Men, divorced, 2, 10; *see also* Father(s)
Mother(s): *see also* Enmeshed relationships; Parent(s); Remarriage
  children's egocentric beliefs about changes in relationship with, 215
  coping with new life of, 215–219
  daughter's relationship with
    emotional separation and independence, 108–109, 195–196
    father–daughter relationship and, 162, 336–337, 339
    parental dating and, 197
    remarriage and, 195–199, 337
  economic pressure on, 188, 331, 333
    anger elicited by, 55
    avoiding discussion of, with child, 220, 222, 223, 224
    depression from, 55
    empathizing with, 219
    fantasies about, 205, 324
    return to work force and, 15
    turning to children for help and, 14, 248
  emotional distress of, 55–58, 219–225
  employment of, 44, 54–55

infant/toddler's attachment to, 108
loss of relationship with, 15
with new live-in partner, 19–21
percentage of minor children living with, 47
perception of diminished love from, displacement communication to correct, 215, 217–219
reactions to ex-spouse's dating, 376
shifts in involvement with children, 54
son's relationship with
  avoidance of closeness in, 152
  difficulties in accepting maternal authority, 340, 345
  displacement technique applied to, 37–39
  emotional distance in, developmentally appropriate, 270–271
  identification with father and, 195
  internal conflict about cooperating with, 361–363
  parental dating and, 266–268
  remarriage and, 268–269
  son's interpersonal conflicts and, 389
Motor activity, regression in, 67, 128

Narcissistic personality disorder, 83
Nervous habits in children, 53, 273–274
Nervousness, diffuse, 132
Nightmares, 103–104, 141, 143, 179–181
Nursery school, 95–97

Pain of divorce, sources of, 114
Parent(s): *see also* Conflict(s), parental; Dating, parental; Father(s); Mother(s); Sexuality, parental; Stages of divorce; Warfare, parental
  abusive, reducing contact with, 368–369
  adolescent's relationship with
    adolescent sexuality and, 382–383
    developmental progress and, 384–385
    emotional separation in, 335, 336–337
    evolving view of, 311
  approach to children's psychological defenses, 280
  children sleeping with, 14
  defensive rage in, 104
  depressed, 55–58, 84–85
  difficulties with using displacement techniques, 39–40
  diminished parenting capabilities of, 10
  emotionally distressed: *see also* Enmeshed relationships

adult-focused resources for, 132, 154, 276–277
dependence on children for support, 175–176
early elementary school children and, 175–181
infants/toddlers and, 83–85
preschoolers and, 133
during short-term aftermath stage, 248–254
emotional responses to initiating divorce, 43
infant/toddler's dependence on, 41–42
living with parents, 188–189, 190
lonely, 14–15, 113–117
noncustodial
buying of new home by, 324, 328
diminished relationship with, 15
identifying with, 279
loss of relationship with, mitigation of, 276
remarriage of, 342
obliviousness to child development, 90
recognition of children's reacting to stress, 394
restructuring of family life by, 181–187
stresses on, 114–117
"Parenting child" phenomenon, 14–15, 22; see also Enmeshed relationships
Peer relations, children's: see also Conflict(s), internal; Social relationships
adolescent, 309, 329
avoidance of, 267, 269, 273
enmeshed mother–son relationship and, 179, 180
loss of father–child relationship and, 120, 122–123
parental warfare and, 295
Personality development, chronic parental warfare and, 232–234
Petition for divorce, 6
Phobias, 202; see also Fear(s)/fearfulness
Physical complaints: see Defense(s), psychological: somatization
Play materials, use in displacement technique, 36
Preschool children, 93–159
cognitive limitations of, 122
coping by, 133–159
consistency in daily schedule and, 133, 136–140

correcting reality-distorting beliefs and fantasies and, 135–140
with dating and remarriage, 155–158
discussing divorce with child and, 134–135
displacement techniques to assist in, 36
help for emotionally distressed custodial parent and, 132
with loss of father–child relationship, 145–148
with parent's emotional distress, 151–155
reduction of parental conflicts and, 123, 140–145
with visiting relationship, 148–151
developmental capabilities of, 93–95, 127
egocentric logic/beliefs in, 93, 100, 113, 122, 133–140
immediate crisis stage of divorce and, 95–104
child care arrangements during, 95–97
fantasizing during, 98–100
parental conflicts during, 100–104
long-range period of divorce and, 117–127
absence of noncustodial father during, 119–123
changes of residence during, 118
parental conflicts during, 118–119
remarriage by custodial mother during, 123–127
main environmental and internal stressors on, 95, 133–134
need for consistency, 96
recognizing distress in, 127–132
anger, 130–131
anxiety, 132
emotional lability, 129–130
failure to achieve developmentally appropriate levels, 129
fear, 131–132
internal sources, 133–134
normal and abnormal signs, 132
regression, 128–129
sadness, 132
withdrawal and listlessness, 132
short-term aftermath stage of divorce and, 104–117
escalation of parental conflicts during, 104–108
father–child relationship during, 108–113
loneliness of single parent during, 113–117
temperament of, 94, 97, 101, 141

Projective tests, 63
Psychotherapy, cases requiring, 281–290, 294, 344–345, 363, 384, 388–389
Puberty, 309

Rage, 104, 319, 322; *see also* Anger in children
Reaction formation, 247–248
Reality-fantasy distinction in preschoolers, 93
Reconciliation wishes of children, 9, 173, 324–330
    displacement communication to dispel, 373–375
    parental dating as obstacle to, 370, 372
    parent's new live-in partner as threat to, 19
Regression, 66–67
    in early elementary school children, 202
    in infancy and toddlerhood, 71
    in preschoolers, 128–129
Rejection, retaliatory, 253
Religious institutions, 154
Remarriage, 18–19, 342; *see also* Stepparent
    anger over, 198–199, 236, 337–338, 378, 379–380
    coping with
        by adolescents, 376–384
        by early elementary school children, 234–239
        by late elementary school children, 298–307
        by preschoolers, 155–158
        stress reduction during, 234–235, 237
    as corrective model for intimate adult relationships, 22
    late elementary school children and, 260, 268–269, 298–307
    mother–daughter relationship and, 195–199, 334–335, 337
    of noncustodial parent, 342
    reactions to
        by adolescents, 376
        developmentally related, 189, 190, 376
        internal conflicts, 301–302
        by preschoolers, 123–127
    salutary effects of, 305
    stressors from, 18–19, 21–22
Residence: *see* Home(s)/house(s)
Resonance, emotional, 42, 79, 90, 100, 101, 103, 140
Resonance mechanism, 69
Resources, adult-focused, 154
Retaliatory rejection, 253

Rivalry with stepfather, 123–127, 156, 234, 331, 339, 370
    minimizing, 64, 65
    sense of displacement from parent's affection and, 304
Rivalry with new partner/lover, 371–372, 376–377
Routines, daily: *see* Schedule, daily
Running away from home, 349

Sadness in children, 2, 98, 100, 274; *see also* Depressive reaction(s) in children
    at being told about divorce, normality of, 207
    conversion into anger, 242
    denial of, 209
    displacement communication to empathize with, 208–209, 210
    in early elementary school, 163, 164–166, 171–173, 185, 200
    elicited by visits, 175
    parental warfare and, 164–166, 225
    in preschool, 132
Schedule, daily: *see also* Consistency
    consistency in, 50, 51, 74–79, 133, 136–140
    disrupted, 104
        from changes in child care arrangements, 95–97
        easing stress caused by, 137
        infants and toddlers and, 50, 51
        preschoolers and, 133
        from preschoolers' own fantasies, 98–100
School, 329, 349
Self-blaming beliefs: *see* Egocentric logic/beliefs
Self-esteem
    loss in child of, 2, 167, 173, 200, 206
    positive father–daughter relationship and, 253–254
Self-injuring behavior, 349
Sexuality, adolescent, 309, 335, 336–337, 378
    male, maternal intimacy and, 316
    mother's new romantic interest and, 377
    parental dating and, 330, 383
    parental sexuality and, 338
    parent's handling of, 382–383
    promiscuous/precocious, 349
Sexuality, parental, 334; *see also* Dating, parental
    adolescents and, 376–377, 382
    adolescent sexuality and, 338

child's developmental level and acceptance of, 16
later elementary school children's awareness of, 302
premature recognition of, 260–261, 265
Shoplifting, 348
Short-term aftermath stage of divorce: *see specific child developmental stages;* Stages of divorce
Side-taking: *see under* Conflict(s), internal
Single-parent household, stressors in, 22
Sleeping arrangements, adjustment of parent–child, 14
Sleeping problems, 50, 66, 103, 128, 185
Socialization, early, 47
Social relationships: *see also* Peer relations, children's
isolation, 114
mother–daughter enmeshment and, 251–252
regression in, 129
uneasiness in, 131–132
withdrawal from, in late elementary school children, 273
Somatization: *see under* Defense(s), psychological
Stability, adolescent's need for, 328–329
Stages of divorce, 5–23; *see also specific child developmental stages*
adolescent reactions to dating/remarriage and, 376
children's coping and, 5
immediate crisis stage, 5–12
depression during, 9–10
environmental characteristics of, 95
financial distress during, 10
"friendly" divorces and, 8–9
nonresident parent's relationship with children, 11
parental conflicts during, 6–8
as period of diminished parenting capabilities, 10
long-range period, 5, 17–23
new live-in partner during, 19–21
parental conflicts during, 17–18
remarriage during, 18–19, 21–22
single-parentage during, 22
persistence of psychological distress in children through, 73–74
short-term aftermath stage, 5, 6, 12–17
diminished relationship with parents during, 15
parental conflicts during, 12–13

parents' sexuality and, 16
recruitment of children as allies and supports, 13–15
resources available to parents during, 17
social isolation during, 114
Stepparent: *see also* Remarriage
adolescents' rejection of, 378
adolescent stepchildren and, 335
avuncular role adopted by, stress reduction through, 235
conflicted reactions to, 21
establishing relationship with, 155–158
evolving role of, 305–307
masculine identity problems and lack of fit with personality of, 346
rivalry with, 123–127
tendency to become too parental/authoritarian, 335, 337, 378–379, 383
Stepsiblings, 21
Stomachaches, 272
Stranger anxiety, 69
Stress(es) and stressor(s), psychosocial, 5; *see also specific child developmental stages*
adjusted sleeping arrangements and, 14
communication and, 23
difficulty in recognizing, 394
diminished parenting capabilities and, 10
diminished relationship with parents and, 15
economic, on mothers, 188, 331, 333
anger elicited by, 55
avoiding discussion of, with child, 220, 222, 223, 224
depression from, 55
empathizing with, 219
fantasies about, 205, 324
return to work force and, 15
turning to children for help and, 14, 248
environmental, 276–277, 354, 357, 394; *see also* Conflict(s), parental; Dating, parental; Father(s); Parent(s): emotionally distressed; Remarriage; Warfare, parental
from "friendly" divorce, 9
internal, 159, 277–278, 354–355, 357, 394; *see also* Egocentric logic/beliefs; Fantasy(ies); Conflict(s), internal
joint physical custody and, 12
loss of one parent, 11–12, 15
new live-in partner and, 19–21
from parental conflicts, 6–7, 12–14, 17–18
parental dating and sexuality, 16

Stress(es) and stressor(s) (*cont.*)
  remarriage, 18–19, 21–22
  single-parent household, 22
  step- or half-sibling relationships, 21
  temperament and response to, 42
Structure, adolescent's need for, 328–329
Substance abuse, 101–104, 255–256, 348, 349
Suicidal feelings in adolescents, 321, 323, 348
Surgery, divorce as social, 2
Suspension from school, 349

Tasks assigned to children. *See* Chores assigned to children
Teenagers: *see* Adolescents
Temperament
  of infants and toddlers, 42, 52, 90
  of preschoolers, 94, 97, 101, 141
  response to stress and, 42
Temper tantrums, 42, 48
"Tender years doctrine," 47
Tests, projective, 63
Toddlers: *see* Infants and toddlers
Toilet training, regression in, 67, 128–129

Unlovable-unworthwhile feelings, 9

Visit(s) to non-custodial parent, 58–59
  changes in schedule, 119–121
  discontinuation to punish ex-spouse, 151
  refusal or reluctance, 290, 293–294
    infant/toddler's, 58–63
      due to lack of "father feelings," 58–62
      due to mistreatment or abuse, 62–63
    mother–daughter enmeshment and, 252

sadness elicited by, 175
stresses from, 148–151

Warfare, parental, 6–8; *see also* Conflict(s), parental
  chronic, child's personality development and, 144–145, 232–234
  coping with, 276
    by adolescents, 363–369
    by early elementary school children, 225–234
    by late elementary school children, 295–298
    by preschoolers, 140–143
  custody disputes, 317–323
  effects on children of
    adolescents, 332
    aggressive behavior, 225
    anger, 245–246, 295–298, 363–364
    depressive reactions, 225, 226–227
    in early elementary school, 164–166, 174, 190–195
    fear, 46, 52–53, 79, 103–104, 191, 193
    in late elementary school, 242–247, 254–260
    peer relationships and, 295
    in preschool, 118–119
    sadness, 164–166, 225
    sense of loss, 225
  enlistment into, 254–260, 277, 295, 318–323
Wife abuse, 188
Withdrawal, 70, 71, 132
Women, divorced, 2, 10; *see also* Mother(s)